	DATE DUE		
1/3/05			

OVERDUE FINE
$0.10 PER DAY

Donated by

***Friends of
The Woodbridge
Library***

Pie

300 Tried-and-True Recipes

for Delicious Homemade Pie

KEN HAEDRICH

The Harvard Common Press • Boston, Massachusetts

The Harvard Common Press
535 Albany Street
Boston, Massachusetts 02118
www.harvardcommonpress.com

Printed in the United States

LIBRARY OF CONGRESS CATALOGING-IN-PUBLICATION DATA

Haedrich, Ken
  Pie : 300 tried-and-true recipes for delicious homemade pie / Ken
  Haedrich.
      p. cm.
  Includes index.
  ISBN 1-55832-253-1 (hc : alk. paper) — ISBN 1-55832-254-X pbk :
  alk. paper)
  1. Pies. I. Title.
  TX773.H2195 2004
  641.8'652—dc22   2004003635

Special bulk-order discounts are available on this and other Harvard
Common Press books. Companies and organizations may purchase
books for premiums or resale, or may arrange a custom edition, by
contacting the Marketing Director at the address above.

10 9 8 7 6 5 4 3 2 1

Interior design by Richard Oriolo
Cover design by Night & Day Design
Photographs by Eric Roth Photography
Food preparation and styling by Mary Bandereck
Illustrations by Jackie Aher

This book is dedicated to my 15-year-old son, Sam, cursed with the father's too-large feet but blessed with a heart of gold. Thanks for all the cooking advice you've offered me, solicited or otherwise, over the years. Now it's my turn.

1. "Tons of snowboarding" may not look as good on the "other interests" section of your college application as you might hope.
2. Cars, gas, and insurance cost more than you make in a couple of weekends.
3. That shorthand u use in ur emails is fine 4 ur buds, but i like regulr english. so clean it up, bub. ☺
4. Unless you plan to become a plumber, I wish you'd reconsider the location of your waist.
5. I will start to look a little smarter as you start to look a little older. Promise.

With love,
Your father

CONTENTS

Here I go again, expressing my gratitude to those who have extended a helping hand in the writing of this book, as well as others—my supporting cast of characters—whose ongoing love, employment, and tolerance have helped make this possible. They include: • Cindy Littlefield, at *FamilyFun* magazine, with whom I've had the pleasure of working on a regular basis for quite a few

ACKNOWLEDGMENTS

years now. Also at *FamilyFun*, Jon Adolph, as well as David Sokol at *Disney Magazine*, *FamilyFun*'s sister publication. • I also wish to thank a number of other editors who, despite my regular whining about deadline extensions, have kept me in their good graces: Kristine Kidd, Barbara Fairchild, and Sarah Tenaglia at *Bon Appétit*; Georgia Orcutt, formerly of *Yankee*; Patsy Jamieson of *Eating Well*; Jenny Rosenstrach at *Real Simple*; and John Riha, Nancy Wall Hopkins, and Sandra Mosley at *Better Homes and Gardens*. • My agent, Meg Ruley, of the Jane Rotrosen Agency, has done a stellar job of hawking my writing wares for some fifteen years now. Thank you, Meg. Thanks, too, to Don Cleary of the Jane Rotrosen Agency.

To the hard-working crew of The Harvard Common Press, who do such a fine job of producing cookbooks: Bruce Shaw, Pam Hoenig, Valerie Cimino, Skye Stewart, Sunshine Erickson, Jodi Marchowsky, Abbey Phalen, Liza Beth, Betsy Young, Christine Alaimo, Dana Garczewski, Megan Weireter, Pat Jalbert-Levine, and Virginia Downes. And, of course, to Barbara Jatkola, my tireless copyeditor.

To all the rest whose recipes, tips, and input have enriched this volume in countless ways: Niel Koep, Rachel van Leer and Sarah Adolph, Friske Orchards, Mayor Barbara Skinner, Jeff and Jayne Rose, Joyce White, Van Eure, Tom Douglas and Shelley Lance, Alice Colombo, Maria Roman, Nancy Byal, Rose Calello, Jeanne Kelley, Dolores Kostelni, Vid and Annie Valdmanis, Betty Zaiger, Andrea Chesman, Robert Stehling, Jeff Paige, Diane Worthington, the late Richard Sax, Liz Reiter, Liz Smothers, Robert Rankin, Deborah Madison, Marion Cunningham, Jim and Linda Nolte, Michele Scicolone, Opal Lyons, Bill and Linda Biard, Marian Clark, Jerry Bechard, Patti's Restaurant, Robert Eichorn, and Joan and Thom Gorman.

To my children, Ben, Tess, Ali, and Sam; know that I'm tremendously proud to be your father; my parents, Warren and Muriel, who taught me what pie making is all about; and my siblings, Joe, Barb, Tom, Bill, Joanne, and Mary, and their wonderful families. A fellow could not have grown up with a better bunch. Many thanks, too, to my stepson, Bryan Moss, who sampled most everything in these pages, but wishes they had all be pumpkin.

Finally, to my wife, Bev Moss Haedrich, the hardest-working real-estate agent in Annapolis, Maryland. Only someone as faithful, loving, and loyal as she would have put up with almost two years' worth of pie buffet dinners, during which—horrors!—she claims to have gained nearly two full pounds.

Recently, I had the good fortune to give a talk at the Smithsonian Institution in Washington, D.C.—not far from my home in Annapolis, Maryland—to a group of young, aspiring food writers. Their hope—and my purpose for being there—was that I might pass on some useful nuggets of career wisdom based on my nearly quarter of a century as a food writer. Not far into my pres-

entation, one earnest young lady raised her hand and asked if I had any advice to offer on the sort of topics she should write about. My response was immediate, if not entirely original: Write about what you love. Convey some passion for your subject matter, and readers will naturally want to hear what you have to say. • The book you're holding should be ample evidence that I don't take my own advice lightly. Pie, in a word, is my passion. Since as far back as I can remember, watching my mom and dad make their apple pies together every fall as a young boy, I have simply loved pie. I can't really explain why. If one loves poetry, or growing orchids, or walking along the beach at sunset, the why isn't all that important. To me, pie is poetry that makes the world a better place.

Only it's better than actual poetry, some might say, because at the end of an hour or so, there emerges from your oven, or refrigerator, something really good to eat. That's where this book will come in handy, especially if you, like many home cooks I talk to, are a little less than confident when it comes to your pie-making skills. Being fully aware of this, one of my main objectives with this collection of recipes has been to build your confidence by first talking you through the process (starting on page 1) and giving you frequent pointers throughout on what to expect during the assembly and baking stages.

Note the phrase I just used—*build your confidence*. That's an important point, because pie-making mastery does not visit you overnight. It's put in place one piece at a time, like a cinder block wall, until you're left with a solid foundation. At least that's the way it was with me. Today, after decades of regular baking, I can make a good pie pretty much without fail. But I can tell you that the road here has been littered with some ugly ones, too. The great things about pie, however, are that even the ugly ones taste wonderful and, at least in my opinion, you can become about 85 percent proficient as a pie maker in short order. The other 15 percent you'll acquire over a lifetime.

A Pie for All Seasons and All Reasons

This is, to my knowledge, the single most comprehensive book that's ever been written on the subject of sweet pies. And if it pleases me to call that to your attention, I wouldn't be the least bit surprised if the breadth of this collection has left you wondering where you should begin. So perhaps a few words are in order to point you in the right direction.

I've always thought that the best pie making occurs within a context—that the context guides the cook, and the cook, in turn, rises to the challenge and does his or her best work. It's an organic process, predicated on circumstance.

The most obvious of contexts is the season, the logical starting point for many pie-making decisions. Let's say, for example, that it's getting to be late fall and your local farm stand shelves are sagging under the weight of crisp fresh apples. Well, it stands to reason that your baking plans are probably going to include an apple pie rather than a blueberry one, especially since blueberries are being flown in from afar and selling for $5 a half pint.

But season is by no means the only reliable context. How about expediency? Again, it's late fall, the middle of apple season. It's nine o'clock on a Monday evening and your

10-year-old son blithely hands you a flyer—one that's been crumpled up in his knapsack for a week—informing you that tomorrow is the class bake sale and you need to send in a pie. Sure, it may be apple season, but you're out of apples, and the only supermarket that's open is 20 miles away. The only fruit in sight is a bag of frozen blueberries in the freezer. Blueberry pie it is. Or maybe peanut butter pie, if that's what's in the cupboard. I think you get the point.

You don't have to search far to find a context for any pie: a special chocolate pie to honor a chocolate-loving guest; chess pie to take on a drive south to visit the family; custard pie, because you know it will look and taste gorgeous garnished with some berries from the garden. A simple craving will do. I've made more buttermilk pies than I can count, just because I was hungry for one.

Remember, Pie Making is Not Rocket Science, and You Don't Need a Lab to Bake One

It's just amazing how many cooking gizmos there are on the market today. Believe me, I like a clever kitchen tool as much as the next guy. But one of the things that has always appealed to me so much about pie making is the fact that you don't have to own a lot of fancy or expensive equipment to make one: a bowl, a paring knife, a rolling pin, a whisk, a pie pan. Remember, home cooks were making darn good pies long before gourmet shops were around. Same for ingredients: no matter how bare your cupboard, I can virtually guarantee that at this very moment, you have the necessary supplies on hand to make some sort of pie. Of course, when pie making becomes a regular part of your life, you'll stock your shelves accordingly—with flour, frozen fruit, cornstarch, chocolate, vanilla, sugar, and the like—so you can indulge your pie fancy whenever you please.

Although I've made every effort to consider the time constraints most of us are under these days, including taking a generous position toward refrigerated pie pastry and other convenience products, this is not a book of "instant" or "effortless" pies. I, for one, am a little wary of this widespread "instant-homemade" movement: you take a tub of whipped topping, stir in a can of this, and pour it into a pie shell. That's okay on occasion, but I believe most home cooks bake a pie because they want to engage their senses, do something that's tactilely rewarding. Pie making is a craft, after all, and one we can be proud of. Indeed, one of the most satisfying things about making a pie is showing it off just a little, then sharing what we've created. In the absence of effort and skill, there's little to feel particularly proud of. How much pride would you take in a dress you "made" if all you did was remove a pre-made front and premade back from a package, then stitch them together in two minutes? Very little, I imagine.

So go ahead, proceed fearlessly, and make some pie. Whether you're a beginner or a seasoned expert, I hope this book will serve as your trusted pie companion for years to come. May you discover recipes that delight, techniques that prove useful, and a word or two of wisdom that leads to a lifetime of happy pie baking for you and yours.

I'm one of those cookbook authors who has, for years, been admonishing readers to *please* read the recipe through before starting it. It's no mystery why: I find that if I take a comfortable seat, kick back, and let the visual steps of the recipe start to develop in my mind while I read, I inevitably bring more confidence and precision to the tasks at hand. It's sort of like looking at a

Required Reading: What It Takes to Make the Perfect Pie

map before beginning a journey to a place you've never been. • What follows are some general guidelines for making a successful pie, from mixing the pastry to getting it out of the oven. For the reasons I've just mentioned, I hope you'll take a few minutes to read these important pages. If you're at home, slide into a cozy chair. If you're at a bookstore, grab a latte and find a quiet corner. Imagine doing each of the steps outlined, then gather your confidence, get yourself into the kitchen, and start baking!

Of *Mise en Place* and Pies

ASK ANY CULINARY SCHOOL STUDENT about the meaning of the French term *mise en place*, and he or she will dive right into a thorough explanation. *Mise en place*—translated as "everything in its place"—is a core concept of the professional kitchen. It means, more or less, that before you so much as turn on a burner, you'd better gather all your ingredients, measure them out, and have the equipment you need ready to go. And while you're at it, sharpen your knife. *Mise en place* is the antithesis of—and antidote for—chaos and confusion in the kitchen.

The home cook would do well to borrow the concept and apply it to pie making. There's much to do before you actually turn on the oven, and the more organized you are, the more you'll enjoy making pies. I speak from experience: it's no fun to get halfway into the preparations for a crumb-topped apple pie, only to find you're out of butter. Or cinnamon.

Here, then, are some of my *mise en place* rules for baking a pie.

▶ Read the recipe first. Actually, read it twice. Not only will this familiarize you with the ingredients list, but it also will help you gauge the recipe's suitability. Do you have everything it calls for? Also, just as important, you'll start developing the mental photographs that will help you make the pie. In addition, reading the recipe will give you an idea when you'll be able to serve the pie. Does it need to be refrigerated overnight? Or can it be served more or less right away?

▶ Check your supplies of ingredients against the recipe's ingredients list. Procure the items you need.

▶ Measure and stage the necessary ingredients. If a recipe calls for cold shortening, put it on a plate in the freezer while you're making other preparations. Remember, your goal—once you start working on a recipe—is to be able to walk right through it without taking detours or making pit stops.

▶ Finally, make plans for your pie. Don't let it linger on the counter or in the fridge, slowly slipping past its prime. Once you've eaten your immediate share, determine how much of it to refrigerate (for short-term storage), freeze, or give away. Pies topped with whipped cream should be eaten the same day, if possible. If that means giving some to your neighbors, so be it.

Making the Perfect Pastry

If you already knew how to make a perfect pastry, chances are you wouldn't be reading this. So let's assume, for our purposes, that you have certain misgivings about making a respectable pie crust. Perhaps you've tried, only to fail miserably. Perhaps you've never even bothered to try, certain that you were born without the all-important "pie pastry gene." Maybe you *are* a real pro, but you're curious about what I have to say on the subject. Whatever the case may be, let's begin by taking a closer look at making good pie dough and see if you can gather the courage to dive right in and make your own perfect pastry. It is, I assure you, not a difficult thing to do.

Simply put, pie pastry is a blend of flour, sugar (sometimes), salt, fat—typically in the form of butter or solid vegetable shortening (such as Crisco)—and water. When these ingredients are properly mixed and handled, the result is a pie crust with a flaky texture and good flavor. For many of the pastries in this book, I have provided instructions for making the pastry three different ways: by hand, in a food processor, and with an electric mixer. Let's look at all three ways.

Making Pastry by Hand

For the beginner, making pastry by hand is the best way to learn. The process is very deliberate, and you won't get ahead of yourself the way you might with a machine. You'll also begin to develop the intuitive "touch" that all good pastry makers possess. You'll get a feel for how much to cut in the fat, the amount of water to add, and how much force to use when handling the dough.

To make pastry by hand, simply mix the dry ingredients in a bowl—something large enough to get your hands down into. Add the fat in pieces, then toss it with the flour. I talk more about the baking qualities of various fats in the headnote to each pastry recipe. But in a nutshell, vegetable shortening will give you great flakiness but little flavor. Butter will result in less flakiness and more flavor. And a blend of the two will give you both. Lard, which has fallen out of fashion and is no longer widely appreciated by home cooks, makes an excellent crust, yielding the ultimate in flakiness.

Before you start cutting in the fat with your pastry blender, break it up by hand so that the pieces aren't so large. Then start pushing down into the mixture with the pastry blender, literally cutting the fat into the flour. After every three or four pushes, stop and toss the mixture up from the bottom of the bowl by hand. What you're doing with all of this cutting is creating little pockets of fat. When these pockets are flattened—when the dough is rolled—they create, essentially, fissures of fat. In the heat of the oven, the fat melts and the moisture in it causes the dough to expand, creating the flaky network that characterizes a good crust. Note that there are many fine home bakers who don't bother with a pastry blender at all. They simply rub the fat into the flour by hand, a method you might want to try if, indeed, you don't own a pastry blender.

When the fat is sufficiently cut in—leaving clumps the proverbial "size of small peas"—water is added to help bind the pastry. The mark of an experienced pastry maker is knowing just how much water to add, leaving the pastry neither too moist nor too dry. There are different schools of thought on how best to add the water. One of the most gifted pie makers I know, contrary to popular wisdom, stirs it in all at once with excellent results. Others add it a tablespoon at a time. I take the middle ground, usually adding half of it at first, then the rest about a tablespoon at a time. The risk of adding it too slowly is that you'll overmix the dough, activating the gluten in the flour—the stuff that makes dough elastic, which is fine in bread dough but an absolute no-no when making a pie crust. With my approach, you give the dough an overall dampening, then you incrementally bring it to the right consistency, but not too incrementally. Just a couple of stirring strokes with a big fork (see the box at left) after each bit of water should do it.

I hesitate to say this, but if you're a beginner and have to err when you're adding the water, err on the side of a bit too much rather than too little. Neither is ideal, but it's slightly easier and less frustrating to handle a dough that's too damp than one that's too dry and prone to cracking and crumbling. If your dough is dampish, make sure you use plenty of flour on your rolling pin and pastry to keep it from sticking.

Making Pastry in a Food Processor

Most cooks have no idea how simple it is to use a food processor to make pie pastry. I know this for a fact because, before every pie-making demonstration I give, I ask how many people in the crowd already do so. Maybe three or four out of a hundred will raise their hands. By the time the demonstration is over, most of the crowd has been converted to the food processor method.

Let me preface my comments by saying that unless you have a large-capacity food processor—the biggest (14-cup capacity) model Cuisinart makes—don't even bother. A smaller machine will not do a thorough, even job of mixing up a double-crust pastry. You can, however, make a single batch of pastry in a smaller machine.

The food processor does essentially the same thing you do by hand when you cut the fat into the flour. The difference is that the food processor is much more efficient. It works many times faster, and it cuts more sharply, with less of a rubbing action than you get by hand. You'll still get a flaky crust with a food processor, but the flakes tend to be smaller.

The key to making a good food processor pastry is the pulse button. The entire pastry is made with quick little pulses. Pulsing is crucial because that starting and stopping of the machine keeps tossing the mixture up from the bottom of the bowl, ensuring that the pastry is evenly mixed. All it takes is about five pulses to cut in the fat, after which I remove the lid and fluff the mixture with a fork. I do this because, even with the pulsing, the processor will start to compact some of the pastry under the blade. Fluffing frees it up.

As with pastry made by hand, the water is added in stages—first half of it, then the remainder. After all the water is added, continue to pulse the machine just until it forms large clumps that can be packed. If the pastry balls up around the blade, you've mixed it too much. Overprocessing often results in a pastry that's not as tender as it should be, so try not to do that next time.

Making Pastry with an Electric Mixer

Only in the past few years have I started making pastry with my electric mixer. I like this method, but since I came to it later in my pie-making career, I can't say I've become a real convert. There are, after all, only so many methods a fellow needs to make pastry. My preference, if I had to choose, would be one of the techniques I've just described. Still, perhaps you'd like to give it a try, and if you do, my observations may prove useful.

I use my KitchenAid stand mixer, which, unlike many cheaper hand mixers, has the slow speeds required for mixing the pastry sufficiently without overmixing it.

Begin by combining your dry ingredients in the mixer bowl. Toss them by hand or turn on the mixer to combine them. Add the fat in pieces. With the mixer on low speed, start mixing—or cutting—the fat and flour together. I've known cooks who use the flat beater attachment for this, but I think the wire whip better emulates the cutting action required. Blend the pastry on low speed for about 10 seconds, then stop the machine and fluff the mixture up from the bottom with a rubber spatula. As with the food processor, some of the pastry will settle and compact in the bottom of the bowl; your aim is to put it back into circulation.

Turn the machine back on low speed and continue to blend for a few more seconds. Sprinkle half of the water over the pastry and blend for a few seconds. Add the remaining water a tablespoon at a time, blending briefly after each addition. Stop the machine and gather up the pastry.

No matter the method you use, wrap and refrigerate your pastry as instructed in each recipe. As I often say, refrigerating a pastry is probably the single most important step you can take to achieve a dough that is easy to roll, is relatively easy to handle, and turns out good and flaky.

Convenience Pie Pastry

In a perfect world, we would all make our own pastry, all the time. And if that's the ideal, we sometimes fall a little short of the mark. We may have planned to make a pastry from scratch, only for life to intervene: A child falls ill. The dog gets sprayed by a skunk. A husband is rushed to the emergency room when the TV remote fuses to his hand and has to be surgically removed. This or, let's be honest, in spite of my rousing pep talk about how simple it is to make a good pastry from scratch, you just aren't buying it.

Okay, fine. I'm here to tell you that you can make a homemade pie on your own terms, without a homemade pastry. The answer is as close as the refrigerator case or frozen food section of your local supermarket.

Refrigerated Pie Pastry

Truth be told, I am a relative newcomer to refrigerated pie pastry. A dedicated pie maker since my late teens, I have always considered it a matter of pride that I made my own pastry from scratch, no matter the other demands on my time. I simply wasn't interested.

That changed one day when, working on an assignment for one of the magazines I write for, I was asked to make some pies with refrigerated pastry. And darned if I wasn't pretty impressed: The crusts came out flaky and tender. The flavor was good, if not quite homemade. And, well, you just couldn't beat the ease of it all: just unfold, line the pan, fill, and bake.

In the course of writing this book, I used a number of refrigerated pie pastries to test recipes. Here are some things I picked up along the way.

- Take the pastry out of the refrigerator about 15 minutes before you line your pan. The pastry will be more pliable and easier to handle when it isn't too cold. Refrigerate or freeze the pie shell while you make the filling.

- The pastry is meant to be used primarily in a 9-inch standard pie pan. There's not enough of it for most deep-dish pans. (See page 8 for the definitions and descriptions of various pie pans.) Used thus, there's just the right amount of pastry to sculpt an upstanding ridge on single-crust pies, which helps contain the filling.

- If the pastry cracks at one of the seams when you're unfolding it, don't worry. Just pinch it back together.

- Refrigerated pastry, I've noticed, has a tendency to brown faster than most homemade pastries I make. If you find that to be the case, simply place a piece of aluminum foil loosely over the pie during the last 10 to 15 minutes of baking to deflect the heat.

- You can, if you wish, use refrigerated pie pastry for virtually any pie in this book that specifies a 9-inch standard (not deep-dish) pie shell.

Frozen Pie Shells

In terms of convenience, frozen pie shells are even more cook-friendly than refrigerated pie pastry. But there are a few limitations and pet peeves worth mentioning.

The first is their size. Even frozen pie shells labeled "deep-dish" don't have the capacity of a 9-inch standard pie pan. Typically, they don't hold more than about 3 cups of fruit, maybe 4 if you're using apples or pears—fruit that isn't too juicy. Most pie recipes in general, including the ones in this book, will not fit very well into a frozen pie shell.

My second beef is the nature of the disposable aluminum pans they come in. Such pans not only deflect the heat, making a properly baked, well-browned crust difficult to achieve, but they also can be tricky to handle because they're so flimsy and tend to bend when they contain a hot pie. Indeed, rather than try to lift one of them out of the oven, I usually slide a rimless cookie sheet under the pan, using it like a giant spatula.

Finally, frozen pie shells tend to get pretty banged up en route to your supermarket. It's not unusual to find edges broken off or gaping holes, like puzzle pieces that have gone missing. The upshot? Choose carefully. And if you do take the frozen pie shell option, here are a few pointers to consider.

▶ I've tried a number of brands, and the one I like best is Marie Callender's. This company's pans are relatively sturdy and a little deeper than most, and the product tastes good, too. I also like Mrs. Smith's shells, perhaps the most sturdily packaged and therefore the least prone to damage.

▶ To get the best possible bottom crust, which is to say as browned as possible, bake the pie on a low oven rack. If you have a dark, heavy baking sheet, preheat it in the oven on a low rack and bake the pie directly on it.

▶ The filling for most 9½-inch deep-dish pies can be divided between two 9-inch frozen pie shells.

Choosing Your Pie Pan

As you might imagine, I own a number of pie pans. Not a ridiculous number—maybe a couple of dozen or so; heck, some guys own that many cars—but enough of them, in various materials and designs, to have formed some opinions about which ones I like and care to recommend.

First, let's look at the three pan sizes I recommend for the vast majority of the pies in this book: the *9-inch standard pan, the 9½-inch deep-dish pan, and the 9½- to 10-inch extra-deep-dish pie pan.*

Pie Equipment: Here's What's Selling

If anyone knows what pie bakers are buying these days, it's Cindy Fountain, retail director for the King Arthur Flour Baker's Store in Norwich, Vermont—possibly the biggest all-baking store in the country. Legions of dedicated bakers flock to it from all around the country every year. I sat down and talked to Cindy about what today's pie bakers want. Here's what she had to say.

"First of all, pies are back. There's a real resurgence of interest in baking a homemade pie nowadays. Presentation is more important to today's pie bakers than it was to past generations. We sell lots of the standard aluminum pans, but the gorgeous Polish pottery pie pans are really hot, too. For some reason, pie birds (see page 217) are all the rage now. People tell me they remind them of their grandmothers. Apparently, everyone's grandmother used to have one. The flour wands are big; this is something you fill with flour and shake over the dough to keep your pin from sticking (see page 319). As for rolling pins, we have a Vermont-made marble pin that's great for rolling. I have one myself, and I love the weight: three or four rolls, and I'm done. Our stainless steel pie chain is another steady seller. You use this as you would dried beans to weight down your pastry when you're prebaking a crust without a filling. Lots of people buy our mini pastry cutters so they can dress up their top crusts. And, of course, pie carriers: someone makes a beautiful pie, and they want a way to transport it so it doesn't get damaged en route."

To view some of these items, go to www.kingarthurflour.com.

The majority of pie recipes I see are written around the 9-inch standard pan. I say standard, but in fact there seem to be few standards when it comes to pie pans, a dilemma I wish Congress would remedy by enacting a new law. Anyway, a 9-inch standard pan is about 9 inches in diameter—measured across the opening—and 1 to $1\frac{1}{4}$ inches deep. Perhaps the best-selling pan of this design is the Pyrex 9-inch clear tempered-glass pan, which you see every time you walk down the baking aisle of your supermarket. Nearby, you'll also find the thin, shiny aluminum pans of roughly the same size. You can make a good pie in both of these pans, but given the choice, I would nearly always choose the Pyrex pan. It isn't sexy or particularly attractive, but for most everyday pies, you get excellent results— which is to say a nicely browned and evenly baked crust—with a glass pie pan. Glass tends to be a little slow in heating up, but once it does, it does a great job of browning.

The thin, shiny aluminum pan is less desirable. Thin aluminum tends to reflect a lot of heat without absorbing much of it—think of those aluminum shields we put in our car windshields. Believe me, I've upended many a pie, turning the whole thing out just to check a crust (oh, the things I do in the name of research), and time and again I've discovered an underdone crust baked in shiny aluminum. (I've also discovered that upended pie tastes just fine, thank you.)

Now if you shop at a fancier kitchenware store, you have a couple of more choices, including a heavier aluminum pan, still shiny, and a darker (usually nonstick) one. One big manufacturer of these pans is Chicago Metallic, which also makes stuff for the bakery trade, so you know its pans are sturdy. I've been a fan of this company's products for years.

When a shiny pan is heavier, you get better results because even if the pan reflects a certain amount of heat, it also absorbs it, thus the bottom crust browns better. The darker pan is better yet. Dark absorbs heat efficiently—the reason you don't wear a black top in the summer—and you wind up with a nicely browned crust, sometimes a little too browned, especially near the upper edge, but it usually isn't enough to quibble about.

Bottom line: if you're not satisfied with your current 9-inch pie pan, try a Pyrex pan or a heavier metal pan.

A 9-inch standard pan holds a certain amount of filling—about 4 cups give or take, a bit more if you're using firm, not-too-juicy fruit such as apples or pears. I think it makes a suitable pie for a small to medium-size family, with a few pieces left over for the next day. Sometimes you want a little extra pie, however—bigger slices, or a pie that's suitable for a larger family or a potluck supper. For those pies, I often use the next size up, a 9½-inch deep-dish pan.

For uniformity's sake, all of the pies in this book that call for such a pan were baked at least once in the one pan I know you can find no matter where you live: the Pyrex 9½-inch deep-dish pan. It measures 9½ inches across the opening and nearly 1¾ inches deep. That may not sound much bigger than a standard pan, but it will hold nearly half again as much filling, with a capacity of about 6 cups. The pan I'm describing has a sloping side and a very distinctive ruffled upper edge. If you can't find one at the supermarket, you can most certainly find one at a kitchenware store. This is my first choice for big, seasonal fruit pies, especially apple, pear, and peach. This pan also has something I wish more pie pans had: handles. They aren't particularly big, but they sure help when you're trying to take a hot pie out of the oven and place it on a cooling rack.

When I want to go really big, I turn to what I call my extra-deep-dish pie pans. This is not a standard term, but one I use to describe several oversize pans I've picked up along the way. These are just slightly larger than the regular deep-dish pans and can be used nearly interchangeably. (If you have too much filling for a pie pan, by the way, just put the little bit extra in a custard cup and bake it without a crust.)

Apart from these common and identifiable pans, there are many enameled pottery pans that not only do a fine job of browning the crust but also are very attractive and make for a lovely presentation. My favorites in this category are the Emile Henry pie plates you can find at Williams-Sonoma (see box) and other gourmet kitchen stores, as well as the lovely Polish pottery pie pans, with a capacity nearly equivalent to the deep-dish pan described above. These pans aren't cheap, put I think they're worth the outlay simply because everyone needs at least one pan that's a real looker. I buy mine from Twins Polish Pottery at www.twinspolishpottery.com.

Finally, there's one pan that I suggest you avoid: the disposable aluminum kind. This type of pan is okay in a pinch, but the flimsiness of the pan and the shininess of the material usually result in an underdone crust.

Rolling Your Pastry

Your pastry is made and chilled, your pan is standing by. Now what's the best way to roll your pastry and get it into the pan without the blessed thing falling apart?

There are, in fact, many ways to do just that. Whenever I give a pie-making demonstration and walk through the method I'm about to describe, several people will, inevitably, describe their own methods. Perhaps one likes to roll her dough on a marble counter, another likes a certain rolling pin, and a third has a favorite method for lifting the pastry into the pan. And I say bravo to that! If you have a way of doing this that already works just fine, stick with it. But if you're relatively new to rolling pastry or not satisfied with your method, this is the way I do it.

Emile Henry Pie Plates

In France, sweet pies as we know them don't exist. It's ironic, then, that a Frenchman named Jacques Henry was granted a U.S. patent for an American pie pan that's become something of a trendsetter.

The pans, with their graceful scalloped edges, are manufactured by Emile Henry, located in Marcigny, Burgundy, France. Burgundy clay is known for its superb heat diffusion and retention—qualities that help promote even browning and make these pans so superior for pies. Jacques Henry, a fifth-generation descendant of the founder, was inspired to create the pan from a turn-of-the-century baking dish he spotted in an old family photo.

Rugged, attractive, and roomy, the standard six-cup pie pan works for any deep-dish pie in this collection. I own several and use them often, especially when presentation counts. You can find Emile Henry pans in gourmet retail stores across the country.

Pins for Your Pies

Walk into any well-stocked kitchen store, and you're liable to find a half dozen or more rolling pins to choose from. How is a pie maker to choose? Here are some guidelines.

- Polished maple is the best hardwood for a rolling pin. It has a close, tight grain that won't absorb moisture or flavors from other foods you might use it on.

- Some bakers I know swear by their heavy marble pins. They like the weight because it does some of the work. Chill a marble pin before rolling out your pastry; the coolness will help.

- The handles are key. They shouldn't be stuck into the pin, or they're liable to break off when you bear down on a cold pastry. On better pins, a heavy metal rod extends through the barrel and well into each handle. Ball bearing construction is a must.

- It's nice to have more than one pin. Tapered French-style pins are good for starting cold pastry dough, but I prefer to finish rolling with a larger American-style pin. A 12- to 15-inch barrel is a good size for home pie makers.

- Avoid flea market pins. You don't know how or where they've been used. If you want to hang them on a wall, fine. A good rolling pin costs $25 to $30, and it's worth every penny.

Before you do anything else, butter or grease your pie pan. It isn't mandatory, and, in theory at least, there's plenty of fat in the pastry to prevent the crust from sticking. But some of my pans don't know this—especially the glass and pottery ones—so I do it anyway.

Now take a piece of waxed paper about 13 inches long and place it on your counter, with the curl down. Dust it *lightly* with flour. If you have a Formica-type counter, waxed paper has a tendency to skid around on it, so you can do one of two things. You can buy a Silpat baking mat (see page 14) and put it down first, under the waxed paper, or use it in place of the waxed paper. Or you can wipe the counter with a *slightly* damp dishrag, which will keep the waxed paper in place. I recommend the first option.

Put your cold but not too hard pastry in the center of the waxed paper and dust the top of it with flour. If you're making a double-crust pie, you've already been instructed to make one half of the pastry (for the shell) a little larger than the other. So make sure you have the correct disk of dough. Flour your rolling pin and roll it over the top of the pastry

From My "Overrated Techniques" File

I hate to break ranks on this, but I'm not a fan of rolling pastry between two pieces of plastic wrap, advice I see dispensed frequently. Why? Because the top piece inevitably sticks to the pastry, crimps, and buckles, requiring you to stop and straighten out the plastic after each pass of your rolling pin. It's not worth the hassle. It's far easier to use a single sheet of waxed paper underneath your pastry and a liberal-enough dusting of flour on top of the pastry—and on your pin—to prevent the dough from sticking. The pastry won't buckle if you use this method, and as long as it has been refrigerated, you shouldn't have any problem with it sticking to the pin. If you want to use two sheets of something (if you're a pastry novice, you may appreciate the added no-stick security), use a second sheet of waxed paper. I find it less troublesome than plastic wrap.

a couple of times, just to wake it up. At this point in the rolling, I sometimes use my tapered French-style pin, because the dough responds to it a little better than it does to my big pin, which is preferable once the dough starts to expand. The thin pin also gives me good directional control, so if I'm rolling along and my pastry starts to look like the state of Florida, I can use short passes to get it back in shape.

One of the key reasons for using waxed paper is that you can rotate the dough easily, just by turning the paper. You don't have to lift the dough itself off the counter, thereby risking a major tear or other catastrophe. Anyway, start pushing down on the dough, directly away from you, once or twice. When you've made a little progress, give the waxed paper a quarter turn and roll a couple of more times, always rolling more or less straight away from you. Keep in mind that you will need to adjust the degree of pressure you use depending on the type of pastry you've made: the higher the proportion of butter, the firmer the chilled pastry will be. A pastry made with all shortening will be relatively soft by comparison. As you roll, keep dusting the pastry and rolling pin with flour, as necessary, to keep them from sticking together. When the dough seems to be about halfway there, switch to your bigger rolling pin if you've started with a thin one—my big pin has a 3-inch-diameter by 12-inch-long roller—and finish rolling.

As you start to roll, don't be concerned if the dough cracks a little around the edge; it probably will. If it starts to get out of hand, however, just stop rolling and pinch the edge back together around the entire perimeter. That will make you feel better and limit the amount of future cracking. Also, always roll from the center out and ease up ever so slightly

The Silpat Solution

So there you are rolling along, 11 inches into a perfect 12-inch circle of pastry, when you discover that your dough is hopelessly stuck to the counter. What's a home baker to do? There's always waxed paper (see page 12), my favorite low-tech surface for rolling out pie pastry. But you might want to consider the Silpat, too. A relative newcomer to the market, the Silpat is a silicone-treated material that's both heat-resistant and virtually nonstick. Primarily intended as a reusable baking sheet liner, the Silpat's nonstick perform-ance makes it a natural for rolling pastry. Simply roll your dough directly on the Silpat, invert it over your pie pan (just as you do with waxed paper), and peel off the Silpat. No need to flour it or apply oil.

Even if you still prefer waxed paper, you might consider the Silpat. Waxed paper has a tendency to slide around on Formica-type counters, and the Silpat can be used as a nonskid surface underneath the waxed paper. An 11 x 16-inch Silpat mat costs about $20 and can be found at housewares stores such as Bed Bath & Beyond and Sur La Table.

on the pressure as you approach the edge. One common error I've noticed with novice rollers is that they tend to press harder as they get near the edge, leaving the pastry too thin there and almost impossible to shape or sculpt. When you're done rolling, your entire circle of dough should be a uniform thickness.

Another reason I like waxed paper is because it has a built-in measure that let's you know when you're done rolling: it's 12 inches wide, the perfect size bottom pastry for a 9-inch standard pie pan. You know you've rolled enough when, provided your circle is actually round, you've reached the edges of the paper. To make a bottom pastry for a 9½-inch deep-dish pan, roll it 13 inches or even a tad wider, just a little off the paper on the factory edges.

Getting Your Pastry into the Pan

Now the challenge is to get the pastry safely into the pan without mishap. This could not be easier. With your pan nearby, put one hand over the pastry, fingers outstretched to better support it. Then in one fluid motion, invert the pastry and waxed paper directly over the pan. Using your fingers to check, center the pastry over the pan, then gently peel off the paper. Pull at a sharp angle, rather than in an upward motion, to keep the pastry from shift-ing position.

As you lift on the overhanging dough with one hand (to take the tension off the dough), gently tuck the pastry into the pan; your two hands will be directly opposite each other as you do this, working in concert. Don't blithely jam your fingers into the dough, or you'll stretch and perhaps tear it. Rather, nudge it into the bottom of the pan without stretching it. Continue in this fashion all around the pan. If you've rolled a pretty good circle and centered the dough nicely, you should have a relatively even overhang all around the pan. If the overhang is not quite even, don't worry. If it is extremely uneven and certain places have no overhang at all, snip some excess dough from another part of the pastry, moisten one side of it with a wet fingertip, and pinch it into place to fill in the gap. Finally, use a pastry brush to sweep any excess flour off the pastry edge.

If you're making a double crust pie, you'll want to keep that overhanging dough in place so that you can attach the top crust to it. Just put the pan directly in the refrigerator as is, taking care not to catch the edge of the pastry on anything. If I don't have room on a shelf, I usually put it on top of a bowl, above harm's way.

Forming the Pastry Edge

If you aren't attaching a top crust to your pie, you'll need to do something with that overhang before you go any further. You have several options.

In many if not most cases, in particular when you have a juicy fruit filling or another liquidy filling, you will want the added height of the pastry edge to help contain the filling. That extra one-half inch of height can mean the difference between a filling that stays where it should and one that spills over the edge, sending you looking for the oven cleaner.

To make what I call an *upstanding ridge*, fold the overhanging dough back, which is to say away from the inside of the pan. Pinch the dough against itself, sculpting it into a ridge. Mold it as you would clay. As you do this, you'll find that the edge will be thicker in some places, thinner in others. One thing you can do when you run into a thick spot is simply squeeze harder to push the excess farther out along the edge. Your goal in all this sculpting is a more or less uniform ridge about one-half inch high, perhaps a little less. You can leave the

UPSTANDING RIDGE CRUST

Ever see that trick, recommended in countless magazines and books, for rolling your pastry around your pin and then unrolling it over your pie pan? Well, I think it's a very cool idea, but it's not at all easy to execute. For starters, it requires you to hold a very heavy rolling pin in one hand while you somehow guide/roll the pastry around the pin with the other. Rolling or unrolling, the odds of your pastry tearing en route are much higher than you'd like. Instead, just roll your pastry out onto a sheet of waxed paper, invert it over your pie pan, and peel off the paper (see page 14).

edge just like that—your basic upstanding ridge—or you can make a scalloped edge, as shown in the picture at right.

In any event, place the pie shell in the refrigerator or freezer. Not only will this make the pastry more durable against the possibility that you'll knock the edge with your hand or a utensil and damage it while you're filling the pie, but it also will firm up the fat, which will help to keep the pastry flaky as it bakes.

SCALLOPED EDGE CRUST

Prebaking the Pie Shell

For certain types of pies, you'll need to prebake the pastry, sometimes *partially*—as when the pie will be filled and then baked, such as with most custard pies—and other times *fully*—as when the pie will require no further baking, such as with cream pies.

I know it's not particularly convenient to prebake a pie shell. Even I get a little impatient with the process, especially if I'm in a hurry. But I think it's really worth the added time in the final analysis. Whenever I'm served a pie and the bottom crust is soggy or undercooked, I know the crust wasn't prebaked, and I consider the pie something of a failure. I'm not likely to say that—"Hey, lovely meal. Thanks for having us. But what gives with your bottom crust?"—but I can't help feeling that if you're going to take the time to bake a pie, you should do what you can to make sure it is properly baked.

You only need a couple of things to prebake a pie shell: aluminum foil and something to weight the foil and pastry down. The weight is necessary to hold the pastry in place so that it doesn't puff up, become misshapen, and not bake properly. Some bakers like special pie weights to hold the pastry down, but I just use dried beans. I have, I'm embarrassed to say, been using the same dried beans for about seven or eight years now. I keep them in an oatmeal box in my baking cupboard. They smell a little toasty—my wife, Bev, always asks me what's burning when I use them—but they're in fine shape otherwise, so I see no reason to throw them out.

Tear off a piece of aluminum foil about 16 inches long. That's more than you'll need to fit into your pan, but the excess makes the foil easy to lift when you're removing the beans. By the way, don't use heavy-duty foil; it's a little too rigid to shape easily. Center the foil over your pie shell and, just as you tucked the pastry into the pan, tuck the foil into the pie shell. (One of the reasons I like to freeze the pastry for 15 minutes is that you won't damage or change the shape of a pastry that's frozen firm when you're tucking and molding.) The bottom edge should be well defined, as should the sides. Basically, the foil should fit the pie shell like a second skin. Let the excess foil on the ends just flare out like wings. Don't bunch it around the pie pan, or you'll deflect heat away from the sides. Pour in enough dried beans to reach the top of the pan.

With your oven preheated to 400°F, bake the pie shell on the center rack for 15 minutes. This first stage of baking really sets the crust—not fully baking it, but allowing it to settle and take on the shape of the pan. You don't want to skimp on this part of the process, or the pastry will be more inclined to shrink when the weights are removed.

After 15 minutes, slide out the rack—you don't have to remove the pie from the oven—and slowly lift up on the sides of the foil to remove the weights. You may not even need oven mitts to do this because as soon as the aluminum foil hits the room-temperature air, it cools right off (this being a perfect illustration of why I don't like flimsy aluminum pans; they don't hold heat). Put the foil and weights on the counter, somewhere out of the way. Take a fork and prick the pastry all over the bottom, perhaps seven or eight times, covering as much area as possible. As you stick the fork in, give it a little twist to enlarge the holes slightly, because small holes have a way of closing up. I generally don't worry about pricking the side of the pastry unless I see it start to puff; then I open the oven door and stick a fork in to deflate it.

Lower the oven temperature to 375°F and continue to bake the pie shell for 10 to 12 minutes for a *partially prebaked* pie shell or 15 to 17 minutes for a *fully prebaked* pie shell. Check on the pie shell once or twice during this time to make sure it isn't puffing up; if it is, prick the problem spot with a fork. Look for visual clues that the pastry is properly baked. A *partially prebaked* pie shell will just be starting to brown, ever so lightly. A *fully prebaked* pie shell will be golden brown and look fully baked. Bear in mind that these times for the second phase of the baking (without the beans) are approximate. For instance, the type of pastry may affect the baking time. Just use your best judgment.

As soon as you remove the pie shell from the oven, use the back of a spoon to gently press the side crust back into position anywhere it might have sagged or slightly puffed. Take care not to push so hard that you break the crust, leaving a place where the filling can run out. Also, whisk an egg white until frothy, then paint it over the holes you've poked to prevent the filling from leaking. Put the pie shell back in the hot oven to bake the egg white to a hard finish, about 2 minutes. Remove the pie shell from the oven and put it on a wire rack to cool.

Filling and Sealing a Double-Crust Pie

Of course, with most fruit pies, you won't be prebaking anything; the filling goes right into the uncooked pie shell. Let's first look at how double-crust pies, typically fruit pies, are handled.

Earlier I said to refrigerate the pastry for a double-crust pie. That will firm it up and make the pastry less likely to turn soggy when juicy fruit filling is added. Unlike the procedure for a single-crust pie, however, you don't freeze the bottom pastry, because the overhang would get too firm to attach to the top crust.

So here's where you stand: Your pie shell is in the refrigerator. Your fruit filling awaits. The assembly can begin, but first you must roll your top pastry.

The top pastry is rolled just as the bottom one was, only you don't have to roll it so large—just large enough to cover the pie plus enough for the overhang. Each recipe tells you just how large this is. Roll the pastry on the waxed paper and have it standing by. If, by chance, the phone rings and you're delayed for any reason, slide the paper and pastry onto a baking sheet and stick it in the fridge until you're ready to proceed. And if you want to make decorative cutouts in the top pastry, put the rolled dough in the freezer for 10 minutes to firm it up, then cut as desired.

The pastry is easier to handle when cool, so without delay get the filling into the refrigerated pie shell. If your filling contains apples, pears, or anything with edges that jut up and might tear the crust, smooth it out with your hands, laying those slices down flat. Now take a pastry brush and moisten the entire rim of the pie shell with water; this acts as the glue to help seal the pastries together. While you're at it, brush excess flour off your top pastry.

Pastry Cutouts

One of the easiest ways to give your pies that decorative edge, figuratively and literally, is by using cookie cutters to make pastry cutouts. You can use large cutters to make a centerpiece on your pie—for example, a big apple in the center of your double-crust apple pie—or smaller cutters to make a leaf border or to spell out a message such as "Happy Halloween." Look for cutters at your local arts and crafts store. If this sounds like fun—and if you have kids, I can assure you it will be—here are some tips to keep in mind.

- For just a few cutouts, use your pastry scraps to cut from. Roll the dough onto a sheet of waxed paper, then slide the paper and dough onto a baking sheet and freeze for 15 minutes. Cold dough cuts much easier than room-temperature dough.

- With double-crust pies, simply place the cutouts right on the top crust after you've brushed it with milk.

- To make a decorative border on a single-crust pie, your cutouts can't be much larger than the rim of the pie pan, or they won't have enough support. Leaves work well because they can drape down into the pie shell and still look quite natural.

- Alternatively, you can make a cutout garland by baking the cutouts separately. Start with enough pastry for a single crust and roll it as above. Make the cutouts and transfer them to a greased baking sheet. Brush with 1 egg white beaten with 1 tablespoon water; try not to get the glaze on the sheet. Keep in mind that you'll need quite a few cutouts to go around the entire pie. Bake the cutouts in a preheated 375°F oven until golden brown, 10 to 15 minutes. Brush the edge of the baked pie shell with corn syrup and press the cutouts into place.

DECORATIVE BORDER WITH CRUST CUTOUTS

A Nice Set of Mini Cutters

My favorite tin of mini cookie cutters is a collection of six autumn designs: pumpkin, apple, oak leaf, maple leaf, acorn, and some sort of generic leaf, none more than about an inch wide. They're great for dressing up fall fruit pies, pumpkin pies, and maple pies (see Maple Cream Pie on page 476). When I'm not using them for pies, they're great for sugar cookies or special cutouts for gingerbread houses.

Here's a little tip for keeping all your cutters in top form. Since they're often made from tin, cutters will develop rust spots if you let water droplets sit on them after washing. To prevent this, place the just-washed cutters on a baking sheet and put them in the oven while it's cooling down. They'll dry right off.

You can find plenty of sources for mini cookie cutters online. Just use those three words to search. One company that seems to have an extensive collection of mini cutters is www.foosecookiecutters.com.

Just as you did earlier when you inverted your pie shell into the pan, invert the top pastry over the pie, center it, and remove the waxed paper. Press where you've moistened to seal. If you plan to make an upstanding ridge (see page 15), take a pair of scissors and trim the overhang so that it is about one-half inch wider than the top of the pan. Then turn the excess pastry back and pinch it into an upstanding ridge. Make a scalloped edge, if desired. Your other choice is to simply trim the pastry flush with the outside edge of the pan. Using a paring

FORK-PRESSED FLUSH EDGE CRUST

knife, held perpendicular to the counter, run the blade around the edge of the pie; the excess pastry will fall right off. Press the tines of a fork around the edge to make an attractive seal. Both methods—upstanding edge and flush trim—have their pros and cons. An upstanding ridge is better insurance against the pie splitting at a seam and bubbling over, and it leaves quite a hefty edge of crust, which is fine if you like that. A flush-trimmed pastry is a little more likely to split at the seam, but you don't have that thick crust there. Either way, don't sweat it: in the grand scheme of things, these are minor concerns, and experience will dictate the choices you make.

Baking Your Pie

It might look like little more than a metal box, but your oven is a dynamic entity. You may think it just sits there, acting like a perfect gentleman. But it's fluctuating all the time: it heats up, gets real hot and then—after the temperature spikes—the heat levels off. When you open the oven to peak at a roast, the temperature in the oven falls, then rises, then levels off again. Some parts of your oven are hotter than others. Most ovens are hotter near the back, the top, and the bottom, and a little less so in the center and front.

So if you're going to bake a pie, you can't do it passively, just shoving the pie in and hoping for the best. You have to get to know your oven and its quirks, then take whatever steps are required to bake the perfect pie.

By and large, the ideal place to bake a pie is in the center of the oven. Nearly all of the recipes in this book instruct you to bake your pie on the center oven rack, and that's where you should start. In some ovens, the rack is slightly high or low of center. If that's the case, go with the slightly lower position. It's more important that the bottom of your pie get hot faster, to help set the crust, than the top of the pie.

Let's say, however, that after you've baked a few pies, you notice that the top keeps getting too brown too quickly. If so, your pie is telling you to bake it on the next lower rack. That should help. If problems persist with chronic overbrowning, your temperature gauge is not accurate and your oven needs to be recalibrated. Call in a pro and have it done. You can check this on your own by buying a good oven thermometer.

Now, when you're out on the beach on a hot summer day, you do your best to tan evenly: you turn over frequently, apply suntan lotion, angle yourself this way and that to get the job done. We don't fuss quite that much with our pies, but there is a little something you can do to facilitate even browning and baking. About halfway through the baking, rotate your pie 180 degrees, "so that the part of the pie that faced the back of the oven now faces forward." Those are the words I use in nearly all of my recipes. The reason you should do this is that most ovens are hotter in the back than they are in the front, and this little rotating exercise acts as an equalizer. You can check for yourself. Thirty minutes into the baking, peek at your pie. The edge of the crust will be several shades darker toward the back.

When I'm baking a fruit pie, I do something else midway through: I slide an aluminum foil–lined baking sheet onto the rack below the pie to catch any spills. I don't put it on the same rack for a couple of reasons. For one, it slows down the baking by temporarily cutting off the direct heat to the bottom of the pan. Second, if the pie does bubble over, the juice runs down the side and oozes under it, making a sticky mess on the bottom of the pan. When the foil-lined sheet is one rack below, the worst that can happen is that the juice will run onto part of the oven rack and harden there, and you can then rub it off with a stiff brush.

The time to start checking your pie is about 10 minutes before it's supposed to be done. Don't open the oven, if you can help it; just turn on the light and look in. With experience, you'll be able to tell if you're on schedule. A custard pie will be just slightly soupy; you will have to nudge it to check. A fruit pie will be showing the first evidence of bubbling juice along the edge. Pecan and pumpkin pie will be starting to swell. These are the little signs that I look for and have tried to clue you in on wherever possible.

Cooling Your Pie

When I was a boy and my mom and dad would bake their wonderful apple pies, I would loiter near the kitchen, ever hopeful for instant pie gratification. No, my dad would tell me, the pie has to cool down first. It was a hard lesson for a kid to swallow, but now I have a better understanding of just how right he was.

Very few pies are fit to be eaten straight out of the oven. A custard pie, for instance, will have little of the tight, creamy texture and mellow flavor it develops as it cools. Warm pecan pie is limp-gooey, not firm-gooey, the way it should be. Fruit pies lack body and flavor nuance if they're served too hot, and the juices are very likely to leak out everywhere if you cut into the pie too soon.

A trip to the cooling rack—followed by a stint in the fridge, if necessary—will take care of all that. A cooling rack is such an ordinary item, but it serves such an important function by allowing air to circulate under the bottom of the pie, which in turn keeps the pie crust from becoming soggy. If I can use the beach analogy again, it's the difference between lying directly on your towel in the sand—your back gets sweaty—and swinging on a rope hammock—your back stays dry. So never skip this step, even if you can put hot pots and pans right on your kitchen counter.

Cooling a fruit pie enables a couple of things to happen: it allows some of the juice to reabsorb into the fruit, and it allows the rest of it to thicken. The cooler the pie gets, the firmer it becomes. Thus, when to eat your fruit pie becomes something of a judgment call,

The Shelf Life of Pies

Fresh homemade pie has a life expectancy that's typically measured in hours, not days. Still, there are times when you'll want to bake a pie ahead or save a slice or two for an arriving visitor. That said, here are my recommendations for keeping pies.

▶ **Fresh fruit pies:** Best served the same day, fresh fruit pies made without dairy products (other than butter) in the filling will keep at average room temperature for 2 days. If you think you'll need to keep a pie longer, immediately refrigerate it. You'll buy an extra day.

▶ **Dried fruit pies:** If they contain no dairy products, they'll typically last 2 to 3 days at average room temperature and 5 or 6 days in the refrigerator.

▶ **Custard pies:** Immediately refrigerate them after cooling. Finish the last slice by day 3.

▶ **Cream pies:** The filling will be fine for up to 3 days, provided you immediately refrigerate them once they are cooled. The whipped cream toppings are far less stable. A topped pie should be eaten within 24 hours. One way to extend this time is to top only the served slices with freshly whipped cream.

▶ **Nut pies:** That pecan pie you love so much will keep in the fridge for 3 or 4 days.

▶ **Pumpkin pies:** Refrigerated, they will keep for 2 or 3 days.

since the ideal texture is somewhere between firm and juicy. You don't want the juice to run all over creation when you serve it, but you also don't want the filling to be overly taut. For most fruit pies, I find that the best filling consistency is reached after about two hours of cooling. At that point, the pie is still warmish. There is still a little free-floating juice, but the slice has just enough body to support itself. That's the ideal slice. Throughout this collection, I've advised how long to cool and/or refrigerate each pie. You may not always agree with me, but at least you'll have someplace to start.

It's Time to Bake

That's quite enough talking about pies. Now it's time to actually bake one. If this is your first time, proceed fearlessly, beginning with one of the traditional pastries, such as Basic Shortening Pie Pastry (page 30) or Basic Flaky Pie Pastry (page 31). Use the hand method for mixing the pastry, then graduate up to the food processor; it's good to learn by touch first. Start with a fruit pie—perhaps one of the apple pies or double-crust summer fruit pies. Don't worry too much about looks in the beginning. Your ability to make a pretty pie will evolve as you master the various skills involved. And be patient with yourself. Even if things don't work out perfectly the first time, it won't be long before you're the best pie baker in the neighborhood and every pie you bake is perfect.

If the following 11 chapters of pie recipes are the flesh of this book, this chapter is the backbone: the recipes here support and give shape to the good pies that follow. Although their role is more or less a supporting one, their importance is not to be underestimated. Simply note, if you will, the crucial role of a supporting cast in a successful film. One good starring performance

Pie Pastries and Crumb Crusts

is rarely enough to make a great film. The same goes for pie: a good filling is key, but without a decent crust, your pie isn't going to win top honors. • Now that I've set the bar rather high, let me put you at ease by telling you that making a good crust is well within your capabilities. For the life of me, I can't understand why pastry making is made out to be such a difficult task. When you consider how few ingredients are involved, how quickly the dough is mixed, how little it is handled, and how effortless it is to roll, there's simply nothing intimidating about it. It's like learning to tie your shoes: it took a few tries, but once you learned the technique, you never forgot it.

For the most part, the following recipes can be divided into two categories: those you roll, the pastry crusts, and those you pat into the pan, the crumb crusts. Although most rolled pie pastries are based on a more or less similar formula, the recipes here represent a range of textures and flavors, achieved by some simple adjustments of the basic ingredients. One of your goals as a pie maker should be a working familiarity with a variety of pastries, leaving you better equipped to decide which sort of pastry to use with a given pie. Looking back on my own pie-making history, I seem to have gone through phases where I preferred one sort of pastry over another. I might have spent the better part of a year making butter pastry, then another stretch when I preferred shortening pastry. There's no irrefutable way to proceed. Although each of the pies in this collection has one or more recommended pastries that I think work well, in time you may decide that you prefer something else. My recommendation will get you started, but it is by no means the last word on the matter.

Crumb crusts aren't really pastries per se. They're loose mixtures, generally made with graham cracker or cookie crumbs, mixed with butter, and patted into your pie pan. These crusts aren't as versatile as pastry crusts, but they are very easy to prepare and require no rolling. Although the crusts themselves are usually prebaked, they're generally used with pies that will require no further cooking—cream pies, for instance, or ice cream pies.

Finally, there is one other type of pastry here, something of a cross between the two I've just mentioned: a press-in pastry.

Whatever your level of expertise as a pastry maker, I suggest that you read the previous chapter before starting out. If you haven't made pastry before or it's been a while, I think you'll find some words of encouragement there to shore up your self-confidence. Even if you are an old pro, I think it's always a good idea to weigh your own experience against someone else's. Even now, with more than 30 years of pie making behind me, I pick up new ideas when I talk to other pie makers.

With that, let me wish you the best of luck with all your pastries and leave you with a few important tips to remember (see box on next page).

Pointers for Perfect Pastry

▶ When all-purpose flour is called for in a pastry, be sure to use just that: bleached all-purpose flour. Do not use unbleached flour, bread flour, or any other flour unless recommended. Other flours often contain too much gluten-forming proteins, which will make dough elastic and may contribute to a tough crust.

▶ When butter is called for, make sure it is fresh and of good quality. I like saving money as much as the next fellow, but I'm generally less than pleased with store brand or other generic butters. Almost exclusively, I used Land O Lakes unsalted butter for the pastries in this collection. I believe this is the gold standard for home cooks.

▶ When vegetable shortening is called for, I like Crisco, and I've become partial to the stick form because it's so easy to measure. If you're using the bulk canned variety, pack it firmly into dry measuring cups and level off the top. Note that I said *firmly*; you don't want any air gaps that may result in a short measure.

▶ Unless otherwise noted, refrigerate all pastries for at least 45 minutes before rolling. They'll be much more cooperative if they've had a chance to chill.

▶ Food processor pastries should not be overprocessed, or they will not be as flaky or as tender as you would like. Pay close attention to the processing instructions with each recipe.

▶ For ease of handling, always roll your pastry on floured waxed paper. The pastry will be a cinch to maneuver and will not stick to the counter and need to be pried off. Also don't forget to flour your rolling pin.

All-Butter Pie Pastry

I'm very fond of this all-butter pastry for a number of reasons. One, with all the butter you just can't argue with the flavor. The butter also gives it a nice gold color, even more so if you make the sturdy version with the egg yolk (see Recipe for Success). It's easy to roll and handle, too, which is why I often choose to use this pastry at my baking demonstrations. It isn't as flaky as some of the other crusts—all-butter pastries never are—but the advantages make this a good pastry to have in your repertoire. Of all the pastries in this collection, I think this is the easiest one to make in a food processor.

MAKES A SINGLE OR DOUBLE CRUST FOR A 9-INCH STANDARD PIE OR 9¹/₂-INCH DEEP-DISH PIE

FOR A SINGLE CRUST

1¹/₂ cups all-purpose flour

1¹/₂ teaspoons sugar

¹/₂ teaspoon salt

¹/₂ cup (1 stick) cold unsalted butter, cut into ¹/₄-inch pieces

¹/₄ cup cold water

FOR A DOUBLE CRUST

2³/₄ cups all-purpose flour

1 tablespoon sugar

1 teaspoon salt

1 cup (2 sticks) cold unsalted butter, cut into ¹/₄-inch pieces

About ¹/₂ cup cold water

1. TO MAKE IN A FOOD PROCESSOR Put the flour, sugar, and salt in the food processor. Pulse several times to mix. Scatter the butter over the dry ingredients and pulse 7 or 8 times to cut the butter in well. Remove the lid and fluff the mixture with a fork, lifting it up from the bottom of the bowl. Drizzle half of the water over the dry ingredients. Pulse 5 or 6 times, until the mixture is crumbly. Fluff the pastry and sprinkle on the remaining water. Pulse 5 or 6 times more, until the pastry starts to form clumps. Overall, it will look like coarse crumbs. Dump the contents of the processor bowl into a large bowl.

TO MAKE BY HAND Combine the flour, sugar, and salt in a large bowl. Toss well, by hand, to mix. Scatter the butter over the dry ingredients and toss to mix. Using a pastry blender, 2 knives, or your fingertips, cut or rub the butter into the flour until it is broken into pieces the size of split peas. Sprinkle half of the water over the dry mixture. Toss well with a fork to dampen the mixture. Add the remaining water in 2 stages and continue to toss and mix, pulling the mixture up from the bottom of the bowl.

TO MAKE WITH AN ELECTRIC MIXER Combine the flour, sugar, and salt in a large bowl. Add the butter, tossing it with the flour. With the mixer on low speed, blend the butter into the flour until you have what looks like coarse, damp meal. Turning the mixer on and off, add half of the water. Mix briefly on low speed. Add the remaining water, mixing slowly until the dough starts to form large clumps. If you're using a stand mixer, stop periodically to stir the mixture up from the bottom of the bowl. Do not overmix.

2. Test the dough by squeezing some of it between your fingers; if it seems a little dry and not quite packable, drizzle a teaspoon or so of cold water over the dough and work it in with your fingertips. Using your hands, pack the dough into a ball (or 2 balls if you are making a double crust) as you would pack a snowball. If you're using this to make a double-crust pie, make one ball slightly larger than the other; this will be your bottom crust. Knead each ball once or twice, then flatten the balls into 3/4-inch-thick disks on a floured work surface. Wrap the disks in plastic and refrigerate for at least an hour or overnight before rolling.

Recipe for Success

▶ Make sure the butter is good and cold—right from the fridge—especially if you're making this in a food processor, because the friction created by the machine softens it fairly quickly.

▶ Remember not to let the pastry ball up around the food processor blade. You want to stop running the machine when the pastry is still in clumps.

▶ All-butter pastry turns pretty firm in the fridge. If it's refrigerated for more than an hour, give it 5 to 10 minutes at room temperature before rolling. Note that the dough can be frozen for up to a month.

▶ To make a sturdier pastry, one with slightly more durability—useful, say, when you're making a freeform pie—add 2 large egg yolks to the double-crust recipe and 1 large egg yolk to the single-crust recipe. Put them in a glass measuring cup and add enough water to equal the required amount of liquid for that recipe. Blend with a fork, then add to your pastry as usual.

Butter Bits

▶ The word "butter" comes from the Greek *bous*, meaning "cow," and *tyros*, meaning "cheese." As early as 1850, the expression "to butter" meant to flatter. It didn't become "butter up" until the late 1930s.

▶ By government edict, all butter must contain at least 80 percent milkfat.

▶ The remaining 20 percent of butter is made up of 18 to 18.5 percent water and 1 to 2 percent curd, or milk solids.

▶ "Sweet butter" is a term used for unsalted butter.

Basic Shortening Pie Pastry

This is a fairly standard shortening pastry, the one that I grew up with and that my dad made so deftly. It produces a flaky, tender crust that's suitable for most of the pies you'll make. It's particularly wonderful with double-crust fruit pies. Unlike butter, solid vegetable shortening is soft and easy to combine with the dry ingredients. I don't even bother to give food processor directions for mixing the dough, since it is almost as fast to make it by hand. (I do, however, give electric mixer directions.) Once you've mastered this recipe, you'll feel a boost of confidence about your pie-making skills.

MAKES A SINGLE OR DOUBLE CRUST FOR A 9-INCH STANDARD PIE OR 9¹/₂-INCH DEEP-DISH PIE

FOR A SINGLE CRUST

1¹/₂ cups all-purpose flour

1 tablespoon sugar

¹/₂ teaspoon salt

¹/₂ cup cold vegetable shortening, cut into pieces

¹/₄ cup cold water

FOR A DOUBLE-CRUST

2³/₄ cups all-purpose flour

1 tablespoon sugar

1 teaspoon salt

1 cup cold vegetable shortening, cut into pieces

6 to 8 tablespoons cold water

1. TO MAKE BY HAND Put the flour in a large, wide bowl that you'll have no trouble getting both hands into as you mix the dough. Add the sugar and salt. Mix well, tossing with your hands. Add the shortening here and there. Using your fingertips, a pastry blender, or 2 knives, rub or cut the shortening into the dry ingredients until the mixture resembles coarse, damp meal. You want to end up with both large and small clumps in the mixture. With a fork in one hand and your cold water in the other, add half of the water to the pastry. You needn't measure it; you can just pour. Mix the dough with the fork, pulling up the dry ingredients from the bottom of the bowl and pushing down to mix everything well. Add the remaining water in 2 stages, mixing until the dough coheres. The dough should feel dampish but not wet. Don't add more water than you need.

TO MAKE WITH AN ELECTRIC MIXER Combine the flour, sugar, and salt in a large bowl. Add the shortening, breaking it into smaller pieces and tossing it with the flour. With the mixer on low speed, blend the shortening into the flour until you have what looks like coarse, damp meal, with both large and small clumps. Sprinkle on half of the water. Turning the machine on and off, mix briefly on low speed. Add the remaining water in 2 stages, mixing slowly until the dough starts to form large clumps. If you're using a stand mixer, stop periodically to stir the mixture up from the bottom of the bowl. Do not overmix.

2. Dust your work surface with flour and turn the dough out onto it. If you're making a double crust, divide the dough into 2 pieces, one—the piece you'll use for the bottom pastry—somewhat larger than the other. Place each piece on a sheet of plastic wrap. Flatten the dough, with floured hands, into disks about ³/₄ inch thick. Wrap them in plastic and refrigerate for at least an hour or overnight before rolling.

FRIED PIE PASTRY The pastry we use to make fried pies is essentially this one, with a bit less fat and 1 egg added—both of which make the dough a little sturdier. Make the following changes to the double-crust recipe: Reduce the shortening to ³/₄ cup. Place 1 large egg in a 1-cup glass measure and beat, then add enough water to make ¹/₂ cup liquid. Use as much of the liquid as necessary to make the dough.

Recipe for Success

▶ To make the dough easy to handle, I like to cut my shortening (I use the easy-to-measure-and-cut sticks) and put it on a plate before I do anything else. This goes in the freezer for about 10 minutes while I'm preparing the rest of my ingredients.

▶ Shortening really sticks to your hands when you're rubbing it to make pastry. For the easiest cleanup, wipe off the excess with paper towels before running your hands under hot water.

▶ The dough may be frozen for up to a month.

Basic Flaky Pie Pastry

This pie pastry is used frequently throughout this collection because it yields such excellent results. I sometimes call it a half-and-half pastry, referring to the equal amounts of vegetable shortening and butter—the former for flakiness, the latter for flavor. It can be made in a food processor if you have a large-capacity machine. But I'll repeat my usual advice, which is to make it by hand or with an electric mixer if you don't. Both methods are quite easy. If you could have only one pastry to work with, this would probably be it.

MAKES A SINGLE OR DOUBLE CRUST FOR A 9-INCH STANDARD PIE OR 9¹/₂-INCH DEEP-DISH PIE

1¹/2 cups all-purpose flour

1 tablespoon sugar

¹/2 teaspoon salt

¹/4 cup (¹/2 stick) cold unsalted butter, cut into ¹/4-inch pieces

¹/4 cup cold vegetable shortening, cut into pieces

¹/4 cup cold water

3 cups all-purpose flour

1 tablespoon sugar

1 teaspoon salt

¹/2 cup (1 stick) cold unsalted butter, cut into ¹/4-inch pieces

¹/2 cup cold vegetable shortening, cut into pieces

¹/2 cup cold water

1. TO MAKE IN A FOOD PROCESSOR Put the flour, sugar, and salt in the food processor. Pulse several times to mix. Scatter the butter over the dry ingredients and pulse the machine 5 or 6 times to cut it in. Fluff the mixture with a fork, lifting it up from the bottom of the bowl. Scatter the shortening over the flour and pulse 5 or 6 times. Fluff the mixture again. Drizzle half of the water over the flour mixture and pulse 5 or 6 times. Fluff the mixture and sprinkle on the remaining water. Pulse 5 or 6 times more, until the dough starts to form clumps. Overall, it will look like coarse crumbs. Dump the contents of the processor bowl into a large bowl. Test the pastry by squeezing some of it between your fingers. If it seems a little dry and not quite packable, drizzle a teaspoon or so of cold water over the pastry and work it in with your fingertips.

TO MAKE BY HAND Combine the flour, sugar, and salt in a large bowl. Toss well, by hand, to mix. Scatter the butter over the dry ingredients and toss to mix. Using a pastry blender, 2 knives, or your fingertips, cut or rub the butter into the flour until it is broken into pieces the size of small peas. Add the shortening and continue to cut until all of the fat is cut into small pieces. Sprinkle half of the water over the mixture. Toss well with a fork to dampen the mixture. Add the remaining water, 1¹/2 to 2 tablespoons at a time, and continue to toss and mix, pulling the mixture up from the bottom of the bowl on the upstroke and gently pressing down on the downstroke. Dough made by hand often needs a bit more water. If necessary, add water 1 or 2 teaspoons at a time until the pastry can be packed.

TO MAKE WITH AN ELECTRIC MIXER Combine the flour, sugar, and salt in a large bowl. Add the butter, tossing it with the flour. With the mixer on low speed, blend the butter into the flour until you have what looks like coarse, damp meal, with both large and small clumps. Add the shortening and repeat. Turning the mixer on and off, add half of the water. Mix briefly on low speed. Add the remaining water, mixing slowly until the dough starts to form large clumps. If you're using a stand mixer, stop periodically to stir the mixture up from the bottom of the bowl. Do not overmix.

2. Using your hands, pack the pastry into a ball (or 2 balls if you are making a double crust) as you would pack a snowball. If you're making a double crust, make one ball slightly larger than the other; this will be your bottom crust. Knead each ball once or twice, then flatten the balls into ³/₄-inch-thick disks on a floured work surface. Wrap the disks in plastic and refrigerate for at least an hour or overnight before rolling.

WHOLE WHEAT PIE PASTRY Follow the basic recipe above, substituting 1 cup whole wheat flour for 1 cup of the all-purpose flour for a double crust, ¹/₂ cup whole wheat flour for a single crust. Proceed as directed.

CHEDDAR CHEESE PIE PASTRY Reduce the flour to 2³/₄ cups in the double-crust recipe. (Do not reduce the flour for a single crust.) When using a food processor, after you've added the shortening, pulse 3 or 4 times. Add 1 cup (¹/₂ cup for single crust) finely shredded sharp cheddar cheese and pulse 3 or 4 times more. Add the water and proceed as directed above. When making the dough by hand or with an electric mixer, add the cheese after you have cut or mixed in all of the fat. Toss with your hands to mix, then add the water as instructed for each method.

Recipe for Success

▶ I use this pastry so often that I tend to make it in large batches. More than half of the time required to make pastry is spent getting out the ingredients, putting them away, and washing the utensils. That said, I may make a double batch of crust, 3 or 4 times over, then freeze it for up to a month. I wrap each disk in plastic, then in aluminum foil. I take the dough out of the freezer the day before I plan to use it and let it thaw in the fridge. It works like a charm.

And You Thought You Had Pastry Problems

"I have had a number of small horrors . . . mostly involving pie crust, something I haven't quite gotten the knack of. One of my pies fell apart. One was so odd-looking my husband took a picture of it, and one had the texture and resilience of old parchment."

—Laurie Colwin, *Home Cooking* (Knopf, 1992)

Extra-Flaky Pie Pastry

This is perhaps the best behaving of all the pastries in this collection, thanks to the addition of cake flour. The benefit of cake flour is twofold: it makes the pastry more shrink-resistant when it is prebaked, and it makes the pastry extra tender and flaky, due to the soft nature of the wheat used in the flour. This pastry can be used for just about any pie, but it's a particularly good choice when the filling is somewhat refined or delicate. Make it by hand or with an electric mixer if you don't have a large-capacity food processor.

MAKES A SINGLE OR DOUBLE CRUST FOR A 9-INCH STANDARD PIE OR 9½-INCH DEEP-DISH PIE

FOR A SINGLE CRUST

1 cup all-purpose flour

2/3 cup cake flour

1 tablespoon sugar

1/2 teaspoon salt

1/4 cup (1/2 stick) cold unsalted butter, cut into 1/4-inch pieces

5 tablespoons cold vegetable shortening, cut into pieces

1/4 cup cold water

FOR A DOUBLE CRUST

2 cups all-purpose flour

1 cup cake flour

1 tablespoon sugar

1 teaspoon salt

1/2 cup (1 stick) cold unsalted butter, cut into 1/4-inch pieces

1/2 cup plus 2 tablespoons cold vegetable shortening, cut into pieces

1/2 cup cold water

1. **TO MAKE IN A FOOD PROCESSOR** Put the flours, sugar, and salt in the food processor. Pulse several times to mix. Scatter the butter over the dry ingredients and pulse 5 or 6 times to cut it in. Fluff the mixture with a fork, lifting it up from the bottom of the bowl. Scatter the shortening over the flour and pulse 5 or 6 times. Fluff the mixture again. Drizzle half of the water over the flour mixture and pulse 5 or 6 times. Fluff the mixture and sprinkle on the remaining the water. Pulse 5 or 6 more times, until the dough starts to form clumps. When it reaches this point, do not continue to process. Empty the crumbs into a large bowl.

TO MAKE BY HAND Combine the flours, sugar, and salt in a large bowl and mix well. Scatter the butter over the dry ingredients and cut or rub it in, using a pastry blender, 2 knives, or your fingertips until the butter is broken into fine pieces. Add the shortening and repeat. Sprinkle half of the water over the dry mixture. Toss well with a fork to dampen the mixture. Add the remaining water in 2 stages and continue to toss and mix.

Add more water if needed. Typically, hand-mixed pastry will require a little more water than machine-mixed.

TO MAKE WITH AN ELECTRIC MIXER Combine the flours, sugar, and salt in a large bowl. Add the butter and toss with the flour. With the mixer on low speed, blend the butter into the flour until you have what looks like coarse, damp meal, with both large and small clumps. Add the shortening and repeat. Turning the mixer on and off, add half of the water and mix briefly on low speed. Add the remaining water, mixing until the dough starts to form large clumps. If you're using a stand mixer, stop periodically to stir the mixture up from the bottom of the bowl. Do not overmix.

2. Using your hands, pack the dough as you would a snowball. If making a double crust, divide the dough in half, making one half—for your bottom crust—a little larger than the other. Knead each piece 2 or 3 times. Put each in the center of a piece of plastic wrap and flatten it into a disk about ³/₄ inch thick. Wrap in the plastic and refrigerate until firm enough to roll, about an hour or overnight.

Recipe for Success

▶ If you don't have cake flour, substitute ¹/₄ cup cornstarch for ¹/₄ cup of the all-purpose flour. Sift it into the flour, then proceed as directed.

▶ The dough may be frozen for up to a month.

Those Pastry Trimmings

Every time you trim the edge of a double-crust pie, you're left with a small handful of dough. What should you do with it? It's not enough to make another pie, and if you're not making decorative cutouts, it seems simpler just to toss it.

Here's a better idea. Flatten it into a ¹/₄-inch-thick disk, wrap it in plastic, slide it into a zipper-topped plastic storage bag, and put it in the freezer. After you've done this 3 or 4 times, you'll have enough dough to make another pie shell. Just take the bag out of the freezer the day before you plan to use it and leave it in the fridge. Then unwrap and stack the disks, loosely cover with plastic wrap, and let sit at room temperature until they're soft enough to roll; they'll fuse together as you do. Don't worry if the pastries aren't all the same sort; nobody will notice the difference.

Lard Pie Pastry

Whoever said that lard makes the flakiest pie crust is absolutely right. If you've never had a lard crust—and there was a time in this country when it would have been nearly the only kind you would have had—you'll be amazed at just how much flake there is. For the uninitiated, one challenge you'll have to master is knowing how much water to add to the pastry. This can be a bit tricky at first, because lard has an oily, elastic texture like that of solid vegetable shortening (only more so) and it's less apparent when sufficient water has been added. The solution is to stick to one brand of lard and the same pastry recipe, then adjust the water each time you make it until you've got it down pat. This is an excellent pastry for any double-crust fruit pie.

MAKES A SINGLE OR DOUBLE CRUST FOR A 9-INCH STANDARD PIE OR 9^1/$_2$-INCH DEEP-DISH PIE

FOR A SINGLE CRUST
1^1/$_4$ cups all-purpose flour

^{1}/$_2$ teaspoon salt

^{1}/$_2$ cup cold lard, cut into pieces

3 to 4 tablespoons cold water, as needed

FOR A DOUBLE CRUST
2^1/$_2$ cups all-purpose flour

1 teaspoon salt

1 cup cold lard, cut into pieces

^{1}/$_3$ to ^{1}/$_2$ cup cold water, as needed

1. TO MAKE IN A FOOD PROCESSOR Put the flour and salt in the food processor. Pulse several times to mix. Scatter the lard over the dry ingredients and pulse 5 or 6 times to cut it in. Fluff the mixture with a fork, lifting it up from the bottom of the bowl. Drizzle 1^1/$_2$ tablespoons (3 tablespoons for double crust) of the water over the mixture and pulse 5 or 6 times. Fluff the mixture and sprinkle on another 1^1/$_2$ tablespoons (2^1/$_2$ tablespoons for double crust) water. Pulse 3 or 4 times more, until the dough starts to form clumps. Overall, it will look like coarse crumbs. Dump the contents of the processor bowl into a large bowl. Test the dough by squeezing it between your fingers. If it seems a little dry, drizzle more water over it, about ^{1}/$_2$ tablespoon at a time, working it in by hand.

TO MAKE BY HAND Combine the flour and salt in a large bowl. Toss well, by hand, to mix. Scatter the lard over the flour and toss to mix. Using a pastry blender, 2 knives, or your fingertips, cut or rub the lard into the flour until it is broken into small clumps. Drizzle 1^1/$_2$ tablespoons (3 tablespoons for double crust) of the water over the mixture and combine, then sprinkle on another 1^1/$_2$ tablespoons (2^1/$_2$ tablespoons for double crust) water and combine.

TO MAKE WITH AN ELECTRIC MIXER Combine the flour and salt in a large bowl. Blend briefly to mix. Add the lard. With the mixer on low speed, blend it into the flour until you have what looks like coarse, damp meal. Turning the mixer on and off, blend in 1½ tablespoons (3 tablespoons for double crust) of the water, mixing briefly on low speed. Sprinkle on another 1½ tablespoons (2½ tablespoons for double crust) water, mixing slowly until the dough forms large clumps. If you're using a stand mixer, stop periodically to stir the mixture up from the bottom of the bowl.

2. Using your hands, pack the pastry into a ball (2 if you're making a double crust) as you would pack a snowball. If you're making a double crust, make one ball slightly larger than the other; this will be your bottom crust. Knead each ball once or twice, then flatten the balls into ³/₄-inch-thick disks on a floured work surface. Wrap the disks in plastic and refrigerate for at least an hour or overnight before rolling.

Recipe for Success

▶ I think this is a good pastry for beginning pie makers. A chilled lard crust has more plasticity—moldability, essentially—than just about any other pastry. It's less likely to crack and holds its shape very nicely. So don't shy away from this one, thinking you need to possess some sort of old-fashioned wisdom to try it.

▶ Not all lard is created equal. The best is known as leaf lard, which comes from the fat around a pig's kidneys. There are discernible flavor differences among brands of lard, and the only way to find a lard you like is to bake with several. Bottom line: the pastry should have a rich, pleasant taste that's more or less neutral and not overpowering. Commonly sold in both tubs and bricks, lard has a shortening-like consistency and, like shortening, is best measured by firmly packing it into the appropriate dry measure and leveling the top.

▶ The dough may be frozen for up to a month.

Crisco Chronology	
1911	Crisco introduced.
1912	First Crisco ad and cookbook.
1923	Crisco available in hermetically sealed cans.
1930	First Crisco Jewish cookbook.
1949	First Crisco TV commercial.
1981	Butter Flavor Crisco introduced.
1991	Crisco available in sticks.

Maria's Shortbread Pie Pastry

Maria Roman's pastry, which I use for her wonderful walnut pie on page 343, is somewhat different from other shortbread pastries. The main difference is the proportion of butter to flour. There's less fat in this one, so the crust is a little drier and sturdier than some, particularly around the edge of the walnut pie, where it is almost biscotto-like in texture. Nonetheless, I think you'll agree that it's just the right pastry for this pie, and you may well end up using it for other enclosed pies. Note that this pastry is best made with a heavy-duty stand mixer. Lacking one, I suggest starting with a hand-held mixer, then working in the flour by hand (see Recipe for Success).

MAKES A DOUBLE CRUST FOR A 9-INCH STANDARD PIE OR 9½-INCH DEEP-DISH PIE

10 tablespoons (1½ sticks) unsalted butter, slightly softened

¾ cup sugar

1 large egg

1½ teaspoons finely grated lemon zest

¼ teaspoon salt

3 cups all-purpose flour

2 tablespoons cold water

1. Using an electric mixer, beat the butter, sugar, egg, lemon zest, and salt together in a large bowl until well blended. Gradually add the flour, about ½ cup at a time, until all of it has been added and the mixture comes together into a ball. Add the water and slowly beat it in or work it in by hand.

2. Put the dough on a lightly floured surface and divide it into 3 pieces, 2 of them just a little larger than the third. Wrap each of the 2 larger pieces in plastic and refrigerate for 30 minutes before rolling. Divide the smaller piece into 2 equal-size balls, wrap them in the same piece of plastic, and refrigerate.

Recipe for Success

▶ There's just too much dough here to make this from start to finish with a hand-held mixer; it will clump up between the beaters and stress the motor. If that's all you have, however, go ahead and beat the butter, sugar, egg, lemon zest, and salt in a large bowl as instructed. Then simply work in the flour by hand, adding about ½ cup at a time.

Yeasted Butter Pastry

Here is the pastry I use for Fresh Peach and Brown Sugar Pizza Pie (page 99). If you've ever eaten a French *galette*—an open-faced tart with a fruit or custard topping—you have some idea of what to expect: a slightly bready, rich dough that's sturdy yet tender. This dough is easily made in the food processor, followed by a quick hand-kneading.

MAKES ENOUGH PASTRY FOR 1 LARGE PIE

1/2 cup lukewarm water

1 package (about 2 teaspoons) active dry yeast

2 cups all-purpose flour

1 1/2 tablespoons sugar

1/2 teaspoon salt

5 tablespoons cold unsalted butter, cut into 1/4-inch pieces

1 large egg yolk

1. Measure the water in a 1-cup glass measure. Sprinkle the yeast over the water, mixing briefly with a fork. Set aside for 5 minutes to dissolve.

2. Meanwhile, place the flour, sugar, and salt in a food processor and pulse several times to mix. Scatter the butter over the dry mixture and pulse 7 or 8 times, until the butter is broken into very small pieces.

3. Add the egg yolk to the yeast mixture and blend with a fork. Add the liquid to the food processor and pulse repeatedly, until the dough coheres, then run the machine non-stop for 8 to 10 seconds to knead the dough.

4. Place the dough in an oiled medium-size bowl, rotating the dough to coat the entire surface. Cover the bowl with plastic wrap and set aside to rise in a warmish spot for 1 hour. If for some reason you need to delay the rising, simply put the dough in the refrigerator.

Recipe for Success

▶ To end up with the best texture, make sure that your butter is good and cold and that you don't overprocess the dough while you're mixing it.

Cornmeal Pie Pastry

I often make this pastry during the holidays. It just seems to fit in with what I think of as early American pies, such as cranberry, pumpkin, and apple. It contains just enough butter to have a great flavor, but what I like best is the little bit of cornmeal crunch. Be aware that a crust made from this pastry may turn a deep golden brown around the edge. Cornmeal will toast up like that, but it's seldom serious, and the darkening is limited to a very small area. One thing you can do to mitigate the browning somewhat is to use an aluminum foil shield like the one described in Recipe for Success.

MAKES A SINGLE OR DOUBLE CRUST FOR A 9-INCH STANDARD PIE OR 9¹/₂-INCH DEEP-DISH PIE

FOR A SINGLE CRUST

1 cup plus 2 tablespoons all-purpose flour

1/4 cup fine yellow cornmeal

1 tablespoon sugar

1/2 teaspoon salt

2 tablespoons cold unsalted butter, cut into 1/4-inch pieces

1/4 cup cold vegetable shortening, cut into pieces

1/4 cup cold buttermilk

FOR A DOUBLE CRUST

2¹/4 cups all-purpose flour

1/2 cup fine yellow cornmeal

2 tablespoons sugar

1 teaspoon salt

1/4 cup (1/2 stick) cold unsalted butter, cut into 1/4-inch pieces

1/2 cup cold vegetable shortening, cut into pieces

1/2 cup cold buttermilk

1. TO MAKE IN A FOOD PROCESSOR Put the flour, cornmeal, sugar, and salt in the food processor. Pulse several times to mix. Scatter the butter over the dry ingredients and pulse 5 or 6 times to cut it in. Fluff the mixture with a folk, lifting it up from the bottom of the bowl. Scatter the shortening over the flour and pulse 5 or 6 times. Fluff the mixture again. Drizzle half of the buttermilk over the flour mixture and pulse 4 or 5 times. Fluff the mixture and sprinkle with the remaining buttermilk. Pulse again, briefly, until the dough forms clumps. It will be damper than some crusts you've seen because of the buttermilk. Dump the contents of the processor into a large, shallow bowl.

TO MAKE BY HAND Combine the flour, cornmeal, sugar, and salt in a large bowl. Toss well, by hand, to mix. Scatter the butter over the dry ingredients and toss to mix. Using a pastry blender, 2 knives, or your fingertips, cut or rub the butter into the flour until it is broken into pieces the size of split peas. Add the shortening and continue to cut until all the fat is cut into small pieces. Sprinkle half of the buttermilk over the dry mixture. Toss well with a fork to dampen the mixture. Add the remaining buttermilk and continue to toss and mix, pulling the mixture up from the bottom of the bowl on the upstroke and gently pressing down on the downstroke. If it seems necessary, add a bit more buttermilk until the pastry can be packed.

TO MAKE WITH AN ELECTRIC MIXER Combine the flour, cornmeal, sugar, and salt in a large bowl. Add the butter, tossing it with the flour. With the mixer on low speed, blend the butter into the flour until you have what looks like coarse, damp meal, with both large and small clumps. Add the shortening and repeat. Turning the mixer on and off, add half of the buttermilk. Mix briefly on low speed. Add the remaining buttermilk, mixing slowly until the dough starts to form large clumps. If you're using a stand mixer, stop periodically to stir the mixture up from the bottom of the bowl. Do not overmix.

2. Using your hands, pack the pastry into a ball (or 2 if you're making a double crust) as you would pack a snowball. If you're making a double crust, make one ball slightly larger than the other; this will be your bottom crust. Knead each ball once or twice, then flatten the balls into ¾-inch-thick disks on a floured work surface. Wrap the disks in plastic and refrigerate for at least an hour or overnight before rolling.

Recipe for Success

▶ There are times when I like to use a coarse, stone-ground cornmeal in baking, but this is not one of them. The coarser the grind, the more likely it is you'll have trouble with this pastry cracking apart as you handle it. I suggest using Quaker brand cornmeal here.

▶ This pastry will keep in the freezer for up to a month.

▶ To prevent overbrowning of the crust, make a foil shield. Tear off a sheet of aluminum foil about 3 feet long. Fold it lengthwise into thirds and wrap it around the pan. It will stand up on its own. Simply overlap the ends; there's no reason to pinch them together. When the pie is done, remove the shield and save it for future use.

Nutty Pie Pastry

Nut pastries are suitable for all sorts of pies. The flavor teams up nicely with fruit, in particular pears, figs, and apples, as it does with chocolate and, of course, nuts. Nut pastries tend to be a little trickier to handle than others, given the added coarseness of the ground nuts. It is important that the nuts be very finely ground—here with the sugar to help keep them from turning oily—and then inspected by hand for larger bits that might impede rolling. Give the pastry time to chill so that the butter can firm up, but not too much time: the more solid a nut pastry becomes, the more likely it is that it will crack. About 45 minutes in the refrigerator is just right. If you need only half of this recipe, you can freeze the other half for up to 2 months.

MAKES 2 SINGLE CRUSTS OR 1 DOUBLE CRUST FOR A 9-INCH STANDARD PIE OR 9 1/2-INCH DEEP-DISH PIE

2/3 cup pecan or walnut halves or whole blanched almonds

1 1/2 tablespoons sugar

2 1/2 cups all-purpose flour

1 teaspoon salt

3/4 cup (1 1/2 sticks) cold unsalted butter, cut into 1/4-inch pieces

2 tablespoons cold vegetable shortening, cut into pieces

About 5 tablespoons cold water

1. Combine the nuts and sugar in a food processor, grinding the nuts in a succession of long bursts. They should not become flour-fine, but almost. (Almonds are likely to require more chopping than walnuts or pecans.) Carefully minding the blade, reach in and feel around for any large pieces of nuts, breaking them up by hand or removing them and chopping them with a knife. Add the flour and salt to the machine and pulse to mix. Scatter the butter over the dry ingredients and pulse 4 or 5 times. Fluff the mixture with a fork, lifting it up from the bottom. Scatter the shortening over the flour and pulse 4 or 5 times. Fluff again. Drizzle 3 tablespoons of the water over the flour mixture and pulse 5 or 6 times. Fluff the pastry and sprinkle on the rest of the water. Pulse 5 or 6 more times, until the dough starts to form clumps. Dump the contents of the processor bowl into a large bowl.

2. Using your hands, pack the pastry into 2 balls as you would pack a snowball. If you're making a double crust, make one ball slightly larger than the other; this will be your bottom crust. If you're making 2 single crusts, make the balls the same size. Knead each one once or twice, then flatten them into 3/4-inch-thick disks on a floured work surface. Wrap the disks in plastic and refrigerate for about 45 minutes before rolling.

Recipe for Success

▶ Perhaps the most important aspect of making a nut crust is getting the consistency of the ground nuts just right. They should be finely ground but not to a powdery or flour-like consistency, or they'll start to turn into something like nut butter. Adding the sugar helps keep the texture granular. Keep an eye on the texture as you pulse the machine (don't keep it running), and stop to inspect the nuts often to monitor your progress.

▶ Thanks to the added fat in the form of nut oil, this pastry requires less water than other recipes of this size. Expect the dough to seem more buttery than some pastries as you near the end of the mixing cycle. It feels similar to a rich tart pastry, if you're familiar with that.

Jeffrey Steingarten on Making the Perfect Pastry

"Perfect American piecrust must be seven things at once—flaky, airy, light, tender, crisp, well browned, and good tasting. The tricky ones are flaky, tender, and crisp—because these are independent virtues. Getting flaky, tender, and crisp to happen at the same time in the same pie seems nearly impossible. Yet millions of American women and men in the early 1900s could do it in their sleep, and probably tens of thousands can today."

—*The Man Who Ate Everything* (Knopf, 1997)

Louise Piper's Oil Pastry

This recipe was given to me by Louise Piper, a perennial winning pie maker at the Iowa State Fair. She tells me she's been using this recipe for nearly 40 years. It's very simple to prepare and needs no refrigeration. Expect to roll it very thin, which will help you achieve a surprisingly flaky crust. This makes just enough dough for a double-crust 9-inch standard pie.

MAKES A DOUBLE CRUST FOR A 9-INCH STANDARD PIE

2 cups all-purpose flour

1 teaspoon salt

1/2 cup vegetable oil (Louise uses Wesson)

1/4 cup cold whole or reduced-fat (2%) milk

1. Combine the flour and salt in a large bowl. Measure the oil and milk into the same glass measuring cup, but do not stir. Add to the flour and mix briskly to combine. The dough will pull together into a ball.

2. Divide the dough in half, making one half—for the bottom pastry—a little larger than the other. Wrap the smaller half in plastic wrap and leave it at room temperature. Roll the larger half right away and line your pie pan with it. Roll the other half of the pastry as directed in your recipe.

Recipe for Success

▶ Because it is made with oil instead of solid fat, this pie pastry can be—and should be—rolled right away.

▶ Elizabeth's Pie (page 192) instructs you to roll the pastry between 2 sheets of waxed paper. Typically, I use only 1 sheet to roll on, but it works well to use the 2 with that recipe.

"Promises and piecrust are made to be broken."

—JONATHAN SWIFT

Louise Piper, Iowa Pie Maker

As pie makers go, Louise Piper is something of a legend in the modern-day annals of the Iowa State Fair. It takes a bit of prying, but when pressed, this modest registered nurse will tell you that she's won more than her share of ribbons at the fair, one of the largest in the country. In 1992 and 1997, she took home the pie sweepstakes, the prize awarded to the winner of the most blue ribbons in the division. She's won the best pie overall "two or three times" and a fistful of second- and third-place ribbons. Her recipe for Elizabeth's Pie (page 192) won a second-place red ribbon in 2003.

With that sort of resumé, I thought that Louise would be a good one to ask about what it takes to make a prize-winning pie. She was happy to share some advice.

- "Make your edges as attractive as possible." Louise has learned that appearance really counts and an attractive edge always scores with the judges. She makes a pretty straightforward scalloped edge, using essentially the same technique I do (see page 16).

- "Use pastry cutouts" (see page 19)—again, because they add to the overall good looks of the pie. She likes to arrange six leaf cutouts in a circle on top of a pie, about one inch in from the edge. She adds them to the top crust about halfway into the baking so that they don't get too dark.

- "Bake only one pie at a time." It takes longer that way, especially if you're entering more than one pie, "but the pie bakes and browns more evenly."

- "Use sugar and milk for the glaze." Nothing fancy, she says, but the combination does a good job of making a golden crust. She sprinkles the sugar first, then drizzles on the milk.

- "Do something a little different." You get points for originality. If she wins a prize for one of her pies, she won't enter the same recipe again in successive years.

- "Use the best fruit and ingredients you can. Most of us who enter pies agree that the closer to home you get your ingredients, the better the pie."

Tender Cream Cheese Pastry

When I have a very delicate filling or a pie that doesn't require the sturdiest of crusts, I often turn to this pastry. Rich, with a slightly tangy flavor, it's great for turnovers and other little pies. Be aware that cream cheese pastry has a tendency to soften up fairly quickly when you roll it. The warm summer months can wreak havoc on this dough in an un-air-conditioned kitchen. If the dough does start to get soft and sticks to your rolling pin, simply slide the pastry—waxed paper and all—onto a baking sheet and put it in the fridge for five minutes before proceeding. The best way to mix this is with a large stand mixer. If you don't have one, use the hand method.

MAKES A SINGLE OR DOUBLE CRUST FOR A 9-INCH STANDARD PIE OR 9¹/₂-INCH DEEP-DISH PIE

FOR A SINGLE CRUST
¹/₂ cup (1 stick) unsalted butter, softened

4 ounces (half an 8-ounce package) full-fat cream cheese, softened

¹/₄ teaspoon salt

1 tablespoon confectioners' sugar, sifted

1¹/₂ cups all-purpose flour

FOR A DOUBLE CRUST
1 cup (2 sticks) unsalted butter, softened

One 8-ounce package full-fat cream cheese (don't use lowfat or nonfat), softened

¹/₂ teaspoon salt

2 tablespoons sifted confectioners' sugar

2³/₄ cups all-purpose flour

1. **TO MAKE WITH AN ELECTRIC MIXER** Combine the butter, cream cheese, and salt in the bowl of a stand mixer fitted with the flat beater attachment. Blend for 30 to 45 seconds on medium-low speed. Stop once or twice, if necessary, to scrape the build-up from the beater. Stopping the machine before each addition, first add the confectioners' sugar and ¹/₂ cup (1 cup for double crust) of the flour. With the mixer on low, blend until the flour is incorporated. Add another ¹/₂ cup (1 cup for double crust) of the flour and blend. Add the remaining flour. When all of the flour has been added and the dough starts to ball up around the beater, stop the machine. Remove the bowl and scrape the dough onto a lightly floured work surface.

TO MAKE BY HAND Using a wooden spoon, cream the butter, cream cheese, and salt together in a large bowl. Stir in the confectioners' sugar, then add the flour about ¹/₂ cup at a time, stirring well after each addition. When the dough coheres, turn it out onto a floured surface.

2. Gently knead 2 or 3 times. Divide the dough into 2 pieces. If you're making a double crust, make one piece—the bottom pastry—a little larger than the other. If you're

making a single crust, make the pieces the same size. Knead each piece into a ball, then flatten it into a disk about ³/₄ inch thick. Wrap the disks in plastic and refrigerate for at least an hour, preferably longer, until firm enough to roll but not too solid.

Recipe for Success

▸ The temperature of the butter and cream cheese will have an impact on how easily and successfully the dough is mixed. Be sure the butter is yielding but not squishy soft. The same goes for the cream cheese. If the ingredients are too cold, you run the risk of overmixing the dough, resulting in a tough crust. If they're too warm, the butter will start to melt into the dough, resulting in a less tender pastry.

▸ The dough may be frozen for up to a month.

Patsy's Cottage Cheese Pastry

This is the pastry that my friend Patsy Jamieson uses for her freeform pies (see pages 158 and 187). As she says, it's pretty much foolproof and it's a cinch to make in a food processor. I recommend it for just about any *crostata*-like pie, but do note that it contains a fair amount of sugar and browns easily. Keep a close eye on it during the last few minutes of baking, and cover the pie with aluminum foil if it starts to get too dark.

MAKES ENOUGH PASTRY FOR 1 LARGE FREEFORM PIE

2 cups all-purpose flour

2 teaspoons baking powder

¹/₂ teaspoon salt

4 teaspoons cold unsalted butter, cut into ¹/₄-inch pieces

³/₄ cup lowfat cottage cheese

¹/₂ cup sugar

¹/₄ cup canola oil or other vegetable oil

2 tablespoons lowfat milk

1¹/₂ teaspoons vanilla extract

1. In a medium-size bowl, combine the flour, baking powder, and salt. Whisk well to mix. Add the butter and blend with a pastry blender or rub between your fingers until the mixture is crumbly and the butter is broken into small bits.

2. Purée the cottage cheese in a food processor. Add the sugar, oil, milk, and vanilla. Process until smooth, stopping once or twice to scrape down the bowl. Add the dry

mixture to the processor bowl and pulse several times, just until the dough clumps together. Do not overmix.

3. Turn the dough out onto a lightly floured work surface and knead several times. Shape the dough into a ball, then flatten it into a thick disk. Sprinkle the dough with flour, then wrap in plastic. Refrigerate for at least 30 minutes or up to 3 hours before rolling.

Recipe for Success

▶ Patsy is the food editor of *Eating Well* magazine, which specializes in healthy, lowfat cooking. Thus, she uses lowfat dairy products for this dough. I've also used full-fat products, which work equally well.

Dolores's Skillet Crust

Here is a simple, made-in-a-skillet pie crust that, as my friend Dolores Kostelni says, even skittish pie makers will find a dream to prepare. She uses it with her strawberry and rhubarb pie on page 144, but I see no reason why it wouldn't work for all kinds of fruit pies.

MAKES ENOUGH FOR A CRUMB-TOPPED 9¹/₂-INCH DEEP-DISH PIE

2¹/₄ cups all-purpose flour

1 cup sugar

¹/₄ teaspoon salt (Dolores doesn't call for it, but I suggest a little)

³/₄ cup (1¹/₂ sticks) unsalted butter

1 teaspoon vanilla extract

1. Combine the flour, sugar, and salt in a medium-size bowl. Set aside.

2. Melt the butter in a very large skillet over medium to low heat. Stir in the vanilla. Add the dry mixture and turn off the heat. Stir the flour and butter with a wooden spoon until the mixture is evenly mixed. Be patient: it will be a little clumpy, but just keep working it. Set the crumbs aside to cool for several minutes.

3. When the crumbs are cool enough to handle, transfer about two-thirds of them to a buttered 9¹/₂-inch deep-dish pie pan. Press them into the bottom and up the side of the pan.

Recipe for Success

▶ Make sure to use a large skillet, preferably one with tall, straight sides, so that the mixture doesn't spill over the edge when you stir.

▶ Do melt the butter gently. You're not trying to brown it.

Simple Press-In Pie Pastry

Press-in pastry, sometimes called pat-in pastry, can be made any number of ways. Some recipes start with soft butter, and some—such as this one—start with cold. This is fairly similar to the other pastries in this collection, with a couple of differences: it has more sugar and more butter, which makes the dough a little easier to handle and keeps it good and tender. The extra sweetener also allows you to use part of the pastry, if you like, for a crumb topping. A food processor makes short work of the preparation.

MAKES ENOUGH FOR ONE 9¹/₂-INCH DEEP-DISH PIE SHELL, ONE 9-INCH STANDARD PIE SHELL AND CRUMB TOPPING, OR SEVERAL INDIVIDUAL-SIZE PIES

1³/₄ cups all-purpose flour

¹/₄ cup sugar

¹/₂ teaspoon salt

10 tablespoons (1¹/₄ sticks) cold unsalted butter, cut into ¹/₄-inch pieces

2¹/₂ tablespoons cold water

1. Combine the flour, sugar, and salt in a food processor. Pulse to mix. Scatter the butter over the dry ingredients and pulse until thoroughly combined. The butter should be nearly undetectable. Sprinkle the water over the mixture. Pulse 4 or 5 times, then fluff with a fork. Continue to pulse until the mixture forms fine crumbs that can be pressed together.

2. Transfer the crumbs to a pie pan and press them evenly into the bottom and up the side of the pan. For fruit pies, place in the freezer for 15 minutes before filling. For cream pies and other pies, place in the freezer for 15 minutes, then fully prebake and let cool according to the instructions on page 16.

Recipe for Success

▶ This isn't necessary, but when I'm saving half of this for a crumb topping, I like to mix the reserved portion with an additional 2 tablespoons sugar, rubbing it in gently. It makes for a slightly sweeter topping, more like the others in this collection.

▶ Note that the butter and dry mixture are blended more thoroughly here than in other pastry recipes. This makes for a crust that's a little more crumbly in texture and less likely to suffer the toughening consequences of overhandling.

Meringue Pie Crust

This meringue crust is the shell for my angel pies (see pages 188 and 419), so named because they're nearly light enough to float away. A meringue crust can be baked in a pie pan, but I've experimented with a variety of methods and this is by far the most successful, with a sheet of parchment paper placed between the meringue and the baking sheet. You have to shape the crust somewhat with your rubber spatula, and flare up the sides to help contain the filling, but that's child's play. Once you've mastered this recipe, you'll be looking for excuses to make it frequently.

MAKES 1 LARGE PIE SHELL

4 large egg whites, at room temperature

1/4 teaspoon cream of tartar

1/2 cup superfine sugar

1 teaspoon vanilla extract

1. Preheat the oven to 250°F. Get out a large baking sheet and line it with parchment paper. Grease the parchment very lightly. Set aside.

2. Using an electric mixer, beat the egg whites in a clean, dry large bowl on medium-high speed until they hold soft peaks. Beat in the cream of tartar. Gradually add the sugar, 1 tablespoon at a time, until the whites are thick and glossy but not dry. Add the vanilla and beat briefly.

3. Using a large rubber spatula, mound the meringue in the center of the parchment paper. Smooth it into a large, flat circle about 11 inches in diameter. Flare the edges upward, creating sidewalls. They needn't be too tall unless your filling is on the runny side. (The ones in this book are not.)

4. Place on the center oven rack and bake, without opening the oven, until the shell has a medium-golden color and a good crisp exterior, about 1½ hours. Let the pie shell cool in the closed oven for 1 hour.

5. Carefully transfer the shell, on the paper, to a cooling rack. Let cool thoroughly, then fill and serve. If you're not using it right away, wrap well in plastic and store at room temperature.

Recipe for Success

▶ Remember the rule for separating eggs: do it while they're cold, but beat the whites when they're at room temperature. To hasten the warming process, you can put your bowl of egg whites inside another bowl of very warm water. Stir them with a wooden spoon to warm them evenly. Use a metal bowl for the whites if you're doing this. It will warm the whites much more quickly than a glass or ceramic bowl.

▶ Even if you have a large nonstick baking sheet, I recommend using the parchment paper. It makes handling the meringue that much easier.

Graham Cracker Crumb Crust

Graham cracker crumb crusts are great for all kinds of pies, especially creamy pies and ice cream pies. If you find yourself making this kind of crust often, keep a box of graham cracker crumbs on hand rather than starting with crackers and grinding them yourself. It's just faster and a lot more convenient that way. By the way, to make $1^3/_4$ cups graham cracker crumbs, you'll need to use about 12 whole crackers. Grind them to a fine meal in a food processor, or stick them in a zipper-topped plastic storage bag and roll over them with a rolling pin.

MAKES ENOUGH FOR ONE 9-INCH STANDARD OR 9$^1/_2$-INCH DEEP-DISH PIE SHELL

$1^3/_4$ cups graham cracker crumbs

2 tablespoons firmly packed light brown sugar

$^1/_2$ teaspoon ground cinnamon

Big pinch of salt

6 tablespoons ($^3/_4$ stick) unsalted butter, melted

1. Preheat the oven to 350°F. Lightly butter your choice of pie pan and set aside.

2. Combine the graham cracker crumbs, brown sugar, cinnamon, and salt in a large bowl. Mix briefly with your fingers. Add the butter and incorporate well, mixing first with a fork, then with your hands, rubbing thoroughly to form evenly dampened crumbs.

3. Spread the crumbs evenly and loosely in the pan, pressing them into the bottom and up the side. Refrigerate for 5 to 10 minutes.

4. Place on the center oven rack and bake for 7 minutes. Let cool on a wire rack before filling. For ice cream pies and other icebox pies, refrigerate the thoroughly cooled pie shell for 10 minutes before filling.

VANILLA WAFER CRUMB CRUST Substitute 1³/₄ cups finely ground vanilla wafers for the graham cracker crumbs. (You'll need to start with about 4 cups crumbled cookies. I use Nabisco Nilla Wafers.) Add 2 tablespoons flour to the dry mixture and mix as above, adding 1 to 2 teaspoons water to help hold it together.

Recipe for Success

▶ I like brown sugar rather than granulated sugar in my graham cracker crusts, because brown sugar has a certain amount of stickiness that helps hold the crust together. Incidentally, a tiny bit of water will make a graham cracker crust easier to press into the pan. While you're mixing your crust and your hands are still covered with crumbs, dampen your fingertips under running water, then shake them into the crumb mixture. Continue to mix; you'll see the difference right away.

Those Crumbly Crumb Crusts

You know how graham cracker and other crumb crusts can sometimes be a little crumbly and resist your best efforts to press them into the pan? Well, here's a little tip. If that happens to you, mix 1 tablespoon flour into the dry ingredients, then add about 1 teaspoon water along with the butter. Mix well, using your hands to rub everything together thoroughly. Modest amounts of these 2 ingredients can make a once uncooperative crumb crust behave splendidly.

Nutty Graham Cracker Crust

This nut variation can be used wherever a plain graham cracker crust is specified. It tastes delicious and has, as you might expect, a distinct nutty flavor that complements many pie fillings. Try it using walnuts, pecans, dry-roasted peanuts, or natural (undyed) pistachios.

MAKES ENOUGH FOR ONE 9-INCH STANDARD OR 9^1/$_2$-INCH DEEP-DISH PIE SHELL

^{3}/$_4$ cup coarsely chopped nuts of your choice

2 tablespoons firmly packed light brown sugar

2 tablespoons all-purpose flour

1 cup plus 2 tablespoons graham cracker crumbs

^{1}/$_4$ teaspoon ground cinnamon

Big pinch of salt

^{1}/$_4$ cup (^{1}/$_2$ stick) unsalted butter, melted

1. Preheat the oven to 350°F. Lightly butter your choice of pie pan and set aside.

2. Combine the nuts, brown sugar, and flour in a food processor and process in a number of long bursts until the nuts are very finely chopped. Dump the mixture into a large bowl. Run your fingers through them, breaking up any bigger pieces the machine might have missed. Stir in the graham cracker crumbs, cinnamon, and salt. Add the butter and incorporate well. Mix first with a fork, then with your hands, and rub everything together thoroughly to form evenly dampened crumbs.

3. Spread the crumbs evenly and loosely in the pie pan, pressing them into the bottom and up the side. Refrigerate for 5 to 10 minutes.

4. Place on the center oven rack and bake for 7 minutes. Let cool on a wire rack before filling. For ice cream pies and other icebox pies, refrigerate the thoroughly cooled pie shell for 10 minutes before filling.

Recipe for Success

▸ If you happen to have a small amount of several different nuts on hand or you just want to mix things up, this crust tastes great made with more than one kind of nut. Simply use ^{3}/$_4$ cup total.

Chocolate Wafer Crumb Crust

Here is a good, basic recipe to use whenever you want an easy-to-make chocolate crust. I prefer Nabisco Famous Chocolate Wafers.

MAKES ENOUGH FOR ONE 9-INCH STANDARD OR 9¹/₂-INCH DEEP-DISH PIE SHELL

30 chocolate wafers

2 tablespoons firmly packed light brown sugar

1 tablespoon all-purpose flour

Big pinch of salt

¹/₄ cup (¹/₂ stick) unsalted butter, melted

1. Preheat the oven to 350°F. Lightly butter your pie pan.

2. Combine the wafers, brown sugar, flour, and salt in a food processor. Using long pulses, grind the wafers to a very fine texture. They should be both slightly gritty and floury. Dump the crumbs into a large bowl and add the butter. Mix, first with a fork, then with your hands, rubbing thoroughly to blend. If the mixture still seems a little crumbly, drizzle on ¹/₂ teaspoon water and rub again.

3. Spread the crumbs evenly in the pie pan, pressing them into the bottom and up the side. Refrigerate for 5 to 10 minutes.

4. Place on the center oven rack and bake for 6 minutes. Let cool on a wire rack before filling. For ice cream pies and other icebox pies, refrigerate the thoroughly cooled pie shell for 10 minutes before filling.

Recipe for Success

▶ I like to refrigerate all my crumb crusts for 5 to 10 minutes before I bake them. It helps firm up the crumbs and keep them in place while the crust bakes.

Julia Child's Rolling Pins

"When Julia declared (while tossing one over her shoulder) that the rolling pins found in most American kitchens were 'toys,' she proceeded to show her television viewers what real French rolling pins ('the sports car of the pin world') were all about. She pulled out a heavy wooden pin, a solid piece of smooth dense wood with no handles measuring over 19 inches long. Julia stored her rolling pins in a copper stock pot on top of a counter in the pastry pantry, just off the main kitchen. There are six rolling pins—each distinctive—in the collection."

—Julia Child's Kitchen at the Smithsonian, www.americanhistory.si.edu/juliachild

Oreo Crumb Crust

I like this simple crumb crust, using one of America's favorite cookies, for many of my icebox and ice cream pies. It's a snap to make in a food processor.

MAKES ENOUGH FOR ONE 9-INCH STANDARD OR 9¹/₂-INCH DEEP-DISH PIE SHELL

3 cups coarsely broken Oreo cookies (18 to 20 cookies)

Pinch of ground cinnamon

2 tablespoons unsalted butter, melted

2 to 3 teaspoons milk

1. Preheat the oven to 325°F.

2. Combine the Oreo cookies and cinnamon in a food processor. Pulse repeatedly in long bursts to make fine crumbs. Transfer the crumbs to a large bowl. Add the butter and mix well, first with a fork, then with your hands, rubbing the mixture until evenly combined. Add the milk and rub again until the crumbs clump together when pressed between your fingers.

3. Transfer the crumbs to a 9-inch standard or 9¹/₂-inch deep-dish pie pan, pressing them into the bottom and about halfway up the side—higher if using the smaller pan. Refrigerate for 5 to 10 minutes.

4. Place on the center oven rack and bake for 6 minutes. Transfer to a wire rack and let cool thoroughly. Refrigerate for 10 minutes before filling.

Recipe for Success

▶ If you're improvising an ice cream pie made with Oreo cookies, use more Oreos in the filling and on top. Just smooth a thick layer of ice cream in the shell, embed a thick layer of broken cookies, and add more ice cream. Sprinkle the top—especially if the top layer is whipped cream—with finely ground Oreos. You'll never hear any complaints about too many Oreos.

Amaretti Crumb Crust

Here's a clever idea for a pie crust from my friends at the Millbrook Inn in Waitsfield, Vermont. The pie they make with this crust (see page 565) has a delicious amaretto fudge filling—a perfect match with the dry little Italian cookies known as amaretti. If you can't find amaretti at your local supermarket, ask if the store will order them for you.

MAKES ENOUGH FOR ONE 9¹/₂-INCH DEEP-DISH PIE

6 tablespoons (³/₄ stick) unsalted butter, cut into pieces

1 ounce unsweetened chocolate, coarsely chopped

1¹/₄ cups amaretti crumbs (see Recipe for Success)

2 tablespoons sugar

1. Combine the butter and chocolate in a small saucepan over low heat, stirring until melted. Let cool to room temperature.

2. Meanwhile, combine the amaretti crumbs and sugar in a medium-size bowl. Add the chocolate mixture and stir well to combine. Transfer the crumbs to a pie pan, pressing them into the bottom and up the side. Refrigerate for 5 to 10 minutes.

Recipe for Success

▶ If you can't find the amaretti at your supermarket, try an Italian market. Some places carry them only around the holidays.

▶ To crush the amaretti, simply put them in a sturdy zipper-topped plastic storage bag and roll them thoroughly with a rolling pin.

▶ If you like, you can make this crust in a 9- or 9¹/₂-inch (3-inch-deep) springform pan. Simply press the crumbs into the pan as described above. During baking, put a large aluminum foil–lined baking sheet on the rack below to catch any butter that might leak out of the pan.

Choco-Nut Press-In Pie Crust

This recipe was given to me by the good folks at the Patchwork Quilt Country Inn in Middlebury, Indiana. They use it to make their wildly popular Coffee Toffee Pie, an exquisite dessert. As I explain in the pie recipe (see page 538), this is something of an unorthodox crust, but it works well. Although I haven't tried it, I think it would also work with many of the icebox and ice cream pies in this collection, especially those featuring chocolate.

MAKES ENOUGH FOR ONE 9-INCH STANDARD OR 9$^1/_2$-INCH DEEP-DISH PIE SHELL

2 ounces unsweetened chocolate, coarsely chopped

$^1/_2$ cup firmly packed light brown sugar

$^3/_4$ cup coarsely chopped walnuts

1 box Jiffy pie crust mix

2 to 2$^1/_2$ tablespoons cold water, as needed

$^1/_2$ teaspoon vanilla extract

1. Preheat the oven to 350°F. Lightly butter the pie pan of your choice.

2. Put the chocolate in a food processor and pulse until well ground. Add the brown sugar and pulse again, grinding the chocolate more finely. Add the walnuts and pulse briefly to finely chop the nuts. Dump the mixture into a large bowl and add the pie crust mix. Toss well with your hands until evenly mixed. Blend 2 tablespoons of the water and the vanilla together in a cup. Drizzle the mixture over the dry ingredients and mix thoroughly until the crumbs can be easily packed. If necessary, add another $^1/_2$ tablespoon water to make a packable mixture.

3. Spread the crumbs evenly in the prepared pan, pressing them evenly into the bottom and up the side. Refrigerate for 10 minutes.

4. Place on the center oven rack and bake until the crust turns a shade or two darker, about 12 minutes. Let cool on a wire rack before filling. For ice cream pies and other icebox pies, refrigerate the thoroughly cooled pie shell for 10 minutes before filling.

Recipe for Success

▶ As you work the mixture with your hands once you've added the water, it may still seem dry. If so, don't be shy about adding that last $^1/_2$ tablespoon water. The real test is whether the mixture can be packed, since it needs to stay in place against the side of the pan. Pinch it to find out.

Pie in the Eye

According to reports by CNN and the British Broadcasting Corporation (BBC), an increasing number of world figures are being targeted by subversive bakers with a penchant for pie throwing. High-profile victims of pie attacks include Bill Gates, former Canadian prime minister Jean Chrétien, and Dutch finance minister Gerrit Zalm, who was beaned with an organic banana cream pie at the opening of the Amsterdam Stock Exchange in 1999. One observer, Rodney Barker of the London School of Economics, thinks it's the anarchist's way of knocking down the high and mighty a notch or two. "The whole thing about cream pies," he reportedly told CNN, "is that it allows you to make your point without actually hurting anybody."

Lest you believe these pie throwers are without scruples, activists abide by a "pie wielder's code." The pie must be "deposited lovingly" rather than simply thrown. The attacker should try to wear some sort of silly costume. And the attack should humiliate but not injure.

Of course, the pie can't be second-rate. "We use only the finest patisserie," one pie thrower told a reporter for Britain's *Observer* newspaper, "ordered at the last minute from small local bakeries. Quality is everything."

For home pie bakers like you and me, summer arrives bearing far more quandaries than answers—most of them, of course, arising from the embarrassment of possible pie choices. Strawberry or strawberry-rhubarb? Plain peach, white peach, or peach-cherry? Double crust or almond crumb topping? Should a home cook be inclined to devote an entire summer to little else than

A Profusion of Summer Fruit Pies

the baking of fruit pies—and I've come pretty darn close—it would still be nearly impossible to cover all the bases. • Nonetheless, we give it our best shot, because this window of opportunity doesn't last forever. Indeed, against summer's typically casual stride, keeping pace with the steady parade of glorious summer fruits is a challenge to even the most dedicated pie baker. Mini fruit seasons arrive in full glory, collide with one another, and then depart until next year. Experienced pie makers anticipate and seize these fleeting moments.

Given the rather generous section that follows, I'm afraid I've done little to help you narrow your summer pie-making choices (especially when you consider that I don't even include berry pies here; they have their own chapter). The aforementioned peach pies are covered quite thoroughly, as are cherry, plum, apricot, and rhubarb—alone and in combination with one another. Many sport crumb toppings, while others have full top crusts or lattice crusts—always a head-turning way to finish a fruit pie. So, you have some serious pie-baking decisions to make.

Let me leave you with this one piece of advice—and it's not the only time you'll hear me mention it—to help you narrow your choices: time your pies to the market. Get the best fruit you can at the peak of its season and only then pick a pie to bake. As any experienced pie baker will tell you, choosing good fruit is about 75 percent of the battle.

Tips for Baking Sensational Summer Fruit Pies

▶ If possible, buy fruit the same day you plan to make your pie. Scrutinize it carefully. If you're buy-ing a quantity of fruit, inspect each piece for signs of spoilage or mold.

▶ Don't hesitate to take a bite out of a piece of fruit to check the flavor and texture. I do this fre-quently (and, of course, always offer to pay the cashier a dime for my sampling). I'd rather buy one lousy peach than eight, then have to return them.

▶ Store your fruit properly once you get it home. Fresh fruit is so expensive these days that few of us can afford to lose any of it due to our own neglect. Don't store peaches and other stone fruit in a bag in one big jumble on the counter. Separate the fruit so it doesn't touch and bruise.

▶ Summer fruit can be very juicy, so always put a large aluminum foil–lined baking sheet on the rack below the pie during the second half of the baking to catch any spills.

▶ Don't underbake juicy summer fruit pies. The thickener needs time to "take" so that the juice develops the proper body. Underbaked pies may also have a raw-thickener flavor.

▶ Don't forget the lemon juice in summer fruit pies. Rare is the fruit pie that doesn't benefit from the slight tang of lemon.

▶ As with other fruit pies, let summer fruit pies cool for at least one hour, preferably two or more, before slicing. Otherwise, the filling will be runny and the slices not nearly as neat.

All-Rhubarb Pie

Alaskan Eskimos and Afghans—Waverly Root tells us in *Food* (Simon and Schuster, 1980)—eat rhubarb raw. The rest of us, when we eat it at all, like it cooked in a pie. (Rhubarb is, after all, also known as pie plant.) Here's a pie recipe for those who like their rhubarb straight up, with-out infringement from other fruit such as strawberries or raspberries, two common pie com-panions. There's a fair amount of sugar in the pie, to counter rhubarb's tart flavor, and a little orange juice and zest for added zing. Rhubarb gives off a lot of juice, so do let the pie rest for several hours before serving to give the juices plenty of time to set.

MAKES 8 SERVINGS

1 recipe Basic Flaky Pie Pastry, Double Crust (page 32) or Tender Cream Cheese Pastry, Double Crust (page 46), refrigerated

FILLING

5 cups fresh rhubarb stalks sliced crosswise 1/2 inch thick

11/4 cups plus 2 tablespoons sugar

2 tablespoons orange juice

Grated zest of 1/2 orange

Big pinch of salt

1/4 teaspoon ground nutmeg

3 tablespoons cornstarch

2 tablespoons cold unsalted butter, cut into small pieces

GLAZE

Milk or light cream

Sugar

1. If you haven't already, prepare the pastry and refrigerate until firm enough to roll, 1 to 1½ hours.

2. On a sheet of lightly floured waxed paper, roll the larger portion of the pastry into a 12-inch circle with a floured rolling pin. Invert the pastry over a 9-inch standard pie pan, center, and peel off the paper. Gently tuck the pastry into the pan, without stretching it, and let the overhang drape over the edge. Place in the refrigerator for 15 minutes.

3. Combine the rhubarb, 1¼ cups of the sugar, the orange juice, orange zest, salt, and nutmeg in a large bowl. Mix well, then set aside for 20 minutes. Preheat the oven to 400°F.

4. Combine the remaining 2 tablespoons sugar and the cornstarch in a small bowl, then stir the mixture into the rhubarb. Turn the filling into the chilled pie shell and smooth the top of the fruit with your hands. Dot the filling with the butter.

5. Roll the other half of the pastry into a 10-inch circle on a sheet of lightly floured waxed paper. Moisten the outer edge of the pie shell with a pastry brush. Invert the top pastry over the filling, center, and peel off the paper. Press the top and bottom pastries together along the dampened edge. Using a pair of scissors, trim the pastry to an even ½-inch overhang all around. Turn the pastry back and under, sculpting the edge into an upstanding ridge. Poke several steam vents in the top of the pie with a fork or paring knife, including a couple along the edge so you can check the juices there later. To glaze the pie, brush the top pastry with a little milk and sprinkle lightly with sugar.

6. Place the pie on the center oven rack and bake for 30 minutes. Reduce the oven temperature to 375°F and rotate the pie 180 degrees, so that the part that faced the back of the oven now faces forward. Just in case, slide a large aluminum foil–lined baking sheet onto the rack below to catch any spills. Continue to bake until the pie is golden brown,

about 25 minutes. When done, you should notice thick juices bubbling out of the steam vents along the edge.

7. Transfer the pie to a wire rack and let cool for at least 3 hours, preferably longer, before serving.

Recipe for Success

▶ Because of the red color, rhubarb makes an attractive lattice-top pie. Follow the lattice weaving instructions on page 71.

▶ Even though this is an all-rhubarb pie, feel free to substitute a cup or two of raspberries for an equal amount of sliced rhubarb.

▶ If your rhubarb comes with leaves attached, do not eat them. They contain something called oxalic acid, which can cause sickness or even death.

Sumner, Washington, Rhubarb Custard Pie

I had seen several references to Sumner, Washington, declaring the town to be the rhubarb pie capital of the country. I love that sort of boast, so I called the mayor, Barbara Skinner, and asked her if she'd care to comment. She told me, quite frankly, that she wasn't sure where the pie title came from. But she informed me that Sumner—a town of 8,800 in the southern Puget Sound area, where she was born and raised—is in the fertile Puyallup Valley, which produces 90 percent of the rhubarb grown in this country. Fair enough. As the town's mayor, would she be willing to share the best local recipe for rhubarb pie? Indeed, she would, and by the end of the day, she'd sent me this recipe from the local St. Andrew's Church cookbook, adding a note that "everyone in the church is a good cook." They must be, because the pie is quite excellent—a thick layer of rhubarb on top of a very light custard. I think you'll enjoy this quite a bit.

MAKES 8 SERVINGS

1 recipe Basic Flaky Pie Pastry, Single Crust (page 31), refrigerated

FILLING
3 cups diced fresh rhubarb stalks
1 1/2 cups sugar
3 tablespoons all-purpose flour
Big pinch of salt

1/2 teaspoon ground nutmeg
2 large eggs
2 tablespoons milk
1 tablespoon cold butter, cut into small pieces

GARNISH
Fresh Whipped Cream (page 605)

1. If you haven't already, prepare the pastry and refrigerate until firm enough to roll, about 1 hour.

2. On a sheet of lightly floured waxed paper, roll the pastry into a 12-inch circle with a floured rolling pin. Invert the pastry over a 9-inch standard pie pan, center, and peel off the paper. Tuck the pastry into the pan, without stretching it, and sculpt the edge into an upstanding ridge. Place in the freezer for 15 minutes. Preheat the oven to 375°F.

3. Combine the rhubarb, sugar, flour, salt, and nutmeg in a large bowl. Toss well, then set aside for several minutes to juice. Whisk the eggs and milk together in a small bowl. Add to the fruit, stirring well to combine. Scrape the filling into the chilled pie shell, smoothing the top of the fruit with a spoon. Dot the filling with the butter.

4. Place the pie on the center oven rack and bake until the top is crusted over and the filling is set, 50 to 55 minutes, rotating the pie 180 degrees halfway through the baking, so that the part that faced the back of the oven now faces forward.

5. Transfer the pie to a wire rack and let cool. Serve barely warm, at room temperature, or chilled, with a dollop of whipped cream.

Recipe for Success

▶ I didn't try this, but Barbara mentioned that adding a couple of drops of red food coloring to the pie will give it a more rhubarb red color.

▶ Don't expect this to bake up like other custard pies. The "custard" here is more of a translucent jelly that settles on the bottom of the pie, not a traditional creamy custard surrounding the fruit.

▶ Be aware that the leaves of the rhubarb plant are toxic and should never be consumed.

Fresh Sweet Cherry Pie with Coconut-Almond Crunch Topping

For most of us, fresh cherry pie is serious business. First, the fruit is generally expensive. Then, even after we've plunked down our cash, there's the matter of the pits, which need to be removed one by one, an undertaking requiring an investment of time and one rather extensive apron to guard against errant juice (see Recipe for Success). With so much at stake, a fresh cherry pie is, justifiably, one of early summer's rare and enduring pleasures. This version incorporates some of my favorite tricks to bring out the best cherries have to offer. I think a shot of cherry liqueur or peach schnapps is a great flavor enhancement, as are a few drops of vanilla. All of it works great in a double crust, but I think a better choice is a classic coconut-almond crunch topping. Do serve this slightly warm, with a big scoop of vanilla ice cream.

MAKES 8 SERVINGS

1 recipe Basic Flaky Pie Pastry, Single Crust (page 31) or Basic Shortening Pie Pastry, Single Crust (page 30), refrigerated

FILLING

4^1/$_2$ cups fresh sweet cherries, stemmed and pitted

^{1}/$_3$ cup plus 3 tablespoons sugar

3 tablespoons cherry liqueur or peach schnapps

2 teaspoons fresh lemon juice

^{1}/$_4$ teaspoon vanilla extract

2 tablespoons cornstarch

COCONUT-ALMOND CRUNCH TOPPING

^{1}/$_2$ cup sugar

^{1}/$_4$ cup whole, slivered, or sliced almonds

^{3}/$_4$ cup all-purpose flour

^{1}/$_2$ cup sweetened flaked coconut

^{1}/$_4$ teaspoon salt

5 tablespoons cold unsalted butter, cut into ^{1}/$_4$-inch pieces

GARNISH

Vanilla ice cream

1. If you haven't already, prepare the pastry and refrigerate until firm enough to roll, about 1 hour.

2. On a sheet of lightly floured waxed paper, roll the pastry into a 12-inch circle with a floured rolling pin. Invert the pastry over a 9-inch standard pie pan, center, and peel off the paper. Tuck the pastry into the pan, without stretching it, and sculpt the edge into an upstanding ridge. Place in the freezer for 15 minutes. Preheat the oven to 400°F.

3. Combine the cherries, ^{1}/$_3$ cup of the sugar, the cherry liqueur, lemon juice, and vanilla in a large bowl. Stir well, then set aside for 15 minutes to juice. In a small bowl, combine the remaining 3 tablespoons sugar and the cornstarch, then stir the mixture into the fruit. Turn the filling into the chilled pie shell, smoothing the top with a spoon. Place the pie on the center oven rack and bake for 30 minutes.

4. Meanwhile, make the topping. Combine the sugar and almonds in a food processor and pulse until the nuts are chopped. Add the flour, coconut, and salt. Pulse briefly to mix. Scatter the butter over the top and pulse until the mixture starts to form gravelly

crumbs. Dump the crumbs into a large bowl and rub between your fingers until the mixture forms large, buttery crumbs. Refrigerate until ready to use.

5. Remove the pie from the oven and reduce the temperature to 375°F. Carefully dump the crumbs in the center of the pie, spreading them evenly over the surface with your hands. Tamp them down lightly. Return the pie to the oven, placing it so that the part that faced the back of the oven now faces forward. Just in case, slide a large aluminum foil–lined baking sheet onto the rack below to catch any spills. Bake until the juices bubble thickly around the edge, about 30 minutes. If the top starts to get too brown, cover loosely with aluminum foil for the last 15 minutes.

6. Transfer the pie to a wire rack and let cool. Serve while still barely warm with a scoop of ice cream.

Recipe for Success

▸ **To mitigate the juice spatter that always accompanies cherry pitting, I often do this outside on the picnic table. When that's not possible, I work inside a large plastic bag.**

Sing a Song of Sixpence

Sing a song of sixpence,
A pocket full of rye,
Four-and-twenty blackbirds
Baked in a pie.
When the pie was opened,
The birds began to sing,
Wasn't that a dainty dish
To set before the king?

Pitting Cherries

One of my good editor friends swears by the paper clip method for pitting cherries. You take a paper clip, bend it open, stick it into the cherry, and give a gentle push. The pit comes right out, she says. Or maybe you're supposed to pull, not push—I forget. What I do remember is that when she first told me about this trick several years ago, I tried it several times and never could get the knack of it.

When I'm pitting cherries, I like to do it outside at the picnic table, if I can, this being one of the most spatter-prone activities a cook can tackle. Inside or out, I think the best way to pit cherries is to work with your hands inside a plastic bag to help contain the juice. I simply pull off the stems, throw a few cherries in a large clear plastic bag, and give them a good squeeze—not hard enough to crush the cherries, just flatten them somewhat. If the cherries are ripe, this squeeze will free up the pits, although you may have to coax them out with a finger. If the cherries aren't ripe, the pits won't be quite as cooperative.

It's a bit tiresome putting the cherries inside the bag, then taking them out. But if you pick a nice sunny summer day, you'll lose track of time and enjoy yourself thoroughly.

Rainier Cherry Pie with a Grated Top Crust

How could you not like a cherry that tastes something like a peach? That, at least, was my thought when I tasted a Rainier cherry for the first time at my local supermarket. Unlike any other cherry you've ever seen, a Rainier cherry has a peachy yellow skin and flesh, with just a mottled blush of red. To my taste buds, the flavor of the cherry has a hint of vanilla, which I play up with a smidgen of vanilla extract in the filling. This exquisite pie is excellent with peach or vanilla ice cream. Incidentally, if you've never made a grated top crust before, I think you'll be pleasantly surprised. Instead of rolling, you simple grate—or shred—the block of pastry onto the fruit. It's quite easy and attractive.

MAKES 8 TO 10 SERVINGS

1 recipe All-Butter Pie Pastry, Double Crust (page 28) or Basic Flaky Pie Pastry, Double Crust (page 31), modified as instructed in step 1 and refrigerated

FILLING

5 cups fresh Rainier cherries, stemmed and pitted

1/3 cup plus 2 tablespoons granulated sugar

1 tablespoon fresh lemon juice

1/4 teaspoon vanilla extract

2 1/2 tablespoons cornstarch

GLAZE

About 1 tablespoon coarse sugar (see page 69) or granulated sugar

GARNISH

Vanilla or peach ice cream

1. If you haven't already, prepare the pastry. Shape the smaller half into a block rather than a disk. Refrigerate the larger half until firm enough to roll, about 1 hour, and place the other half—the block—in the freezer (see Recipe for Success).

2. On a sheet of lightly floured waxed paper, roll the larger half of the pastry into a 13-inch circle with a floured rolling pin. Invert the pastry over a 9 1/2-inch deep-dish pie pan, center, and peel off the paper. Tuck the pastry into the pan, without stretching it, and sculpt the edge into an upstanding ridge. Place in the freezer for 15 minutes. Preheat the oven to 400°F.

3. In a large bowl, combine the cherries, 1/3 cup of the granulated sugar, the lemon juice, and vanilla. Mix well, then set aside for 10 minutes to juice. Combine the remaining 2 tablespoons granulated sugar and the cornstarch in a small bowl, then stir the mixture into the fruit. Turn the filling into the chilled pie shell and smooth the top of the fruit with your hands or a spoon.

4. Using the large holes of a box grater, grate the other half of the pastry over the top of the fruit, as if it were a block of cheese, covering the filling more or less evenly. Sprinkle the coarse sugar evenly over the pastry.

5. Place the pie on the center oven rack and bake for 30 minutes. Reduce the oven temperature to 375°F and rotate the pie 180 degrees, so that the part that faced the back of the oven now faces forward. Just in case, slide a large aluminum foil–lined baking sheet onto the rack below to catch any spills. Continue to bake until the top is golden brown and the juices bubble thickly around the edge, 25 to 30 minutes.

6. Transfer the pie to a wire rack and let cool for at least 2 hours before serving. Garnish with ice cream.

Recipe for Success

▶ If you have kids who like to bake with you, one of the nice things about making a Rainier cherry pie is the absence of cherry red juices squirting all over creation as you pit the cherries. It's sort of a kid-proof cherry.

▶ Rainier cherries lack the tartness of some cherries, so consider adding an additional $^1/_2$ tablespoon fresh lemon juice for a little more pucker.

▶ The consistency of the pastry "block" should be firm but not frozen solid.

Coarse Sugar

Granulated sugar is fine for sprinkling on pie pastry. It gives your top crust a fetching golden finish and sandy-sugary texture. When you want a bit more crunch, however, try coarse sugar, also known as sanding sugar. The crunchy texture is especially nice when you have a soft fruit filling, as in the recipe opposite. Keep coarse sugar in a jar or other tightly covered container and store it in your pantry. It's available in several shades of white and golden brown at specialty food stores and from the King Arthur Flour Baker's Catalogue, available online at www.kingarthurflour.com. Try it on muffins, too.

Lattice-Top Deep-Dish Sour Cherry Pie

Sour cherries are prized for the wonderful pies they make. They have a special flavor and unique tartness not found in other types of cherries. In many parts of the country, the trickiest part of making a sour cherry pie is finding the cherries. Not only are they somewhat fragile, but their tartness isn't embraced by consumers who, for the most part, expect cherries to be sweet. If your local supermarket doesn't carry them, check farmers' markets. The key to making a good sour cherry pie, I believe, is to add just enough sugar to tame the tartness, not overwhelm it. The other trick is to use sufficient thickening to gel the prodigious amount of juice. Other than that, I keep the filling fairly simple, with a little lemon juice and zest, a dab of butter, and a pretty lattice top so the bright red cherries can peek through. Do use an extra-deep-dish pie pan, if you have one. This is a very juicy pie, and the added depth will help contain the juice.

MAKES 8 TO 10 SERVINGS

1 recipe Basic Flaky Pie Pastry, Double Crust (page 31) or All-Butter Pie Pastry, Double Crust (page 28), modified as instructed in step 1 and refrigerated

FILLING

6 cups fresh sour cherries, stemmed and pitted

1¼ cups plus 3 tablespoons sugar

¼ cup cornstarch

2 teaspoons fresh lemon juice

Grated zest of 1 lemon

2 tablespoons cold unsalted butter, cut into small pieces

GLAZE

Milk or light cream

Sugar

1. If you haven't already, prepare the pastry as directed, making one half of it just slightly larger than the other. Shape the larger half into a disk and the other half into a square, both about ³/₄ inch thick. Wrap the pastry as usual and refrigerate until firm enough to roll, about 1 hour.

2. On a sheet of lightly floured waxed paper, roll the disk of pastry into a 13½-inch circle with a floured rolling pin. Invert the pastry over a 9½-inch deep-dish pie pan (see Recipe for Success), center, and peel off the paper. Gently tuck the pastry into the pan, without stretching it, and sculpt the overhang into an upstanding ridge. Place in the refrigerator for 15 minutes.

3. Place the cherries in a large bowl. Mix the sugar and cornstarch together in a small bowl, then stir the mixture into the fruit. Stir in the lemon juice and zest. Set aside for 10 minutes to juice. Preheat the oven to 400°F.

4.   On another sheet of lightly floured waxed paper, roll the remaining pastry into a 12 x 10-inch rectangle. With a pastry wheel or pizza cutter, cut the pastry into 8 lengthwise strips, each 1¼ inches wide. (In other words, you should have 8 strips measuring 12 inches long and 1¼ inches wide.) Set aside.

Figure 1

5.   Turn the filling into the chilled pie shell, moistening the rim of the shell slightly. Smooth the top of the filling with your hands or a spoon. Dot the filling with the butter. Lay 5 pastry strips vertically across the pie, evenly spaced, as shown in figure 1. Fold back strips 2 and 4 and lay another strip directly across the center of the pie, as shown in figure 2. Unfold the folded strips, then fold back strips 1, 3, and 5. Lay another perpendicular strip across the pie, as shown in figure 3. Unfold the folded strips, then fold up strips 1, 3, and 5 on the other side of the pie. Place another perpendicular strip across the pie, as shown in figure 4, then unfold strips 1, 3, and 5. Trim the strips, then pinch the ends of the strips into the edge of the pastry. Lightly brush the pastry strips with milk and sprinkle the top of the pie with sugar.

Figure 2

6.   Place the pie on the center oven rack and bake for 30 minutes. Reduce the oven temperature to 375°F and rotate the pie 180 degrees, so that the part that faced the back of the oven now faces forward. Just in case, slide a large aluminum foil–lined baking sheet onto the rack below to catch any spills. Continue to bake until the top is golden brown and any visible juices bubble thickly, 35 to 40 minutes.

Figure 3

7.   Transfer the pie to a wire rack and let cool for at least 2 hours before serving.

Recipe for Success

Figure 4

▸   Ripe sour cherries are very easy to pit. After you pull off the stem, you can simply squeeze the pit out of the stem end.

▸   Don't omit the lemon juice and zest, thinking the cherries will be tart enough. The lemon flavor is very good with the cherries.

About Lattice-Top Pies

Whenever I give a pie-baking demonstration, the part of the program that really brings the house down is when I make a lattice-top pie. The audience is there to learn the nuances of making flaky pastry and how to roll it out without a catastrophe—information they absorb with appreciation. But more often than not, they actually break into applause when they see me assemble a lattice-top pie.

No small part of their exuberance has to do with the fact that they can't believe how easy it is. Most cooks, I'm afraid, believe that nobody other than food stylists and culinary school graduates can actually make a lattice crust. But after they see me demonstrate just how simple it is, they realize this is something they, too, can do right in their own kitchens. (To see just how easy, turn to the diagrams on page 71.)

Here, then, are a few tips for making foolproof lattice-top pies.

- For clean, even cutting, make sure the dough has been well chilled after rolling. Dough that's room temperature won't have the same clean lines.

- Don't, however, try to weave the lattice until the chilled strips have warmed up slightly. Otherwise, they'll be stiff, not flexible enough to weave.

- You'll probably figure this out, but use the shorter strips on the edge of your pie and the longer ones in the center.

- Don't use whole-grain or nut pastries to make a lattice, if possible. The coarse particles tend to make these pastries prone to crumbling when handled too much.

- Colorful fruit tends to make the prettiest lattice-top pies, given the greater contrast between the lighter crust and the dark filling, but don't limit yourself in this way. Some of my favorite lattice pies are made with apples.

Dense Cherry-Almond Coffeecake Pie

I have in my files all manner of almond cakes, all of which I'm wild about, from chocolate tortes to moist sour cream coffeecakes. I also have this: a pie in the tradition of the latter, just moist and dense enough to require a pastry to contain it. We begin by putting a single layer of cherries in a partially prebaked pie shell. Then a rich sour cream filling, thickened with almond meal and eggs, is poured over the fruit. As it bakes, a delicious cake-like filling forms around the cherries, leaving a lovely golden almond crust on top. Rich and tasty as it is, I love this served just barely warm, with a bit of coffee or vanilla ice cream.

MAKES 10 SERVINGS

1 recipe Basic Flaky Pie Pastry, Single Crust (page 31) or Basic Shortening Pie Pastry, Single Crust (page 30), refrigerated

FILLING
2 cups pitted sweet cherries, fresh or individually frozen (not packed in syrup), partially thawed

1 cup whole almonds

1/3 cup all-purpose flour

1 1/3 cups granulated sugar

1/4 teaspoon salt

3 large eggs, at room temperature

2 large egg yolks, at room temperature

1 cup full-fat sour cream

2 tablespoons firmly packed light brown sugar

2 tablespoons unsalted butter, melted

1 teaspoon vanilla extract

1/4 teaspoon almond extract

1. If you haven't already, prepare the pastry and refrigerate until firm enough to roll, about 1 hour.

2. On a sheet of lightly floured waxed paper, roll the pastry into a 13-inch circle with a floured rolling pin. Invert the pastry over a 9½-inch deep-dish pie pan, center, and peel off the paper. Tuck the pastry into the pan, without stretching it, and sculpt the edge into an upstanding ridge. Place in the freezer for 15 minutes, then partially prebake and let cool according to the instructions on page 16. Reduce the oven temperature to 350°F.

3. Place the cherries on a double layer of paper towels and set them aside for 15 minutes. Meanwhile, combine the almonds, flour, 1/3 cup of the granulated sugar, and the salt in a food processor and pulse until the mixture resembles coarse meal. Set aside.

4. Using an electric mixer, lightly beat the eggs, egg yolks, sour cream, the remaining 1 cup granulated sugar, and the brown sugar until smooth. Blend in the butter and

extracts. Stir the almond flour into the liquid, blending until smooth. Arrange the cherries in a single layer in the cooled pie shell. Ladle the filling over the cherries.

5. Place the pie on the center oven rack and bake for 30 minutes, then rotate the pie 180 degrees, so that the side that faced the back of the oven now faces forward. Continue to bake until the filling is set in the center and the surface of the pie is a rich, uniform golden brown, 25 to 30 minutes.

6. Transfer the pie to a wire rack and let cool. Serve just barely warm or at room temperature.

Recipe for Success

▶ Typically, you wouldn't want to drain or blot off any juice when you're making a cherry pie. Because of the cake-like texture of the filling, however, this one is a little different. If too much cherry juice bleeds into the filling, it loses some of its cake-like texture. That's why we drain the cherries first.

▶ Make sure to refrigerate leftovers, but gently rewarm the pie before serving, especially if you're planning to serve it with ice cream.

If You Happen to Get Bored Waiting for Your Cherry Pie to Bake . . .

. . . try knotting cherry stems with your tongue. But you'll have to be fast to break the record, set in 1999 in Orlando, Florida. In three minutes, Al Gliniecki of Gulf Breeze, Florida, managed to do 39 of them, enough to twist, turn, and ultimately tongue-tie his way into the *Guinness Book of World Records*.

Friske Orchards' Michigan Balaton Cherry Pie

One of the new varieties of cherries available in this country is the Balaton, a European favorite named for a lake in its native Hungary. It has the tangy taste of a sour cherry, but the smooth, satisfying flavor of a sweet one, and a deep burgundy color that makes for a striking pie. After years of experimental plantings in the United States, Balaton cherries are now commercially grown in Michigan, Wisconsin, New York, and Utah. One Michigan farm that does a brisk business in Balaton cherries is Friske Orchards, run by Richard Friske and his family (see box, next page). In addition to selling spectacular homegrown fruit, Friske Orchards produces delicious pies to showcase that fruit. Here is the Balaton cherry pie the Friskes bake, and when you try it, you'll know why they sell as many as 100 of these on a busy fall weekend day. So do try to get your hands on some Balatons, but be advised: once you've tried these cherries, you may not be satisfied with any other kind. Note that the Friskes make this with both a top crust and the very cinnamony crumb topping used here.

MAKES 8 TO 10 SERVINGS

1 recipe Basic Shortening Pie Pastry, Single Crust (page 30) or All-Butter Pie Pastry, Single Crust (page 28), refrigerated

FILLING

4 cups fresh Balaton cherries, stemmed and pitted

1/2 cup granulated sugar

1 1/2 tablespoons cornstarch

1/4 teaspoon almond extract

CINNAMON CRUMB TOPPING

3/4 cup all-purpose flour

1/2 cup quick-cooking rolled oats

1/2 cup firmly packed light brown sugar

2 teaspoons ground cinnamon

1/2 cup (1 stick) cold unsalted butter, cut into 1/4-inch pieces

1. If you haven't already, prepare the pastry and refrigerate until firm enough to roll, about 1 hour.

2. On a sheet of lightly floured waxed paper, roll the pastry into a 12-inch circle with a floured rolling pin. Invert the pastry over a 9-inch standard pie pan, center, and peel off the paper. Tuck the pastry into the pan, without stretching it, and sculpt the overhang into an upstanding ridge. Place in the freezer for 15 minutes.

3. Place the cherries in a large bowl. Mix the granulated sugar and cornstarch

together in a small bowl, then stir the mixture into the fruit. Stir in the almond extract. Set aside for 10 minutes. Preheat the oven to 400°F.

4. Scrape the filling into the chilled pie shell, smoothing the fruit with a spoon. Place the pie on the center oven rack and bake for 25 minutes.

5. Meanwhile, make the topping. Combine the flour, oats, brown sugar, and cinnamon in a food processor and pulse to mix. Scatter the butter over the dry ingredients and pulse until the mixture resembles fine crumbs. Transfer to a large bowl and rub the mixture between your fingers to make large, buttery crumbs. Refrigerate until ready to use.

6. After 25 minutes, remove the pie from the oven and reduce the temperature to 375°F. Carefully dump the crumbs in the center of the pie and spread evenly over the surface with your hands. Tamp them down lightly. Return the pie to the oven, placing it so that the part that faced the back of the oven now faces forward. Just in case, slide a large aluminum foil–lined baking sheet onto the rack below to catch any spills. Continue to bake until the juices bubble thickly around the edge, about 25 minutes.

7. Transfer the pie to a wire rack and let cool for at least 2 hours before serving.

Recipe for Success

▶ At Friske Orchards, they use a shortening crust, but the European heritage of the Balaton suggests a buttery partnership as well. That's why I also recommend the all-butter crust.

▶ The flavor of the fruit really carries this pie, so little is needed by way of enhancements. The little bit of almond extract is the perfect, subtle touch. Even if you like the flavor of almond, don't be tempted to add more, or it may intrude.

▶ These are very juicy cherries, so do have your foil-lined baking sheet in place to catch any spills.

Friske Orchards

Richard Friske knows good pie fruit. He should. His family-owned Friske Orchards grows more than 300 hundred acres' worth in northwestern Michigan's fruit country: red sour cherries, black sweet cherries, Red Haven peaches, and Northern Spy apples. Much of this fruit is sold fresh at Friske's farm stand, a lot goes into the hundreds of homemade pies the orchard sells, and the rest is frozen. Friske is something of a pioneer in the marketing of what's known as IQF—individually quick frozen—fruit. Properly handled and frozen, Richard says, IQF fruit is as close to using fresh fruit as possible.

"To make a superior pie, you have to start with superior fruit," he advises. That requires thoughtful stewardship of the land and intensive orchard management. Friske's cherry trees, for instance, are pruned aggressively to allow for as much sunlight as possible in order to yield fruit with a deeper color.

If you live in Michigan, you're in luck: Friske Orchards sells its frozen fruit, including sliced apples—which, Richard says, are indistinguishable from fresh in a baked pie—through a network of food markets in the state. The rest of us can have his frozen fruit shipped overnight. For price information and availability, call Friske Orchards at (231) 599-2604, or visit Friske's Web site, www.friske.com.

"Floating Top" Cherry–Vanilla Bean Pie

Here are a couple of neat tricks you can use on a lot of fruit pies. The first is including a vanilla bean in the filling. I usually keep a vanilla bean or two around the kitchen for one reason or another. Sometimes I'll have a slit section, or a section I've scraped the seeds from but haven't discarded, since there's still a lot of flavor to be gleaned from it. Baking a section of slit bean in a fruit filling releases the vanilla flavor nicely. I particularly like the flavor it adds to cherry, peach, and pear pies. The other thing I do here is use a "floating" top crust. A floating crust is not attached to the sides. Rather, a circle of dough—slightly smaller than the top of the pie—is simply placed over the filling; it just floats there, in other words. The juice bubbles up and makes a ring around the pie: the darker the fruit, such as blackberries or cherries, the more striking the effect.

MAKES 8 TO 10 SERVINGS

1 recipe Basic Flaky Pie Pastry, Double Crust (page 31) or Extra-Flaky Pie Pastry, Double Crust (page 34), refrigerated

FILLING

4 cups fresh sweet cherries, stemmed and pitted

1/3 cup plus 2 tablespoons sugar

2 teaspoons fresh lemon juice

2 tablespoons cornstarch

Pinch of ground nutmeg

One 3- to 4-inch section of vanilla bean, slit lengthwise

GLAZE

Milk or light cream

Sugar

1. If you haven't already, prepare the pastry and refrigerate until firm enough to roll, about 1 hour.

2. On a sheet of lightly floured waxed paper, roll half of the pastry into a 12-inch circle with a floured rolling pin. Invert the pastry over a 9-inch standard pie pan, center, and peel off the paper. Tuck the pastry into the pan, without stretching it, and sculpt the edge into an upstanding ridge. Place in the freezer for 15 minutes. When the 15 minutes are up, preheat the oven to 400 degrees.

3. Combine the cherries, 1/3 cup of the sugar, and the lemon juice in a medium-size bowl. Mix well, then set aside for 10 minutes to juice. Mix together the remaining 2 table-spoons sugar and the cornstarch in a small bowl, then stir the mixture into the fruit along with the nutmeg. Set aside.

4. On another sheet of floured waxed paper, roll the other half of the pastry into a 10-inch circle. If you're not particularly steady-handed, use a bowl or another template for the next step. Cut a 7-inch circle in the pastry using a paring knife or pastry wheel. Remove the outer pastry scraps and save for another use. Keep the circle of pastry nearby.

5. Turn the filling into the chilled pie shell, smoothing the top with a spoon. Bury the vanilla bean in the fruit, right in the center of the pie (so you can find it easily later). Invert the top pastry over the filling, center, and peel off the paper. Brush the top pastry with milk and sprinkle with sugar.

6. Place the pie on the center oven rack and bake for 30 minutes. Reduce the oven temperature to 375°F and rotate the pie 180 degrees, so that the part that faced the back of the oven now faces forward. Just in case, slide a large aluminum foil–lined baking sheet onto the rack below to catch any spills. Bake until the top of the pie is golden brown and the juices bubble thickly all around the edge, 25 to 30 minutes.

7.   Transfer the pie to a wire rack and let cool for at least 2 hours. Remove the vanilla bean before serving.

Recipe for Success

▶   Another attractive way to do this is to use decorative pastry cutouts (see page 19), such as diamonds or circles, to "attach" the floating crust to the rim. Lay 6 or 8 cutouts evenly around the perimeter, placing them partly on the floating pastry and partly on the rim, spanning the fruit filling.

Poetic Pies

From the oven hot and steaming,

With the ruby bubbles gleaming,

As they boil up through the craters in little puffs and sighs,

There's restless invitation

To the palate's delectation

In the odor and the look of those "poetic" cherry pies.

Oh, their juice than wine is richer!

It is poured from out the pitcher

Where is stored the luscious nectar distilled at summer's prime.

Show these pies to Doctor Tanner,

He would forthwith strike his banner

And put off the fasting racket to a more convenient time.

—Ellen P. Allerton, *Walls of Corn and Other Poems*

Double-Cherry Pie

This delicious pie is from the Cherry Marketing Institute, whose job it is to promote the use of sour cherries, also known as pie cherries or tart cherries. (The most common variety, incidentally, is the Montmorency.) This recipe includes two kinds of sour cherries—fresh and dried—along with sugar and just a bit of butter, nutmeg, and almond extract to highlight the flavor of the cherries.

MAKES 8 TO 10 SERVINGS

1 recipe Basic Flaky Pie Pastry, Double Crust (page 31) or Tender Cream Cheese Pastry, Double Crust (page 46), refrigerated

FILLING

4^1/$_2$ cups pitted sour cherries, fresh, individually frozen (not packed in syrup; partially thawed), or canned (drained)

1 cup dried sour cherries

1 cup sugar

2 tablespoons quick-cooking tapioca

^{1}/$_2$ teaspoon almond extract

^{1}/$_4$ teaspoon ground nutmeg

1 tablespoon cold unsalted butter, cut into small pieces

GLAZE

Milk or light cream

Sugar

1.   If you haven't already, prepare the pastry and refrigerate until firm enough to roll, about 1 hour.

2.   On a sheet of lightly floured waxed paper, roll the larger portion of the pastry into a 13-inch circle with a floured rolling pin. Invert the pastry over a 9^1/$_2$-inch deep-dish pie pan, center, and peel off the paper. Gently tuck the pastry into the pan, without stretching it, and let the overhang drape over the edge. Place in the refrigerator for 15 minutes.

3.   Combine the pitted cherries, dried cherries, sugar, tapioca, and almond extract in a large bowl and mix well. Set aside for 10 minutes to juice. Preheat the oven to 375°F.

4.   Roll the other half of the pastry into a 10-inch circle on a sheet of lightly floured waxed paper. Turn the filling into the chilled pie shell, smoothing the top of the fruit with a spoon. Sprinkle the nutmeg over the fruit and dot the filling with the butter. Moisten the edge of the pie shell with a pastry brush. Invert the top pastry over the filling, center, and peel off the paper. Press the top and bottom pastries together along the dampened edge. Using a knife, trim the pastry flush with the edge of the pan, then crimp the edge with a fork. Poke several steam vents in the top of the pie with a paring knife, twisting the knife

to enlarge the holes slightly. Put a couple of the holes along the edge so you can check the juices there later. To glaze the pie, brush a little milk over the pastry and sprinkle lightly with sugar.

5. Place the pie on the center oven rack and bake for 30 minutes, then rotate the pie 180 degrees, so that the part that faced the back of the oven now faces forward. Just in case, slide a large aluminum foil–lined baking sheet onto the rack below to catch any drips. Continue to bake until the juices bubble thickly up through the steam vents, 30 to 35 minutes. If the top starts to get too brown, loosely drape a piece of aluminum foil over the pie during the last 15 minutes.

6. Transfer the pie to a wire rack and let cool for at least 2 hours. This is best eaten slightly warm or at room temperature.

Recipe for Success

▶ **Do try to find sour cherries to make this pie, but don't neglect it if all you can find are sweet cherries. When using sweet, reduce the sugar by about half and add 1 tablespoon fresh lemon juice to the filling.**

▶ **At the very least, you should be able to find the dried sour cherries, most likely at a gourmet or health food store. They're rather expensive, but they're worth the price of admission to make this great pie.**

The Ultimate Four-Cherry Pie

I can't resist a profusion of fresh cherries in the market, a situation that often finds me with several bags of my favorite pie cherries on hand simultaneously: sweet, sour, and the Rainier cherries I like so much for pies. Rummaging further in my pantry, I can nearly always find a partial bag of dried cherries. When all of these are combined in a pie, it makes what I consider the ultimate cherry pie, one in which no one cherry dominates but all contribute to a unique flavor. Add a top crust if you like, but my first choice is this brown sugar topping.

MAKES 8 TO 10 SERVINGS

1 recipe Extra-Flaky Pie Pastry, Single Crust (page 34) or Basic Flaky Pie Pastry, Single Crust (page 31), refrigerated

FILLING

2 cups fresh sour cherries, stemmed and pitted

2 cups fresh Rainier cherries, stemmed and pitted

1 cup fresh sweet cherries, stemmed and pitted

1/2 cup dried sour or sweet cherries

1/2 cup plus 2 tablespoons granulated sugar

1 tablespoon fresh lemon or orange juice

Grated zest of 1/2 orange

1 teaspoon vanilla extract

3 tablespoons cornstarch

BROWN SUGAR TOPPING

1/2 cup firmly packed light brown sugar

1/2 cup all-purpose flour

Big pinch of salt

1/4 cup (1/2 stick) cold unsalted butter, cut into 1/4-inch pieces

1. If you haven't already, prepare the pastry and refrigerate until firm enough to roll, about 1 hour.

2. On a sheet of lightly floured waxed paper, roll the pastry into a 13-inch circle with a floured rolling pin. Invert the pastry over a 9½-inch deep-dish pie pan, center, and peel off the paper. Gently tuck the pastry into the pan, without stretching it, and sculpt the overhang into an upstanding ridge. Place in the freezer for 15 minutes. Preheat the oven to 400°F.

3. In a large bowl, combine all the cherries, ½ cup of the granulated sugar, the lemon juice, orange zest, and vanilla. Mix well and set aside for 10 to 15 minutes to juice. Mix the remaining 2 tablespoons granulated sugar and the cornstarch together in a small bowl, then stir the mixture into the fruit. Turn the filling into the chilled pie shell and smooth the top of the fruit with a spoon. Place the pie on the center oven rack and bake for 30 minutes.

4. Meanwhile, make the topping. Combine the brown sugar, flour, and salt in a food processor and pulse to mix. Scatter the butter over the dry ingredients and pulse until the mixture resembles fine crumbs. Empty the crumbs into a large bowl and rub them between your fingers to make large, buttery crumbs. Refrigerate until ready to use.

5. Remove the pie from the oven and reduce the temperature to 375°F. Carefully dump the crumbs in the center of the pie, spreading them over the surface with your hands. Tamp them down lightly. Return the pie to the oven, placing it so that the part that faced the back of the oven now faces forward. Just in case, slide a large aluminum

A Crash Course in Cherries

▶ The leading producer of sour cherries is Michigan, producing about 75 percent of the annual crop, or some 200 to 250 million pounds.

▶ The primary variety of sour cherry grown in the United States is the Montmorency, prized for preserves, jelly, juice, and—of course—pie.

▶ Most sweet cherries are grown in the Pacific Coast states, although Michigan does produce 20 percent of the annual crop.

▶ There are more than 1,000 varieties of sweet cherries. The most famous sweet cherry is the Bing.

▶ Pie makers take note: the third week of July is usually the peak of the harvest.

▶ The average cherry tree produces 7,000 cherries. It takes about 250 of them to make a pie.

foil–lined baking sheet onto the rack below to catch any spills. Bake until the top is dark golden brown and the juices bubble thickly around the edge, about 30 minutes.

6. Transfer the pie to a wire rack and let cool for at least 2 hours before serving.

Recipe for Success

▶ You'll diminish the subtle cherry notes if you oversweeten this pie, so resist the temptation (if you're so inclined) to add more sugar to the filling.

▶ Pitting cherries (see page 67) usually leaves them broken, somewhat crushed, or in several pieces. That's about as chopped as they need to be, so don't worry about cutting them further.

▶ For the purest, clearest cherry flavor, omit the vanilla extract in the filling and substitute granulated sugar for the brown sugar in the topping.

Double-Crust Cherry-Blackberry Pie

A pound each of frozen cherries and frozen blackberries go into this any-time-of-year fruit pie. The filling is berry-dark and juicy, and it tastes particularly delicious in the cream cheese pastry.

1 recipe Tender Cream Cheese Pastry, Double Crust (page 46), refrigerated

FILLING

One 1-pound bag individually frozen pitted sweet cherries (not packed in syrup), partially thawed

One 1-pound bag individually frozen blackberries (not packed in syrup), partially thawed

1/2 cup plus 2 tablespoons granulated sugar

1 tablespoon fresh lemon juice

Grated zest of 1 lemon

3 tablespoons cornstarch

1/4 teaspoon ground nutmeg

1/4 teaspoon ground ginger

GARNISH

Confectioners' sugar

1. If you haven't already, prepare the pastry and refrigerate until firm enough to roll, about 1¹/₂ hours.

2. On a sheet of lightly floured waxed paper, roll the larger portion of the pastry into a 12-inch circle with a floured rolling pin. Invert the pastry over a 9-inch standard pie pan, center, and peel off the paper. Gently tuck the pastry into the pan, without stretching it, and let the overhang drape over the edge. Place in the refrigerator for 15 minutes.

3. Combine the cherries, blackberries, ¹/₂ cup of the granulated sugar, the lemon juice, and lemon zest in a large bowl. Mix gently several times (see Recipe for Success) and set aside for 10 minutes. Preheat the oven to 400°F.

4. In a small bowl, combine the remaining 2 tablespoons granulated sugar, cornstarch, nutmeg, and ginger. Add to the fruit and mix briefly.

5. On another sheet of lightly floured waxed paper, roll the other half of the pastry into an 11-inch circle. Turn the filling into the chilled pie shell and smooth with a spoon. Lightly moisten the rim of the pie shell with a wet finger or pastry brush. Invert the top pastry over the filling, center, and peel off the paper. Press the top and bottom pastries together along the dampened edge. Trim the pastry with scissors or a paring knife, leaving

an even ½-inch overhang all around, then sculpt the overhang into an upstanding ridge. Poke several steam vents in the top of the pie with a fork or paring knife. Put a couple of the vents near the edge of the crust so you can check the juices there later.

6. Place the pie on the center oven rack and bake for 30 minutes. Reduce the oven temperature to 375°F and rotate the pie 180 degrees, so that the part that faced the back of the oven now faces forward. Just in case, slide a large aluminum foil–lined baking sheet onto the rack below to catch any spills. Continue to bake until the top is golden brown and any juices visible at the steam vents bubble thickly, 30 to 35 minutes.

7. Transfer the pie to a wire rack and let cool for 15 to 20 minutes. While it is still quite warm, dust the top lightly with confectioners' sugar. Once the pie has cooled completely, dust it again. Let the pie cool for at least 1 hour before serving.

Recipe for Success

▶ Frozen blackberries, like fresh, tend to be quite juicy and fragile once they have partially thawed. That said, avoid the temptation to overmix the fruit. Too much mixing will cause the berries to break up, leaving the pie with fewer whole berries and less textural interest.

All-Peach Pie with Coconut-Almond Crumb Topping

We all know that the season for truly good, ripe peaches is short—far shorter than the amount of time they occupy supermarket produce aisles during the summer months. When the quality of peaches is not what it should be, I like to use frozen fruit instead. Frozen peaches are a relative bargain, compared to fresh or canned, and the quality is very good. I'll repeat here what I say elsewhere: the quality of frozen produce in this country is quite often superior to that of fresh, in large part because there is very little time between harvesting and processing. That said, you can make an excellent peach pie with frozen fruit. I like to add a good amount of lemon juice and zest, both of which lend an aura of freshness, and a little nutmeg and vanilla to replace those subtle flavor notes that get lost in the processing.

MAKES 8 TO 10 SERVINGS

1 recipe Basic Flaky Pie Pastry, Single Crust (page 31), refrigerated

FILLING

Two 1-pound bags frozen sliced peaches, partially thawed

1 1/2 tablespoons fresh lemon juice

Finely grated zest of 1 lemon

1/3 cup plus 3 tablespoons sugar

2 tablespoons cornstarch

1/2 teaspoon vanilla extract

1/4 teaspoon ground nutmeg

COCONUT-ALMOND CRUMB TOPPING

1 cup all-purpose flour

2/3 cup sugar

1/4 teaspoon salt

1/2 cup sliced almonds

1/2 cup sweetened flaked coconut

6 tablespoons (3/4 stick) cold unsalted butter, cut into 1/4-inch pieces

1 tablespoon milk

1. If you haven't already, prepare the pastry and refrigerate until firm enough to roll, about 1 hour.

2. On a sheet of lightly floured waxed paper, roll the pastry into a 13-inch circle with a floured rolling pin. Invert the pastry over a 9 1/2-inch deep-dish pie pan, center, and peel off the paper. Gently tuck the pastry into the pan, without stretching it, and sculpt the overhang into an upstanding ridge. Place in the freezer for 15 minutes.

3. Combine the peaches, lemon juice, lemon zest, and 1/3 cup of the sugar in a large bowl and toss well to mix. Set aside for 10 minutes to juice. Preheat the oven to 400°F.

4. In a small bowl, mix the cornstarch with the remaining 3 tablespoons sugar. Sprinkle this mixture over the fruit and mix well. Stir in the vanilla and nutmeg. Turn the filling into the chilled pie shell and smooth the filling with your hands to even it out. Place the pie on the center oven rack and bake for 35 minutes.

5. Meanwhile, make the topping. Combine the flour, sugar, salt, almonds, and coconut in a food processor and pulse several times to mix. Scatter the butter over the top and pulse until the mixture resembles fine crumbs. Add the milk and process again until the crumbs are gravelly. Transfer to a large bowl and rub gently between your fingers to make the crumbs uniform in texture. Refrigerate until ready to use.

6. Remove the pie from the oven and reduce the temperature to 375°F. Carefully dump the crumbs in the center of the pie and spread them evenly with your hands. Press on the crumbs gently to compact them. Return the pie to the oven, placing it so that the part that faced the back of the oven now faces forward. Just in case, slide a large aluminum

foil–lined baking sheet onto the rack below to catch any spills. Bake until the juices bubble thickly around the edge, about 30 minutes.

7. Transfer the pie to a wire rack and let cool for at least 1 hour before serving.

Recipe for Success

▶ The juiciest pies, such as this one, seem to need a very thick layer of crumb topping, the way we do it here. If you use too little topping, it tends to just soak into the juice, and you end up with a sludge-topped pie rather than a crumb-topped pie. Don't worry if you think there's too much topping. Use all of it, and the pie will be great.

Peaches and Cream Pie

This open-faced pie tastes like peach ice cream—not surprising, since the three main ingredients are peaches, cream, and confectioners' sugar. In summer, try to use fresh peaches if you have them, but you'll get an excellent pie with frozen peaches as well. The finishing touch is a sprinkling of brown sugar that goes on for the last 15 minutes of baking, giving the pie a delicious caramel coating. Plan ahead, because you have to chill this pie before serving.

MAKES 8 TO 10 SERVINGS

1 recipe Basic Flaky Pie Pastry, Single Crust (page 31), All-Butter Pie Pastry, Single Crust (page 28), or Tender Cream Cheese Pastry, Single Crust (page 46), refrigerated

FILLING

2 1/2 to 3 cups peeled, pitted, and sliced ripe peaches or one 1-pound bag frozen sliced peaches, partially thawed

1 cup heavy or whipping cream

1/2 cup confectioners' sugar, sifted

Big pinch of salt

1/2 teaspoon vanilla extract

1/2 cup firmly packed light brown sugar

1. If you haven't already, prepare the pastry and refrigerate until firm enough to roll, about 1 hour.

2. On a sheet of lightly floured waxed paper, roll the pastry into a 13-inch circle with a floured rolling pin. Invert the pastry over a 9 1/2-inch deep-dish pie pan, center, and peel off the paper. Tuck the pastry into the pan, without stretching it, and sculpt the edge so

it is more or less flush with the top of the pan. Place in the freezer for 15 minutes. Preheat the oven to 400°F.

3. Distribute the peach slices evenly in the chilled shell. Combine the cream, confectioners' sugar, salt, and vanilla in a medium-size bowl and whisk to blend. Slowly pour the cream over the peaches. Use a fork, if necessary, to rearrange the peach slices evenly in the shell.

4. Place the pie on the center oven rack and bake for 30 minutes. Remove from the oven and reduce the temperature to 350°F. Sprinkle the brown sugar evenly over the pie, then return it to the oven, placing it so that the part that faced the back of the oven now faces forward. Bake until the filling is bubbly and the top is caramel-colored, 15 to 20 minutes. The filling will still be liquidy.

5. Transfer the pie to a wire rack and let cool thoroughly. Cover with loosely tented aluminum foil and refrigerate for at least 4 hours or overnight before serving.

Recipe for Success

▶ Unlike other similar recipes, this is not a custard pie, because it contains no eggs. Thus, as I indicate in the recipe, the filling typically looks liquidy when the pie comes out of the oven. Don't bake the pie longer, though, in hopes that the filling will firm up. The thickening occurs as the pie cools.

How to Blanch a Peach

One bite of a peach is all it takes to tell whether you'll want to peel your pie-bound fruit: If the skin is thick and chewy, peel it. If not, you probably don't have to bother.

If you're going to peel, you can, of course, use a sharp paring knife. If you're good, you won't remove much of the precious flesh underneath. If you're not, you may want to consider blanching.

To blanch your peaches, bring 2 to 3 quarts of water to a boil in a large saucepan. Using a slotted spoon, lower the peaches into the boiling water one at a time. Count to 15, then remove the peach. Let it cool briefly, then just slide off the skin. The first one is your test peach: if the skin doesn't slip right off, give the next one 30 seconds. The trick is to submerge the peach just long enough to loosen the skin, but not so long that the flesh underneath gets too soft, making it difficult to handle when you slice it.

Peach-Mascarpone Cream Pie

There are other peach custard pies in this collection, but this one is no doubt the richest, thanks to the mascarpone cheese, heavy cream, and unabashed number of egg yolks. That said, I think of it as a once-a-year proposition, made with only the softest and juiciest summer peaches. The tender peaches almost melt into the golden custard, obscuring the boundary between the two. The edge of the pie has a slightly dry texture, like New York–style cheese-cake, while the center is creamy and moist. This is a decadent and caloric pie, but it's also deli-cious, light, and far from the ordinary.

MAKES 8 TO 10 SERVINGS

1 recipe Basic Flaky Pie Pastry, Single Crust (page 31), refrigerated

FILLING

3 cups peeled, pitted, and sliced ripe peaches

²/₃ cup plus 2 tablespoons sugar

3 tablespoons all-purpose flour

5 large egg yolks

³/₄ cup heavy or whipping cream

1 teaspoon vanilla extract

8 ounces (about 1 cup) mascarpone cheese

1.   If you haven't already, prepare the pastry and refrigerate until firm enough to roll, about 1 hour.

2.   On a sheet of lightly floured waxed paper, roll the pastry into a 13-inch circle with a floured rolling pin. Invert the pastry over a 9½-inch deep-dish pie pan, center, and peel off the paper. Gently tuck the pastry into the pan, without stretching it, and sculpt the overhang into an upstanding ridge. Place in the freezer for 15 minutes.

3.   Combine the peaches, 2 tablespoons of the sugar, and the flour in a medium-size bowl. Mix well and set aside.

4.   Combine the egg yolks and remaining ²/₃ cup sugar in the top of a double boiler set over, not in, barely simmering water. Whisk the yolks until they're thick and lemon-colored, 7 to 8 minutes. Remove from the heat and whisk in the cream and vanilla. Set aside for 10 minutes to cool. Preheat the oven to 375°F.

5.   Put the mascarpone and ½ cup of the custard in a large bowl. Using an electric mixer, blend briefly until smooth. Blend in the remaining custard, ½ cup at a time, until all of the custard is added.

6. Transfer the peaches to the chilled pie shell, smoothing the fruit with a spoon. Slowly pour the mascarpone custard over the peaches. Using a fork, move the peaches around slightly so that the custard flows under and around them.

7. Place the pie on the center oven rack and bake for 10 minutes. Reduce the oven temperature to 350°F and continue to bake until the custard is set and the top is golden brown, though perhaps not uniformly so, about 35 minutes. Rotate the pie 180 degrees, so that the part that faced the back of the oven now faces forward, about 15 minutes before it is finished baking. To check for doneness, give the pie a little nudge. The filling shouldn't seem soupy at the center.

8. Transfer the pie to a wire rack and let cool. Serve barely warm or at room temperature. Or cover the cooled pie with loosely tented aluminum foil, refrigerate, and serve cold.

Recipe for Success

▶ It isn't really the same, by a long shot, but in a pinch you could substitute 1/2 cup each full-fat sour cream and cream cheese for the mascarpone cheese.

▶ If you don't have ripe peaches, try another peach pie, one that's not so dependent on perfect summer fruit. Consult the index for some ideas.

Lemonade-Peach Pie

Fresh peaches and lemonade concentrate give this pie an unmistakable summer flavor. The store-bought frozen pie shell lets you get this in the oven in a thrice. The crunchy streusel topping takes less than five minutes to prepare and adds a delicious finish.

MAKES 8 SERVINGS

1 store-bought frozen 9-inch deep-dish pie shell

FILLING

4 cups peeled, pitted, and thinly sliced ripe peaches

1/3 cup frozen lemonade concentrate, thawed

1/4 cup sugar

2 1/2 tablespoons quick-cooking tapioca

STREUSEL TOPPING

3/4 cup all-purpose flour

1/3 cup sugar

1/4 teaspoon ground cinnamon

1/8 teaspoon salt

5 tablespoons cold unsalted butter, cut into 1/4-inch pieces

1. Remove the pie shell from the package but leave it in the freezer. Preheat the oven to 400°F.

2. Combine all the filling ingredients in a medium-size bowl. Turn the filling into the frozen pie shell and smooth the top with a spoon. Place the pie on the center oven rack and bake for 25 minutes.

3. Meanwhile, make the topping. Put the flour, sugar, cinnamon, and salt in a food processor and pulse several times to mix. Scatter the butter over the top and pulse until the mixture resembles fine crumbs. Empty the crumbs into a medium-size bowl and rub between your fingers to make large, buttery crumbs. Refrigerate until ready to use.

4. Remove the pie from the oven and reduce the temperature to 375°F. Carefully dump the crumbs on the pie, spreading them evenly over the surface with your hands. Tamp them down lightly. Return the pie to the oven, placing it so that the part that faced the back of the oven now faces forward. Just in case, slide a large aluminum foil–lined baking sheet onto the rack below to catch any drips. Continue to bake until the topping is golden brown and the juices bubble thickly around the edge, about 25 minutes.

5. Transfer the pie to a wire rack and let cool for at least 2 hours before serving.

Recipe for Success

▸ Remember to be careful when handling store-bought pie shells, because the edges tend to get brittle as they bake. The best way to get them in and out of the oven is by using a small rimless baking sheet as an oversize spatula, sliding it under the pan.

▸ Instead of peaches, substitute fresh nectarines, if you like.

Peachy Peach Butter Pie with Sour Cream Topping

One of the best ways to make a really peachy peach pie is to add peach butter. If you've never tried it, peach butter is like apple butter—a thick fruit spread made primarily from the fruit itself, with some sugar, lemon juice, and spices added for good measure. I use Kauffman's peach butter, out of Bird-in-Hand, Pennsylvania. (Don't you love that name?) I get it at the Pennsylvania Dutch Market here in Annapolis, Maryland, although I've seen peach butters sold elsewhere as well. I combine it with juicy fresh peaches, sugar, spices, and flour and bake the pie until it's bubbly and thick. Once it cools down, I spread brown sugar–sweetened sour cream over the top, which makes a great creamy contrast to the chunky fruit filling.

MAKES 8 TO 10 SERVINGS

1 recipe All-Butter Pie Pastry, Single Crust (page 28) or Basic Flaky Pie Pastry, Single Crust (page 31), refrigerated

FILLING

4 cups peeled, pitted, and sliced ripe peaches

1 cup peach butter

1/2 cup granulated sugar

Grated zest of 1 lemon

2 tablespoons all-purpose flour

1/2 teaspoon ground cinnamon

1/4 teaspoon ground nutmeg

SOUR CREAM TOPPING

1 1/4 cups sour cream, preferably full-fat

1/4 cup firmly packed light brown sugar

1/2 teaspoon vanilla extract

1. If you haven't already, prepare the pastry and refrigerate until firm enough to roll, about 1 hour.

2. On a sheet of lightly floured waxed paper, roll the pastry into a 13-inch circle with a floured rolling pin. Invert the pastry over a 9 1/2-inch deep-dish pie pan, center, and peel off the paper. Gently tuck the pastry into the pan, without stretching it, and sculpt the overhang into an upstanding ridge. Place in the freezer for 15 minutes.

3. In a large bowl, combine all the filling ingredients. Set aside for 10 minutes to juice. Preheat the oven to 400°F.

4. Pour the filling into the chilled pie shell, smoothing the top of the fruit with a spoon. Place on the center oven rack and bake for 30 minutes. Reduce the oven temperature to 375°F and rotate the pie 180 degrees, so that the part that faced the back of the oven now faces forward. Continue to bake until the filling bubbles thickly, 30 to 35 minutes.

5. Transfer the pie to a wire rack and let cool for 2 hours. Cover with loosely tented aluminum foil and refrigerate for at least 2 hours.

6. At least 30 minutes before serving, make the topping. Combine the sour cream and brown sugar in a small saucepan over low heat. Heat, stirring continuously, until the sour cream is runny, 2 to 3 minutes. Do not let the mixture boil. Remove from the heat and stir in the vanilla. Slowly pour the mixture over the center of the pie, gently shaking

and tilting the pie so that the topping runs up to the edge. Refrigerate for 30 minutes before serving.

Recipe for Success

▶ As I mentioned earlier, some brands of peach butter already contain spices. Taste yours to see how spicy it is. If the spices are bold, reduce the amount of cinnamon and nutmeg added to the filling here.

▶ This filling may appear to have thickened after 30 to 40 minutes, but don't be tempted to remove the pie from the oven before you see it bubble. It won't be as juicy as a traditional fruit pie, but it should be bubbly-thick in several locations.

Triple Vanilla Bean–Scented All-Peach Pie

The sweet, delicate flavor of summer peaches pairs up beautifully with vanilla. So when I'm feeling extravagant and totally in the thrall of the summer peach harvest, I slit open a vanilla bean, scrape out the seeds, and grind them with a cup of sugar. Then I use this vanilla sugar three different ways: to sweeten the filling, to sprinkle over the pie crust when it comes out of the oven, and to flavor the whipped cream I serve with the pie. It's a little indulgent—vanilla beans costing what they do—but worth every penny for this best-of-summer peach pie.

MAKES 8 TO 10 SERVINGS

1 recipe Basic Flaky Pie Pastry, Double Crust (page 31) or Basic Shortening Pie Pastry, Double Crust (page 30), refrigerated

FILLING

1 plump vanilla bean

1 cup sugar

3 tablespoons cornstarch

5 cups peeled, pitted, and thickly sliced ripe peaches

2 teaspoons fresh lemon juice

2 tablespoons cold unsalted butter, cut into small pieces

GARNISH

1 cup cold heavy or whipping cream

1. If you haven't already, prepare the pastry and refrigerate until firm enough to roll, about 1 hour.

2. On a sheet of lightly floured waxed paper, roll the larger portion of the pastry into a 12-inch circle with a floured rolling pin. Invert the pastry over a 9-inch standard pie pan,

center, and peel off the paper. Gently tuck the pastry into the pan, without stretching it, and let the overhang drape over the edge. Place in the refrigerator for 15 minutes.

3. Slit the vanilla bean lengthwise. With the blade of a paring knife, scrape the seeds out of the bean and into a food processor. Add the sugar and process for about 1 minute. (If the machine sends up a cloud of sugar dust through the feed tube, just cover the tube with your hand.) Transfer the vanilla sugar to a small bowl. Mix $1/2$ cup of the vanilla sugar with the cornstarch in another bowl and keep it nearby.

4. Combine the peaches, sugar-cornstarch mixture, and lemon juice in a large bowl. Mix well and set aside. Preheat the oven to 400°F.

5. On another sheet of floured waxed paper, roll the other half of the pastry into a 10-inch circle with a floured rolling pin. Turn the filling into the chilled pie shell, smoothing the top with your hands or a spoon. Dot the top of the fruit with the butter. Lightly moisten the rim of the pie shell. Invert the top pastry over the filling, center, and peel off the paper. Press the top and bottom pastries together along the dampened edge. Using the back of a butter knife or pastry knife, trim the pastry flush with the edge of the pan. Poke several steam vents in the top of the pie with a fork or paring knife. Put a couple of the vents near the edge of the crust so you can check the juices there later.

6. Place the pie on the center oven rack and bake for 30 minutes. Reduce the oven temperature to 375°F and rotate the pie 180 degrees, so that the part that faced the back of the oven now faces forward. Just in case, slide a large aluminum foil–lined baking sheet onto the rack below to catch any spills. Continue to bake until the top is a deep golden brown and the juices visible at the side vents bubble thickly, about 30 minutes.

7. Transfer the pie to a wire rack and immediately sprinkle half the remaining vanilla sugar (about $1/4$ cup) over the top. Set aside on the wire rack to cool for at least 2 hours.

8. Shortly before serving, using a chilled medium-size bowl and chilled beaters, whip the cream with an electric mixer until it holds soft peaks. Add the remaining vanilla sugar and continue to beat until stiff but not grainy. Serve a large dollop of whipped cream with each slice of pie.

Picking and Handling Those Perfect Pie Peaches

The most important step in making the best peach pie—and this goes for nearly all fruit pies—is choosing good fruit. And that's not always as easy as you might think. Looks alone aren't necessarily an accurate indicator: the best-looking fruit can often disappoint. Here, then, are some things to keep in mind when selecting peaches.

> ▶ Use your nose. A good peach will have a sweet, peachy smell.

> ▶ Apply gentle finger pressure. Peaches should yield slightly. If they're rock hard—and they often are—just wait until better fruit comes along. Or use frozen.

> ▶ Stay away from greenish peaches. They were picked too early and won't make a good pie.

> ▶ Buy only enough ripe peaches for your immediate use. Ripe peaches are delicate and won't last more than a day or two once you get them home.

> ▶ Store fully ripe peaches in the refrigerator, in a single layer. Use within 1 to 2 days. Store slightly underripe fruit at room temperature, again in a single layer. Turn frequently to minimize bruising.

Recipe for Success

> ▶ Make sure to choose a fat, supple vanilla bean about 8 inches long, meaning it's fully mature. It should have a clear, lovely fragrance and should not smell of smoke, which could be an indication of improper curing.

> ▶ Do sprinkle the vanilla sugar on the pie as soon as it comes out of the oven so that some of it can "melt" into the top crust. Expect much of it to remain gritty, however.

Adolph Family Peach Swirl Pie

For our purposes, a pie is some sort of sweet filling with a pastry or crumb crust under, over, or around it. And with one or two exceptions, I've clung steadfastly to that definition. But not here, for two good reasons. Good Reason #1: this is delicious, and it does, after all, have what you'd call a *cake* crust and is baked in a pie pan. Good Reason #2: the recipe was given to me by Jon Adolph, the editor of *FamilyFun* magazine, where I am a contributing editor—a position I'd just as soon keep. All kidding aside, this really is a wonderful pie, a family favorite often baked by Jon's mother-in-law, Rachel van Leer, and his wife, Sarah. A layer of cream cheese custard bakes up in pockets within the coffeecake crust. That's topped with a layer of peaches and a sour cream and brown sugar glaze, which go on for the last five minutes of baking. Call it just plain scrumptious. Serve it for breakfast or dessert.

MAKES 8 TO 10 SERVINGS

CAKE CRUST

1 cup all-purpose flour, sifted

1 teaspoon baking powder

1/2 teaspoon salt

1/2 cup (1 stick) unsalted butter, softened

2/3 cup granulated sugar

2 large eggs, at room temperature

1 teaspoon vanilla extract

1 tablespoon reserved syrup from canned peaches (see topping)

CREAM CHEESE CUSTARD

One 3-ounce package full-fat cream cheese, softened

1/3 cup granulated sugar

1/4 cup full-fat sour cream

1 large egg

1/4 teaspoon salt

TOPPING

1 cup full-fat sour cream

2 tablespoons firmly packed light brown sugar

One 29-ounce can sliced peaches in syrup, drained but 1 tablespoon syrup reserved for crust

1. Butter a 9½-inch deep-dish pie pan. Preheat the oven to 325°F.

2. To make the cake crust, combine the flour, baking powder, and salt in a medium-size bowl. Set aside. Using an electric mixer, cream the butter in a large bowl, gradually adding the granulated sugar. Beat in the eggs, one at a time, beating well after each addition. Blend in the vanilla and peach syrup. Stir in the dry mixture until evenly blended. Scrape the batter into the prepared pie pan, smoothing it evenly over the bottom and about halfway up the side. Set aside.

3. To make the cream cheese custard, use an electric mixer to beat the cream cheese, granulated sugar, sour cream, egg, and salt together in a medium-size bowl. Slowly pour the mixture over the cake crust. Place on the center oven rack and bake for 30 minutes. Meanwhile, as the pie bakes, blend the sour cream and brown sugar for the topping in a small bowl.

4. Remove the pie from the oven and arrange the peaches on top. Put a few in the center and arrange the rest of them like the spokes of a wheel, radiating out from the center. Spoon the sour cream topping over and around the peaches, smoothing it with the back of the spoon. Put the pie back in the oven and bake for 5 minutes.

5. Transfer the pie to a wire rack and let cool to room temperature before serving.

Recipe for Success

▶ The Adolph family recipe calls for canned peaches, but I don't see any reason you couldn't make this with peeled fresh peach slices. Use a tablespoon of their juice in place of the reserved syrup.

▶ For that matter, I think you could use many other fresh summer fruits here as well, from nectarines to fresh berries.

▶ Sarah says she sometimes substitutes up to half plain yogurt for an equal measure of sour cream in the cake. That's handy to know, especially if you don't have enough sour cream on hand.

Colonial Rose Inn's Peach Custard Pie

This one really hits my personal bull's-eye, because it has everything I like in a pie: peaches, custard, and crumb topping. As the pie bakes, the various elements almost melt into one, forming a sort of peach custard. Use very ripe and juicy summer peaches. My thanks to Jeff and Jayne Rose, owners of the Colonial Rose Inn in Grand Detour, Illinois, for providing this recipe.

MAKES 8 TO 10 SERVINGS

1 recipe Basic Flaky Pie Pastry, Single Crust (page 31) or All-Butter Pie Pastry, Single Crust (page 28), refrigerated

FILLING

1 cup full-fat sour cream

1 cup sugar

3 large egg yolks

1/4 cup all-purpose flour

1 teaspoon vanilla extract

4 large ripe peaches, peeled, pitted, and thickly sliced

STREUSEL TOPPING

1/2 cup all-purpose flour

1/2 cup sugar

1/4 cup (1/2 stick) cold unsalted butter, cut into 1/4-inch pieces

1. If you haven't already, prepare the pastry and refrigerate until firm enough to roll, about 1 hour.

2. On a sheet of lightly floured waxed paper, roll the pastry into a 13-inch circle with a floured rolling pin. Invert the pastry over a 9 1/2-inch deep-dish pie pan, center, and peel off the paper. Tuck the pastry into the pan, without stretching it, and sculpt the edge into an upstanding ridge. Place in the freezer for 15 minutes. Preheat the oven to 425°F.

3. In a large bowl, whisk together the sour cream, sugar, egg yolks, flour, and vanilla until smooth. Set aside. Arrange the peach slices in the chilled pie shell in tight, stacked concentric circles. You don't have to make it look perfect, just relatively neat. Slowly and evenly pour the sour cream mixture over the peaches. Gently shake the pan to help the mixture settle between the peaches. Place the pie on the center oven rack and bake for 30 minutes.

4. Meanwhile, make the streusel topping. Combine the flour, sugar, and butter in a large bowl, tossing to blend. Using your fingers, rub the butter into the dry ingredients until the mixture resembles coarse crumbs. Refrigerate until ready to use.

5. Remove the pie from the oven and reduce the temperature to 400°F. Dump the streusel in the center of the pie, spreading it evenly over the top with your hands. Tamp it down very gently. Return the pie to the oven, placing it so that the part that faced the back of the oven now faces forward. Continue to bake until the topping is golden brown, about 25 minutes. If the top starts to get too dark, cover with loosely tented aluminum foil during the last 10 minutes.

6. Transfer the pie to a wire rack and let cool for at least 2 hours. I prefer this pie cold, but it's also very good at room temperature or slightly warm. Once the pie has cooled to room temperature, cover with loosely tented aluminum foil and refrigerate before serving.

Recipe for Success

> ▶ Jeff Rose bakes this a little hotter than I typically bake custard pies, but the density of the sour cream filling seems to protect the custard from "breaking" and becoming watery.

> ▶ This same denseness of filling makes it a little difficult to judge when the pie is done. Jeff suggests sticking a knife in the center of the pie. If it comes out clean, the pie is done.

Fresh Peach and Brown Sugar Pizza Pie

This is probably closer to a pizza than it is to a pie, but you won't much care once you've tried it. The pastry bakes up bready and buttery and makes a good sturdy base for the sliced peach topping. A brown sugar and flour mixture is sprinkled over the crust to absorb the juice from the peaches. Then a little more of it is rubbed together with butter and spread over the peaches, creating a caramel-like streusel topping. It's different and delicious—a little too bready, perhaps, for dessert after a filling meal, but perfect following a light meal or as a summer baking project with the kids, who'll finish this off with their friends in no time flat.

MAKES 8 TO 10 SERVINGS

1 recipe Yeasted Butter Pastry (page 39)

Cornmeal

FILLING

4 cups peeled, pitted, and thickly sliced ripe peaches

3 tablespoons granulated sugar

¹/₃ cup firmly packed light brown sugar

¹/₄ cup all-purpose flour

¹/₄ teaspoon ground cinnamon

2 tablespoons cold unsalted butter, cut into small pieces

1. If you haven't already, prepare the pastry and let it rise for 1 hour according to the pastry directions. Meanwhile, lightly oil a large baking sheet and dust it with cornmeal.

2. After an hour of rising, punch the dough down gently once or twice, but not vigorously as you would a regular yeast dough. Put the dough on a floured work surface and dust it lightly with flour. Gently roll the pastry into a 13- to 14-inch circle, keeping it, as best you can, of even thickness. Transfer the pastry to the prepared baking sheet, pinching the edge of the dough into an upstanding ridge. Refrigerate for 15 minutes. Preheat the oven to 425°F.

3. Combine the sliced peaches and granulated sugar in a medium-size bowl and toss gently. Set aside for 10 minutes to juice. Meanwhile, mix the brown sugar, flour, and cinnamon together in a small bowl.

4. Remove the pastry from the refrigerator and sprinkle 2 tablespoons of the brown sugar mixture over it. By hand, lift the peaches out of their juice and arrange them in a single, random layer on the pastry. (Reserve the peach juice for another use, if you like; there won't be much of it.) Wash and dry your hands, then add the butter to the remaining brown sugar mixture and rub it in until you have coarse, buttery crumbs. Spread the crumbs evenly over the peaches.

5. Put the baking sheet on the center oven rack and bake for 15 minutes. Reduce the oven temperature to 375°F and rotate the baking sheet 180 degrees, so that the part that faced the back of the oven now faces forward. Continue to bake until the crust is golden brown and the juices bubble thickly on top, 10 to 12 minutes.

6. Slide the pizza onto a large wire rack. Let cool for 10 to 15 minutes, then slice and serve.

Recipe for Success

▶ You could, if you like, make this with a combination of stone fruits: apricots, peaches, and nectarines.

▶ Given the bread-like texture of this pastry, it really is best eaten as soon as possible—preferably within 30 minutes, but up to a couple of hours, of coming out of the oven.

Peach and Damson Plum Preserves Pie

You can, on occasion, get around the problem of inferior—or nonexistent—fresh fruit by using preserves in your pie filling. Such was the case here when I needed to make a plum pie but couldn't get my hands on any decent fresh plums. I substituted a jar of quality damson plum preserves, adding moisture and a fruit touch with some ripe peaches. I could have added a top crust, but since I was using the walnut pastry, I decided to go with a walnut crumb topping. The pie came out splendidly, as I trust you'll agree.

MAKES 8 TO 10 SERVINGS

1/2 recipe Nutty Pie Pastry (page 42) made with walnuts, refrigerated

FILLING

1 1/2 cups peeled, pitted, and diced ripe peaches

1 1/2 tablespoons granulated sugar

1 tablespoon all-purpose flour

1 1/4 cups damson plum preserves

WALNUT CRUMB TOPPING

3/4 cup all-purpose flour

3/4 cup finely chopped walnuts

1/3 cup rolled oats (old-fashioned or quick-cooking)

1/3 cup firmly packed light brown sugar

1/2 teaspoon ground cinnamon

1/4 teaspoon salt

5 tablespoons unsalted butter, melted

1.   If you haven't already, prepare the pastry and refrigerate until firm enough to roll, about 45 minutes. It's best not to overchill nut pastries or they can be tricky to handle.

2.   On a sheet of lightly floured waxed paper, roll the pastry into a 12-inch circle with a floured rolling pin. Invert the pastry over a 9-inch standard pie pan, center, and peel off the paper. Tuck the pastry into the pan, without stretching it, and sculpt the edge into a ridge that's just slightly higher than the edge of the pan. Place in the freezer for 15 minutes. Preheat the oven to 400°F.

3.   Combine the peaches, granulated sugar, and flour in a small bowl. Toss to mix.

4.   Spread half of the preserves evenly in the chilled pie shell. Spoon the peach mixture over the preserves, smoothing it with a spoon. Dab the remaining preserves here and there on top of the peaches, then smooth. Place the pie on the center oven rack and bake for 15 minutes.

5.   Meanwhile, make the topping. Combine the flour, walnuts, oats, brown sugar, cinnamon, and salt in a large bowl. Toss with your hands to mix. Stir in the butter, mixing first with a fork, then with your hands. Rub the topping until you have evenly mixed, coarse crumbs. Refrigerate until ready to use.

6.   Remove the pie from the oven and reduce the temperature to 375°F. Dump the crumbs in the center of the pie, spreading them over the top with your hands. Tamp them down slightly. Return the pie to the oven, placing it so that the part that faced the back of the oven now faces forward. Continue to bake until the fruit bubbles thickly around the edge and the topping is golden brown, 30 to 35 minutes.

7. Transfer the pie to a wire rack and let cool. Serve just barely warm or at room temperature.

Recipe for Success

▶ Using the same basic formula, consider your other filling options. Fig preserves are wonderful with diced pears, as are peach preserves with diced apples. Both are great with this nut pastry.

▶ If you'd like to alter the construction of the pie, assemble it as for Linzer Pie (page 577), adding strips of pastry across the top. You'll need the full pastry recipe. It looks very pretty with the dark red plum preserves peeking up through the lattice.

Pennsylvania Dutch Market Peach and Sour Cherry Pie

One of my favorite places to shop in Annapolis, Maryland, where I live, is the Pennsylvania Dutch Market. An impressive assemblage of food vendors under one roof, the market attracts shoppers from miles around and for good reason: the food and selection are always good, the portions large, and the prices what you would have expected to pay 10 or 15 years ago. Come summer, the market is one of the few in the area where I can find the sour cherries I love so much in pies—right when the Lancaster County, Pennsylvania, peaches come to market as well. I love combining the two in this pie—the tartness and color of the cherries providing a perfect contrast to the sweetness of the peaches. It's one of those classic summer pies I like to take along when we're invited for a cookout or patio party, always with a half gallon of good vanilla ice cream.

MAKES 8 TO 10 SERVINGS

1 recipe Basic Flaky Pie Pastry, Single Crust (page 31) or All-Butter Pie Pastry, Single Crust (page 28), refrigerated

FILLING

4 cups peeled, pitted, and sliced ripe peaches

2 cups ripe fresh sour cherries, stemmed and pitted

2/3 cup granulated sugar

1 tablespoon fresh lemon juice

1/4 cup firmly packed light brown sugar

3 tablespoons cornstarch

Big pinch of ground nutmeg

OATMEAL CRUMB TOPPING

1 cup all-purpose flour

$^1/_2$ cup rolled oats (old-fashioned or quick-cooking)

$^2/_3$ cup firmly packed light brown sugar

$^1/_2$ teaspoon ground cinnamon

$^1/_4$ teaspoon salt

$^1/_2$ cup (1 stick) cold unsalted butter, cut into $^1/_4$-inch pieces

1. If you haven't already, prepare the pastry and refrigerate until firm enough to roll, about 1 hour.

2. On a sheet of lightly floured waxed paper, roll the pastry into a 13-inch circle with a floured rolling pin. Invert the pastry over a $9^1/_2$-inch deep-dish pie pan, center, and peel off the paper. Gently tuck the pastry into the pan, without stretching it, and sculpt the overhang into an upstanding ridge. Place in the freezer for 15 minutes.

3. Combine the peaches, cherries, granulated sugar, and lemon juice in a large bowl. Mix well, then set aside for 10 minutes to juice. Preheat the oven to 400°F.

4. In a small bowl, combine the brown sugar and cornstarch. Stir the mixture into the fruit along with the nutmeg. Turn the filling into the chilled pie shell and smooth the top of the fruit with your hands. Place the pie on the center oven rack and bake for 30 minutes.

5. Meanwhile, make the crumb topping. Put the flour, oats, brown sugar, cinnamon, and salt in a food processor and pulse several times to mix. Scatter the butter over the top and pulse until the mixture resembles fine crumbs. Empty the crumbs into a large bowl and rub them between your fingers until you have large, buttery crumbs. Refrigerate until ready to use.

6. Remove the pie from the oven and reduce the temperature to 375°F. Carefully dump the crumbs in the center of the pie, spreading them over the surface with your hands. Tamp them down lightly. Return the pie to the oven, placing it so that the part that faced the back of the oven now faces forward. Just in case, slide a large aluminum foil–lined baking sheet onto the rack below to catch any spills. Continue to bake until the top is dark golden brown and the juices bubble thickly at the edge, 35 to 40 minutes. If the topping starts to get too dark, loosely cover the pie with tented aluminum foil during the last 15 minutes of baking.

7. Transfer the pie to a wire rack and let cool for at least 2 hours before serving.

Recipe for Success

- If you can't find fresh sour cherries, look for frozen. Drained canned sour cherries also will do in a pinch.

- Either peel the peaches by hand or use the blanching method described on page 88.

- Feel free to substitute another streusel-like topping if you don't have oats or simply prefer something else.

Peach-Blueberry Cobbler Pie

Those of you who own a copy of my previous pie book, *Apple Pie Perfect* (Harvard Common Press, 2002), will remember that the cobbler pie is an invention I credit to my wife, Bev. Long story short: When I was writing my last book, Bev insisted that I include a recipe for an apple cobbler. I reminded her that it was a book of pies and cobblers didn't fit the profile. She told me, in so many words, that if I just put a crust under it, it would still be a pie. So I did, and it was wonderful—wonderful enough to invent this peach and blueberry version. Adding a cobbler topping is not really that much of a stretch. The topping simply replaces the top crust, and if it's a little heavier than pastry, no one seems to mind. Indeed, the biscuit-like topping is right at home on the juicy peaches and blueberries, flavored with lemon and nutmeg. You'll think of this as a new summer classic.

MAKES 8 TO 10 SERVINGS

1 recipe Extra-Flaky Pie Pastry, Single Crust (page 34) or Basic Flaky Pie Pastry, Single Crust (page 31), refrigerated

FILLING

3 1/2 cups peeled, pitted, and thickly sliced ripe peaches

1 1/2 cups fresh blueberries, picked over for stems

1/3 cup plus 2 tablespoons sugar

1 tablespoon fresh lemon juice

2 teaspoons grated lemon zest

1/4 teaspoon ground nutmeg

1 1/2 teaspoons cornstarch

COBBLER TOPPING

1 1/4 cups all-purpose flour

5 tablespoons sugar

1/2 teaspoon baking soda

1/2 teaspoon baking powder

1/4 teaspoon salt

1/4 cup (1/2 stick) cold unsalted butter, cut into 1/4-inch pieces

2/3 cup buttermilk

1 large egg

1/2 teaspoon vanilla extract

GARNISH

Fresh Whipped Cream (page 605)

1. If you haven't already, prepare the pastry and refrigerate until firm enough to roll, about 1 hour.

2. On a sheet of lightly floured waxed paper, roll half the pastry into a 13- to 13 1/2-inch circle with a floured rolling pin. Invert the pastry over a 9 1/2- to 10-inch extra-deep-dish pie pan, center, and peel off the paper. Tuck the pastry into the pan, without stretching it, and sculpt the edge into an upstanding ridge. Place in the freezer for 15 minutes.

3. Combine the peaches, blueberries, 1/3 cup of the sugar, the lemon juice, lemon zest, and nutmeg in a large bowl. Toss to combine, then set aside for 10 minutes. Preheat the oven to 400°F.

4. In a small bowl, combine the remaining 2 tablespoons sugar and the cornstarch, then stir the mixture into the fruit. Turn the filling into the chilled pie shell, smoothing the fruit with your hands. Place on the center oven rack and bake for 30 minutes. Reduce the oven temperature to 375°F and rotate the pie 180 degrees, so that the part that faced the back of the oven now faces forward. Continue to bake for 10 minutes.

5. Meanwhile, make the topping. Sift the flour, 4 tablespoons of the sugar, the baking soda, baking powder, and salt together in a medium-size bowl. Add the butter and rub it into the flour with your fingers or cut it in with a pastry blender until the mixture resembles coarse crumbs. Blend the buttermilk, egg, and vanilla together in a small bowl. Make a well in the dry mixture and add the liquid. Stir the batter until evenly blended.

6. Remove the pie from the oven and spoon the cobbler topping evenly over the fruit. Sprinkle the topping with the remaining 1 tablespoon sugar. Return the pie to the oven, placing it so that the part that faced the back of the oven now faces forward. Just in

case, slide a large aluminum foil–lined baking sheet onto the rack below to catch any spills. Bake until the top is golden brown, 23 to 25 minutes.

7. Transfer the pie to a wire rack and let cool for at least 20 minutes before serving. This is best served within an hour or so (see Recipe for Success). Garnish with a dollop of whipped cream.

Recipe for Success

▶ If you like, substitute nectarines for the peaches.

▶ This is best eaten within about an hour because after that, the porous cobbler topping tends to absorb the juices, almost like a sponge. The pie still tastes great after that happens, but it isn't as juicy.

Fresh Peach and Red Currant Pie

Here's a pie I generally make only once or twice a year, depending on the availability and quality of fresh currants. When I lived in New Hampshire, I had a secret spot where, if I was willing to patiently pick these fragile berries one by one, I could count on finding just enough for a pie or two. These days, when they're available, I buy them at the Whole Foods Market here in Annapolis, Maryland. (Generally speaking, their fragility is a problem for marketers, and thus few retailers carry them.) If you've never had a fresh currant, they're extremely tart, so much so that it's a puckery challenge to eat them right off the bush. That tartness makes them a good addition to this peach pie. Look for both of these fruits in the market at about the same time— July or August, when they're at their best.

MAKES 8 TO 10 SERVINGS

1 recipe Basic Flaky Pie Pastry, Double Crust (page 31) or Tender Cream Cheese Pastry, Double Crust (page 46), refrigerated

FILLING
5 cups peeled, pitted, and sliced ripe peaches

1 cup sugar

2¹/₂ to 3 tablespoons cornstarch

1 tablespoon fresh lemon juice

¹/₄ teaspoon ground cinnamon

2 cups fresh red currants, picked over for stems

GLAZE
Milk or light cream

Sugar

1. If you haven't already, prepare the pastry and refrigerate until firm enough to roll, 1 to 1½ hours.

2. On a sheet of lightly floured waxed paper, roll the larger portion of the pastry into a 13-inch circle with a floured rolling pin. Invert the pastry over a 9½-inch deep-dish pie pan, center, and peel off the paper. Gently tuck the pastry into the pan, without stretching it, and let the overhang drape over the edge. Place in the refrigerator for 15 minutes. Preheat the oven to 400°F.

3. Put the peaches in a large bowl. In a small bowl, mix together the sugar and cornstarch, using the larger amount if the peaches seem very juicy. Add the mixture to the peaches and toss well to mix. Stir in the lemon juice and cinnamon. Add the currants and toss once or twice. Don't overdo it, because they're fragile, and you don't want them to fall apart.

4. On another sheet of lightly floured waxed paper, roll the top pastry into an 11-inch circle. Turn the filling into the chilled pie shell and smooth the top with your fingers. Dampen the edge of the pie shell with a wet fingertip or pastry brush, then invert the top pastry over the filling, center, and peel off the paper. Press the top and bottom pastries together along the dampened edge. Trim the pastry, leaving an even ½-inch overhang all around, then sculpt the overhang into an upstanding ridge. Poke several steam vents in the top with a fork or paring knife. Put a couple of the vents near the edge of the crust so you can check the juices there later. Brush the top with a little milk and sprinkle lightly with sugar.

5. Place the pie on the center oven rack and bake for 30 minutes. Reduce the oven temperature to 375°F and rotate the pie 180 degrees, so that the part that faced the back of the oven now faces forward. Just in case, slide a large aluminum foil–lined baking sheet onto the rack below to catch any spills. Continue to bake until the juices visible at the steam vents bubble thickly, 30 to 35 minutes.

6. Transfer the pie to a wire rack and let cool for at least 1 hour. Serve warm or at room temperature.

Recipe for Success

▶ **If the asking price for 2 cups of currants seems exorbitant, simply buy fewer and add another cup of sliced peaches. Reduce the sugar by about ¼ cup if you do. The pie will still be wonderful.**

Deep-Dish Nectarine Pie
with Almond Crumb Topping

Here's a little tip: all of the stone fruits—peaches, nectarines, apricots, and plums—have an affinity for almonds, a flavor that can be used to your advantage. This juicy, summer-fresh nectarine pie flavored with almond extract and topped with an almond streusel is one of the pies I most look forward to making come midsummer. Choose your nectarines carefully. If they have a green tinge, they will not ripen properly. Like peaches, they should yield to gentle finger pressure but not feel mushy, as they sometimes do, given their habit of overripening quickly. There's no need to peel the skins; they soften up nicely as the pie bakes.

MAKES 8 TO 10 SERVINGS

1 recipe Basic Flaky Pie Pastry, Single Crust (page 31) or Extra-Flaky Pie Pastry, Single Crust (page 34), refrigerated

FILLING

6 cups pitted and sliced ripe nectarines, unpeeled

Scant $1/2$ cup plus 2 tablespoons sugar

$1 1/2$ tablespoons fresh lemon juice

2 teaspoons grated lemon zest

$2 1/2$ tablespoons cornstarch

$1/4$ teaspoon almond extract

ALMOND CRUMB TOPPING

$3/4$ cup whole or slivered almonds

$1/2$ cup sugar

$1/2$ cup all-purpose flour

$1/4$ teaspoon salt

6 tablespoons ($3/4$ stick) cold unsalted butter, cut into $1/4$-inch pieces

1. If you haven't already, prepare the pastry and refrigerate until firm enough to roll, about 1 hour.

2. On a sheet of lightly floured waxed paper, roll half of the pastry into a 13-inch circle with a floured rolling pin. Invert the pastry over a $9 1/2$-inch deep-dish pie pan, center, and peel off the paper. Tuck the pastry into the pan, without stretching it, and sculpt the edge into an upstanding ridge. Place in the freezer for 15 minutes. Preheat the oven to 400°F.

3. In a large bowl, combine the nectarines, $1/2$ cup of the sugar, the lemon juice, and lemon zest. Set aside for 10 minutes to juice. Combine the remaining 2 tablespoons sugar

and the cornstarch in a small bowl, then stir the mixture into the fruit. Stir in the almond extract. Scrape the filling into the chilled pie shell, smoothing the fruit with a spoon. Place the pie on the center oven rack and bake for 30 minutes.

4. Meanwhile, make the topping. Combine the almonds and sugar in a food processor, pulsing in short bursts to chop the almonds well. Add the flour and salt and pulse briefly to mix. Scatter the butter over the dry ingredients and pulse until the mixture looks like fine crumbs. Dump the crumbs into a large bowl and rub between your fingers to make large, buttery crumbs. Refrigerate until ready to use.

5. Remove the pie from the oven and reduce the temperature to 375°F. Carefully dump the crumbs in the center of the pie, spreading them evenly and tamping them lightly with your hands. Return the pie to the oven, placing it so that the part that faced the back of the oven now faces forward. Just in case, slide a large aluminum foil–lined baking sheet onto the rack below to catch any spills. Continue to bake until the juices bubble thickly around the edge, 30 to 40 minutes.

6. Transfer the pie to a wire rack and let cool for at least 2 hours before serving.

Recipe for Success

▶ **The same filling can be used in a double-crust pie or with a different crumb topping.**

▶ **If you'd like to try a nectarine-blueberry combination, reduce the nectarines by 2 cups and add 2 cups ripe fresh blueberries.**

No-Peel Nectarine-Lime Pie

By using a store-bought frozen pie shell and not peeling the nectarines, you can make a fresh summer pie that's as simple as it is delicious and crowd-pleasing. Another timesaving grace: I use a melted-butter streusel, about the easiest sort of topping there is. Lemon is wonderful in just about any fruit pie, but lime—I use both the juice and the zest here—has a little more pizzazz, and I like the sassy accent it gives to the nectarines.

MAKES 8 SERVINGS

1 store-bought frozen 9-inch deep-dish pie shell

FILLING

4 cups pitted and sliced ripe nectarines, unpeeled

1/3 cup plus 2 tablespoons sugar

1 tablespoon fresh lime juice

1/2 teaspoon grated lime zest

1 1/2 to 2 tablespoons cornstarch

Pinch of ground nutmeg

STREUSEL TOPPING

1 cup all-purpose flour

1/2 cup sugar

1/4 teaspoon salt

Pinch of ground cinnamon

1/2 teaspoon grated lemon zest (optional)

5 tablespoons unsalted butter, melted

1. Remove the pie shell from its package but leave it in the freezer until you're ready to fill it.

2. Combine the nectarines, 1/3 cup of the sugar, the lime juice, and lime zest in a large bowl and mix well. Set aside for 15 minutes to juice. Preheat the oven to 400°F.

3. After 15 minutes, check the accumulated juice. If the nectarines are pretty much covered with juice, use 2 tablespoons of the cornstarch. If not, use 1 1/2 tablespoons. In a small bowl, mix the cornstarch with the remaining 2 tablespoons sugar. Stir the mixture into the fruit along with the nutmeg. Turn the filling into the frozen pie shell, smoothing the top with a spoon. Place the pie on the center oven rack and bake for 30 minutes.

4. Meanwhile, make the topping. Combine the flour, sugar, salt, cinnamon, and lemon zest (if using) in a medium-size bowl. Pour the butter over them. Mix first with a fork to blend, then switch to your hands and rub gently until the mixture has the texture of gravelly crumbs. Refrigerate until ready to use.

5. Remove the pie from the oven and reduce the temperature to 375°F. Carefully dump the topping in the center of the pie and spread evenly over the surface with your hands. Tamp the crumbs down lightly. Return the pie to the oven, placing it so that the part that faced the back of the oven now faces forward. To catch any spills, slide a large aluminum foil–lined baking sheet onto the rack below. Bake until you see the juices bubbling thickly at the edge, 25 to 35 minutes. If the top starts to get too brown, cover loosely with aluminum foil for the last 10 minutes.

6. Transfer the pie to a wire rack and let cool for at least 1 hour before serving.

Recipe for Success

▶ Use only ripe fresh nectarines, and be selective about the ones you choose. Like peaches, they should yield to gentle finger pressure. Each nectarine should have a light but distinct fruity fragrance and feel weighty—which is to say juicy—in proportion to its size.

Easy Apricot Pie with Simple Press-In Pastry

Come summer, sometimes it's just less trouble to forget about a rolled pastry and opt for the press-in kind. That's what I do here, filling the shell with ripe fresh apricots. This shell is not prebaked—just refrigerated, to help firm it up before the fruit goes in. As for the filling, I keep that simple, too: apricots, sugar, lemon juice, and cornstarch. I add an oatmeal crumb topping during the last part of the baking, then brown it lightly. Feel free to use peaches in place of some of the apricots.

MAKES 8 TO 10 SERVINGS

1 recipe Simple Press-In Pie Pastry (page 49), refrigerated

FILLING

5 cups pitted and sliced fresh apricots (see Recipe for Success), unpeeled

1/2 cup plus 2 tablespoons sugar

1 tablespoon fresh lemon juice

2 tablespoons cornstarch

OATMEAL CRUMB TOPPING

2/3 cup all-purpose flour

1/2 cup rolled oats (old-fashioned or quick-cooking)

1/2 cup sugar

1/4 teaspoon salt

5 tablespoons cold unsalted butter, cut into 1/4-inch pieces

1.   Prepare the pastry and press it into the bottom and most of the way up the side of a 9 1/2-inch deep-dish pie pan. Place in the freezer for 15 minutes.

2.   Combine the apricots, 1/2 cup of the sugar, and the lemon juice in a large bowl. Set aside for 10 minutes to juice. Preheat the oven to 375°F.

3.   In a small bowl, combine the remaining 2 tablespoons sugar and the cornstarch, then stir the mixture into the fruit. Scrape the filling into the chilled pie shell, smoothing the top with a spoon. Place the pie on the center oven rack and bake for 30 minutes.

4.   Meanwhile, make the topping. Combine the flour, oats, sugar, and salt in a food processor and pulse to chop the oats well. Scatter the butter over the top and pulse until

the mixture resembles fine crumbs. Transfer the mixture to a medium-size bowl and rub between your fingers to make large, buttery crumbs. Refrigerate until ready to use.

5. Remove the pie from the oven and carefully dump the crumbs in the center of the pie, spreading them evenly over the surface with your hands. Tamp them down lightly. Return the pie to the oven, placing it so that the part that faced the back of the oven now faces forward. Just in case, slide a large aluminum foil–lined baking sheet onto the rack below to catch any drips. Continue to bake until the top is golden brown and any juices visible near the edge bubble thickly, 20 to 25 minutes.

6. Transfer the pie to a wire rack and let cool for at least 2 hours before serving.

Recipe for Success

▶ Fresh apricots can sometimes be a little dry. If you find that even after 20 minutes, your apricots aren't all that juicy, add a tablespoon or so of orange juice or lemonade.

▶ Some people find the flavor of an all-apricot pie a little too forward. You can soften the flavor with peaches, sliced apples, or even raspberries or blueberries, for a mixed-fruit pie.

Apricot-Strawberry Pie

This may seem like an unlikely combination for a fruit pie, but it actually works quite nicely, with the soft and sweet strawberry flavor gently subduing the more pronounced taste of the apricots. I like to serve this with vanilla or a fruit-flavored ice cream.

MAKES 8 TO 10 SERVINGS

1 recipe Extra-Flaky Pie Pastry, Double Crust (page 34) or Tender Cream Cheese Pastry, Double Crust (page 46), refrigerated

FILLING

3 cups pitted and sliced fresh apricots, unpeeled

1/3 cup plus 3 tablespoons sugar

1 tablespoon fresh lemon juice

2 tablespoons cornstarch

1 1/2 cups hulled and sliced fresh strawberries

GLAZE

Milk or light cream

Sugar

GARNISH

Vanilla, peach, or strawberry ice cream

1. If you haven't already, prepare the pastry and refrigerate until firm enough to roll, about 1 hour.

2. On a sheet of lightly floured waxed paper, roll the larger portion of the pastry into a 12-inch circle with a floured rolling pin. Invert the pastry over a 9-inch standard pie pan, center, and peel off the paper. Gently tuck the pastry into the pan, without stretching it, and let the overhang drape over the edge. Place in the refrigerator for 15 minutes.

3. Combine the apricots, ⅓ cup of the sugar, and the lemon juice in a large bowl. Mix well and set aside to juice for 30 minutes. In a small bowl, combine the remaining 3 tablespoons sugar and the cornstarch, then stir the mixture into the apricots. Add the strawberries and mix gently. Preheat the oven to 400°F.

4. Roll the other half of the pastry into a 10-inch circle on a sheet of lightly floured waxed paper. Turn the filling into the chilled pie shell, smoothing the top with your hands or a spoon. Lightly moisten the rim of the pie shell. Invert the top pastry over the filling, center, and peel off the paper. Press the top and bottom pastries together along the dampened edge. Using the back of a butter knife or pastry knife, trim the pastry flush with the edge of the pan and crimp the edge with a fork. Poke several steam vents in the top of the pie with a fork or paring knife. Put a couple of the vents near the edge of the crust so you can check the juices there later. To glaze the pie, lightly brush the pastry with milk and sprinkle with sugar.

5. Place the pie on the center oven rack and bake for 30 minutes. Reduce the oven temperature to 375°F and rotate the pie 180 degrees, so that the part that faced the back of the oven now faces forward. Just in case, slide a large aluminum foil–lined baking sheet onto the rack below to catch any spills. Continue to bake until the top is golden brown and any visible juices bubble thickly through the steam vents, about 30 minutes.

6. Transfer the pie to a wire rack and let cool for at least 2 hours. Serve with ice cream.

Recipe for Success

▶ **If you're fonder of strawberries than you are of apricots, adjust the balance of fruit accordingly, up to equal portions of both.**

▶ **This is more of a spring than a summer combination, but you could reduce the amount of apricots and include a thinly sliced stalk of rhubarb in their place.**

▶ **The reason for the longer than usual juicing of the fruit here has to do with the typical dryness of apricots. Thirty minutes allows more time for the sugar to draw out a good amount of juice from the apricots and thus yield a juicy pie.**

Catoctin Mountain Apricot-Blueberry Pie

When you think of Maryland, you probably think of blue crab, which is, of course, our more or less official state comestible. But out in the western part of the state, and a distance from the Chesapeake Bay, Maryland has some great farm country and orchards, where the determined traveler and pie maker can find excellent fruit for pies. My wife, Bev, and I stumbled upon several of these farm stands and orchards on a trip to an area known as Catoctin Mountain Park, where we hiked and swam in a lovely mountain lake. At a tidy operation called Catoctin Mountain Orchard, run by the Black family, we found excellent fresh apricots, blueberries, plums, and sour cherries—alongside the family's own orchard-baked pies. One pie that caught our eye was the apricot-blueberry, which was the inspiration for this pie. We made it with the orchard's fruit, and it was one of the best pies of the summer.

MAKES 8 TO 10 SERVINGS

1 recipe Basic Shortening Pie Pastry, Single Crust (page 30) or Basic Flaky Pie Pastry, Single Crust (page 31), refrigerated

FILLING

3 cups pitted and sliced fresh apricots, unpeeled

2 cups fresh blueberries, picked over for stems

^{2}/$_3$ cup plus 2 tablespoons granulated sugar

1 tablespoon fresh lemon juice

3 tablespoons cornstarch

^{1}/$_4$ teaspoon ground nutmeg

BROWN SUGAR TOPPING

^{1}/$_2$ cup firmly packed light brown sugar

^{1}/$_2$ cup all-purpose flour

^{1}/$_4$ teaspoon ground cinnamon

Big pinch of salt

^{1}/$_4$ cup (^{1}/$_2$ stick) cold unsalted butter, cut into ^{1}/$_4$-inch pieces

1.   If you haven't already, prepare the pastry and refrigerate until firm enough to roll, about 1 hour.

2.   On a sheet of lightly floured waxed paper, roll the pastry into a 13-inch circle with a floured rolling pin. Invert the pastry over a 9^1/$_2$-inch deep-dish pie pan, center, and peel off the paper. Gently tuck the pastry into the pan, without stretching it, and sculpt the overhang into an upstanding ridge. Place in the freezer for 15 minutes.

3.   In a large bowl, combine the apricots, blueberries, ^{2}/$_3$ cup of the granulated sugar, and the lemon juice. Mix well and set aside for 30 minutes to juice. Near the end of the 30 minutes, preheat the oven to 400°F.

4. In a small bowl, combine the cornstarch and remaining 2 tablespoons granulated sugar. Stir the mixture into the fruit along with the nutmeg. Turn the filling into the chilled pie shell, leveling the top of the fruit with a spoon. Place the pie on the center oven rack and bake for 30 minutes.

5. Meanwhile, make the topping. Combine the brown sugar, flour, cinnamon, and salt in a food processor and pulse several times to mix. Scatter the butter over the dry ingredients and pulse until the mixture resembles fine crumbs. Empty the crumbs into a large bowl and rub them between your fingers to make large, buttery crumbs. Refrigerate until ready to use.

6. Remove the pie from the oven and reduce the temperature to 375°F. Carefully dump the crumbs in the center of the pie, spreading them over the surface with your hands. Tamp them down lightly. Return the pie to the oven, placing it so that the part that faced the back of the oven now faces forward. Just in case, slide a large aluminum foil–lined baking sheet onto the rack below to catch any spills. Bake until the top is dark golden brown and the juices bubble thickly at the edge, 35 to 40 minutes. If the topping starts to get too dark, cover the pie with loosely tented aluminum foil during the last 15 minutes of baking.

7. Transfer the pie to a wire rack and let cool for at least 2 hours before serving.

Recipe for Success

▸ **This makes a gorgeous double-crust pie. Indeed, the one we saw at the orchard had a top crust. I've also made it with a lattice crust, which is perhaps the best-looking option of all.**

▸ **The reason for the longer than usual juicing of the fruit here has to do with the typical dryness of apricots. Thirty minutes allows more time for the sugar to draw out a good amount of juice from the apricots and thus yield a juicy pie.**

Apricot-Mango Pie with Coconut Crumb Topping

If you're looking for a pie with distinctly tropical overtones, this is it. Given the unreliability of out-of-season fresh apricots, I consider this a summer pie—although I have had pretty good results with drained canned apricots. For the mango, you can use fresh fruit, of course (see Recipe for Success), but for convenience you can't beat those jars of long mango slices found in the produce section of the grocery store. Just drain and cut into chunks.

MAKES 8 TO 10 SERVINGS

1 recipe Basic Flaky Pie Pastry, Single Crust (page 31), refrigerated

FILLING

4 cups pitted and sliced fresh apricots, unpeeled

2 cups peeled mango chunks

1/3 cup plus 1 tablespoon sugar

1 tablespoon fresh lemon juice

1 teaspoon grated lemon zest

1 tablespoon cornstarch

COCONUT CRUMB TOPPING

2/3 cup all-purpose flour

1/2 cup sugar

1/2 cup sweetened flaked coconut

1/4 teaspoon salt

5 tablespoons cold unsalted butter, cut into 1/4-inch pieces

1. If you haven't already, prepare the pastry and refrigerate until firm enough to roll, about 1 hour.

2. On a sheet of lightly floured waxed paper, roll the pastry into a 12-inch circle with a floured rolling pin. Invert the pastry over a 9-inch standard pie pan, center, and peel off the paper. Tuck the pastry into the pan, without stretching it, and sculpt the edge into an upstanding ridge. Place in the freezer for 15 minutes.

3. Combine the apricots, mango, 1/3 cup of the sugar, the lemon juice, and lemon zest in a large bowl. Toss well, then set aside for 15 minutes. Preheat the oven to 400°F.

4. Combine the remaining 1 tablespoon sugar and the cornstarch in a small bowl, then stir the mixture into the fruit. Turn the filling into the chilled pie shell and smooth the top with your hands. Place the pie on the center oven rack and bake for 30 minutes.

5. Meanwhile, make the topping. Combine the flour, sugar, coconut, and salt in a food processor, pulsing to mix. Scatter the butter over the top and pulse until the mixture resembles fine crumbs. Empty the crumbs into a large bowl and rub gently between your fingers to make buttery, gravelly crumbs. Refrigerate until ready to use.

6. Remove the pie from the oven and reduce the temperature to 375°F. Carefully dump the crumbs in the center of the pie and spread them evenly over the surface with your hands. Press down gently to compact them. Return the pie to the oven, placing it so that the part that faced the back of the oven now faces forward. Just in case, slide a large aluminum foil–lined baking sheet onto the rack below to catch any spills. Continue to bake until the top is golden brown and the juices bubble thickly at the edge, about 30 minutes. If necessary, cover with loosely tented aluminum foil during the last 15 minutes to prevent the pie from browning too much.

7. Transfer the pie to a wire rack and let cool for at least 2 hours before serving.

Recipe for Success

▶ To peel a fresh mango, slice the skin lengthwise and remove the peel. Cutting lengthwise and avoiding the large pit in the center, cut off a large slab of flesh on either side. Cut the remaining flesh off the pit in chunks.

Fresh Plum and Port Pie

Juicy, ripe plums are one of the best summer fruits to eat out of hand: the flavor is sweet-tart, refreshing, and wonderfully subtle. But a lot of people don't realize that in addition to being a fine uncooked fruit, plums make a swell pie. Indeed, the French adore their fresh plum tarts. Here's a plum pie made with reduced port, which adds a fruity accent to the sweet fruit and provides an ample amount of juice for the plums to cook in and become melt-in-your-mouth soft. To finish things off, the crumb topping gives the pie an irresistible flavor and crunch.

MAKES 8 TO 10 SERVINGS

1 recipe Basic Flaky Pie Pastry, Single Crust (page 31) or All-Butter Pie Pastry, Single Crust (page 28), refrigerated

FILLING

1/2 cup ruby port

7 cups pitted and sliced plums, unpeeled

1/2 cup sugar

1/4 cup quick-cooking tapioca

2 tablespoons raspberry preserves (optional)

1 tablespoon fresh lemon juice

1/2 teaspoon grated lemon zest

COCONUT-ALMOND CRUMB TOPPING

3/4 cup all-purpose flour

1/2 cup sugar

1/4 teaspoon salt

1/3 cup sliced almonds

1/3 cup sweetened flaked coconut

6 tablespoons (3/4 stick) cold unsalted butter, cut into 1/4-inch pieces

1 tablespoon milk

1. If you haven't already, prepare the pastry and refrigerate until firm enough to roll, about 1 hour.

2. On a sheet of lightly floured waxed paper, roll the pastry into a 13-inch circle with a floured rolling pin. Invert the pastry over a 9½-inch deep-dish pie pan, center, and peel off the paper. Gently tuck the pastry into the pan, without stretching it, and sculpt the overhang into an upstanding ridge. Place in the freezer for 15 minutes.

3. Bring the port to a boil in a medium-size nonreactive saucepan. Continue to boil until reduced by roughly one-half; check by pouring it into a heatproof measuring cup. Combine the plums, sugar, and reduced port in a large bowl. Set aside for 10 minutes. Preheat the oven to 400°F.

4. Stir the tapioca, raspberry preserves (if using), lemon juice, and lemon zest into the fruit. Turn the filling into the chilled pie shell and smooth the top with your hands. Place the pie on the center oven rack and bake for 30 minutes.

5. Meanwhile, make the topping. Put the flour, sugar, salt, almonds, and coconut in a food processor and pulse several times to mix. Scatter the butter over the top and pulse until the mixture resembles fine crumbs. Add the milk and process again until the crumbs are gravelly. Transfer the crumbs to a medium-size bowl and rub gently between your fingers to make them uniform in texture. Refrigerate until ready to use.

6. Remove the pie from the oven and reduce the temperature to 375°F. Carefully dump the crumbs in the center of the pie, spreading them over the surface with your hands. Tamp down gently to compact them. Return the pie to the oven, placing it so that the part that faced the back of the oven now faces forward. Just in case, slide a large alu-

minum foil–lined baking sheet onto the rack below to catch any drips. Continue to bake until the juices bubble thickly at the edge, 30 to 35 minutes. If necessary, cover with loosely tented aluminum foil during the last 20 minutes to prevent the pie from browning too much.

7. Transfer the pie to a wire rack and let cool for at least 1 hour before serving.

Recipe for Success

❱ The best advice I can give you for making plum pie is pretty straightforward: wait for the best-of-summer plums. I know I've said that about other fruit, but it bears repeating here. Plums are perhaps the trickiest of fruits to buy because even though the skins may look dark, ripe, and inviting, the flesh may be disappointing. Even the finger pressure test will often fail, because yielding flesh is not necessarily an indicator of peak ripeness. Instead, the plum might just be old and mushy.

Italian Prune Plum Pie

Little Italian prune plums aren't only good for turning into prunes. They're good fresh—compact, tasty, easy to handle—and even better baked in a pie. With a couple of pounds of plums and some refrigerated pie pastry, you can have this pie in the oven in minutes. If you need a pie on the fly for a pool party or an early fall tailgate party, this is a great choice.

MAKES 8 SERVINGS

2 store-bought refrigerated pie pastries

FILLING

4 cups halved (lengthwise) and pitted prune plums

$^{1}/_{3}$ cup plus 2 tablespoons sugar

1 tablespoon fresh lemon juice

$1^{1}/_{2}$ tablespoons cornstarch

1. Line a 9-inch standard pie pan with 1 round of the pastry. Tuck the pastry into the pan, without stretching it, and let the overhang drape over the edge. Place in the refrigerator for 15 minutes. Preheat the oven to 400°F.

2. Combine the plums, $^{1}/_{3}$ cup of the sugar, and the lemon juice in a large bowl. Set aside for 5 minutes to juice. Combine the remaining 2 tablespoons sugar and the corn-

starch in a small bowl, then stir the mixture into the fruit. Turn the filling into the chilled pie shell, smoothing the top of the fruit with a spoon. Moisten the edge of the pie shell with a pastry brush. Place the other round of pastry over the filling, pressing along the edge to seal. Trim the pastry with scissors, leaving an even ½-inch overhang. Sculpt the pastry into an upstanding ridge. Using a fork or paring knife, poke several steam vents in the top pastry. Put a few of the vents near the edge so you can check the juices there later.

3.   Place the pie on the center oven rack and bake for 30 minutes. Reduce the oven temperature to 375°F and rotate the pie 180 degrees, so that the part that faced the back of the oven now faces forward. Just in case, slide a large aluminum foil–lined baking sheet onto the rack below to catch any spills. Continue to bake until the juices bubble thickly at the edge and the top is golden brown, about 25 minutes.

4.   Transfer the pie to a wire rack and let cool. Serve just barely warm or at room temperature.

Recipe for Success

▶   Choose prune plums that are uniformly dark and yielding without being overly so. Avoid fruit with soft, mushy spots. Incidentally, if you have young children, buy extra plums for eating out of hand. Children really like the kid-friendly size.

▶   If you're looking for a fast way to turn this into a crumb pie, use a store-bought frozen 9-inch deep-dish pie shell. Bake for 30 minutes with the fruit, then reduce the oven temperature to 375°F and bake with any of the crumb toppings in this book. One that works particularly well is the topping for The Easiest Apple Pie on page 197.

Deep-Dish Pluot Pie with Oatmeal-Walnut Crumb Topping

I was shopping at my local Whole Foods Market one early-summer day and happened upon a display of Pluots, also sold as plumcots, which, though I had never tasted one, I knew to be a cross between a plum and an apricot. The produce manager was kind enough to offer me a taste, and I was immediately smitten. It was sweeter than any plum I'd ever had and juicier than an apricot, but with the delicate flavor of both. Back home, I called Leith Zaiger, whose family owns the trademarked name of Pluot. They've developed about 30 commercially viable varieties, with many more still under development. Leith told me that Pluots are quickly catching up with plums in terms of sales. Consumers like the same things about Pluots that I did when I first tasted them: sweet flavor, nice texture. After our discussion and a little lesson on using Pluots in pies, I took to the kitchen and baked this pie. Leith's mother, Betty, the resident pie maker in the Zaiger family, also gave me her favorite Pluot pie recipe (see page 122). Do try it, too.

MAKES 8 TO 10 SERVINGS

1 recipe Basic Flaky Pie Pastry, Single Crust (page 31) or Basic Shortening Pie Pastry, Single Crust (page 30), refrigerated

FILLING

5 1/2 to 6 cups pitted and sliced Pluots (see Recipe for Success)

1/2 cup plus 2 tablespoons sugar

1 tablespoon fresh lemon juice

1 teaspoon grated lemon zest

Big pinch of ground nutmeg

3 tablespoons cornstarch

OATMEAL-WALNUT CRUMB TOPPING

3/4 cup all-purpose flour

3/4 cup finely chopped walnuts

1/3 cup rolled oats (old-fashioned or quick-cooking)

1/2 teaspoon ground cinnamon

1/4 teaspoon salt

6 tablespoons (3/4 stick) unsalted butter, melted

1. If you haven't already, prepare the pastry and refrigerate until firm enough to roll, about 1 hour.

2. On a sheet of lightly floured waxed paper, roll the larger portion of the pastry into a 13 1/2-inch circle with a floured rolling pin. Invert the pastry over a 9 1/2- to 10-inch extra-deep-dish pie pan, center, and peel off the paper. Gently tuck the pastry into the pan, without stretching it, and sculpt the overhang into an upstanding ridge. Place in the freezer for 15 minutes.

3. Combine the Pluots, 1/2 cup of the sugar, lemon juice, lemon zest, and nutmeg in a large bowl. Mix well, then set aside for 15 minutes to juice. Preheat the oven to 400°F.

4. Combine the remaining 2 tablespoons sugar and the cornstarch in a small bowl, then stir the mixture into the fruit. Turn the filling into the chilled pie shell and smooth the top with a spoon. Place the pie on the center oven rack and bake for 30 minutes.

5. Meanwhile, make the topping. Combine the flour, walnuts, oats, cinnamon, and salt in a large bowl. Toss with your hands to mix. Pour the butter over the top and stir with

a fork to combine. Then switch to your hands and rub the mixture gently to make uniform gravelly crumbs. Refrigerate until ready to use.

6. Remove the pie from the oven and reduce the temperature to 375°F. Carefully dump the crumb topping in the center of the pie and spread evenly over the surface with your hands. Tamp the crumbs down lightly. Return the pie to the oven, placing it so that the part that faced the back of the oven now faces forward. To catch any spills, slide a large aluminum foil–lined baking sheet onto the rack below. Bake until you see the juices bubbling thickly at the edge, 25 to 35 minutes. If the top starts to get too brown, cover loosely with aluminum foil for the last 10 minutes.

7. Transfer the pie to a wire rack and let cool for at least 2 hours before serving.

Recipe for Success

▶ Pluots tend to be very juicy, which is why I recommend the extra-deep-dish pan. If you only have a standard deep-dish pan, you may want to limit the fruit to 5 to 5 1/2 cups.

▶ You can blanch Pluots, like peaches (see page 88), to remove the skins, but they tend to bake up fairly soft, and I don't think it's necessary. Also, a lot of the deep burgundy color is in the skin, so you will lose some of that color if you peel them. Still, if you'd rather, blanch them for about 15 seconds, and the skins will slide right off.

Betty Zaiger's Pluot Pie

Betty Zaiger is the matriarch of the family that has bred more than 30 commercial varieties of the Pluot, a cross between a plum and an apricot. (Read more about Pluots, pages 120–121.) Betty's pie is a little different from my own crumb-topped Pluot pie (see page 120). For one, she uses no top crust or crumb crust. Rather, she cooks the filling on top of the stove, thickens it with cornstarch, and pours it directly into a fully prebaked crust. To boost the flavor of the fruit, she swears by peach schnapps, so a healthy dose is added along with the cornstarch. Betty says she often serves this pie at her family's Wednesday meeting with fruit growers, and she says it creates quite a stir when word gets out that her Pluot pie is on the menu. For a simple garnish, do what Betty does: serve it with a dollop of whipped cream.

MAKES 8 TO 10 SERVINGS

1 recipe Basic Flaky Pie Pastry, Single Crust (page 31) or Basic Shortening Pie Pastry, Single Crust (page 30), refrigerated

FILLING

4 cups pitted and sliced Pluots

2/3 cup water

1/2 to 3/4 cup sugar, to your taste

1/3 to 1/2 cup peach schnapps, to your taste

2 tablespoons cornstarch

Big pinch of ground nutmeg

1. If you haven't already, prepare the pastry and refrigerate until firm enough to roll, about 1 hour.

2. On a sheet of lightly floured waxed paper, roll the pastry into a 13-inch circle with a floured rolling pin. Invert the pastry over a 9½-inch deep-dish pie pan, center, and peel off the paper. Tuck the pastry into the pan, without stretching it, and sculpt the edge into an upstanding ridge. Place in the freezer for 15 minutes, then fully prebake and let cool according to the instructions on page 16.

3. Combine the Pluots, water, and sugar in a medium-size nonreactive saucepan. Bring to a boil, then cook at a low boil until the fruit is soft, about 10 minutes. Meanwhile, combine the peach schnapps and cornstarch in a small bowl, blending well. When the fruit is soft, stir in the cornstarch mixture. Continue to cook at a low boil for 1 minute, then remove from the heat and stir in the nutmeg. Let the filling cool for several minutes, then turn it into the cooled pie shell, smoothing the top with a spoon.

4. Transfer the pie to a wire rack and let cool thoroughly. Cover with loosely tented aluminum foil and refrigerate until quite firm, at least 2 hours. Serve chilled.

Recipe for Success

▸ Review the tips for fully prebaking a pie shell on page 16. One pointer that bears repeating is the importance of baking the crust until it is golden brown on the bottom. If you don't, the pastry may taste a little raw.

▸ In my Pluot pie recipe (see page 120), I speak briefly about peeling the Pluots. Betty says she never bothers, because once the fruit is simmered for 10 minutes, the skins are very soft and unobtrusive.

Champagne Grape Pie

Those pearl-size champagne grapes that you see in the produce department are actually a variety known as Black Corinth. Dried, they're called currants, and you've probably used them to bake into muffins, buns, or scones. They've become quite popular in recent years, in part because of their petite size and sweet flavor and in part because those of us who entertain think they look so attractive on a cheese and fruit platter. Not surprisingly, they make a very good fresh pie, and—sweet as they are—they require little added sugar. A bit of lemon juice and a delicate pastry, and you have a delicious, pure-grape pie you'd be proud to serve your family or guests. Look for champagne grapes starting in late July or early August.

MAKES 8 TO 10 SERVINGS

1 recipe Extra-Flaky Pie Pastry, Double Crust (page 34), refrigerated

FILLING

4 cups champagne grapes, stemmed (see Recipe for Success)

1/4 cup plus 1 1/2 tablespoons sugar

1 tablespoon fresh lemon juice

2 1/2 tablespoons cornstarch

GLAZE

Milk or light cream

Sugar

1.   If you haven't already, prepare the pastry and refrigerate until firm enough to roll, about 1 hour.

2.   On a sheet of lightly floured waxed paper, roll the larger portion of the pastry into a 12-inch circle with a floured rolling pin. Invert the pastry over a 9-inch standard pie pan, center, and peel off the paper. Gently tuck the pastry into the pan, without stretching it, and let the overhang drape over the edge. Place in the refrigerator for 15 minutes.

3.   In a medium-size bowl, combine the grapes, 1/4 cup of the sugar, and the lemon juice. Mix well and set aside to juice for 10 minutes. Preheat the oven to 400°F.

4.   On another sheet of floured waxed paper, roll the other half of the pastry into a 10-inch circle. Combine the remaining 1 1/2 tablespoons sugar and the cornstarch in small bowl, then stir the mixture into the fruit. Turn the filling into the chilled pie shell, smoothing the top with a spoon. Lightly moisten the rim of the pie shell. Invert the top pastry over the filling, center, and peel off the paper. Press the top and bottom pastries together along the dampened edge. Using the back of a butter knife or pastry knife, trim the pastry flush with the edge of the pan, then pinch the edges together to seal. Poke several steam vents

in the top of the pie with a fork or paring knife. Put a couple of the vents near the edge of the crust so you can check the juices there later. To glaze the pie, lightly brush the pastry with milk and sprinkle with sugar.

5.   Place the pie on the center oven rack and bake for 30 minutes. Reduce the oven temperature to 375°F and rotate the pie 180 degrees, so that the part that faced the back of the oven now faces forward. Just in case, slide a large aluminum foil–lined baking sheet onto the rack below to catch any spills. Continue to bake until the top is golden brown and any visible juices bubble thickly through the steam vents, 25 to 30 minutes.

6.   Transfer the pie to a wire rack and let cool for at least 2 hours before serving.

Recipe for Success

▶   Champagne grapes sometimes have a white "bloom" on them, which could be mistaken for mold. The bloom, however, is an indication of ripeness and need not be avoided.

▶   The easiest way to remove the grapes from the stems is to "rake" them off with a wide-set fork or, lacking one of those, your hands.

▶   Although you set the fruit aside to juice, you may not actually get all that much juice until the pie is baked.

Seedless Black Grape Pie

It's not easy in most parts of the country to find the sort of grapes needed to make a flavorful pie. Most are firm and less than ripe. If you keep your eyes open, however, you will occasionally find some that are softer, sweeter, and juicer than usual. When you do, consider turning them into a pie. I've added a few tablespoons of reduced red wine to the filling to provide some of that winy flavor your taste buds might expect to find in a pie such as this.

MAKES 8 TO 10 SERVINGS

1 recipe Basic Flaky Pie Pastry, Double Crust (page 31), refrigerated

FILLING

1/2 cup Merlot, Cabernet Sauvignon, or other dry red wine

51/2 cups halved seedless black grapes

1/3 cup plus 2 tablespoons sugar

2 teaspoons fresh lemon juice

21/2 tablespoons cornstarch

2 tablespoons cold unsalted butter, cut into small pieces

1. If you haven't already, prepare the pastry and refrigerate until firm enough to roll, about 1 hour.

2. On a sheet of lightly floured waxed paper, roll the larger portion of the pastry into a 12-inch circle with a floured rolling pin. Invert the pastry over a 9-inch standard pie pan, center, and peel off the paper. Gently tuck the pastry into the pan, without stretching it, and let the overhang drape over the edge. Place in the refrigerator for 15 minutes.

3. Bring the wine to a boil in a medium-size nonreactive saucepan. Boil rapidly for several minutes, until reduced to 2 to 3 tablespoons. Keep a heatproof measuring cup nearby to check. Combine the grapes, reduced wine, 1/3 cup of the sugar, and the lemon juice in a medium-size bowl. Mix well, then set aside for 10 minutes to juice. Preheat the oven to 400°F.

4. Combine the cornstarch and remaining 2 tablespoons sugar in a small bowl. Stir the mixture into the fruit. Turn the filling into the chilled pie shell and smooth the top with a spoon. Dot the filling with the butter.

5. Roll the other half of the pastry into a 10-inch circle on a sheet of lightly floured waxed paper. Moisten the outer edge of the pie shell with a pastry brush. Invert the top pastry over the filling, center, and peel off the paper. Press the top and bottom pastries together along the dampened edge. Using the back of a butter knife, trim the pastry flush with the edge of the pan. With the back of a fork, press the tines all along the edge to seal. Using the fork, poke several steam vents in the top of the pie, including a couple along the edge so you can check the juices there later.

6. Place the pie on the center oven rack and bake for 30 minutes. Reduce the oven temperature to 375°F and rotate the pie 180 degrees, so that the part of the pie that faced the back of the oven now faces forward. Just in case, slide a large aluminum foil–lined baking sheet onto the rack below to catch any spills. Continue to bake until golden brown, about 25 minutes. When done, you may notice thick juices bubbling out of the steam vents along the edge.

7. Transfer the pie to a wire rack and let cool for at least 2 hours before serving.

Recipe for Success

▶ **Grapes can be deceiving when it comes to juiciness. They might not look all that juicy even after they've been sugared and set aside for 10 minutes. But don't let that fool you into using less cornstarch. My experience is that grape pies are very juicy—remember, most grapes are grown for their juice—and you'll need every bit of the cornstarch recommended here to achieve the proper texture.**

Grape and Fig Pie

I think the best fruit to mix with fresh black grapes is dried figs. You end up with a gorgeous deep purple filling and juice, aromatically suggestive of the Mediterranean. Instead of poaching the figs, as I sometimes do when I'm using them in pies, I simply steam them for a few minutes. That softens them but leaves them sufficiently absorbent to soak up the copious juice that bakes out of the grapes. Garnished with sweetened mascarpone, this is a wonderful pie to follow a light Mediterranean meal.

MAKES 8 TO 10 SERVINGS

1 recipe Basic Flaky Pie Pastry, Double Crust (page 31), refrigerated

FILLING

1 1/2 cups stemmed and diced dried Black Mission figs (see Recipe for Success)

4 cups halved seedless black grapes

1/2 cup sugar

2 teaspoons fresh lemon juice

1 teaspoon grated lemon zest

1 1/2 tablespoons Frangelico or 1/2 teaspoon vanilla extract (optional)

1 1/2 tablespoons cornstarch

1 tablespoon cold unsalted butter, cut into small pieces

GARNISH

Sweetened Mascarpone Cheese (page 606)

1. If you haven't already, prepare the pastry and refrigerate until firm enough to roll, about 1 hour.

2. On a sheet of lightly floured waxed paper, roll the larger portion of the pastry into a 12-inch circle with a floured rolling pin. Invert the pastry over a 9-inch standard pie pan, center, and peel off the paper. Gently tuck the pastry into the pan, without stretching it, and let the overhang drape over the edge. Place in the refrigerator for 15 minutes.

3. Place the figs in a steamer basket set in a saucepan (or directly in the saucepan) and add about 1/2 inch of water to the pan. Cover tightly and bring the water to a boil. Reduce the heat slightly and simmer-steam the figs for 5 minutes. Drain in a colander or sieve.

4. In a large bowl, combine the grapes, figs, all but about 2 tablespoons of the sugar, the lemon juice, lemon zest, and Frangelico (if using). Mix well, then set aside for 15 minutes. Preheat the oven to 400°F.

5. Mix the cornstarch and remaining 2 tablespoons sugar together in a small bowl. Sprinkle the mixture over the fruit and stir to combine. Turn the filling into the chilled pie shell and smooth the top. Dot the filling with the butter.

6. Roll the other half of the pastry into a 10-inch circle on a sheet of lightly floured waxed paper. Moisten the outer edge of the pie shell with a pastry brush. Invert the top pastry over the filling, center, and peel off the paper. Press the top and bottom pastries together along the dampened edge. Using the back of a butter knife, trim the pastry flush with the edge of the pan. With the back of a fork, press the tines all along the edge to seal. Using the fork, poke several steam vents in the top of the pie, including a couple along the edge so you can check the juices there later.

7. Place the pie on the center oven rack and bake for 30 minutes. Reduce the oven temperature to 375°F and rotate the pie 180 degrees, so that the part of the pie that faced the back of the oven now faces forward. Just in case, slide a large aluminum foil–lined baking sheet onto the rack below to catch any spills. Continue to bake until the pie is golden brown, about 25 minutes. When done, you may notice thick juices bubbling out of the steam vents along the edge.

8. Transfer the pie to a wire rack and let cool for at least 2 hours before serving. Garnish each slice with sweetened mascarpone.

Recipe for Success

▶ Other types of dried figs will work, too, including Turkish figs, but I prefer the Black Mission variety. Lacking figs altogether, you can substitute pitted prunes.

▶ If your figs are pleasantly moist—that is, it doesn't feel like a workout to eat them—you can actually skip the steaming.

Watermelon Rind Pie

When you eat a piece of watermelon, you take the last juicy bite and toss out the rind, right? Well, not if you want to bake one of the more unusual pies in this collection. A holdover from the days when thrifty farm wives were reluctant to waste a scrap of food, this pie gets its primary ingredient not from the flesh of the watermelon—like Watermelon Chiffon Pie (page 485)—but from the peeled rind. First you cook the diced rind in lightly sugared water until tender. Then you combine it with raisins, nuts, brown sugar, vinegar, and spices. Does it taste anything like watermelon? Not really. It's actually something like mock mincemeat, making this more of a fall pie than a summer one. Serve this to your family and friends and see if they can guess what's in it.

MAKES 8 TO 10 SERVINGS

1 recipe Basic Flaky Pie Pastry, Double Crust (page 31) or Basic Shortening Pie Pastry, Double Crust (page 30), refrigerated

FILLING

3 cups peeled and diced watermelon rind

3/4 cup granulated sugar

1/2 cup dark raisins

1/2 cup chopped walnuts or pecans

3 tablespoons cider vinegar

2 tablespoons firmly packed light brown sugar

1 tablespoon all-purpose flour

1/2 teaspoon ground cinnamon

1/4 teaspoon ground cloves

1/4 teaspoon ground nutmeg

1/4 teaspoon salt

GLAZE

1 large egg white, lightly beaten

Granulated sugar

1. If you haven't already, prepare the pastry and refrigerate until firm enough to roll, about 1 hour.

2. Combine the watermelon rind and 1/4 cup of the granulated sugar in a large saucepan. Add water just to cover. Bring to a boil, partially cover, and continue to boil until the rind is tender and translucent, 20 to 25 minutes. Drain well, then transfer the rind to a large bowl and let cool.

3. On a sheet of lightly floured waxed paper, roll the larger portion of the pastry into a 12-inch circle with a floured rolling pin. Invert the pastry over a 9-inch standard pie pan, center, and peel off the paper. Gently tuck the pastry into the pan, without stretching it, and let the overhang drape over the edge. Place in the refrigerator for 15 minutes. Preheat the oven to 400°F.

4. Stir the remaining 1/2 cup granulated sugar into the cooled rind. Stir in the raisins, nuts, vinegar, and brown sugar, then stir in the flour, spices, and salt.

5. On another sheet of floured waxed paper, roll the other half of dough into a 10-inch circle. Turn the filling into the chilled pie shell, smoothing the top with your hands or a spoon. Lightly moisten the rim of the pie shell. Invert the top pastry over the filling, center, and peel off the paper. Press the top and bottom pastries together along the dampened edge. Trim the pastry with scissors or a paring knife, leaving an even 1/2-inch overhang all around, then sculpt the overhang into an upstanding ridge. Poke several steam vents in the top of the pie with a fork or paring knife; put a couple of the vents near the edge of the crust so you can check the juices there later. To glaze the pie, lightly brush the pastry with the beaten egg white and sprinkle lightly with granulated sugar.

6. Place the pie on the center oven rack and bake for 30 minutes. Reduce the oven temperature to 375°F and rotate the pie 180 degrees, so that the part that faced the back of the oven now faces forward. Just in case, slide a large aluminum foil–lined baking sheet onto the rack below to catch any spills. Continue to bake until the top is dark golden brown, 25 to 30 minutes. This is not a particularly juicy pie, so you may or may not see juices bubbling up through the steam vents.

7. Transfer the pie to a wire rack and let cool for at least 1 hour. Serve slightly warm or at room temperature.

Recipe for Success

▶ When you peel the rind, be sure to remove all of the outermost skin with a sharp peeler, since it's the toughest part of the skin. Don't undercook the rind, thinking it will soften further as it bakes. Because of the vinegar in the filling, this isn't likely to happen.

Crumb-Topped Zapple Pie

Here's an idea I borrowed from *The Classic Zucchini Cookbook*, published by my friends at Storey Books (2002). Zapple pie, if you're wondering, is the name of a sweet zucchini pie that tastes like an apple pie—or reasonably close to it. Zucchini doesn't taste like anything, and if you add enough cinnamon, nutmeg, and lemon juice to something that tastes like nothing, then throw on a crumb topping, you'll have an approximation of a real apple pie—kind of like a vegetable version of mock apple pie (see page 246). Anyway, I was intrigued by the whole idea of a sweet zucchini pie, so with the authors' recipe as my blueprint, I started playing around with variations of my own. I added apple juice concentrate to increase its apple credibility, as well as apple cider vinegar for tang. I also added some raisins, because I thought they belonged. In the end, you may not think it's real apple pie, but I think you'll enjoy it nonetheless, especially if you—like many gardeners—have more zucchini in the summer than you know what to do with.

MAKES 8 TO 10 SERVINGS

1 recipe Basic Shortening Pie Pastry, Single Crust (page 30), refrigerated

FILLING

6 cups peeled, halved lengthwise, and thinly sliced zucchini

2/3 cup granulated sugar

2 tablespoons frozen apple juice concentrate, thawed

1 teaspoon ground cinnamon

1/4 teaspoon ground nutmeg

1/4 teaspoon salt

2 tablespoons cornstarch

1/3 cup fresh lemon juice

1 tablespoon cider vinegar

CRUMB TOPPING

1/2 cup all-purpose flour

1/2 cup firmly packed light brown sugar

1/2 cup pecan halves

1/4 teaspoon salt

1/4 cup (1/2 stick) cold unsalted butter, cut into 1/4-inch pieces

1. If you haven't already, prepare the pastry and refrigerate until firm enough to roll, about 1 hour.

2. On a sheet of lightly floured waxed paper, roll the pastry into a 13-inch circle with a floured rolling pin. Invert the pastry over a 9½-inch deep-dish pie pan, center, and peel off the paper. Tuck the pastry into the pan, without stretching it, and sculpt the edge into an upstanding ridge. Place in the freezer for 15 minutes. Preheat the oven to 400°F.

3. Meanwhile, in a large, heavy soup pot, combine the zucchini, sugar, apple juice concentrate, cinnamon, nutmeg, and salt over medium-high heat and gradually heat, stirring occasionally, until the liquid starts to boil. Reduce the heat slightly and simmer until the zucchini is tender but not mushy, about 10 minutes.

4. Blend the cornstarch and lemon juice together in a small bowl, stirring until smooth. When the zucchini is tender, stir the cornstarch slurry into the pot and cook, stirring nonstop to prevent sticking, for 1 to 1½ minutes. The juice will thicken noticeably. Remove the pan from the heat and stir in the vinegar.

5. To make the crumb topping, combine the flour, brown sugar, pecans, and salt in a food processor and pulse several times to chop the nuts. Scatter the butter over the dry ingredients and pulse until the mixture resembles fine crumbs. Transfer to a bowl and rub between your fingers to make large, buttery crumbs.

6. Spoon the filling into the chilled pie shell, smoothing the top with a spoon. Dump the crumbs in the center of the pie, spreading them evenly over the top. Tamp them down gently with your hands. Place the pie on the center oven rack, reduce the temperature to 350°F, and bake for about 40 minutes, rotating the pie 180 degrees halfway through the

baking, so that the part that faced the back of the oven now faces forward. When done, you may or may not see thick juice bubbling around the edge. The best indication of doneness is total elapsed time.

7.   Transfer the pie to a wire rack and let cool. Serve slightly warm, at room temperature, or chilled. This is best served the same day it is made.

Recipe for Success

▶   **Choose small to medium-size zucchini for the filling. The flesh will be firmer, more apple-like, and better able to hold its shape.**

▶   **Do watch the amount of time you cook the zucchini. This pie is charming when there's a little texture to it and slightly less so if the zucchini is overcooked.**

▶   **The pie can be made with a top crust instead of the crumb topping.**

Fruits of the Forest Pie (Fruit Version) with Coarse Sugar Glaze

I'd been hearing about various "fruits of the forest" pies for some time before I actually started researching recipes. When I finally did, I found that they fall into two distinct categories—nut fillings (see page 356) and fruit fillings. My guess is that the nut versions came first, since one might well consider them fruits of the forest. Then, I imagine, someone appropriated the fanciful name and applied it to a delicious mixed-fruit pie, and the idea caught on in spite of the geographic misrepresentation. This, obviously, falls into the latter category. And if the blueberries are, perhaps, the closest this pie gets to the forest, we'll overlook that because it's so delicious. For the glaze, I use coarse sugar, which offers some good crunchy contrast to the soft filling. The best time to make this pie is mid- to late summer.

MAKES 8 TO 10 SERVINGS

1 recipe Basic Shortening Pie Pastry, Double Crust (page 30), refrigerated

FILLING

2 medium-size ripe peaches, peeled, pitted, and sliced

1 large ripe pear, peeled, cored, and sliced

1 large Granny Smith or other tart apple, peeled, cored, and sliced

1 cup fresh blueberries, picked over for stems

1 cup hulled and sliced fresh strawberries

1/2 cup chopped pineapple, fresh or canned (drained)

1/2 cup plus 3 tablespoons granulated sugar

1/2 teaspoon ground ginger

1/4 teaspoon ground nutmeg

1 tablespoon fresh lemon juice

3 tablespoons cornstarch

GLAZE

Milk or light cream

Coarse sugar (see page 69)

1. If you haven't already, prepare the pastry and refrigerate until firm enough to roll, about 1 hour.

2. On a sheet of lightly floured waxed paper, roll the larger portion of the pastry into a 13-inch circle with a floured rolling pin. Invert the pastry over a 9½-inch deep-dish pie pan, center, and peel off the paper. Gently tuck the pastry into the pan, without stretching it, and let the overhang drape over the edge. Place in the refrigerator for 15 minutes.

3. In a large bowl, combine the fruit, ½ cup of the granulated sugar, the ginger, nutmeg, and lemon juice. Toss well to mix, then set aside for 10 minutes to juice. Mix the remaining 3 tablespoons granulated sugar and the cornstarch together in a small bowl, then stir the mixture into the fruit. Preheat the oven to 400°F.

4. On another sheet of lightly floured waxed paper, roll the other half of the pastry into an 11-inch circle. Turn the filling into the chilled pie shell, smoothing the fruit with a spoon. Lightly moisten the rim of the pie shell. Invert the top pastry over the filling, center, and peel off the paper. Press the top and bottom pastries together along the dampened edge. Trim the pastry with scissors or a paring knife, leaving an even ½-inch overhang all around, then sculpt the overhang into an upstanding ridge. Poke several steam vents in the top of the pie with a fork or paring knife. Put a couple of the vents near the edge of the crust so you can check the juices there later. To glaze the pie, lightly brush the pastry with milk and sprinkle with coarse sugar.

5. Place the pie on the center oven rack and bake for 30 minutes. Reduce the oven temperature to 375°F and rotate the pie 180 degrees, so that the part that faced the back

of the oven now faces forward. Just in case, slide a large aluminum foil–lined baking sheet onto the rack below to catch any drips. Bake until the juices bubble thickly at the steam vents and the top is golden brown, 35 to 45 minutes. If the top of the pie starts to get too dark, cover with loosely tented aluminum foil during the last 10 to 15 minutes.

6. Transfer the pie to a wire rack and let cool for at least 2 hours before serving.

Recipe for Success

▶ This is the combination of fruits I like best in this pie, but there is a lot of room for flexibility here. You can use blackberries or raspberries in place of the strawberries, nectarines in place of the peaches, and 2 apples instead of a pear and an apple.

▶ If you happen to have fruit cookie cutters, especially small ones, an arrangement of fruit pastry cutouts (see page 19) on top is very pretty and hints at what's to come.

Robin Hood: Prize Pie Baker?

"Pies, contrary to popular belief, were not invented in North America. Probably every bread-making people of the Old World used dough as a container in which to bake fruit or other food and so make their bread more interesting. Those venison pasties (turnovers) that Robin Hood fed to his merry men were pies of a sort, and the prologue to the Cook's tale in Chaucer's *The Canterbury Tales* tells of an unethical pie dealer who was notorious for selling pasties 'That hath been twies hoot and twies coold.'"

—Jonathan Norton Leonard, *American Cooking: New England* (Time-Life Books, 1970)

"White" Summer Fruit Pie

I love the so-called white summer fruits—white peaches, white nectarines, and the blushing orange-white Rainier cherries—for their unusual shades and unique flavors. (Rainier cherries taste peachy to me, and white peaches have a floral fragrance and flavor I don't find with other peaches.) Bring these fruits together in one crust, and you have a pie with a rather distinct flavor and hue. Here I combine either white peaches or nectarines and Rainier cherries in a streusel-topped pie with an unexpected flavor. The trick to doing this right is simply waiting, patiently, for the two crops to come to market at the same time, in late June and July, before making this pie. But, as you'll discover, it is well worth the wait.

MAKES 8 TO 10 SERVINGS

1 recipe Basic Flaky Pie Pastry, Single Crust (page 31) or All-Butter Pie Pastry, Single Crust (page 28), refrigerated

FILLING

4 cups peeled, pitted, and sliced ripe white peaches or nectarines

2 cups fresh Rainier cherries, stemmed, halved, and pitted

1/3 cup plus 3 tablespoons sugar

1 tablespoon fresh orange or lemon juice

1 teaspoon grated orange or lemon zest

2 1/2 tablespoons cornstarch

Pinch of ground nutmeg

STREUSEL TOPPING

1/2 cup all-purpose flour

1/2 cup sugar

Big pinch of salt

Big pinch of ground cinnamon

1/4 cup (1/2 stick) cold unsalted butter, cut into 1/4-inch pieces

1. If you haven't already, prepare the pastry and refrigerate until firm enough to roll, about 1 hour.

2. On a sheet of lightly floured waxed paper, roll the pastry into a 13-inch circle with a floured rolling pin. Invert the pastry over a 9½-inch deep-dish pie pan, center, and peel off the paper. Tuck the pastry into the pan, without stretching it, and sculpt the edge into an upstanding ridge. Place in the freezer for 15 minutes.

3. In a large bowl, combine the fruit, ⅓ cup of the sugar, the orange juice, and orange zest. Toss gently to combine, then set aside for 10 minutes to juice. Preheat the oven to 400°F.

4. Combine the remaining 3 tablespoons sugar and the cornstarch in a small bowl. Stir the mixture into the fruit along with nutmeg. Turn the filling into the chilled pie shell and smooth the top of the fruit with your hands or a spoon. Place the pie on the center oven rack and bake for 30 minutes.

5. Meanwhile, make the topping. In a large bowl, combine the flour, sugar, salt, and cinnamon. Toss gently to mix. Rub the butter into the dry ingredients until the mixture resembles coarse crumbs. Refrigerate until ready to use.

6. Remove the pie from the oven and reduce the temperature to 375°F. Dump the topping in the center of the pie and spread it evenly over the fruit with your hands. Tamp it down gently. Return the pie to the oven, placing it so that the part that faced the back of the oven now faces forward. Just in case, slide a large aluminum foil–lined baking sheet onto the rack below to catch any spills. Continue to bake until the topping is golden brown and the juices bubble thickly around the edge, 25 to 30 minutes.

7. Transfer the pie to a wire rack and let cool for at least 2 hours before serving.

Recipe for Success

▶ With some of my peach and nectarine pies, I don't bother to peel the fruit, because the skins are very soft. But with this pie and filling, which I consider somewhat refined, I do.

▶ You may be wondering whether you can make this pie with another type of cherry. Of course you can, and it will be delicious, but the flavor will be very different from the one intended.

▶ Remember, there are 2 ways to peel a peach: with a sharp paring knife and by blanching method (see page 88). Either works fine here.

Fresh summer berries are so irresistible in homemade pies that it seemed

only right to give them their own showcase. This chapter is precisely that, and

if you occasionally stumble upon an errant fig, peach, or slice of rhubarb here

and there, remember that the more than two dozen recipes that follow are

connected by a single purpose: to celebrate those black, red, and blue

Berry Good Pies

summer jewels that steal the show in some of our most memorable pies. •

Not that we don't all sometimes rely on not-fresh fruit to tide us over or aug-

ment the berries we have on hand. There are times, after all, when you just

have to have a berry pie and the only reasonably priced fruit to be had is

found in a can or the freezer case. For that reason, a few of these recipes

specify alternatives to fresh. But most of them more or less take for granted

that you're going to be baking with fresh picked. • My intention was to make

this chapter as inclusive as possible, but I make no apologies for that fact that my own bias in berry pies is readily transparent: blueberry pies outnumber all others. I used to grow blueberries at my former home in New Hampshire. What the bears and birds didn't get first, I would turn into pies. And delectable pies they were. This supports my belief that the best pies I've ever eaten have been those made by cooks with local ingredients. That's something to keep in mind as you peruse this chapter. And if blueberry isn't your favorite, you're sure to find a berry pie that's just right for you.

The $900 Pie

The Darby, Montana, Public Library has a friend in Emma Lee Nicholson—81 years old and a lifetime resident of Darby. According to a report in a July 2003 issue of the *Missoulian* newspaper, Emma Lee's sour cream and raisin pie sold for $900 at a pie auction to benefit the construction of a new town library. It was the last pie of the evening to be auctioned, and Emma Lee, who is something of a local pie-baking celebrity, thought it would fetch much less. "I guessed $40," she reportedly told her granddaughter.

The winning bidders, Sharon and Ron Wilkerson of Missoula, took the pie home after the auction, ate a couple of pieces, and served the rest to several guests the following day. The pie auction raised $3,267.50 for the new library, including $300 for one of Emma Lee's strawberry pies.

Tips for Baking Beautiful Berry Pies

▶ **Don't jump on the berry pie bandwagon too early.** The best berries come to market in mid- to late season. For the best price, shop at farmers' markets, where competing vendors will try to undersell one another.

▶ **Inspect baskets of berries carefully.** Find out when the berries were picked. The same day or the day before is best. Fresh berries are the most fragile of fruits and are easily damaged by their own weight and by one or more spoiled berries. I always take a whiff of a berry basket. If I detect a moldy smell, I don't buy it. One or two moldy berries can taint the flavor of an entire pie.

▶ **If you must rinse berries, don't do it until you're ready to use them.** Because raspberries have a cavity, they need to be inverted on paper towels after rinsing to drain the excess water.

▶ **Use berries in pies right away, preferably the same day you buy them.** If you're keeping them overnight, pour them into a wide container so that they don't continue to sit under their own weight.

▶ **Mix all berry fillings very carefully,** or you'll crush the fruit. A few crushed berries are fine, but for the most part you want to maintain their shape and texture.

▶ **Don't overfill a berry pie.** Fresh berries produce a lot of juice, and you'll minimize bubbling over if the pan isn't full.

▶ **As with other fruit pies, don't underbake a berry pie,** or the filling will not thicken properly. The visible juices should be bubbling thickly before you remove the pie from the oven.

▶ **Let your berry pie cool for at least one hour,** preferably two or more, before slicing, to keep the filling from oozing everywhere.

All-Strawberry Pie

As I've said elsewhere, there are those who think that strawberries are, for the most part, unsuitable for pies because they bake up so soft. I say nonsense. Sure, they cook up soft, but so do many other fruits. Just because strawberries don't stay firm doesn't mean you should eliminate them from your pie repertoire. Like so many other fresh fruit pies, I tend to make this one only during local fresh berry season. I like to add some form of mint to the mix, since the two share harvest times and taste so good together. Minced fresh mint is fine, although it tends to turn a little dark in the baking, which may be somewhat unappealing if you're serving the pie to guests. Instead, you might consider a drop or two of mint oil, or, as I use here, white crème de menthe. Along with the nutmeg, it adds a soft flavor to the fruit that everyone seems to like.

MAKES 8 TO 10 SERVINGS

1 recipe Basic Flaky Pie Pastry, Double Crust (page 31), refrigerated

FILLING

4 cups hulled and thickly sliced fresh strawberries

1/2 cup sugar

2 tablespoons cornstarch

1 tablespoon white crème de menthe (optional; see headnote)

1 tablespoon fresh lemon juice

1/4 teaspoon ground nutmeg

1 tablespoon cold unsalted butter, cut into small pieces

GLAZE

Sugar

Milk or light cream

1.　If you haven't already, prepare the pastry and refrigerate until firm enough to roll, about 1 hour.

2.　On a sheet of lightly floured waxed paper, roll the larger portion of the pastry into a 12-inch circle with a floured rolling pin. Invert over a 9-inch standard pie pan, center, and peel off the paper. Gently tuck the pastry into the pan, without stretching it, and let the overhang drape over the edge. Place in the refrigerator for 15 minutes.

3.　Put the strawberries in a large bowl. Mix the sugar and cornstarch together in a small bowl, then add the mixture to the fruit and toss well. Add the crème de menthe (if using), lemon juice, and nutmeg and toss again. Set aside for 10 minutes. Preheat the oven to 400°F.

4. On another sheet of lightly floured waxed paper, roll the other half of the pastry into an 11-inch circle. Turn the filling into the chilled pie shell and smooth the fruit with a spoon. Dot the top with the butter. Lightly moisten the rim of the pie shell. Invert the top pastry over the filling, center, and peel off the paper. Press the top and bottom pastries together along the dampened edge. Trim the pastry with scissors or a paring knife, leaving an even ½-inch overhang all around, then sculpt the overhang into an upstanding ridge. Poke several steam vents in the top of the pie with a fork or paring knife. Put a couple of the vents near the edge of the crust so you can check the juices there later. Sprinkle the top crust evenly with sugar, then with milk.

5. Place the pie on the center oven rack and bake for 30 minutes. Reduce the oven temperature to 375°F and rotate the pie 180 degrees, so that the part that faced the back of the oven now faces forward. Just in case, slide a large aluminum foil–lined baking sheet onto the rack below to catch any drips. Bake until the juices bubble thickly at the steam vents and the top is golden brown, 35 to 45 minutes. If the top of the pie starts to get too dark, cover it with loosely tented aluminum foil during the last 10 to 15 minutes.

6. Transfer the pie to a wire rack and let cool for at least 2 hours to let the juices settle and firm up before serving.

Recipe for Success

▶ **This really is meant to be an all-strawberry pie, with the purity of flavor you hope for from such a pie. But if you just can't resist adding that handful of leftover raspberries or cherries you have hanging around, I'll understand.**

▶ **This also will work as a crumb-topped pie. Simply choose one of the crumb toppings in this collection, adding it halfway through the baking. (If you're uncertain how this is done, read a crumb-topped pie recipe before proceeding.)**

▶ **If your strawberries are a little lackluster, add 2 tablespoons strawberry preserves to the filling to enhance the flavor.**

Strawberry-Rhubarb Crumb Pie

Spring should never pass without at least one or two rhubarb pies issuing from your oven. Rhubarb pie is a rite of spring, and a little later in the season, when the strawberries come along, the two make great partners. Their flavors are so bright and agreeable that you need little more than sugar and lemon to accent them. This makes an excellent lattice-top pie, so try it that way, too. But I really love the way it tastes with the cornmeal crumb topping.

MAKES 8 TO 10 SERVINGS

1 recipe Basic Flaky Pie Pastry, Single Crust (page 31), refrigerated

FILLING

3 cups fresh rhubarb stalks sliced crosswise $1/2$ inch thick

$3/4$ cup granulated sugar

$1 1/2$ tablespoons fresh lemon juice

Grated zest of 1 lemon

4 cups hulled and halved (quartered if large) fresh strawberries

$1/4$ cup quick-cooking tapioca

CORNMEAL CRUMB TOPPING

$3/4$ cup all-purpose flour

$1/4$ cup fine yellow cornmeal

$2/3$ cup firmly packed light brown sugar

$1/2$ teaspoon ground cinnamon

$1/4$ teaspoon salt

$1/2$ cup (1 stick) cold unsalted butter, cut into $1/4$-inch pieces

1. If you haven't already, prepare the pastry and refrigerate until firm enough to roll, about 1 hour.

2. On a sheet of lightly floured waxed paper, roll the pastry into a 13-inch circle with a floured rolling pin. Invert the pastry over a $9 1/2$-inch deep-dish pie pan, center, and peel off the paper. Tuck the pastry into the pan, without stretching it, and sculpt the edge into an upstanding ridge. Place in the freezer for 15 minutes. Preheat the oven to 400°F.

3. Combine the rhubarb, granulated sugar, lemon juice, and lemon zest in a large bowl. Toss well to mix, then set aside for 10 minutes.

4. Add the strawberries and tapioca to the bowl and toss well. Scrape the filling into the chilled pie shell and smooth the top with your hands. Place the pie on the center oven rack and bake for 30 minutes.

5. Meanwhile, make the topping. Combine the flour, cornmeal, brown sugar, cinnamon, and salt in a food processor and pulse several times to mix. Scatter the butter over the top and pulse until the mixture resembles fine crumbs. Empty the crumbs into a medium-size bowl and rub between your fingers to make large, buttery crumbs. Refrigerate until ready to use.

6. Remove the pie from the oven and reduce the temperature to 375°F. Carefully dump the crumbs in the center of the pie, spreading them evenly over the surface with your hands. Tamp them down gently. Return the pie to the oven, placing it so that the part that faced the back of the oven now faces forward. Just in case, slide a large aluminum foil–lined baking sheet onto the rack below to catch any spills. Continue to bake until the juices bubble thickly around the edge, 30 to 40 minutes. If necessary, cover with loosely tented aluminum foil during the last 10 minutes to prevent the top from getting too dark.

7. Transfer the pie to a wire rack and let cool for at least 1 hour before serving.

Recipe for Success

▶ When you're shopping for rhubarb, buy solid, crisp, bright red stalks. If the stalks seem too wide, halve them lengthwise before slicing them crosswise to make the filling. Toss the leaves, if they happen to be attached. They'll make you sick if you eat them.

Dolores's Strawberry and Rhubarb Crumb Pie in a Skillet Crust

I first "met" Dolores Kostelni when she interviewed me about apple pie for her radio show, *The Happy Cook*, on WREL-AM radio out of Lexington, Virginia. Turns out that Dolores also loves to make pies and is a self-described "intrepid lover of desserts." When Dolores found out I was working on a new pie book, she kindly agreed to send me this, one of her favorite pie recipes. I was immediately intrigued: what did she mean by a "skillet crust"? Turns out that her ingenious crust is mixed in, well, a big skillet: you melt butter, add your dry ingredients, and stir it all up. Some of it gets pressed into a large pie pan; the rest is used for a crumb topping. As for the filling, it's a spring classic. Cardamom and ginger, she reminds us, are in the same family, and their flavors are wonderful together, as well as with the strawberries and rhubarb. This is fine pie indeed. (P.S.—Check out Dolores's great cookbook, *Cookies by the Dozen*, published by Warner Books, 1995.)

MAKES 8 TO 10 SERVINGS

1 recipe Dolores's Skillet Crust (page 48)

FILLING

1 1/2 pounds fresh rhubarb stalks, trimmed of any leaves and sliced crosswise 1/4 inch thick (about 4 cups)

2 cups hulled and sliced fresh strawberries

3/4 cup sugar

Juice of 1 lemon

1/4 to 1/3 cup all-purpose flour (see Recipe for Success)

1/2 teaspoon ground cardamom

1/4 teaspoon ground ginger

1. Prepare the crust and press nearly 2 cups of it into the bottom and up the side of a 9 1/2- to 10-inch extra-deep-dish pie pan as directed. Set aside. Reserve the rest of the crust mixture for the topping.

2. In a large bowl, combine the rhubarb, strawberries, sugar, lemon juice, flour, cardamom, and ginger. Set aside for 10 minutes. Preheat the oven to 350°F.

3. Turn the filling into the pie shell, smoothing the top with your hand or a spoon. Crumble the reserved crust mixture evenly over the pie, pressing down on it gently.

4. Place the pie on the center oven rack and bake for 30 minutes, then reduce the oven temperature to 325°F and rotate the pie 180 degrees, so that the part that faced the back of the oven now faces forward. Just in case, slide a large aluminum foil–lined baking

sheet onto the rack below to catch any spills. Continue to bake until the top is golden brown and the juices bubble thickly around the edges, 40 to 50 minutes. If the top starts to get too dark, cover with loosely tented aluminum foil during the last 15 minutes of baking.

5. Transfer the pie to a wire rack and let cool for at least 2 hours before serving.

Recipe for Success

▶ Dolores says, "Older, thicker stalks of rhubarb, like big strawberries, tend to be dry, so use the lesser amount of flour to absorb their juice if this is the case."

▶ Note that because of the large amount of sugar in the crust, Dolores bakes the pie at a relatively low temperature for a fruit pie. Don't increase the oven temperature in an effort to hurry the pie along; you'll just scorch the crust.

Strawberry-Raspberry Mint Pie

I've never bought the conventional wisdom that strawberries don't make a good pie because their texture is too soft and won't hold up to baking. Sure, strawberry pies do have a very soft texture, but I don't really consider that a problem. With enough cornstarch, the filling will indeed firm up as the pie cools, leaving you with the texture of thick preserves. Unless the strawberries are fresh, local, and in season, I often prefer frozen strawberries to fresh, which can be lacking in flavor much of the time. Here we use a bag of frozen strawberries and mix it with a bag of raspberries, and the result is a delicious pie in a tender cream cheese crust. I like to include a little mint, which gives the pie a summery sparkle even in the dead of winter.

MAKES 8 TO 10 SERVINGS

1 recipe Tender Cream Cheese Pastry, Double Crust (page 46), refrigerated

FILLING

One 1-pound bag individually frozen strawberries (not packed in syrup), partially thawed

One 1-pound bag individually frozen raspberries (not packed in syrup), partially thawed

2/3 cup granulated sugar

1/4 cup cornstarch

1 1/2 tablespoons orange liqueur or 1/2 teaspoon orange extract

1 tablespoon fresh lemon juice

1/4 teaspoon ground cinnamon

1/4 teaspoon ground nutmeg

Small handful of fresh mint leaves or 1/2 teaspoon crumbled dried mint

2 tablespoons cold unsalted butter, cut into small pieces

GARNISH

Confectioners' sugar

1.   If you haven't already, prepare the pastry and refrigerate until firm enough to roll, 1 to 1½ hours.

2.   On a sheet of lightly floured waxed paper, roll the larger portion of the pastry into a 12-inch circle with a floured rolling pin. Invert the pastry over a 9-inch standard pie pan, center, and peel off the paper. Gently tuck the pastry into the pan, without stretching it, and let the overhang drape over the edge. Place in the refrigerator for 15 minutes.

3.   If the strawberries are whole or in large pieces, use a sharp knife to cut them in half or into large bite-size pieces. Combine the strawberries and raspberries in a large bowl. Mix the granulated sugar and cornstarch together in a small bowl. Add the mixture to the fruit and mix briefly. Add the orange liqueur, lemon juice, cinnamon, nutmeg, and mint and toss to mix. Set the fruit mixture aside for 15 minutes. Preheat the oven to 400°F.

4.   On another sheet of lightly floured waxed paper, roll the other half of the pastry into an 11-inch circle. Turn the filling into the chilled pie shell and smooth the top with a spoon. Dot the top with the butter. Lightly moisten the rim of the pie shell with a wet finger or pastry brush. Invert the top pastry over the filling, center, and peel off the paper. Press the top and bottom pastries together along the dampened edge. Trim the pastry with scissors or a paring knife, leaving an even ½-inch overhang all around, then sculpt the overhang into an upstanding ridge. Poke several steam vents in the top of the pie with a fork or paring knife. Put a couple of the vents near the edge of the crust so you can check the juices there later.

5.   Place the pie on the center oven rack and bake for 30 minutes. Reduce the oven temperature to 375°F and rotate the pie 180 degrees, so that the part that faced the back of the oven now faces forward. Just in case, slide a large aluminum foil–lined baking sheet onto the rack below to catch any spills. Bake until the top of the pie is golden brown and any juices visible at the steam vents bubble thickly, 30 to 35 minutes.

6.   Transfer the pie to a wire rack and let cool for 15 to 20 minutes. While it is still quite warm, dust the top lightly with confectioners' sugar. Once the pie has cooled, dust it again. Let the pie cool for at least 1 hour before serving.

Recipe for Success

▶ **This filling is quite soft and therefore settles low in the pan. By contrast, the top crust is likely to remain somewhat domed. This is not an unfamiliar situation to pie makers. There is something you can do, however, to shrink the distance between crust and filling so the pastry snuggles up to the fruit. As soon as the** pie comes out of the oven, drape a clean tea towel over it. Let it sit there for 1 minute, steam-softening the crust, then very gently press down on the towel and pastry to collapse it a little. There's no guarantee that the pastry won't shatter or break slightly, but it's usually not a disaster. Note that the more pronounced the pastry dome is, the more difficult it is to do this without serious breakage. The tender cream cheese pastry is probably the best dough to try this little trick on.

Vid and Annie's Fresh Raspberry Crumb Pie

Here's a pie I like to make two or three times a summer. When my New Hampshire friends Vid and Annie Valdmanis would give me boxes of fresh raspberries from their garden, I would quickly turn around and bake those fragile fruits into pies like this, lest they slide past their prime. So I dedicate this pie to Vid and Annie, for all the great berries they generously bestowed on me.

MAKES 8 TO 10 SERVINGS

1 recipe Basic Shortening Pie Pastry, Single Crust (page 30) or Basic Flaky Pie Pastry, Single Crust (page 31), refrigerated

FILLING

4 cups fresh raspberries

1/2 cup plus 3 tablespoons sugar

2 teaspoons fresh lemon juice

1 1/2 tablespoons cornstarch

1/4 teaspoon ground nutmeg

2 to 3 tablespoons seedless raspberry jam (optional)

CRUMB TOPPING

1/2 cup all-purpose flour

1/2 cup sugar

1/2 teaspoon ground cinnamon

1/4 teaspoon salt

1/4 cup (1/2 stick) cold unsalted butter, cut into 1/4-inch pieces

GARNISH

Vanilla, peach, or strawberry ice cream

1. If you haven't already, prepare the pastry and refrigerate until firm enough to roll, about 1 hour.

2. On a sheet of lightly floured waxed paper, roll the pastry into a 12-inch circle with a floured rolling pin. Invert the pastry over a 9-inch standard pie pan, center, and peel off the paper. Tuck the pastry into the pan, without stretching it, and sculpt the edge into an upstanding ridge. Place in the freezer for 15 minutes. Preheat the oven to 400°F.

3. Combine the raspberries, ½ cup of the sugar, and the lemon juice in a large bowl. Toss gently to mix, then set aside for 10 minutes to juice. Meanwhile, combine the remaining 3 tablespoons sugar and the cornstarch and nutmeg in a small bowl. Stir the mixture into the fruit.

4. Spread the raspberry jam, if using, inside the chilled pie shell. Scrape the filling into the shell, smoothing the fruit with a spoon. Place the pie on the center oven rack and bake for 25 minutes.

5. Meanwhile, make the topping. Combine the flour, sugar, cinnamon, and salt in a food processor. Scatter the butter over the dry mixture and pulse until the mixture resembles fine crumbs. Dump the crumbs into a large bowl and gently rub between your fingers to make large, buttery crumbs. Refrigerate until ready to use.

6. Remove the pie from the oven and reduce the oven temperature to 375°F. Carefully dump the crumbs in the center of the pie and spread them evenly over the top with your hands. Return the pie to the oven, placing it so that the part that faced the back of the oven now faces forward. Just in case, slide a large aluminum foil–lined baking sheet onto the rack below to catch any spills. Continue to bake until the juices bubble thickly around the edge of the pie, about 25 minutes.

7. Transfer the pie to a wire rack and let cool. Serve barely warm or at room temperature, accompanied by ice cream.

Recipe for Success

▶ Due to their fragile nature, raspberries are quite prone to mold. For that reason, I always give them the sniff test before purchasing. If I detect any trace of mold, which is often very difficult to see, I pass. Even the smallest amount of mold will taint the flavor of a pie.

▶ Juicy berry pies like this one are sometimes tricky to team up with a crumb topping, as the topping has a tendency to absorb excess juice. If I see a lot of juice in a filling when I'm ready to add the topping, I sprinkle several tablespoons of rolled oats (quick-cooking work best) over the pie and return it to the oven for about 5 minutes. The oats absorb the juice and form something of a barrier. I then add the topping and proceed as usual. It works pretty well.

Breitbach's Raspberry Pie

I had heard that the raspberry pie at Breitbach's Country Dining in Balltown, Iowa—the state's oldest bar and restaurant—had a stellar reputation. So I called Cindy Breitbach, the resident pie maker, to find out what makes her raspberry pie such a hit. I should mention that Cindy, who learned to make pies from her grandmothers—"both fine pie makers"—has been making pies since the age of 10, so one suspects she has that pie maker's touch. The way she tells it, the raspberry pie that everyone raves about could not be easier: it's just raspberries, blackberries, sugar, and tapioca. Lemon juice? No, she thinks there is enough acidity in the fruit itself. And in yet another vote of confidence for frozen fruit, she says that's what she uses. As for the crust, hers is a shortening double crust—"nothing fancy about that either." Maybe not, but the pie is wonderful.

MAKES 8 TO 10 SERVINGS

1 recipe Basic Shortening Pie Pastry, Double Crust (page 30), refrigerated

FILLING

3 cups individually frozen raspberries (not packed in syrup), partially thawed

1 cup individually frozen blackberries (not packed in syrup), partially thawed

1 1/4 cups sugar

3 tablespoons quick-cooking tapioca

GLAZE

Sugar

1. If you haven't already, prepare the pastry and refrigerate until firm enough to roll, about 1 hour.

2. On a sheet of lightly floured waxed paper, roll the larger portion of the pastry into a 13-inch circle with a floured rolling pin. Invert the pastry over a 9 1/2-inch deep-dish pie pan, center, and peel off the paper. Gently tuck the pastry into the pan, without stretching it, and let the overhang drape over the edge. Place in the refrigerator for 15 minutes.

3. In a large bowl, combine the berries, sugar, and tapioca. Toss gently to combine, then set aside for several minutes. Preheat the oven to 350°F.

4. Roll the other half of the pastry into an 11-inch circle on a sheet of lightly floured waxed paper. Turn the filling into the chilled pie shell, smoothing the fruit with a spoon. Lightly moisten the rim of the pie shell. Invert the top pastry over the filling, center, and

peel off the paper. Press the top and bottom pastries together along the dampened edge. Using the back of a butter knife or paring knife, trim the pastry flush with the edge of the pan. Poke several steam vents in the top of the pie with a fork or paring knife. Put a couple of the vents near the edge of the crust so you can check the juices there later. Sprinkle the top of the pie lightly with sugar.

5. Place the pie on the center oven rack and bake for 30 minutes, then rotate the pie 180 degrees, so that the part that faced the back of the oven now faces forward. Just in case, slide a large aluminum foil–lined baking sheet onto the rack below to catch any spills. Continue to bake until the juices bubble thickly at the steam vents, about 45 minutes. Cindy says it is important to give the pie a thorough baking, "so the beads of tapioca disappear."

6. Transfer the pie to a wire rack and let cool. Serve just slightly warm or at room temperature.

Recipe for Success

▶ Cindy uses the same trick I do to prepare frozen fruit for baking. She puts it in a bowl in the microwave and heats it just until the fruit is nearly thawed. Remember that using hard-frozen fruit increases the baking time and often results in an overbaked crust.

New Hampshire Raspberry and Red Currant Pie

This pie always reminds me of my days in New Hampshire, when I would make it a few times each summer. The timing was pretty much preordained: right about the time my secret red currant picking spot would bear fruit, my friends Vid and Annie Valdmanis would start delivering the first of the raspberries from their home garden. Thus blessed, I would always make a double-crust pie of roughly equal amounts of fruit so they could share the limelight. Nowadays, I usually buy my red currants from the local Whole Foods Market here in Annapolis, Maryland. These tart, translucent red jewels team up wonderfully with the raspberries—sweet-tart, brilliant red, and absolutely delicious.

MAKES 8 TO 10 SERVINGS

1 recipe Tender Cream Cheese Pastry, Double Crust (page 46), refrigerated

FILLING

2 1/2 cups fresh raspberries

2 cups fresh red currants, picked over for stems

1/2 cup plus 3 tablespoons sugar

2 tablespoons red currant jelly (optional)

1 teaspoon fresh lemon juice

3 tablespoons cornstarch

1 tablespoon cold unsalted butter, cut into small pieces

GLAZE

Milk or light cream

Sugar

1. If you haven't already, prepare the pastry and refrigerate until firm enough to roll, about 1 hour.

2. On a sheet of lightly floured waxed paper, roll the larger portion of the pastry into a 12-inch circle with a floured rolling pin. Invert the pastry over a 9-inch standard pie pan, center, and peel off the paper. Gently tuck the pastry into the pan, without stretching it, and let the overhang drape over the edge. Place in the refrigerator for 15 minutes.

3. In a large bowl, combine the raspberries, currants, 1/2 cup of the sugar, the jelly (if using), and lemon juice. Toss gently to mix, then set aside for 10 minutes to juice. Preheat the oven to 400°F.

4. Roll the other half of the pastry into a 10-inch circle on a sheet of lightly floured waxed paper. Combine the remaining 3 tablespoons sugar and the cornstarch in a small bowl. Stir the mixture gently into the fruit. Turn the filling into the chilled pie shell, smoothing the top with your hands or a spoon. Dot the filling with the butter. Lightly moisten the rim of the pie shell. Invert the top pastry over the filling, center, and peel off the paper. Press the top and bottom pastries together along the dampened edge. Using the back of a butter knife or pastry knife, trim the pastry flush with the edge of the pan, reserving the scraps for decoration, if desired. Poke several steam vents in the top of the pie with a fork or paring knife. Put a couple of the vents near the edge of the crust so you can check the juices there later. To glaze the pie, lightly brush the pastry with milk and sprinkle with sugar. If you want to add a decorative flourish to the pie, shape a very thin "stem" of a currant branch, 3 or 4 inches long, and lay it in the center of the pie, arching the top gracefully to one side. Make little balls of dough—the currants—about 1/4 inch in diameter and place them in clusters on either side of the stem.

5. Place the pie on the center oven rack and bake for 30 minutes. Reduce the oven temperature to 375°F and rotate the pie 180 degrees, so that the part that faced the back

of the oven now faces forward. Just in case, slide a large aluminum foil–lined baking sheet onto the rack below to catch any spills. Continue to bake until the top is dark golden brown and the juices bubble thickly at the steam vents, about 30 minutes.

6. Transfer the pie to a wire rack and let cool for at least 2 hours before serving.

Recipe for Success

▶ Do toss the fruit gently when you mix it, because both the raspberries and the currants are fragile. Rough handling will turn them into a texture-less mush. By the same token, gently "rake" the currants off the stems with your fingers to avoid mashing them.

▶ If you happen to taste the filling and find the currants quite tart (they are), don't be tempted to add more sugar. Hiding their tartness behind too much sugar detracts from their unique flavor.

Raspberry and Fresh Fig Freeform Pie

Jeanne Thiel Kelley is one of the best home bakers I know. A freelance food writer and contributing editor at *Bon Appétit*, Jeanne lives in California. When I told her I was working on a book of pies and asked her if she had any neat California-style pies in her files, she immediately thought of this one. I'm glad she did, because the combination of fresh figs and raspberries is one I've never considered. Now I'm here to tell you that they work beautifully together. Jeanne likes to add an egg yolk to her pastry, to keep it on the sturdy side, so note that I've modified my All-Butter Pie Pastry to satisfy her requirements. Jeanne tops off this delicious pie with an unusual honey-anise whipped cream that's out of this world.

MAKES 8 SERVINGS

1 recipe All-Butter Pie Pastry, Single Crust (page 28), modified as instructed in step 1 and refrigerated

FILLING

1/4 cup granulated sugar

1/4 cup firmly packed light brown sugar

1 tablespoon all-purpose flour

Two 6-ounce baskets fresh raspberries

2 cups (about 10 ounces) small, fresh black figs, stemmed and quartered

2 tablespoons honey

HONEY-ANISE WHIPPED CREAM

1 cup cold heavy or whipping cream

2 tablespoons honey

2 tablespoons anisette or other anise-flavored liqueur

Words of Pastry Wisdom from a Test Kitchen Pro

Jeanne Thiel Kelley knows about the challenges facing home pie bakers. A contributing editor at *Bon Appétit* and a former staff member of the *Bon Appétit* test kitchen, Jeanne attended La Varenne cooking school in France and has worked on a variety of cookbooks. Her experience, she says, has taught her that the key to mastering pies is a great crust. Here are her tips for building what she calls "crust confidence."

▶ Use a good recipe for classic pie crust, obtained from a reliable resource—a friend or family member with a tried-and-true formula, or one of the recipes here, of course.

▶ Experiment with making the crust by hand and in a food processor. Find the technique that works best for you. There is no right or wrong way.

▶ Practice makes perfect. With time, you'll be able to gauge when the fat is correctly blended into the dry ingredients and just how much liquid to add for a crust that is neither dry and crumbly nor wet and sticky.

▶ A freeform pie is a great choice for the beginning baker. The simple technique allows the novice to focus on the crust and get it right.

Look for Jeanne's *Holiday Baking*, a Williams-Sonoma book (Time-Life, 1999).

---

1. Prepare the pastry as directed, substituting 1 egg yolk for 1 tablespoon of the water; simply blend the yolk with the water. Refrigerate until firm enough to roll, about 1 hour. Position an oven rack in the upper third of the oven and preheat the oven to 400°F.

2. Mix the sugars and flour together in a large bowl. Add three-quarters of the raspberries and all of the figs. Toss gently to combine, then set aside.

3. To make the freeform crust, on a sheet of lightly floured waxed paper, roll the pastry into a 12-inch circle with a floured rolling pin. Invert the pastry onto a rimless baking sheet and peel off the paper, letting the pastry drape over the edge of the sheet, if necessary. Imagine an 8-inch circle in the center of the pastry and spoon the fruit into it. Using a metal spatula or dough scraper to help you lift the pastry, fold the overhanging dough over the filling.

FREEFORM CRUST

4. Place the baking sheet on the upper oven rack and bake until the crust is golden brown and the juice bubbles thickly in the center of the pie, about 35 minutes.

5. Transfer the baking sheet pie to a wire rack and drizzle the honey over the pie. Let cool on the sheet. If the pie has leaked juice, loosen it in those areas with a spatula while the pie is still quite warm.

6. While the pie is still warm, make the whipped cream. Using a chilled medium-size bowl and chilled beaters, beat the cream, honey, and anisette until soft peaks form. Scatter the remaining raspberries over the pie and serve garnished with whipped cream.

Recipe for Success

▶ Jeanne has some good ideas to share about making this pie. She likes to roll the pastry between 2 sheets of parchment paper, then slide it onto the baking sheet. She removes the top sheet of paper but leaves the bottom one in place for the pie to bake on. The parchment, she explains, is also useful for folding the pastry over the filling: just lift up on the parchment and fold it over the fruit.

▶ Keep in mind that the season for making this pie is limited, especially if you live in a place where fresh figs are hard to find. Look for them in late summer.

Blackberry Silk Pie

When I lived in New Hampshire, I spent more time than I should have engaged in one of the most enjoyable, least profitable hobbies a fellow could have: picking wild blackberries. I used to say I did it for the kids—all four of mine loved to come along—but in fact I liked trudging through the thorny bushes as much as they did, always emerging with at least enough berries to make one of my favorite blackberry pies. What I do here is make a blackberry puree, strain it, and then blend it with the usual custard ingredients: cream, eggs, and sugar. The color of the filling is a beautiful dark-berry red, with an ultra-smooth texture that reminds me of silk— thus the name. The best thing about it? You don't need a patch of wild berries down the road to try this. It works equally well with fresh blackberries—ripe and in season—or frozen ones.

MAKES 8 TO 10 SERVINGS

1 recipe Basic Flaky Pie Pastry, Single Crust (page 31), refrigerated

FILLING

1 pint fresh blackberries or one 1-pound bag individually frozen blackberries (not packed in syrup), partially thawed

1 cup sugar

3 large eggs, at room temperature

1 tablespoon cornstarch

1 1/2 cups heavy or whipping cream, at room temperature

1/2 cup light cream, at room temperature

1 teaspoon vanilla extract

GARNISH

Ripe fresh blackberries (optional)

1. If you haven't already, prepare the pastry and refrigerate until firm enough to roll, about 1 hour.

2. On a sheet of lightly floured waxed paper, roll the pastry into a 13-inch circle with a floured rolling pin. Invert the pastry over a 9 1/2-inch deep-dish pie pan, center, and peel off the paper. Tuck the pastry into the pan, without stretching it, and sculpt the edge so it is slightly higher than the rim. Place in the freezer for 15 minutes, then partially prebake and let cool according to the instructions on page 16. Reduce the oven temperature to 300°F.

3. Combine the berries and 1/4 cup of the sugar in a food processor and process for about 30 seconds, long enough to make a smooth puree. Put a mesh sieve over a large bowl and pour the puree into the sieve. Using a rubber spatula, force the puree through the mesh, leaving just the seeds. Discard the seeds.

4. In a large bowl, whisk the eggs until frothy. Add the remaining 3/4 cup sugar and the cornstarch and whisk until well blended. Blend in the heavy cream, light cream, vanilla, and 1 cup of the puree, mixing until evenly blended. (Save the extra puree for another use. It's great on pancakes, with fresh berries, or with cheesecake or crepes.) Ladle the filling into the cooled pie shell.

5. Place the pie on the center oven rack and bake for 50 to 60 minutes, rotating the pie 180 degrees halfway through the baking, so that the part that faced the back of the oven now faces forward. When done, the filling will likely have puffed somewhat. The center may seem a little jiggly; that's fine. If after the allotted time, the pie seems overly puffy and the center a little underdone, turn the oven off and leave the pie in the hot oven for 10 to 15 minutes.

6. Transfer the pie to a wire rack and let cool to room temperature. Cover the pie with loosely tented aluminum foil and refrigerate for at least 2 hours. To serve, spoon some of the leftover puree onto each plate and over each slice and garnish with blackberries, if desired.

Recipe for Success

▶ Since this is essentially a custard pie, you should observe the "low and slow" rule of baking. If you try to rush this pie by raising the oven temperature, the custard will "break" and result in a watery filling.

Sour Cream–Blackberry Pie

Like Marionberry Pie (page 162), this recipe comes courtesy of the Oregon Raspberry and Blackberry Commission. The idea couldn't be more deliciously simple: Just put some berries in the bottom of a pie shell and pour a sweetened sour cream mixture over the top. Dust with streusel and bake. The creamy part of the filling bakes up something like a moist, spongy cake, covering the fruit below. I've tinkered with the commission's original recipe just a little, adding a couple of eggs (for a firmer filling), a pinch of salt, and some orange zest. In addition to blackberries, I've also made this with raspberries. It works beautifully either way, and I can't see any reason why the same basic formula couldn't be adapted to any other berry as well.

MAKES 8 TO 10 SERVINGS

1 recipe Basic Flaky Pie Pastry, Single Crust (page 31) or Tender Cream Cheese Pastry, Single Crust (page 46), refrigerated

FILLING

2 large eggs, at room temperature

2 cups full-fat sour cream, at room temperature

3/4 cup granulated sugar

1/3 cup all-purpose flour

1/2 teaspoon vanilla extract

1/2 teaspoon grated orange zest

Big pinch of salt

3 cups fresh blackberries, raspberries, or other berries

STREUSEL TOPPING

3 tablespoons all-purpose flour

2 tablespoons firmly packed light brown sugar

1 tablespoon unsalted butter, melted

1.   If you haven't already, prepare the pastry and refrigerate until firm enough to roll, about 1 hour.

2.   On a sheet of lightly floured waxed paper, roll the pastry into a 13-inch circle with a floured rolling pin. Invert the pastry over a 9½-inch deep-dish pie pan, center, and peel off the paper. Tuck the pastry into the pan, without stretching it, and sculpt the edge into an upstanding ridge. Place in the freezer for 15 minutes, then partially prebake and let cool according to the instructions on page 16. Reduce the oven temperature to 350°F.

3.   Whisk the eggs in a large bowl just until frothy. Add the sour cream, granulated sugar, flour, vanilla, orange zest, and salt, whisking again until evenly blended. Spread the berries evenly in the cooled pie shell, then ladle the sour cream mixture over them.

4.   To make the streusel, combine the flour and brown sugar in a small bowl and mix with your fingers. Add the butter, stirring with a fork. Switch to your fingers and gently rub the topping until it is crumbly. Add a bit more brown sugar or granulated sugar if the mixture is too clumpy. Sprinkle the topping evenly over the sour cream filling.

5.   Place the pie on the center oven rack and bake until the filling is set, about 35 minutes. When done, the filling will likely have puffed slightly and will no longer seem liquid-loose. Don't expect the top of the pie to brown much, if at all, because it isn't in the oven quite long enough.

6.   Transfer the pie to a wire rack and let cool thoroughly. Serve at room temperature, or cover with loosely tented aluminum foil and refrigerate before serving.

Recipe for Success

▶   **If you rinse your berries in a colander before using them (I suspect you do, unless you grow them or are certain of the source), be sure to drain them well on paper towels to keep the pie filling from getting watery. I start by lining a baking sheet with a double layer of paper towels. I give the berries a quick rinse with cold water, then a shake or two to knock off any excess water. Then I upend them onto the paper towels and gently spread them out to (at least partially) air-dry. If I'm using raspberries, I turn them stem end down so that any water that's trapped in the berries drains out.**

Patsy's Blackberry-Rhubarb Freeform Pie

My friend and colleague Patsy Jamieson, food editor of *Eating Well* magazine, knows her way around pies, as you'll discover when you try this blackberry rhubarb version baked *crostata-*style. She calls this pie a celebration of spring—spring indeed being something to celebrate when you live and work where she does, in northern Vermont. In addition to fresh rhubarb, Patsy uses frozen blackberries, a great complementary flavor and color enhancer. (You can, of course, use fresh blackberries when they're in season.) Since Patsy's specialty is reduced-fat recipes, you'll be delighted how much great flavor there is in this pie with a relatively small amount of butter. Her crumb topping, made with orange juice concentrate, is delicious.

MAKES 10 SERVINGS

1 recipe Patsy's Cottage Cheese Pastry (page 47), refrigerated

FILLING AND TOPPING

2/3 cup all-purpose flour

1/4 cup firmly packed light brown sugar

1/2 teaspoon ground cinnamon

2 teaspoons cold salted or unsalted butter, cut into 1/4-inch pieces

1 tablespoon canola oil or other vegetable oil

1 tablespoon frozen orange juice concentrate, thawed

1/4 cup sliced almonds

3 cups fresh rhubarb stalks sliced crosswise 1/2 inch thick

1 cup individually frozen blackberries (not packed in syrup), partially thawed

3/4 cup plus 1 teaspoon granulated sugar

1 large egg white

1 tablespoon water

1.   If you haven't already, prepare the pastry and refrigerate until firm enough to roll, about 1 hour.

2.   Combine the flour, brown sugar, and cinnamon in a medium-size bowl. Reserve 2 tablespoons of this mixture in a small bowl. Add the butter to the larger portion and rub it into the dry mixture with your fingers until crumbly. Add the oil and orange juice concentrate, tossing lightly with a fork to blend. Add the almonds, then rub the mixture gently between your fingers to form evenly mixed crumbs. Refrigerate until ready to use.

3.   Combine the rhubarb, blackberries, and 3/4 cup of the granulated sugar in a medium-size bowl and place in the refrigerator. Preheat the oven to 425°F. Line a large

baking sheet with lightly oiled parchment paper or aluminum foil. (Juicy fillings like this often spring a leak, and lining the sheet will make the cleanup much easier.)

4.   On a sheet of lightly floured waxed paper, roll the pastry into a 13½-inch circle with a floured rolling pin. Invert the pastry over the baking sheet, center, and peel off the paper. Without upsetting the overhanging dough, put the entire baking sheet in the refrigerator for 5 minutes to refirm the pastry. Imagine an 8-inch circle in the center of the pastry. Sprinkle the 2 tablespoons reserved flour–sugar mixture over this area. Pour the fruit filling over the same area, then even it out with your hands or a fork. Sprinkle the topping evenly over the fruit.

5.   Using a spatula to help you lift the pastry, fold the uncovered portion over the filling. The pastry will sort of self-pleat as you do so. (See the illustration of a freeform crust on page 153 for what this should look like.) Whisk the egg white and water together in a small bowl and brush the mixture over the exposed pastry. Sprinkle with the remaining 1 teaspoon sugar.

6.   Place the pie on the center oven rack and bake for 15 minutes. Reduce the oven temperature to 350°F and continue to bake until the crust is golden brown and the fruit bubbly, 25 to 35 minutes. Rotate the baking sheet 180 degrees, so that the side that faced the back of the oven now faces forward, about 15 minutes before it is done. If the pie starts to get a little too dark, cover with loosely tented aluminum foil.

7.   Transfer the pie, on the sheet, to a wire rack. Let cool for 10 minutes, then slide the pie, with the foil or parchment, onto the rack to finish cooling. Serve warm.

Recipe for Success

▶   It's always best to line your baking sheet with aluminum foil or parchment when you're baking a juicy freeform pie such as this one. Invariably, hot juice will seep through a thin spot in the pastry. There's really no way to stop the leak, and the best thing to do is nothing, because the leaking juice will harden and plug the hole. If you do spring a leak, it helps to run a spatula between the pie and the parchment or foil as soon as the pie comes out of the oven to keep the pie from sticking.

Deep-Dish Blackberry-Peach Double-Crust Pie

This is a favorite pie from my New Hampshire days, when I used to make it with handpicked blackberries and, when I could get my hands on them, Reliance peaches, a delicious cold-hardy peach developed by Dr. Elwyn Meader of Rochester, New Hampshire. It's a very thick summer pie with so much fruit that I bake it in one of my extra-deep-dish pie pans. (You can bake it in a 9½-inch deep-dish pan, but you'll have to reduce the amount of fruit to about 6½ cups.)

Peaches can be peeled by hand, with a sharp paring knife, but here we use another method: blanching them. Blanching really takes no longer than peeling by hand and the upside is you don't lose any of the precious sweet flesh that you're bound to cut off when using a knife. The combination of peaches and blackberries in a flaky double crust is hard to beat.

MAKES 8 TO 10 SERVINGS

1 recipe Basic Flaky Pie Pastry, Double Crust (page 31), refrigerated

FILLING

6 to 8 small to medium-size ripe peaches

4 cups fresh or individually frozen blackberries (not packed in syrup), partially thawed

½ cup plus 3 tablespoons sugar

3½ tablespoons cornstarch

¼ teaspoon ground nutmeg

1 tablespoon fresh lemon juice

1 teaspoon grated lemon zest

2 tablespoons cold unsalted butter, cut into small pieces

GLAZE

Milk or light cream

Sugar

1.   If you haven't already, prepare the pastry and refrigerate until firm enough to roll, about 1 hour.

2.   While the pastry chills, blanch the peaches as described on page 88. After you slip off the skins, slice the peaches into a large measuring cup; you'll need 4 cups. (Reserve any remaining peaches for another use.) Combine the sliced peaches, blackberries, and ½ cup of the sugar in a large bowl. Toss well to combine and set aside for 15 minutes.

3.   On a sheet of lightly floured waxed paper, roll the larger portion of the pastry into a 13½-inch circle with a floured rolling pin. Invert the pastry over a 9½- to 10-inch extra-deep-dish pie pan, center, and peel off the paper. Gently tuck the pastry into the pan,

without stretching it, and let the overhang drape over the edge. Place in the refrigerator for 15 minutes.

4. In a small bowl, mix the remaining 3 tablespoons sugar with the cornstarch. Stir the mixture into the fruit along with the nutmeg, lemon juice, and lemon zest. Preheat the oven to 400°F.

5. On another sheet of lightly floured waxed paper, roll the other half of the pastry into an 11½-inch circle. Turn the filling into the chilled pie shell. Smooth the fruit with a spoon and dot with the butter. Lightly moisten the rim of the pie shell. Invert the top pastry over the filling, center, and peel off the paper. Press the top and bottom pastries together along the dampened edge. Trim the pastry with scissors or a paring knife, leaving an even ½-inch overhang all around, then sculpt the overhang into an upstanding ridge. Poke several steam vents in the top of the pie with a fork or paring knife. Put a couple of the vents near the edge of the crust so you can check the juices there later. To glaze the pie, lightly brush the pastry with milk and sprinkle with sugar.

6. Place the pie on the center oven rack and bake for 30 minutes. Reduce the oven temperature to 375°F and rotate the pie 180 degrees, so that the part that faced the back of the oven now faces forward. Just in case, slide a large aluminum foil–lined baking sheet onto the rack below to catch any drips. Continue to bake until the juices bubble thickly at the steam vents and the top is golden brown, 35 to 45 minutes. If the top starts to get too dark, cover it with loosely tented aluminum foil during the last 15 minutes.

7. Transfer the pie to a wire rack and let cool for at least 2 hours before serving.

Recipe for Success

▶ Whatever pie pan you use, there should be at least ½ to ¾ inch of headroom between the top of the filling and the rim of the pan to minimize spillover.

A Guardian Angel for Pie Bakers

Besides being irresistibly delicious, fruit pies have something else in common: they like to bubble over late in the baking and leave a mess all over the oven floor. You, of course, know this and take precautions, sliding a large aluminum foil–lined baking sheet onto the rack below the pie to catch the spills.

I've recently run across another clever product that doubles nicely for a foil-lined baking sheet. It's called an oven guard, and it looks a little like a dark metal donut with flared edges to contain any spills. You bake your pie right on top of the oven guard; the hole in the center allows direct heat penetration to the center of the pie, so your pie shell browns nicely. I like to use it for the second half of the baking, just as I do my foil-lined sheet. If the pie does spill over, the finish is nonstick and the drips can be easily washed off. Look for an oven guard at kitchenware stores and at www.kingarthurflour.com.

Marionberry Pie

Marionberries, fans say, are a more complex- and delicious-tasting blackberry—"the Cabernet of blackberries," as they're called. Named for Marion County, Oregon, fresh Marionberries are a rarity outside the Northwest. So for advice on making the best Marionberry pie, I went to the Oregon Raspberry and Blackberry Commission and found this great recipe on its Web site, www.oregon-berries.com. (I know it's great because I made it with regular, everyday blackberries and it was wonderful.) This isn't a baked pie; the filling is cooked in a saucepan and poured into a prebaked crust. Half of the berries are cooked and thickened with cornstarch. The other half are folded into the cooked berries, so the filling has a nice blend of cooked and fresh flavors and textures. Since nearly all Marionberries are sold frozen, that's what this pie is made with. If you can't find frozen Marionberries, use blackberries, fresh or frozen. This pie is great served with whipped cream or vanilla ice cream.

MAKES 8 TO 10 SERVINGS

1 recipe Basic Flaky Pie Pastry, Single Crust (page 31), refrigerated

FILLING
5 cups individually frozen Marionberries or blackberries (not packed in syrup)

2 tablespoons fresh lemon juice

1 cup sugar

1/4 cup cornstarch

1.   If you haven't already, prepare the pastry and refrigerate until firm enough to roll, about 1 hour.

2.   On a sheet of lightly floured waxed paper, roll the pastry into a 12-inch circle with a floured rolling pin. Invert the pastry over a 9-inch standard pie pan, center, and peel off the paper. Tuck the pastry into the pan, without stretching it, and sculpt the edge into an upstanding ridge. Place in the freezer for 15 minutes, then fully prebake and let cool according to the instructions on page 16.

3.   Place half of the frozen berries and the lemon juice in a medium-size, preferably nonstick nonreactive saucepan. Using a pastry blender or potato masher, mash the berries well. Place over low heat and start heating the berries gently. Meanwhile, mix the sugar and cornstarch together in a small bowl. When the berries have put off a fair amount of juice, stir in this mixture. Increase the heat slightly and bring the berry mixture to a boil,

stirring often. Boil for 1 minute, stirring virtually nonstop to keep the fruit from spattering. Remove from the heat and scrape the fruit into a shallow bowl. Let cool, then refrigerate for about 1 hour.

4. Gently fold the remaining berries into the chilled fruit. Scrape the filling into the cooled pie shell and smooth the top with a spoon. Cover with loosely tented aluminum foil and refrigerate for at least 1 hour before serving.

Recipe for Success

▶ **As the pie shell gets no further baking, make sure it is fully prebaked to a rich golden brown.**

▶ **This pie is best served the same day. The filling will trap and absorb a certain amount of juice released by the whole frozen berries, but eventually it will start to puddle in the filling.**

Marionberry Pie with Hazelnut Crumb Topping

This pie features two of Oregon's premier agricultural products, Marionberries, considered by some to be the best-tasting type of blackberries, and hazelnuts, the latter toasted and scattered over the fruit in the form of a crumb topping. The hazelnuts—whose flavor components are sometimes compared to those in some wines and Brie cheese—add a sharp toasted flavor to the sweet fruit. It's really a wonderful combination.

MAKES 8 TO 10 SERVINGS

1 recipe Basic Flaky Pie Pastry, Single Crust (page 31), refrigerated

FILLING

4^1/$_2$ cups Marionberries or blackberries, fresh or individually frozen (not packed in syrup), partially thawed

^{2}/$_3$ cup sugar

1^1/$_2$ tablespoons cornstarch

1 tablespoon fresh lemon juice

Pinch of salt

HAZELNUT CRUMB TOPPING

^{3}/$_4$ cup hazelnuts, toasted (see box)

^{1}/$_2$ cup sugar

^{1}/$_4$ teaspoon salt

6 tablespoons (^{3}/$_4$ stick) cold unsalted butter, cut into ^{1}/$_4$-inch pieces

1 tablespoon milk or light cream

1. If you haven't already, prepare the pastry and refrigerate until firm enough to roll, about 1 hour.

2. On a sheet of lightly floured waxed paper, roll the pastry into a 12-inch circle with a floured rolling pin. Invert the pastry over a 9-inch standard pie pan, center, and peel off the paper. Tuck the pastry into the pan, without stretching it, and sculpt the edge into an upstanding ridge. Place in the freezer for 15 minutes. Preheat the oven to 400°F.

3. Put the Marionberries in a large bowl. Mix the sugar and cornstarch together in a small bowl, then stir the mixture into the fruit along with the lemon juice and salt. Set aside for 10 minutes to juice. Scrape the filling into the chilled pie shell and smooth the top with a spoon. Place the pie on the center oven rack and bake for 30 minutes.

4. Meanwhile, make the topping. Combine the hazelnuts, sugar, and salt in a food processor and pulse until the nuts are fairly well chopped. Scatter the butter over the top and pulse again until the mixture resembles fine crumbs. Sprinkle the milk over the mixture and pulse again briefly. Transfer the topping to a medium-size bowl and rub it between your fingers to make damp, gravelly crumbs. Refrigerate until ready to use.

5. Remove the pie from the oven and reduce the temperature to 375°F. Carefully dump the crumbs in the center of the pie, spreading them evenly over the surface with your hands. Tamp them down lightly. Return the pie to the oven, placing it so that the part that faced the back of the oven now faces forward. Just in case, slide a large aluminum foil–lined baking sheet onto the rack below to catch any drips. Continue to bake until the juices bubble thickly around the edge, 30 to 40 minutes. If necessary, cover with loosely tented aluminum foil for the last 15 minutes to keep the top from turning too dark.

6. Transfer the pie to a wire rack and let cool for at least 2 hours before serving.

Recipe for Success

▶ Much as I love the hazelnut's distinctive flavor here, if you'd rather not bother with them and you have other nuts on hand that don't require peeling, such as pecans or walnuts, those will work fine, too.

▶ This recipe works wonderfully as a mixed-fruit pie. If you like, substitute half raspberries or blueberries, or even 2 cups thinly sliced pears, for an equal amount of the Marionberries.

Loganberry Pie with Sour Cream Topping

My favorite book on American Northwest cooking is Janie Hibler's *Dungeness Crabs and Blackberry Cobblers* (Knopf, 1991). I'm sorry to say I've not spent much time in the northwestern states, but with Hibler's book, I have been an enthusiastic armchair traveler there, tasting my way through wild mushroom pizzas, delicious salmon and caper spreads, and wonderful berry pies and tarts. Loganberries, Hibler writes, are a variety of blackberry grown commercially in the Pacific Northwest. Their intense berry flavor and slight tartness, she says, make them perfect candidates for pies and preserves. Although loganberries can add an irresistible splash of color and flavor to mixed-fruit pies, it is a real treat to use them alone in a pie. Here, adapted from a recipe in Hibler's book, is a pie in which I do just that. The pie is first baked open-faced, then cooled briefly and draped with a sweet-tart sour cream coating. It's a great taste of the Northwest and a fine way to enjoy these delicious berries.

MAKES 8 TO 10 SERVINGS

1 recipe Basic Shortening Pie Pastry, Single Crust (page 30) or Basic Flaky Pie Pastry, Single Crust (page 31), refrigerated

FILLING

4 cups loganberries, fresh or individually frozen (not packed in syrup), partially thawed

1 cup sugar

1 tablespoon fresh lemon juice

2 tablespoons cornstarch

SOUR CREAM TOPPING

1¼ cups full-fat sour cream

3 tablespoons sugar

1 teaspoon vanilla extract

1. If you haven't already, prepare the pastry and refrigerate until firm enough to roll, about 1 hour.

2. On a sheet of lightly floured waxed paper, roll the pastry into a 12-inch circle with a floured rolling pin. Invert the pastry over a 9-inch standard pie pan, center, and peel off the paper. Tuck the pastry into the pan, without stretching it, and sculpt the edge into an upstanding ridge. Place in the freezer for 15 minutes.

3. Combine the loganberries, ³/₄ cup of the sugar, and the lemon juice in a large bowl. Mix well and set aside for 10 minutes. Preheat the oven to 400°F.

4. Mix the remaining ¼ cup sugar and the cornstarch together in a small bowl, then stir the mixture into the fruit. Turn the filling into the chilled pie shell and smooth the top of the fruit with a spoon.

5. Place the pie on the center oven rack and bake for 25 minutes. Reduce the oven temperature to 375°F and rotate the pie 180 degrees, so that the part that faced the back of the oven now faces forward. Just in case, slide a large aluminum foil–lined baking sheet onto the rack below to catch any drips. Continue to bake until the juices bubble thickly around the edge and in the center of the pie, 20 to 25 minutes.

6. Transfer the pie to a wire rack and let cool for 30 minutes.

7. To make the topping, combine the sour cream and sugar in a small, heavy saucepan over low heat. Stirring virtually nonstop, gently heat the mixture until it is warm and thin enough to pour, about 3 minutes. Stir in the vanilla. Slowly pour the sour cream over the center of the pie or simply smooth it out with a spoon. Gently jiggle the pie to spread the topping.

8. Put the pie back on the rack and let cool thoroughly. Serve at room temperature or cover with loosely tented aluminum foil and refrigerate until serving. I prefer it slightly chilled.

Recipe for Success

▶ Be careful not to overheat the sour cream mixture or it will curdle in the pan and become unusable.

▶ For a slight caramel flavor, use brown sugar in place of the granulated sugar in the topping.

▶ Don't worry too much if the sour cream and pie juices bleed together when you add the topping. It's bound to happen a bit, and a little berry color in the white sour cream will only whet the appetite.

Blueberry–Sour Cream Pie

This is one of the easiest pies you can make, even more so if you cheat a little and use a store-bought graham cracker crust. A layer of frozen blueberries cooked on the stovetop and thickened with cornstarch goes on top of the crust. Once that has cooled, a layer of blended, sweetened cream cheese and sour cream is spooned on top. And that's all there is to it. It looks, and tastes, almost like an upside-down blueberry cheesecake, but with a lot less effort. If fresh blueberries are in season, you can press a handful of them into the cooked berries when you spoon them into the pie shell. The combination of uncooked and cooked berries is very good.

MAKES 8 TO 10 SERVINGS

1 recipe Graham Cracker Crumb Crust (page 51) or 1 large store-bought graham cracker crust

FILLING

One 1-pound bag individually frozen blueberries (not packed in syrup)

1 1/2 tablespoons fresh lemon juice

1/3 cup granulated sugar

2 tablespoons cornstarch

1/2 teaspoon vanilla extract

Handful of fresh blueberries (optional)

CREAM CHEESE–SOUR CREAM TOPPING

One 8-ounce package full-fat cream cheese, softened

1/3 cup confectioners' sugar, sifted

2 tablespoons granulated sugar

1 teaspoon finely grated lemon zest

1/2 cup full-fat sour cream

1/4 teaspoon vanilla extract

GARNISH

Handful of fresh blueberries or threads of lemon zest (optional)

1. Prepare the crust and press it into the bottom and up the side of a 9½-inch deep-dish pie pan. Refrigerate, prebake, and let cool as directed. If you're using a store-bought crust, prebake as directed on the package and let cool.

2. Combine the frozen blueberries and lemon juice in a medium-size nonreactive saucepan. Cover, and cook over medium to low heat until the blueberries are almost simmering in their own liquid. Mix the granulated sugar and cornstarch together in a small bowl, then stir the mixture into the blueberries. Bring the fruit to a boil, stirring. Once the fruit starts to boil, reduce the heat a little and cook, stirring nonstop, for 1½ minutes. Remove from the heat and stir in the vanilla. Scrape the fruit into a shallow bowl and let cool for 15 minutes.

3. Spoon the partially cooled filling into the cooled pie shell and smooth with a spoon. If you're using fresh berries, scatter them over the fruit and press them into the cooked berries. Refrigerate for 30 to 60 minutes.

4. Meanwhile, make the topping. Using an electric mixer, beat the cream cheese, sugars, and lemon zest together in a medium-size bowl until smooth. Add the sour cream and vanilla and blend briefly until smooth. Spoon the filling over the chilled pie and smooth the top with a spoon. Cover with loosely tented aluminum foil and refrigerate for at least 2 hours.

5. Just before serving, garnish with the blueberries or lemon zest, if desired.

Recipe for Success

▶ When you're spooning the creamy topping over the fruit, take care that all of the topping is in place before you start to smooth it out. That way, you're more likely to avoid dipping the back of your spoon into the fruit filling and smearing blue streaks across the otherwise perfectly white surface. If that does happen and you're bothered by the streaks, you can always crush some vanilla wafers in a food processor or by hand and sprinkle them over the top to hide your boo-boo. Or you can garnish the pie with fresh berries.

Blueberry–Yogurt Cheese Pie

When you drain yogurt of all its whey, or extra liquid, you end up with what's known as yogurt cheese. It's not really cheese, but it does have a soft cream cheese–like consistency that's firm enough to support a layer of cooked blueberries and thus make a fine pie. You'll need to start this pie the day before you plan to serve it, because the yogurt needs plenty of time to drain and get relatively firm. Once this pie is assembled, give it a couple of hours in the fridge to firm up before serving. Instead of making this in a standard 9-inch pie pan, you can also use a large store-bought graham cracker crust.

MAKES 8 TO 10 SERVINGS

1 recipe Graham Cracker Crumb Crust (page 51) or 1 large store-bought graham cracker crust

FILLING

One 1-pound bag individually frozen blueberries (not packed in syrup)

1/4 cup orange juice

1/3 cup plus 2 tablespoons granulated sugar

1 1/2 tablespoons cornstarch

2 teaspoons fresh lemon juice

1 teaspoon minced candied (crystallized) ginger (optional)

One 32-ounce container plain yogurt (see Recipe for Success), drained for at least 12 hours (see box)

1/3 cup confectioners' sugar, sifted

1/4 teaspoon vanilla extract

GARNISH

Long threads of lemon zest (optional)

1. Prepare the crust and press it into the bottom and up the side of a 9-inch standard pie pan. Refrigerate, prebake, and let cool as directed. Or simply prebake a store-bought crust as directed on the package and let cool.

2. About an hour or so before you plan to assemble the pie, combine the frozen blueberries, orange juice, and 1/3 cup of the granulated sugar in a medium-size nonreactive saucepan over medium heat. Cook, stirring occasionally, until hot and the berries have put off a lot of their juice, about 5 minutes. Mix together the remaining 2 tablespoons granulated sugar and the cornstarch in a small bowl. Stir the mixture into the blueberries. Bring the berries to a boil, stirring, and gently boil for about 1 1/2 minutes, until thickened. Remove from the heat and stir in the lemon juice and ginger (if using). Scrape the berries into a wide bowl and let cool to room temperature. Once cooled, refrigerate for at least 30 minutes.

3. To assemble the pie, transfer the drained yogurt to a medium-size bowl. Stir in the confectioners' sugar until smooth, then stir in the vanilla. Spoon the yogurt into the cooled pie shell, smoothing it over the bottom and up the sides. Spoon the cooled blueberries over the yogurt and smooth with a spoon. Garnish, if desired, with long threads of lemon zest. Cover with loosely tented aluminum foil and refrigerate for at least 1 hour or overnight before serving.

Recipe for Success

▶ I've made this pie with full-fat, lowfat, and nonfat yogurt, and they all work. I think you get better results, however, with full-fat yogurt. I'm not sure why, but it seems to drain better—perhaps because of the greater amount of starch in the lowfat and nonfat versions—and yield a firmer yogurt cheese, thus a firmer pie. I prefer Stonyfield Farm yogurt, made in New Hampshire.

Making Yogurt Cheese

The day before you plan to serve this pie, line a colander with cheesecloth or a clean, damp, very thin cotton tea towel. Place the colander in a bowl. Empty the yogurt into the cloth, pull up the sides of the cloth, and gather them on top of the yogurt. Put the bowl in the refrigerator and let the yogurt drain for at least 12 hours.

Wild Blueberry–Maple Pie with a Cornmeal Crust

The fun of writing your own pie cookbook is that you don't have to justify weighting the material toward your personal favorites. So without apology, I present yet another blueberry pie that I simply love. I think of this as a sort of "Best of New England" blueberry pie: small, sweet-tart wild blueberries sweetened with real maple syrup. The earthy cornmeal crust is a nod to earlier times, when cornmeal was much more commonly used in American kitchens. It's crunchy yet tender, the perfect crust when you want a rustic pie for your family or a casual gathering. I like to serve it with vanilla ice cream.

MAKES 8 TO 10 SERVINGS

1 recipe Cornmeal Pie Pastry, Double Crust (page 40), refrigerated (see Recipe for Success)

FILLING

3 cups wild blueberries, canned (drained), frozen (partially thawed), or fresh (picked over for stems)

$1/4$ cup pure maple syrup, preferably light or medium amber

2 tablespoons sugar

$1^1/2$ tablespoons cornstarch

1 tablespoon fresh lemon juice

$1/8$ teaspoon ground cinnamon

1. If you haven't already, prepare the pastry and refrigerate until firm enough to roll, about 1 hour.

2. On a sheet of lightly floured waxed paper, roll the larger portion of the pastry into a 12-inch circle with a floured rolling pin. Please note that this pastry is a little softer than some and the graininess from the cornmeal makes it slightly more fragile, so proceed delicately and with a well-floured pin. Invert the pastry over a 9-inch standard pie pan, center, and peel off the paper. Gently tuck the pastry into the pan, without stretching it, and let the overhang drape over the edge. Place in the refrigerator for 15 minutes.

3. Combine the blueberries and maple syrup in a medium-size bowl. Combine the sugar and cornstarch in a small bowl, then stir the mixture into the blueberries along with the lemon juice and cinnamon. Turn the filling into the chilled pie shell, smoothing the fruit with a spoon. Preheat the oven to 400°F.

4. Roll the other half of the pastry into a 10-inch circle on a sheet of lightly floured waxed paper. Moisten the outer edge of the pie shell with a pastry brush. Invert the top pastry over the filling, center, and peel off the paper. Press the top and bottom pastries together along the dampened edge. Using a knife, trim the pastry flush with the edge of the pan. Pinch and push the pastry slightly down inside the pan so that it sits just below the edge. Doing so will protect the pastry, which has a tendency to overbrown along the edge. Poke several steam vents in the top of the pie with a paring knife, twisting the knife to enlarge the holes slightly. Put a couple of the vents along the edge so you can check the juices there later.

5. Place the pie on the center oven rack and bake for 25 minutes. Reduce the oven temperature to 350°F and rotate the pie 180 degrees, so that the part that faced the back of the oven now faces forward. Just in case, slide a large aluminum foil–lined baking sheet onto the rack below to catch any spills. Continue to bake until the juices bubble thickly along the edge, 25 to 30 minutes. If the top pastry starts to get too brown, cover the pie with loosely tented aluminum foil during the last 10 to 15 minutes.

6. Transfer the pie to a wire rack and let cool for at least 1 hour before serving.

Recipe for Success

▶ If you've never rolled a pie pastry before, it might be better to use another pastry to make this pie—perhaps Basic Flaky Pie Pastry (page 31) or All-Butter Pie Pastry (page 28). Cornmeal pastry is a little temperamental and is better made by someone with a little rolling experience.

▶ Don't worry if the crust develops large cracks as it bakes. It is somewhat brittle because of the cornmeal, and occasionally the buildup of steam in the filling can cause enough pressure to break the crust, usually along the edge.

Spoken Like a True-Blue Yankee

"Cherry pie was never as important in New England as in other parts of the United States. Yankees prefer blueberry pie, which, when properly baked, is a glorious thing. Unfortunately, it is often made badly. Restaurant and store-bought blueberry pies usually have more flour or cornstarch in them than blueberries, and many home-baked blueberry pies are too runny."

—Jonathan Norton Leonard, *American Cooking: New England* (Time-Life Books, 1970)

Wyman's Wild Blueberry Lattice-Top Pie

Wyman's, founded in 1874 in Milbridge, Maine, is a big name in wild blueberry production. If you don't have a local source for wild blueberries, you'll probably end up with canned or frozen Wyman's berries. How are wild blueberries different from cultivated ones? They're smaller, with a more distinctive, sweeter flavor, and they're a little chewier as well. If you've never tried them, you really should. This lattice-top pie, Wyman's house recipe, is a great showcase for their flavor and deep blue color.

MAKES 8 TO 10 SERVINGS

1 recipe Basic Flaky Pie Pastry, Double Crust (page 31) or All-Butter Pie Pastry, Double Crust (page 28), modified as instructed in step 1 and refrigerated

FILLING

5 cups wild blueberries, fresh (picked over for stems), canned (drained), or frozen (partially thawed)

1/2 cup sugar

2 tablespoons cornstarch

1 tablespoon all-purpose flour

1/8 teaspoon ground cinnamon

1/8 teaspoon salt

1/2 teaspoon grated lemon zest

GLAZE

Milk or light cream

Sugar

1.   Prepare the pastry as directed, shaping half of it into a disk and the other half into a square; both should be about 3/4 inch thick. Wrap the pastry as usual and refrigerate until firm enough to roll, about 1 hour.

2.   On a sheet of lightly floured waxed paper, roll the round portion of pastry into a 12-inch circle with a floured rolling pin. Invert the pastry over a 9-inch standard pie pan, center, and peel off the paper. Gently tuck the pastry into the pan, without stretching it, and sculpt the overhang into an upstanding ridge. Place in the refrigerator for 15 minutes.

3.   Place the berries in a large bowl. In a small bowl, combine the sugar, cornstarch, flour, cinnamon, and salt. Stir the mixture into the fruit, then stir in the lemon zest. Preheat the oven to 425°F.

4.   On another sheet of lightly floured waxed paper, roll the square portion of dough into a rectangle about 10 inches square. Using a pastry wheel or pizza cutter and a ruler, cut the pastry into 8 lengthwise strips about 1 inch wide. Turn the filling into the chilled pie shell, smoothing the top with a spoon. Lay 5 strips vertically across the pie, evenly

spaced, as shown in figure 1. Fold back strips 2 and 4, then lay another strip directly across the center of the pie, as shown in figure 2. Unfold the folded dough strips, then fold back strips 1, 3, and 5. Lay another perpendicular strip across the pie, as shown in figure 3. Unfold the folded strips, then fold up strips 1, 3, and 5 on the other side of the pie. Place another perpendicular strip across the pie, as shown in figure 4, then unfold strips 1, 3, and 5. Trim the strips, then pinch the ends into the edge of the pastry. Lightly brush the pastry strips with milk and sprinkle the top of the pie with sugar.

5. Place the pie on the center oven rack and bake for 25 minutes. Reduce the oven temperature to 350°F and rotate the pie 180 degrees, so that the part that faced the back of the oven now faces forward. Just in case, put a large aluminum foil–lined baking sheet onto the rack below to catch any spills. Continue to bake until the top pastry is golden brown and any visible juices bubble thickly near the center, 35 to 40 minutes.

6. Transfer the pie to a wire rack and let cool for at least 2 hours before serving.

Recipe for Success

> ▸ Read about lattice-top pies on page 72 before making this pie.

> ▸ The Wyman's recipe doesn't call for it, but I like to add 1 tablespoon fresh lemon juice to the filling.

> ▸ If you're using Wyman's canned blueberries packed in water, you can boil down 1 cup of the drained juice from the cans to about one-quarter of its volume and add this to the filling for extra flavor. If you do, also add 1 teaspoon cornstarch.

Figure 1

Figure 2

Figure 3

Figure 4

Blueberry-Lime Pie

If you want a simple, low-stress, but delicious blueberry pie that can be made with frozen berries, here it is. To give the pie an unmistakable lime flavor, I use both grated lime zest and frozen limeade concentrate, a convenient product that allows you to use less sugar in the filling. Let this cool well before slicing, or it will be rather runny.

MAKES 8 TO 10 SERVINGS

1 recipe Basic Flaky Pie Pastry, Double Crust (page 31), refrigerated

FILLING

One 1-pound bag individually frozen blueberries (not packed in syrup), partially thawed (see Recipe for Success)

1/3 cup thawed frozen limeade concentrate

3 tablespoons sugar

3 tablespoons quick-cooking tapioca

1 teaspoon grated lime zest

GLAZE

Milk or light cream

Sugar

1. If you haven't already, prepare the pastry and refrigerate until firm enough to roll, about 1 hour.

2. On a sheet of lightly floured waxed paper, roll the larger portion of the pastry into a 12-inch circle with a floured rolling pin. Invert the pastry over a 9-inch standard pie pan, center, and peel off the paper. Gently tuck the pastry into the pan, without stretching it, and let the overhang drape over the edge. Place in the refrigerator for 15 minutes. Preheat the oven to 400°F.

3. Combine the blueberries, limeade concentrate, sugar, tapioca, and lime zest in a large bowl. Mix well, but try not to crush the blueberries. Set aside.

4. On another sheet of lightly floured waxed paper, roll the other half of the pastry into an 11-inch circle. Turn the filling into the chilled pie shell and smooth the top with a spoon. Lightly moisten the rim of the pie shell with a wet finger or pastry brush. Invert the top pastry over the filling, center, and peel off the paper. Press the top and bottom pastries together along the dampened edge. Trim the pastry with scissors or a paring knife, leaving an even 1/2-inch overhang all around, then sculpt the overhang into an upstanding ridge. Poke several steam vents in the top of the pie with a fork or paring knife. Put a couple of the vents near the edge of the crust so you can check the juices there later. Brush the top of the pie lightly with milk and sprinkle with sugar.

5. Place the pie on the center oven rack and bake for 30 minutes. Reduce the oven temperature to 375°F and rotate the pie 180 degrees, so that the part that faced the back of the oven now faces forward. Just in case, slide a large aluminum foil–lined baking sheet onto the rack below to catch any drips. Continue to bake until the top of the pie is golden brown and any juices visible at the steam vents bubble thickly, 20 to 25 minutes.

6. Transfer the pie to a wire rack and let cool for at least 2 hours before serving.

Recipe for Success

▶ It's not necessary to completely thaw the berries before you mix the filling. In fact, slightly cold and firm is okay, because it keeps the berries from turning to mush when you mix them. If you haven't taken them out of the freezer ahead, spread the frozen berries in a glass pie pan or other wide microwave-safe dish and heat them on medium power for about 30 seconds. Check and continue heating, if necessary, until they are partially thawed.

Blueberry-Peach Pie with Pecan Crumb Topping

For as long as I can remember, my favorite two fruits have been blueberries and peaches. And they are, to my pie maker's mind, infallible partners in a mixed-fruit pie. If for some reason I had to choose but one kind of mixed-fruit pie to eat for the rest of my life, this would be it: blueberries and peaches, topped with a pecan crumb topping. I readily admit to making this pie with frozen blueberries and, from time to time, frozen peaches. It's still great but, like most fruit pies, not what it can be with all fresh fruit, in season. My idea of a perfect summer afternoon would be some breezy conversation with friends or family on my deck, all of us nibbling on slices of this pie, with the hum of my ice cream maker in the background churning up a batch of fresh peach or vanilla ice cream.

MAKES 8 TO 10 SERVINGS

1 recipe Basic Flaky Pie Pastry, Single Crust (page 31), refrigerated

FILLING

3 cups wild or regular blueberries, fresh (picked over for stems) or frozen (partially thawed)

3 cups peeled, pitted, and sliced ripe peaches or frozen sliced peaches, partially thawed

1/2 cup plus 2 tablespoons sugar

1 tablespoon fresh lime juice

Grated zest of 1 lime

3 tablespoons cornstarch

PECAN CRUMB TOPPING

3/4 cup all-purpose flour

3/4 cup pecan halves

1/2 cup sugar

1/4 teaspoon salt

6 tablespoons (3/4 stick) cold unsalted butter, cut into 1/4-inch pieces

1 tablespoon milk or light cream

1. If you haven't already, prepare the pastry and refrigerate until firm enough to roll, about 1 hour.

2. On a sheet of lightly floured waxed paper, roll the pastry into a 13-inch circle with a floured rolling pin. Invert the pastry over a 9½-inch deep-dish pie pan, center, and peel off the paper. Tuck the pastry into the pan, without stretching it, and sculpt the edge into an upstanding ridge. Place in the freezer for 15 minutes. Preheat the oven to 400°F.

3. In a large bowl, combine the blueberries, peaches, ½ cup of the sugar, the lime juice, and lime zest. Mix well, then set aside for 10 minutes. Mix together the cornstarch and remaining 2 tablespoons sugar in a small bowl, then stir the mixture into the fruit.

4. Turn the filling into the chilled pie shell, smoothing the top with a spoon or your hands. Place the pie on the center oven rack and bake for 30 minutes.

5. Meanwhile, make the topping. Combine the flour, pecans, sugar, and salt in a food processor. Pulse several times to chop the nuts coarsely. Scatter the butter over the top and pulse again until the mixture resembles fine crumbs. Sprinkle the milk over the mixture and pulse again briefly. Transfer the topping to a medium-size bowl and rub it between your fingers to make damp, gravelly crumbs. Refrigerate until ready to use.

6. Remove the pie from the oven and reduce the temperature to 375°F. Carefully dump the crumbs in the center of the pie, spreading them evenly over the surface with your hands. Tamp them down lightly. Return the pie to the oven, placing it so that the part that faced the back of the oven now faces forward. Just in case, slide a large aluminum foil–lined baking sheet onto the rack below to catch any drips. Continue to bake until the juices bubble thickly around the edge, 30 to 40 minutes. If necessary, cover the pie with loosely tented aluminum foil for the last 15 minutes to keep the top from getting too dark.

7. Transfer the pie to a wire rack and let cool for at least 2 hours before serving.

Recipe for Success

▶ Although you can use either kind of blueberries, I like the small wild ones here. Given the choice, I think I'd choose frozen or canned (drained) wild blueberries over fresh regular ones.

▶ Canned peaches will work fine, too. My first choice would be sliced peaches in syrup, drained of all but a little of the juice.

Blueberries for Sale, 20 Cents a Quart

"Wild blueberries are best for pie. Picking them is still a considerable industry in Maine, where great areas of barren land are covered with low bushes that in season are covered with small, somewhat acid berries. In the rest of New England the bushes do best on burned-over forestland. This was the ravaged condition of much of Cape Cod's interior when I was a boy. Sometimes I picked as many as 20 quarts a day, which I divided between my family, gratis, and the grocery store across Main Street from our house, at 20 cents a quart. . . . The large cultivated berries that grow on big bushes in marshy areas are apt to be too sweet to make perfect pies. Yet even the sweetest can be remedied with a touch of lemon juice."

—Jonathan Norton Leonard, *American Cooking: New England* (Time-Life Books, 1970)

Blueberry-Pineapple Piña Colada Pie

This pie is absolutely delicious, with a tropical island flavor that makes it the perfect dessert for an islands theme party. But don't wait until then to try it! The secret ingredient? Frozen piña colada concentrate. It's great made with frozen or canned blueberries, but do use the little wild ones for the best flavor. This would be the perfect tailgate party pie, even more so at a Jimmy Buffet concert.

MAKES 8 TO 10 SERVINGS

1 recipe Basic Flaky Pie Pastry, Single Crust (page 31), refrigerated

FILLING

3 cups wild blueberries, canned (drained), frozen (partially thawed), or fresh (picked over for stems)

1 cup canned crushed pineapple, drained

1/3 cup thawed frozen piña colada concentrate

1/4 cup sugar

1 1/2 tablespoons cornstarch

1 tablespoon light or dark rum (optional)

1/2 teaspoon coconut or vanilla extract

Pinch of salt

COCONUT CRUMB TOPPING

3/4 cup all-purpose flour

3/4 cup sweetened flaked coconut

1/2 cup sugar

1/4 teaspoon salt

5 tablespoons cold unsalted butter, cut into 1/4-inch pieces

1. If you haven't already, prepare the pastry and refrigerate until firm enough to roll, about 1 hour.

2. On a sheet of lightly floured waxed paper, roll the pastry into a 12-inch circle with a floured rolling pin. Invert the pastry over a 9-inch standard pie pan, center, and peel off the paper. Tuck the pastry into the pan, without stretching it, and sculpt the edge into an upstanding ridge. Place in the freezer for 15 minutes. Preheat the oven to 400°F.

3. Combine the blueberries, pineapple, and piña colada concentrate in a large bowl. Mix the sugar and cornstarch together in a small bowl, then stir the mixture into the fruit. Stir in the rum (if using), coconut extract, and salt. Scrape the filling into the chilled pie shell and smooth the top with a spoon. Place the pie on the center oven rack and bake for 30 minutes.

4. Meanwhile, make the coconut crumb topping. Put the flour, coconut, sugar, and salt in a food processor and pulse briefly to mix. Scatter the butter over the top and pulse until the mixture starts to form gravelly crumbs. Dump the crumbs into a large bowl and rub between your fingers to form large, buttery crumbs. Refrigerate until ready to use.

5. Remove the pie from the oven and reduce the temperature to 375°F. Carefully dump the crumbs in the center of the pie, spreading them evenly over the surface with your hands. Tamp them down lightly. Return the pie to the oven, placing it so that the part that faced the back of the oven now faces forward. Just in case, slide a large aluminum foil–lined baking sheet onto the rack below to catch any spills. Continue to bake until the juices bubble thickly around the edge, about 30 minutes. If the top starts to get too brown, cover loosely with aluminum foil for the last 15 minutes.

6. Transfer the pie to a wire rack and let cool for at least 1 hour before serving.

Recipe for Success

▶ Remember that a pie made with frozen fruit can take as much as 20 to 30 minutes more to bake than one made with fresh. This is enough time to overbake the crust, especially the exposed areas. That why it's important that your fruit not be fully frozen when it goes into the pie shell. Once you've mixed the filling, it won't do any harm to let it sit in the bowl for an extra 15 to 20 minutes at room temperature to let the fruit thaw even longer before you turn it into the shell.

▶ Watch the pie closely during the last 20 minutes. Coconut tends to brown quickly, and the pie may have to be covered with aluminum foil near the end of the baking.

Jumble Berry Pie

Perhaps you've seen jumble berries around your home. Typically, they arrive in the summer when fresh berries are irresistibly in season: first a few leftover pancake blueberries, then some strawberries or a pint of raspberries dropped off by a friend. Before you know it, you have a jumble of berries. When that happens to me, I like to make this five-berry pie, throwing in some frozen cranberries for tartness and taste. (I always keep a few bags in the freezer.) It makes a wonderful finale for any summer meal and a fitting salute to berry season, served with vanilla ice cream. You'll need 5$1/2$ to 6 cups berries, in roughly the proportions given below, but feel free to tilt the balance one way or another as you like. If you enjoy this pie, also try one of the bumble berry pies on pages 184 and 185.

MAKES 8 TO 10 SERVINGS

1 recipe Basic Flaky Pie Pastry, Double Crust (page 31) or Tender Cream Cheese Pastry, Double Crust (page 46), refrigerated

FILLING

1 1/4 cups fresh blueberries, picked over for stems

1 1/4 cups hulled and sliced fresh strawberries

1 cup fresh raspberries

1 cup fresh blackberries

1 cup cranberries, fresh (picked over for stems) or frozen (partially thawed), coarsely chopped

1/2 cup sugar

1 1/2 tablespoons cornstarch

1/4 teaspoon ground nutmeg

Pinch of salt

1 tablespoon fresh lemon juice

1 teaspoon grated lemon zest

GLAZE

Heavy cream (see Recipe for Success)

Sugar

1. If you haven't already, prepare the pastry and refrigerate until firm enough to roll, about 1 hour.

2. On a sheet of lightly floured waxed paper, roll the larger portion of the pastry into a 12-inch circle with a floured rolling pin. Invert the pastry over a 9-inch standard pie pan, center, and peel off the paper. Gently tuck the pastry into the pan, without stretching it, and let the overhang drape over the edge. Place in the refrigerator for 15 minutes.

3. Combine the berries in a large bowl. Mix the sugar and cornstarch together in a small bowl, then stir the mixture into the fruit. Stir in the nutmeg, salt, lemon juice, and lemon zest. Set aside for 10 minutes. Preheat the oven to 400°F.

4. Roll the other half of the pastry into a 10-inch circle on a sheet of lightly floured waxed paper. Turn the filling into the chilled pie shell, smoothing the fruit with a spoon. Moisten the outer edge of the pie shell with a pastry brush. Invert the top pastry over the filling, center, and peel off the paper. Press the top and bottom pastries together along the dampened edge. Trim the edge to an even 1/2 inch all around, then sculpt the overhang into an upstanding ridge. Poke several steam vents in the top of the pie with a fork or paring knife. Put a couple of the vents near the edge so you can check the juices there later. Brush the top of the pie generously with heavy cream and sprinkle with sugar.

5. Place the pie on the center oven rack and bake for 30 minutes. Reduce the oven temperature to 375°F and rotate the pie 180 degrees, so that the part that faced the back of the oven now faces forward. Just in case, slide a large aluminum foil–lined baking sheet onto the rack below to catch any spills. Continue to bake until the juices, most likely visible at the steam vents, bubble thickly, 25 to 30 minutes. If the top pastry starts to get too brown, cover with loosely tented aluminum foil during the last 10 minutes.

6. Transfer the pie to a wire rack and let cool for at least 1 hour before serving.

Recipe for Success

▶ As much as possible, use fresh berries here. When they're not available, frozen is fine, but do let the berries thaw partially first. Some drained canned berries are okay, too.

▶ Using heavy cream, rather than milk or light cream, for the glaze yields a different result. It forms a second skin on top of the pastry—a brittle, blistered layer something like phyllo dough. It's quite delicious and adds another dimension of flavor and interest to any double-crust pie.

Orange-Berry Pie

Another fast pie made with frozen convenience products, this can be in the oven in about 5 minutes if you have a bag of mixed berries on hand. The orange flavor goes particularly well with vanilla ice cream, just the flourish this pie needs.

MAKES 8 TO 10 SERVINGS

1 store-bought frozen 9-inch deep-dish pie shell

FILLING

One 1-pound bag individually frozen mixed berries (not packed in syrup), partially thawed

2 tablespoons thawed frozen orange juice concentrate

1/3 cup sugar

1 1/2 tablespoons cornstarch

Pinch of salt

STREUSEL TOPPING

1/2 cup all-purpose flour

1/2 cup sugar

1/4 teaspoon ground cinnamon

1/8 teaspoon salt

4 tablespoons cold unsalted butter, cut into 1/4-inch pieces

1. Remove the pie shell from the package but leave it in the freezer for now. Preheat the oven to 400°F.

2. Combine the berries and orange juice concentrate in a large bowl. In a small bowl, mix together the sugar, cornstarch, and salt, then stir the mixture into the fruit. Turn the filling into the frozen pie shell. Place the pie on the center oven rack and bake for 25 minutes.

3. Meanwhile, make the topping. Place the flour, sugar, cinnamon, and salt in a food processor and pulse several times to mix. Scatter the butter over the top and pulse until the mixture resembles fine crumbs. Empty the crumbs into a medium-size bowl and rub between your fingers to make large, buttery crumbs. Refrigerate until ready to use.

4. Remove the pie from the oven and reduce the temperature to 375°F. Carefully dump the crumbs over the pie, spreading them evenly over the surface with your hands. Tamp them down lightly. Return the pie to the oven, placing it so that the part that faced the back of the oven now faces forward. Just in case, slide a large aluminum foil–lined baking sheet onto the rack below to catch any drips. Continue to bake until the topping is golden brown and the juices bubble thickly around the edge, about 25 minutes.

5. Transfer the pie to a wire rack and let cool for at least 2 hours before serving.

Recipe for Success

▶ Typically, bags of frozen mixed berries contain large strawberries. If that's indeed the case, be sure to cut each of them into several smaller pieces for better distribution before mixing the filling.

▶ If your berries are frozen solid, you can get them to the partially thawed state by putting them in the microwave on defrost for 2 to 3 minutes.

The Dean of American Cooking Weighs In on Pies

"If winters were cold, pies were made in quantity and put out to freeze. The varieties were limited to the supplies at hand, but dried fruit was always available to the thrifty housekeeper. Sometimes the pies were layered. For instance, fresh or dried and simmered apple slices might be topped with custard or a cottage cheese custard; and mince might be topped with apple, cranberries, pumpkin, or sometimes apple and custard. Such recipes do not appear in cookbooks, but have come down to us in old diaries or literature of the time."

—James Beard, *James Beard's American Cookery* (Little, Brown and Company, 1972)

Dundee Arms Inn Bumble Berry Pie

The Dundee Arms Inn on Prince Edward Island is a Victorian-era home built in 1903 by a prosperous local businessman. Today owner and innkeeper Pat Sands presides over this lovingly restored Charlottetown guest house, well-known for its delicious cuisine. One of the guests' favorite desserts is this version of bumble berry pie. Bumble berry (it's often spelled as one word) refers generally to a mixed-berry pie that often includes rhubarb and apple. In this rather unusual version, the top crust is not rolled. Instead, the pastry is formed into a ball, frozen, and then grated over the filling as if it were a block of cheese. I thought this rather odd at first, but then I was taken by how clever it is—so much so that I've used this trick for several other pies in this collection.

MAKES 8 TO 10 SERVINGS

1 recipe Basic Flaky Pie Pastry, Double Crust (page 31), refrigerated

FILLING

1 cup fresh raspberries

1 cup fresh blueberries, picked over for stems

1 cup hulled and sliced fresh strawberries

1 cup fresh rhubarb stalks sliced crosswise 1/2 inch thick

1 cup granulated sugar

2 tablespoons fresh lemon juice

1/3 cup all-purpose flour

2 tablespoons cold unsalted butter, cut into small pieces

GLAZE

About 1 tablespoon coarse sugar (see page 69) or granulated sugar

1. If you haven't already, prepare the pastry and refrigerate until firm enough to roll, about 1 hour.

2. On a sheet of lightly floured waxed paper, roll the larger half of the pastry into a 13-inch circle with a floured rolling pin. Invert the pastry over a 9½-inch deep-dish pie pan, center, and peel off the paper. Tuck the pastry into the pan, without stretching it, and sculpt the edge into an upstanding ridge. Place in the freezer for 15 minutes. Also place the unrolled pastry in the freezer. Preheat the oven to 400°F.

3. Combine the berries, rhubarb, sugar, and lemon juice in a large bowl. Toss gently to mix. Add the flour and toss again gently. Turn the filling into the chilled pie shell, smoothing the top of the fruit with a spoon. Dot the top of the filling with the butter.

4.   Using the large holes of a box grater, grate the other half of the pastry directly over the fruit, as if it were a block of cheese. Using a fork, gently move the gratings here and there for an even covering. Sprinkle the coarse sugar over the top.

5.   Place the pie on the center oven rack and bake for 30 minutes. Reduce the oven temperature to 375°F and rotate the pie 180 degrees, so that the part that faced the back of the oven now faces forward. Just in case, slide a large aluminum foil–lined baking pan onto the rack below to catch any spills. Continue to bake until the top is golden brown and the juices bubble thickly around the edge, 25 to 30 minutes.

6.   Transfer the pie to a wire rack and let cool for at least 2 hours before serving.

Recipe for Success

▶ **The pastry chef at the Dundee Arms Inn likes to use fresh fruit here, but feel free to substitute some frozen fruit, if necessary. When using fresh fruit, toss gently to maintain the shape of the fruit.**

▶ **Don't be too concerned about making the top of the pastry nice and even. If it's a little clumpy, that's fine. The pastry tends to settle in the heat of the oven, leaving a cobbler-like finish.**

Bumble Berry Pie II

So enamored was I of both the name bumble berry and the Dundee Arms version of this great pie (see page 184) that I decided to create another version that could be made simply, with store-bought pie pastry. In addition to the blackberries and blueberries, this one has a shredded apple, a plum, and cherries. The apple and plum are a little hard to identify once the pie has baked, but they give it a wonderfully complex flavor that I think you'll enjoy.

MAKES 8 TO 10 SERVINGS

2 store-bought refrigerated pie pastries

FILLING

1 cup fresh blueberries, picked over for stems

1 cup fresh blackberries or raspberries

1 cup pitted sweet or sour cherries, canned (drained) or fresh

1 plum or Pluot (see page 120), unpeeled, pitted, and thinly sliced

1 large Granny Smith or other tart apple, peeled, cored, and shredded

1 teaspoon fresh lemon juice

$1/3$ cup plus 3 tablespoons sugar

$2 1/2$ tablespoons cornstarch

$1/8$ teaspoon ground nutmeg

2 tablespoons cold unsalted butter, cut into small pieces

1.   If you haven't already, remove the pie pastries from the refrigerator and let sit at room temperature for 15 to 20 minutes. Remove one of pastries from the package and line a 9-inch standard pie pan with it. Refrigerate.

2.   Combine the fruit and lemon juice in a large bowl. Add $1/3$ cup of the sugar and toss well to mix. Set aside for 10 minutes. Preheat the oven to 400°F.

3.   Combine the remaining 3 tablespoons sugar, the cornstarch, and nutmeg in a small bowl, then stir the mixture into the fruit. Turn the filling into the chilled pie shell, smooth the top, and dot with the butter. Using a wet finger or pastry brush, moisten the rim of the pie shell. Remove the other pastry from the package. Unfold, draping it over the top of the pie. Press the top and bottom pastries together at the dampened edge. Trim the pastry to an even $1/2$ inch all around, then sculpt the overhang into a upstanding ridge. Poke several steam vents in the top of the pie with a fork or paring knife. Put a couple of the vents near the edge so you can check the juices there later.

4.   Place the pie on the center oven rack and bake for 30 minutes Reduce the oven temperature to 375°F and rotate the pie 180 degrees, so that the part that faced the back of the oven now faces forward. Just in case, slide a large aluminum foil–lined baking sheet on the rack below to catch any spills. Bake until the top is dark golden brown and the juices visible at the steam vents bubble thickly, 25 to 30 minutes.

5.   Transfer the pie to a wire rack and let cool for at least 2 hours before serving.

Recipe for Success

▶   **This pie tastes delicious with almost any combination of fresh, frozen, or canned fruit. Try to use at least some fresh fruit, for best flavor and texture. And remember that frozen fruit should be partially thawed prior to mixing the filling.**

▶   **If you prefer a more textured pie, dice the apple rather than grating it.**

Patsy's Mixed-Berry Freeform Pie

Like my friend Patsy Jamieson, food editor of *Eating Well* magazine, I love to mix berries in summer pies. Here she does just that in a freeform pie with a base of cheesecake-like custard, which Patsy says makes a creamy contrast to the berries. Instead of a traditional butter pastry, this one uses Patsy's excellent cottage cheese pastry. In addition to the cottage cheese, it contains oil and baking powder, so the baked texture is more cake-like than crumbly, the way pastry typically is. It tastes delicious and makes a wonderful container for this special summer pie.

MAKES 8 TO 10 SERVINGS

1 recipe Patsy's Cottage Cheese Pastry (page 47), refrigerated

FILLING

4 ounces (half of an 8-ounce package) reduced-fat cream cheese (Neufchâtel cheese), softened

1/4 cup sugar

1 teaspoon cornstarch

1 large egg yolk

2 teaspoons grated lemon zest

1 teaspoon vanilla extract

4 cups fresh mixed berries, such as blackberries, raspberries, and blueberries (picked over for stems)

GLAZE

1 large egg white

1 tablespoon water

2 tablespoons sugar

1. If you haven't already, prepare the pastry and refrigerate for 1 hour, as directed.

2. Line a large baking sheet with lightly oiled parchment paper or aluminum foil. Preheat the oven to 400°F.

3. Using an electric mixer, beat the cream cheese, sugar, and cornstarch together in a medium-size bowl until smooth. Blend in the egg yolk, lemon zest, and vanilla until smooth. Set aside.

4. On a sheet of lightly floured waxed paper, roll the pastry into a 14-inch circle. Invert the pastry over the lined baking sheet, center, and peel off the paper, letting the pastry drape slightly over the edges, if necessary. Without upsetting the overhanging dough, put the entire baking sheet in the refrigerator for 5 minutes to refirm the pastry (see Recipe for Success).

5. Remove the baking sheet and pastry from the refrigerator. Imagine a circle about 8 inches in diameter in the center of the pastry. Spread the cream cheese mixture over that area, leaving a wide border all around. Pile the berries evenly over the mixture. Using

a metal spatula to help you lift it, fold the uncovered perimeter of pastry up and over the filling, enclosing it. The pastry will sort of self-pleat as you do this. (See the illustration of a freeform crust on page 153.)

6. To make the glaze, whisk the egg white with the water in a small bowl. Brush glaze lightly over the exposed portion of the pastry. Sprinkle the berries and pastry with the sugar.

7. Place the pie on the center oven rack and bake until the crust is deep golden brown, about 30 minutes. Transfer the baking sheet and pie to a wire rack and let cool for 10 minutes, then slide the pie, with the lining, onto the rack. Serve slightly warm or at room temperature.

Recipe for Success

▶ Because of the baking powder, Patsy's pastry is a little more delicate than some, which is why I give it an intermediate rest in the fridge to help firm it up for more handling. If you have a small fridge or a rather full one and putting the pastry—on a large baking sheet—in it is impractical, you can use an alternative method. Start rolling the pastry on the waxed paper as directed, until it is 10 or 11 inches in diameter. Slide the dough and paper onto a small baking sheet or tray, cover with plastic wrap, and refrigerate for 10 minutes. Then proceed with the rolling and filling.

Angel Pie with Berries, Cream, and Custard

You don't hear much about angel pie anymore. I think it's quite old-fashioned, and since it's really a dish of the moment—to be enjoyed soon after it's topped—you will rarely find anything like it in restaurants or bakeries. An angel pie is always made with a meringue crust—a good choice when you've just made a dish with lots of yolks and have the whites on hand. You can bake it in a pie pan, but after much trial and error, I've decided the best way to make the crust is freeform, on a parchment-lined baking sheet, to avoid any problems with sticking. The fun part comes after the crisp-cooked meringue is baked and you get to decide how to top it. Here we take a very elegant approach, mounding whipped cream, fresh raspberries and blueberries, and then custard sauce over everything. It's sliced and served right away, so the meringue stays crunchy and delicious. It's good for any occasion, but it's especially fitting for those traditionally female gatherings like tea parties and showers.

MAKES 8 SERVINGS

1 recipe Meringue Pie Crust (page 50)

Fresh Whipped Cream (page 605)

1/2 to 3/4 cup fresh raspberries

1/2 to 3/4 cup fresh blueberries, picked over for stems

Crème Anglaise (page 606)

1. If you haven't already, prepare the meringue crust and set it aside to cool. Note that this is about a 2½-hour proposition from start to finish, because of the extended baking and cooling.

2. When you are ready to serve the pie, carefully place the crust on a large, flat serving platter. Smooth the whipped cream over the crust, then scatter the berries over the cream. Drizzle the top with the crème anglaise, just enough for decorative purposes. Slice and serve the pie in wedges, drizzling each piece with additional crème anglaise.

Recipe for Success

▶ Handle the meringue carefully when you're moving it, or it may shatter; it's somewhat fragile. If the worst happens, don't worry: just put the pieces back together, and when the other ingredients are added, no one will be the wiser.

▶ Use other berries on top, if you like. Small strawberries are great.

▶ If you shape the meringue into a rectangle, you'll have a great flag shape for a patriotic pie. Use white whipped cream and red and blue berries to create your own Fourth of July flag. Kids love this project.

It Must Be the Pie Diet

"When you look at the tremendous quantities of desserts they cook and eat, it's amazing that any Midwesterners are able to fit through a normal size doorway. Strangely enough, the majority of people in the Midwest are quite thin. . . . Many Midwestern community and church cookbooks, instead of starting out conventionally with chapters on appetizers and soups and proceeding through the rest of the meal to dessert and beverages, plunge right in and start off with the sweets. First things first."

—Glenn Andrews, *Food from the Heartland* (Prentice Hall, 1991)

Three-Berry Shortcake Pie

This is similar to Peach-Blueberry Cobbler Pie (page 104), though perhaps even truer to the shortcake theme because it uses all berries. Unlike the other version, the filling here is partially cooked on top of the stove. It's poured into a partially baked pie shell, the topping is spooned on right away, and the pie is baked for about 25 minutes. The shorter baking time helps preserve some of the berries' texture. As for the topping, this one has a little cornmeal for added texture, and it's made with milk instead of buttermilk. This makes a great breakfast, brunch, or dessert pie.

MAKES 8 TO 10 SERVINGS

1 recipe Basic Flaky Pie Pastry, Single Crust (page 31), refrigerated

FILLING

1¹/₂ cups fresh blueberries, picked over for stems

1¹/₂ cups fresh raspberries or blackberries

1¹/₂ cups hulled and thickly sliced fresh strawberries

¹/₃ cup sugar

1 tablespoon fresh lemon juice

¹/₄ cup orange juice

1 tablespoon plus 1 teaspoon cornstarch

SHORTCAKE TOPPING

1 cup all-purpose flour

¹/₄ cup fine yellow cornmeal

¹/₄ cup sugar

1¹/₂ teaspoons baking powder

¹/₂ teaspoon salt

¹/₄ cup (¹/₂ stick) cold unsalted butter, cut into ¹/₄-inch pieces

¹/₂ cup milk

1 large egg

¹/₂ teaspoon vanilla extract

GARNISH

Fresh Whipped Cream (page 605)

1. If you haven't already, prepare the pastry and refrigerate until firm enough to roll, about 1 hour.

2. On a sheet of lightly floured waxed paper, roll half of the pastry into a 13- to 13¹/₂-inch circle with a floured rolling pin. Invert the pastry over a 9¹/₂- to 10-inch extra-deep-dish pie pan, center, and peel off the paper. Tuck the pastry into the pan, without stretching it, and sculpt the edge into an upstanding ridge. Place in the freezer for 15 minutes. Partially prebake and let cool according to the directions on page 16.

3. In a large saucepan, combine the berries, sugar, and lemon juice over medium heat. Slowly heat, stirring occasionally, until the berries put off a good deal of juice, 5 to 7 minutes. In a small bowl, combine the orange juice and cornstarch. Stir the mixture into the fruit. Bring the fruit to a low boil and cook, stirring, for about $1^{1}/_{2}$ minutes, until slightly thickened. Remove from the heat. Preheat the oven to 400°F.

4. To make the topping, sift the flour, cornmeal, sugar, baking powder, and salt together in a medium-size bowl. Add the butter and cut it into the dry ingredients until the mixture resembles coarse crumbs. Beat the milk, egg, and vanilla together in a small bowl. Make a well in the dry ingredients, add the liquid, and stir until evenly mixed. Set aside.

5. Reheat the fruit, bringing it to a boil. Pour the filling into the cooled pie shell. Spoon the topping evenly over the fruit.

6. Place the pie on the center oven rack. Just in case, slide a large aluminum foil–lined baking sheet onto the rack below to catch any spills. Bake until the topping is golden brown and cooked through, 22 to 25 minutes.

7. Transfer the pie to a wire rack and let cool for 20 to 30 minutes before serving. This is best served within 2 hours.

Recipe for Success

> If you have an extra-deep-dish pie pan, now is the time to use it. The combination of the juicy fruit and the cobbler topping raises the level of the liquid considerably. A typical $9^{1}/_{2}$-inch deep-dish pan is barely adequate.

> Nearly any combination of fresh berries will work fine here. Use $4^{1}/_{2}$ to 5 cups fruit.

> If you like whole-grain flours, feel free to substitute up to $^{1}/_{2}$ cup whole wheat flour for an equal amount of the all-purpose flour.

> The shortcake topping for this pie and the cobbler topping on pages 104–105 are interchangeable.

Elizabeth's Pie

Elizabeth is the granddaughter of Louise Piper (see page 45), one of the stellar pie bakers and consistent winners at the Iowa State Fair. This particular pie, a mixed-fruit affair, earned Louise a ribbon at the 2003 fair. The combination of fruit and other filling ingredients was first suggested years earlier by her six-year-old granddaughter. Since then, the pie has become a family tradition. Louise bakes the pie in an oil crust that she's been using for years. It's a little trickier to handle than pastry made with solid fat, but I was very impressed with the flaky, delicate result. For thickening, she uses both quick-cooking tapioca and flour, because, as Louise says, the pie is very juicy. It does, however, set up fairly firm. My personal favorite way to eat this pie is barely warm, when it's still juicy but not runny.

MAKES 8 SERVINGS

1 recipe Louise Piper's Oil Pastry (page 44)

FILLING

1 cup sugar

1/4 cup all-purpose flour

2 tablespoons quick-cooking tapioca

1/2 teaspoon ground cinnamon

1/4 cup honey

1 cup peeled, cored, and diced tart apple (Louise likes Jonathan or Red Rome; Granny Smith is good, too)

1 cup fresh red raspberries

1 cup hulled and sliced fresh strawberries

1 cup diced fresh rhubarb stalks

2 tablespoons cold unsalted butter, cut into small pieces

GLAZE

Sugar

Milk or light cream

1. If you haven't already, prepare the pastry. Wrap in plastic but do not refrigerate. Set aside.

2. Combine the sugar, flour, tapioca, and cinnamon in a large bowl. Toss well to mix. Add the honey, apple, berries, and rhubarb and mix gently but thoroughly. Set aside. Preheat the oven to 375°F.

3. Put the larger half of the pastry between 2 sheets of *unfloured* waxed paper. Using your rolling pin, roll the pastry into a 12-inch circle. Peel off the top sheet of paper. Invert the pastry over a 9-inch standard pie pan, center, and peel off the paper. Gently tuck the pastry into the pan, without stretching or tearing it, and let the overhang drape over the edge. Using the same sheets of waxed paper, roll the other half of the dough into a 10-inch circle. Remove the top sheet of paper.

4. Scrape the filling into the pie shell, smoothing the fruit with a spoon. Dot the fruit with the butter. Dampen the edge of the pie shell with a pastry brush. Invert the top pastry over the filling, center, and slowly peel off the paper, pressing down along the edge to seal. Sculpt the overhanging dough into an upstanding ridge. Sprinkle the top of the pie generously with sugar, then drizzle with milk. Using a fork or paring knife, poke several steam vents in the top of the pie. Put at least one of them along the edge so you can check the juices there later.

5. Place the pie on the center oven rack and bake for 30 minutes, then rotate the pie 180 degrees, so that the part that faced the back of the oven now faces forward. Just in case, slide a large aluminum foil–lined baking sheet onto the rack below to catch any spills. Continue to bake until the top is a rich golden brown and any juices visible at the steam vents bubble thickly, 20 to 25 minutes.

6. Transfer the pie to a wire rack and let cool. Serve just barely warm or at room temperature.

Recipe for Success

▶ I find that Louise's pastry works best if rolled shortly after making it. That's why I don't refrigerate it the way I typically do other pastries.

▶ The dough will need to be rolled very thin to make a 12-inch circle. Don't be surprised if it is a little crumbly at the edge. Just handle it delicately.

▶ I usually glaze my pies with milk first, then with sugar, but Louise does it just the opposite. It makes a slight difference in the texture—the sugar sort of gathers into crunchy waves rather than being uniformly crunchy. I like it. Try it yourself and see.

Piecing Together a Pie Chronology

No one knows for certain who baked the first pie. Some historians believe that it was the Romans. The first written recipe for a pie, they tell us, came from Cato the Censor (234–139 B.C.), who printed a recipe for a goat cheese and honey pie in a rye crust. Here are a few more things we know about the evolution of pie.

▶ *The Oxford English Dictionary* notes that the word "pie" was "evidently a well-known popular word in 1362," although it most likely referred to meat and fowl pies, not dessert pies.

▶ In 1475, the Italian writer Platina offered a recipe for a squash pie sprinkled with sugar and rose water. Could this have been an early ancestor of our pumpkin pie?

▶ Fruit pies likely did not exist much before the 1500s. In Tudor and Stuart times, English pies were made with pears, apples, and quinces.

▶ Pie came to America with the English settlers, who baked their pies in pans known as "coffyns." Pastry crust was not their forte. It was typically meant only to contain the pie, not to be eaten.

▶ Pies have long been a large part of the New England diet. Apple pie for breakfast is a New England tradition. The 1877 diary of a Vermont housewife counts her annual output of pies at 427—and this without refrigerated pie pastry!

▶ Pie is still America's favorite dessert, with apple leading the pack.

Apple is America's signature pie—not just something we love to eat, but one of those rare, universal symbols of things we hold dear. It's no wonder, then, that making an apple pie is one of fall's enduring rites. To a large extent, whether it tastes delicious or is store-bought or homemade is irrelevant: apple pie enjoys iconic stature in this country, and we cherish it all the same.

Make Mine Apple

You may have a single, irrefutable memory of what constitutes a true apple pie—perhaps it was the one your grandmother or mother made—but the most surprising thing about apple pie is just how varied it can be. Nobody knows this better than me. My book *Apple Pie Perfect* (Harvard Common Press, 2002) is a collection of 100 recipes for apple pie. That I was able to add considerably to that total here speaks volumes about apple pie's adaptable nature. • One of the things I love most about apple pie is that it marks the unofficial start of the fall baking season. Relief from the oppressive summer heat arrives, bringing with it a renewed interest in dusting off favorite recipes and baking almost every weekend. Outings are planned to secure the best local apples. Warm, fresh pies are delivered to friends and family, strengthening ties that have been loosened by months of vacations and far-flung endeavors. Apple pie brings us home, in a very real sense, and envelops us in the warmth of domestic well-being.

Here's hoping all your apple pies are memorable.

"If you want to make an apple pie from scratch, you must first create the universe."

—CARL SAGAN

Tips for Baking Delicious Apple Pies

▶ Start with the best fruit you can find. The box on page 233 will point you in the right direction. If you have access to local orchards, talk to the people who grow the apples. They can give you guidance on regional apple varieties that may be perfect for pies.

▶ You can improve the flavor of lackluster fruit with the addition of lemon juice, apple butter, or boiled cider.

▶ To make a more compact pie with a dense filling, cut some of the fruit into slices and some into small chunks. You'll get more fruit into the filling that way.

▶ Avoid using too much sugar in apple pies. Sweetness is fine, but you don't want to obscure the pleasant tart flavor tones of good apples.

▶ Don't underbake your apple pies, or the thickening will not "take," leaving you with a runny mess. In most cases, you want to see thick—not thin—juices bubbling up in the pie filling.

▶ Always cool your pie for at least one hour, preferably two, before slicing it, or the filling will not have ample time to set.

The Easiest Apple Pie

This is an even easier version of a shortcut apple pie that appears in my book *Apple Pie Perfect* (Harvard Common Press, 2002). The idea of a very easy quasi-homemade apple pie appeals to quite a few people, apparently. One of them is interviewer Robin Young at WBUR, a National Public Radio station in Boston. Robin invited me to be on her show, where I actually made a pie live, on the radio, while she interviewed me about apple pie—a first for me. During the interview, she brought out her version of my Easiest Apple Pie of All, which she had baked at the studio shortly before my arrival. It was duly impressive, and I was delighted and flattered that she had tried one of the recipes from my book. Anyway, this is an apple pie for those with neither the time nor the inclination to make a pie from scratch. It makes unabashed use of convenience products, adding just enough homemade touches—including a fresh apple and a scratch crumb topping—to leave your family wondering how much trouble you've actually gone to. If you have a need for speed, or just convenience, this is the pie for you.

MAKES 8 TO 10 SERVINGS

1 store-bought refrigerated pie pastry

FILLING

One and a half 21-ounce cans apple pie filling

1 large Granny Smith or other tart, juicy apple, peeled, cored, and finely chopped

1 tablespoon fresh lemon juice

1/2 cup dark raisins, dried currants, or sweetened dried cranberries (sold as Craisins)

1/4 teaspoon ground cinnamon

CRUMB TOPPING

1/2 cup all-purpose flour

1/2 cup sugar

1/4 teaspoon ground cinnamon

Big pinch of salt

1/4 cup (1/2 stick) cold unsalted butter, cut into 1/4-inch pieces

1. Line a 9-inch standard pie pan with the pastry. Fold the excess pastry back and pinch the edge into an upstanding ridge. Place in the freezer for 15 minutes. Preheat the oven to 400°F.

2. Combine the apple pie filling, apple, lemon juice, raisins, and cinnamon in a medium-size bowl. Turn the filling into the chilled pie shell and smooth the top with your hands or a spoon. Place the pie on the center oven rack and bake for 30 minutes.

3. Meanwhile, make the topping. Put the flour, sugar, cinnamon, and salt in a food processor and pulse several times to mix. Scatter the butter over the dry mixture and pulse until the mixture resembles fine crumbs. Empty the crumbs into a large bowl and rub the mixture between your fingers to make large, buttery crumbs. Refrigerate until ready to use.

4. Remove the pie from the oven and reduce the temperature to 375°F. Carefully dump the crumbs in the center of the pie, spreading them evenly over the surface with your hands. Tamp them down lightly. Return the pie to the oven, placing it so that the part that faced the back of the oven now faces forward. Just in case, slide a large aluminum foil–lined baking sheet onto the rack below to catch any drips. Continue to bake until the juices bubble thickly around the edge, about 25 minutes.

5. Transfer the pie to a wire rack and let cool for at least 1 hour before serving.

Recipe for Success

▸ The purpose of the apple here is to give the canned pie filling a little contrasting texture and fresh flavor. Even with a juicy apple, however, it isn't necessary to add more thickener, because there is already plenty in the canned filling.

My Dad, Warren Haedrich, on Making Apple Pie

"I always started with flour, butter, and Crisco, plus a tin cup filled with cold water and a few ice cubes to keep it cold. I liked working on a large maple board, which I floured so all was ready when I mixed the butter—cut into little squares with several tablespoons of Crisco—into the flour with a wire pastry blender. I would mix this combination with enough cold water to easily handle everything, then make up two balls for chilling in the refrigerator.

"After that, I would help your mother core, peel, and slice the apples. We decided New York State McIntosh were our favorites. I don't remember how many we would cut up. I do remember that there were a lot of sliced apples and we never thought we could get that many in a 9-inch pie plate. We used a glass pie plate at one time, but at some point shifted to a shiny metal one. Those who ate the pie never seemed to mind.

"The apples got a coating of nutmeg (just a small amount) and some cinnamon (a larger amount), a heavy dusting of brown sugar, and the rest of the stick of butter I didn't use for the crust. Then I got busy rolling out the dough using waxed paper until it looked right but was thick enough to handle. I lined the pie plate with the dough, with an extra inch hanging over the edge, then we poured the apples onto the dough. We would put the top layer on, slit the top dough, brush it with milk, dust it with a small amount of sugar, and put it in the oven until it was done. We learned to put foil under the pie rack, to catch the drippings. Altogether, it smelled wonderful and tasted even better."

▶ By the same token, the thickener in canned filling reduces the amount of time needed for cooling. I recommend 1 hour, but you could get by with 30 minutes.

▶ If you prefer a top crust instead of a crumb topping, that will work fine. Simply moisten the edge of the pie shell, drape the top crust over the pie, and seal. Trim and crimp the edge as usual.

Golden Delicious Apple Pie with Oatmeal Crumb Topping

Since my book *Apple Pie Perfect* (Harvard Common Press) was published in 2002, I've traveled quite some distance giving perhaps 50 or more apple pie–baking demonstrations. Many of the questions asked during these demos have to do with pie apples—namely, which ones are best for pies. I spend several minutes discussing a wide variety, but knowing that many cooks feel limited to the 10 or 15 common supermarket varieties, I often put in a word for the good old Golden Delicious apple. Detractors call it insipid, and it can be at its worst. But then again, any apple can be insipid, especially one past its prime. It's been my experience that fresh Golden Delicious apples have a good apple flavor, are reasonably juicy, and hold their shape fairly well in a pie, softening up nicely in the oven. Here's a great basic apple pie built on the Golden Delicious, with the oatmeal crumb topping that's earned this pie its distinction as the "best apple pie I've ever eaten" by more than a few of my friends and neighbors.

MAKES 8 TO 10 SERVINGS

1 recipe Basic Flaky Pie Pastry, Single Crust (page 31), refrigerated

FILLING

7 cups peeled, cored, and thinly sliced Golden Delicious apples

$1/3$ cup plus 1 tablespoon granulated sugar

Juice and grated zest of 1 lemon

$1/4$ teaspoon ground nutmeg

$1 1/2$ tablespoons cornstarch

OATMEAL CRUMB TOPPING

1 cup all-purpose flour

$1/2$ cup rolled oats (old-fashioned or quick-cooking)

$2/3$ cup firmly packed light brown sugar

$1/2$ teaspoon ground cinnamon

$1/4$ teaspoon salt

$1/2$ cup (1 stick) cold unsalted butter, cut into $1/4$-inch pieces

1. If you haven't already, prepare the pastry and refrigerate until firm enough to roll, about 1 hour.

2. On a sheet of lightly floured waxed paper, roll the pastry into a 13-inch circle with a floured rolling pin. Invert the pastry over a $9 1/2$-inch deep-dish pie pan, center, and peel off the paper. Gently tuck the pastry into the pan, without stretching it, and sculpt the edge into an upstanding ridge. Place in the freezer for 15 minutes.

3. Combine the apples, $1/3$ cup of the granulated sugar, and the lemon juice and zest in a large bowl. Mix well, then set aside for 10 minutes. Preheat the oven to 400°F.

4. In a small bowl, mix the remaining 1 tablespoon sugar with the nutmeg and cornstarch. Add the mixture to the apples and stir the fruit well. Turn the filling into the chilled pie shell and smooth with your hands to even it out. Place the pie on the center oven rack and bake for 30 minutes.

5. Meanwhile, make the crumb topping. Put the flour, oats, brown sugar, cinnamon, and salt in a food processor and pulse several times to mix. Scatter the butter over the top.

Pulse repeatedly until the mixture resembles fine crumbs. Empty the crumbs into a large bowl and rub them between your fingers until you have large, buttery crumbs. Refrigerate until ready to use.

6. Remove the pie from the oven and reduce the temperature to 375°F. Carefully dump the crumbs in the center of the pie, spreading them over the surface with your hands. Tamp them down lightly. Return the pie to the oven, placing it so that the part that faced the back of the oven now faces forward. Just in case, slide a large aluminum foil–lined baking sheet onto the rack below to catch any spills. Bake until the top is dark golden brown and the juices bubble thickly at the edge, 30 to 35 minutes. If necessary, cover the pie with loosely tented aluminum foil during the last 15 minutes of baking to keep the top from browning too much.

7. Transfer the pie to a wire rack and let cool for at least 1 hour before serving.

Recipe for Success

▶ **My crumb pies tend to have a lot of crumb topping—perhaps a little too much for some people. I think, at the very least, the crumbs should cover the pie in a compact, thickish layer. You can always use fewer crumbs if you prefer, bagging the extra and freezing them for another pie or muffin recipe.**

An Apple Peeler You'll Really Like

If you're in the market for a new apple peeler—and you certainly should be if yours is dull, slips around in your grip, or is otherwise frustrating to wield—check out the selection of OXO brand peelers at your local kitchenware shop. I own several of them, and I say it's about time someone made a peeler that performs like a tool and not a toy. Most notably, OXO peelers have a substantial slip-proof, rubberized grip that you can really get your hand around. That alone makes these far superior to other peelers. The swivel blade is blessedly sharp and makes for a smooth, shallow cut, perfect for peeling those pie apples without gouging the precious flesh.

Brown Sugar Apple Pie

This pie differs from the previous one in that it is the blueprint for an apple pie you'd make in a 9-inch standard pie pan, as opposed to a 9½-inch deep-dish pan. As such, most of the ingredients are scaled down and the baking time is slightly less, although the techniques involved are virtually identical. One change I've made is using brown sugar instead of granulated, the way my mom and dad used to make their apples pies. Brown sugar adds a caramel note to the pie, which purists disparage for masking the true flavor of the apples and the rest of us simply enjoy. Another obvious difference: you don't get as many slices—six big pieces or eight smaller ones.

MAKES 6 TO 8 SERVINGS

1 recipe Basic Flaky Pie Pastry, Double Crust (page 31), refrigerated

FILLING

6 cups peeled, cored, and thinly sliced Golden Delicious, Gala, Northern Spy, or other apples (see pages 232–233 for recommendations)

½ cup firmly packed light brown sugar

1 tablespoon fresh lemon juice

Big pinch of salt

1 tablespoon granulated sugar

1 tablespoon cornstarch

¼ teaspoon ground cinnamon (optional)

GLAZE

Milk or light cream

Granulated sugar

1. If you haven't already, prepare the pastry and refrigerate until firm enough to roll, about 1 hour.

2. On a sheet of lightly floured waxed paper, roll the larger portion of the pastry into a 12-inch circle with a floured rolling pin. Invert the pastry over a 9-inch standard pie pan, center, and peel off the paper. Gently tuck the pastry into the pan, without stretching it, and let the overhang drape over the edge. Place in the refrigerator for 15 minutes.

3. Combine the apples, brown sugar, lemon juice, and salt in a large bowl. Toss well, then set aside for 15 minutes. Preheat the oven to 400°F. Mix the granulated sugar and cornstarch together in a small bowl. Stir the mixture into the apples along with the cinnamon, if using. Scrape the filling into the chilled pie shell and smooth the top with your hands.

4. Roll the other half of the pastry into a 10-inch circle on a sheet of lightly floured waxed paper. Moisten the outer edge of the pie shell with a pastry brush. Invert the top pastry over the filling, center, and peel off the paper. Press the top and bottom pastries together along the dampened edge. Using the back of a butter knife, trim the pastry flush with the edge of the pan. With the back of a fork, press the tines all along the edge to seal. Using the fork, poke several steam vents in the top, including a couple along the edge so you can check the juices there later. Brush the top with a little milk and sprinkle with granulated sugar.

5. Place the pie on the center oven rack and bake for 30 minutes. Reduce the oven temperature to 375°F and rotate the pie 180 degrees, so that the part of the pie that faced the back of the oven now faces forward. Just in case, slide a large aluminum foil–lined baking sheet onto the rack below to catch any drips. Bake until golden brown, about 25 minutes. When done, you should notice thick juices bubbling out of the steam vents along the edge.

6. Transfer the pie to a wire rack and let cool for at least 2 hours, preferably longer, before serving.

Recipe for Success

▶ **When I'm baking an apple pie and I'm not sure if the apples are done, I often use a long, thin bamboo skewer to check the apples, much the way you would use a toothpick to check a cake. I keep a supply on hand just for this purpose. When I suspect the pie is done, I stick the skewer down into one of the steam vents I've made near the center of the pie (the center always takes the longest to cook). As the skewer enters the apples, there should be almost no resistance. If there is, the pie probably needs at least 10 more minutes of baking.**

Apple Pie with Cheddar Cracker Topping

Combining cheddar cheese and apples is an old New England tradition. (Also see the recipe on page 206.) The filling is pretty standard—apples, a little sugar, some lemon—but the crumb topping, made from cheddar cheese crackers, butter, and cheese, is probably unlike any you've ever had. The topping goes on during the last 20 minutes and bakes up golden and crunchy, in perfect contrast to the soft apple filling.

MAKES 8 TO 10 SERVINGS

1 recipe Basic Flaky Pie Pastry, Single Crust (page 31) or All-Butter Pie Pastry, Single Crust (page 28), refrigerated

FILLING

6 cups peeled, cored, and thinly sliced apples (see pages 232–233 for recommendations)

1/4 cup plus 2 tablespoons sugar

Big pinch of salt

2 teaspoons fresh lemon juice

1/2 teaspoon grated lemon zest

11/2 tablespoons cornstarch

CHEDDAR CRACKER TOPPING

21/2 cups Cheez-It cheddar cheese crackers, preferably the white cheddar variety

1/4 cup (1/2 stick) cold unsalted butter, cut into 1/4-inch pieces

3/4 cup finely shredded sharp white cheddar cheese

1. If you haven't already, prepare the pastry and refrigerate until firm enough to roll, about 1 hour.

2. On a sheet of lightly floured waxed paper, roll the pastry into a 12-inch circle with a floured rolling pin. Invert the pastry over a 9-inch standard pie pan, center, and peel off the paper. Tuck the pastry into the pan, without stretching it, and sculpt the edge into an upstanding ridge. Place in the freezer for 15 minutes. Preheat the oven to 400°F.

3. Combine the apples, 1/4 cup of the sugar, the salt, lemon juice, and lemon zest in a large bowl. Set aside for 10 minutes to juice.

4. Combine the remaining 2 tablespoons sugar and cornstarch in a small bowl, then stir the mixture into the apples. Turn the filling into the chilled pie shell and smooth the top with your hands. Place the pie on the center oven rack and bake for 30 minutes. Reduce the heat to 375°F and bake for 10 minutes more.

5. Meanwhile, make the cracker topping. Place the crackers in a food processor and pulse until you have fairly fine—but not too fine—crumbs. Scatter the butter over the crumbs and pulse again to make a mixture that looks gravelly and buttery. Add the cheese and pulse 2 or 3 times to mix.

6. When the pie has baked for a total of 40 minutes, remove it from the oven. Carefully dump the crumbs over the top, spreading them evenly with your hands. Press gently to compact them. Return the pie to the oven, placing it so that the part that faced the back of the oven now faces forward. Just in case, slide a large aluminum foil–lined baking sheet onto the rack below to catch any drips. Bake until the top is a rich toasted brown and the juices visible at the edge bubble thickly, about 20 minutes. If the topping starts to get too brown, loosely drape a piece of aluminum foil over the top during the last 5 to 10 minutes of baking.

The Search for Granny Smith

Granny Smith is a fine pie apple. But would your real granny make the best Granny Smith? Here's a way to find out. Every year, the Washington Apple Commission launches a search for Granny Smith—a nationwide hunt to find the perfect grandmother to promote the state's famous green fruit. According to the commission's press materials, it's looking for someone who personifies the healthful attributes of Washington's apples. In addition, the candidate should:

> Be sweet to the core and have good moral fiber.

> Be handpicked by children, grandchildren, spouse, or friends.

> Have beauty that's more than skin-deep and just the right amount of maturity.

> Have "a-peel."

If you think your own granny qualifies, go to the Washington Apple Commission's Web site, www.bestapples.com, for more details.

7. Transfer the pie to a wire rack and let cool for 30 minutes to 1 hour. This pie is best served warm.

Recipe for Success

> Try to find juicy apples to use in this recipe, because the topping is dry and crumbly and the pie can use the juice. Adding 1 or 2 Granny Smith apples will help, since they're generally pretty juicy.

> One nice trick to get the most from the cheddar topping is to rewarm the pie in the oven for 5 to 8 minutes before serving. Two to 3 minutes before taking it out of the oven, sprinkle the top with an additional $1/2$ to 1 cup shredded sharp white cheddar cheese. As soon as the cheese melts, take the pie out of the oven and serve right away.

Cheddar-Crusted Apple-Pear Pie

Traditionally, a thick slab of cheddar cheese is placed on top of a hot slice of apple pie, and then, after a brief pause to let the cheese soften, pie and cheese are eaten together. You can still do that with this pie, but for an extra cheddar kick, I bake some cheese right into the crust. It smells great as it bakes, mingling with the fragrance of the apples, and tastes wonderful, too, something like cheese straws, if you're familiar with them. This can be made with all apples if you like, but I like to combine the apples with some sliced pears.

MAKES 8 SERVINGS

1 recipe Cheddar Cheese Pie Pastry, Double Crust (page 33), refrigerated

FILLING

4 cups peeled, cored, and sliced Golden Delicious, Granny Smith, Northern Spy, or other apples (see pages 232–233 for recommendations)

3 cups cored and sliced ripe fresh pears, peeled or unpeeled

$1/3$ cup sugar

$1^1/2$ tablespoons cornstarch

Pinch of salt

2 teaspoons fresh lemon juice

2 tablespoons cold unsalted butter, cut into small pieces

1. If you haven't already, prepare the pastry and refrigerate until firm enough to roll, about 1 hour.

2. On a sheet of lightly floured waxed paper, roll the larger portion of the pastry into a 13-inch circle with a floured rolling pin. Invert the pastry over a $9^1/2$-inch deep-dish pie pan, center, and peel off the paper. Gently tuck the pastry into the pan, without stretching it, and let the overhang drape over the edge. Place in the refrigerator for 15 minutes.

3. Combine the apples, pears, and $1/4$ cup of the sugar in a large bowl. Toss to mix, then set aside to juice for 10 minutes. Preheat the oven to 400°F.

4. Mix the remaining sugar, the cornstarch, and salt in a small bowl. Add the mixture to the fruit and toss well. Stir in the lemon juice.

5. On another sheet of lightly floured waxed paper, roll the other half of the pastry into an $11^1/2$-inch circle. Turn the filling into the chilled pie shell and smooth the top with your hands. Dot the filling with the butter. Lightly moisten the rim of the pie shell. Invert the top pastry over the filling, center, and peel off the paper. Press the top and bottom

pastries together along the dampened edge. Trim the pastry with scissors or a paring knife, leaving an even ½-inch overhang all around, then sculpt the overhang into an upstanding ridge. Poke several steam vents in the top crust with a fork or paring knife. Put a couple of the vents near the edge of the crust so you can check the juices there later.

6. Place the pie on the center oven rack and bake for 30 minutes. Reduce the oven temperature to 375°F and rotate the pie 180 degrees, so that the part that faced the back of the oven now faces forward. Just in case, slide a large aluminum foil–lined baking sheet onto the rack below to catch any drips. Bake until the top is dark golden brown and any juices visible at the steam vents bubble thickly, 35 to 40 minutes.

7. Transfer the pie to a wire rack and let cool briefly before serving.

Recipe for Success

▶ Use a good sharp or extra-sharp cheddar in the pastry because it makes a world of difference in the flavor of the finished pie. There are many fine cheddars on the market, but I think Cracker Barrel is consistently the best.

▶ Because of the cheese, this is one of those pies I prefer to eat while it's still very warm. The more the pie cools, the more muted the flavor of the cheddar becomes. Cool slices can easily be warmed in the microwave or, wrapped in aluminum foil, in a hot oven.

Throw in a Few Dump Trucks of Ben & Jerry's, and That's One Heck of a Pie à la Mode

The world's largest apple pie was baked on August 16, 1997, by 300 volunteers for the North Central Washington Museum in Wenatchee, Washington. The prodigious pie required 32,000 pounds of apples, 7,000 pounds of sugar and flour, and, in the words of one observer, one really strange-looking oven—a 10,000-pound insulated lid that "baked" the pie for 5 hours. Much to the delight of the pastry crew, we suspect, the pie had no top crust. Yield: about 70,000 slices.

Honey Apple-Currant Pie in a Whole Wheat Crust

A lot of good bakers like to incorporate a whole-grain pastry into their fruit pies. There's something entirely apropos about enclosing fresh-picked fall apples, pears, or cranberries in a wholesome pie pastry. Here we take the earthy profile one step further by using honey as the primary sweetener. Honey is sweeter than sugar, so we use a little less sweetener than usual for a pie of this size. I like this with a top crust but another option would be to use this pastry—or perhaps the Nutty Pie Pastry (page 42)—for the bottom crust, then add any of the crumb toppings in this collection about midway through the baking.

MAKES 8 TO 10 SERVINGS

1 recipe Whole Wheat Pie Pastry, Double Crust (page 33), refrigerated

FILLING

7 cups peeled, cored, and sliced apples (see pages 232–233 for recommendations)

3/4 cup dark dried currants

1/3 cup honey

2 tablespoons sugar (optional)

1 1/2 tablespoons fresh lemon juice

Grated zest of 1/2 lemon

2 1/2 tablespoons all-purpose flour

1/2 teaspoon ground cinnamon

2 tablespoons cold unsalted butter, cut into small pieces

GLAZE

Milk or light cream

Sugar

1.   If you haven't already, prepare the pastry and refrigerate until firm enough to roll, about 1 hour.

2.   On a sheet of lightly floured waxed paper, roll the larger portion of the pastry into a 13-inch circle with a floured rolling pin. Invert the pastry over a 9 1/2-inch deep-dish pie pan, center, and peel off the paper. Gently tuck the pastry into the pan, without stretching it, and let the overhang drape over the edge. Place in the refrigerator for 15 minutes.

3.   Combine the apples, currants, honey, sugar (if using), lemon juice, and lemon zest in a large bowl. Toss well, then set aside for 10 minutes. Preheat the oven to 375°F.

4.   On another sheet of lightly floured waxed paper, roll the other half of the pastry into an 11 1/2-inch circle. Add the flour and cinnamon to the fruit and mix well. Turn the filling into the chilled pie shell. Dot the top of the filling with the butter. Moisten the edge

of the pie shell with a wet fingertip or pastry brush. Invert the top pastry over the filling, center, and peel off the paper. Press the pastries together along the dampened edge, then trim the excess dough with scissors or a paring knife to an even ¹/₂ inch all around. Sculpt the edge into an upstanding ridge. Using a fork or paring knife, poke several steam vents near the edge of the pie so you can check the juices there later. Lightly brush the pie with milk and sprinkle with sugar.

5. Place the pie on the center oven rack and bake for 30 minutes. Rotate the baking sheet 180 degrees, so that the part of the pie that faced the back of the oven now faces forward. Just in case, slide a large aluminum foil–lined baking sheet onto the rack below to catch any spills. Continue to bake until the juices bubble thickly at the edge, 30 to 40 minutes.

6. Transfer the pie to a wire rack and let cool for at least 1 hour before serving.

Recipe for Success

▶ **Whole wheat flour contains flecks of oil-rich wheat germ, so whole wheat pie pastry has a tendency to brown faster than pastries made with white flour. When you're making a fruit pie with whole wheat pastry, it's a good idea to bake the pie a little slower. That's why I bake this pie at 375°F for the entire time rather than the usual 400°F for the first 30 minutes.**

Apple and Dried Apricot Pie

Dried fruit is a good way to add an element of surprise and complementary flavor to fresh fruit pies. You can use it right from the box or bag, as is, or you can get a little fancier, as I do here, and poach the fruit first. (Another good example of using dried fruit this way is Very Fig and Walnut Pie on page 316.) Not only does poaching soften the fruit—and some fruits, such as figs, can often use a serious softening—but it also leaves you with a sweet, flavorful poaching liquid, which I like to boil down to a syrup and add to the filling. With apples, dried fruit, and walnuts, this is a good choice for a winter pie, when the supply of good fresh fruit is limited.

MAKES 8 TO 10 SERVINGS

1 recipe Tender Cream Cheese Pastry, Double Crust (page 46), refrigerated

FILLING

1 1/2 cups diced dried apricots

2 cups apple or apricot juice (see Recipe for Success)

2 or 3 lemon slices

5 cups peeled, cored, and sliced Granny Smith or other tart apples

1/3 cup granulated sugar

1/2 cup coarsely chopped walnuts

3 tablespoons all-purpose flour

1 tablespoon fresh lemon juice

1/4 teaspoon ground cinnamon

1 1/2 tablespoons cold unsalted butter, cut into small pieces

GARNISH

Confectioners' sugar

1.   If you haven't already, prepare the pastry and refrigerate until firm enough to roll, for 1 to 1 1/2 hours.

2.   While the pastry is chilling, poach the apricots. Combine the apricots, apple juice, and lemon slices in a medium-size nonreactive saucepan. Bring to a boil, reduce the heat to medium-low, cover, and gently simmer for 20 minutes. Remove from the heat and drain the apricots, reserving the liquid. Return the liquid to the saucepan. Remove the lemon slices from the apricots and discard.

3.   In a large bowl, combine the apples, granulated sugar, walnuts, flour, lemon juice, and cinnamon and toss well. Stir in the apricots. Let stand at room temperature for 15 minutes.

4.   While the fruit sits, bring the poaching liquid to a boil. Continue to boil rapidly until the liquid in the pan is reduced to between 1/4 and 1/3 cup, just enough syrupy liquid to cover the bottom of the pan. Pour the liquid over the fruit and toss well. Set the filling aside. Preheat the oven to 400°F.

5.   On a sheet of lightly floured waxed paper, roll half of the pastry into a 12-inch circle with a floured rolling pin. Invert the pastry over a 9-inch standard pie pan, center, and peel off the paper. Gently tuck the pastry down into the pan, without stretching it, and let the overhang drape over the edge. Place in the refrigerator for 5 minutes.

6.   Roll the other half of the pastry into an 11-inch circle on a sheet of lightly floured waxed paper. Turn the filling into the chilled pie shell and smooth the top with your hands. Dot the filling with the butter. Dampen the edge of the pie shell with a wet fingertip or pastry brush. Invert the top pastry over the filling, center, and peel off the paper. Press the top and bottom pastries together along the dampened edge. Trim the pastry, leaving an

Baking Your Way into the CIA

If you or someone you know is thinking about pursuing a career in the culinary arts, your way with apple pie could earn you a hefty scholarship.

The Culinary Institute of America, thought by many to be the nation's top school of its kind, sponsors what it calls the All-American Apple Pie Recipe Contest. This contest, the institute says, "challenges prospective students to demonstrate their understanding of cooking basics."

Interested applicants, who must be in their junior year of high school or older, are asked to submit a recipe for an original apple pie, a photo of the pie, and a personal statement of up to 100 words describing who they are and what is special about the recipe. The top 20 entrants each receive $4,000 toward their freshman year tuition at the CIA and a free trip to the institute, in Hyde Park, New York, for a VIP visit. In addition, 10 runners-up each receive a $1,500 honorable mention scholarship.

For more information or to receive an official contest packet, call the institute at (800) 285-4627.

even ¹/₂-inch overhang all around, then sculpt this into an upstanding ridge. Poke several steam vents in the top of the pie with a fork or paring knife. Put a couple of the vents near the edge of the crust so you can check the juices there later.

7. Place the pie on the center oven rack and bake for 25 minutes. Reduce the oven temperature to 375°F and rotate the pie 180 degrees, so that the part that faced the back of the oven now faces forward. Just in case, slide a large aluminum foil–lined baking sheet onto the rack below to catch any drips. Continue to bake until the top is golden brown and the juices visible at the steam vents bubble thickly, 25 to 30 minutes.

8. Transfer the pie to a wire rack. While the pie is still hot, dust the top with confectioners' sugar. Let cool for at least 1 hour before serving.

Recipe for Success

▶ Dried apricots have a pretty strong, concentrated flavor—strong enough to dominate the flavor of the apples. If that appeals to you, poach the apricots in apricot juice. Otherwise, use apple juice. You'll still get plenty of apricot flavor, but it won't be quite so forward. In either case, I recommend using unfiltered juice, available at health food stores.

Cinnamon Applesauce Pie

Cooks of another era would often make applesauce pies as their supplies of storage apples dwindled and then ran dry. It's easy to understand why they would have embraced the idea, what with all the other chores to be done, because a jar of applesauce relieves a busy home-maker of the peeling and slicing required for a fresh apple pie. I think you'll like this pie for the same reason. If you have a jar of your own homemade applesauce, by all means use it. Otherwise, just use Mott's or another good-quality brand. You'll need some sugar to sweeten things up, a bit of lemon to kick up the flavor, and some cinnamon to add a little spice. Unless you like hot applesauce, you'll probably (like me) prefer this pie cold.

MAKES 8 SERVINGS

1 recipe Basic Flaky Pie Pastry, Single Crust (page 31), refrigerated

FILLING

2 large eggs, at room temperature

1 large egg yolk, at room temperature

1/3 cup granulated sugar

1/3 cup firmly packed light brown sugar

2 cups sweetened applesauce

1/4 cup (1/2 stick) unsalted butter, melted

1 tablespoon fresh lemon juice

1 teaspoon grated lemon zest

1/2 teaspoon ground cinnamon

1/4 teaspoon salt

1. If you haven't already, prepare the pastry and refrigerate until firm enough to roll, about 1 hour.

2. On a sheet of lightly floured waxed paper, roll the pastry into a 12-inch circle with a floured rolling pin. Invert the pastry over a 9-inch standard pie pan, center, and peel off the paper. Tuck the pastry into the pan, without stretching it, and sculpt the edge into an upstanding ridge. Place in the freezer for 15 minutes. Preheat the oven to 400°F.

3. Combine the eggs, egg yolk, and sugars in a large bowl. Using an electric mixer, blend the ingredients on medium speed until well mixed, about 30 seconds. Add all the remaining ingredients and beat again until evenly blended. Carefully pour the filling into the chilled pie shell.

4. Place the pie on the center oven rack and bake for 15 minutes. Reduce the oven temperature to 350°F. and continue to bake until the filling is set, about 30 minutes more. Rotate the pie 180 degrees, so that the part that faced the back of the oven now faces

forward, about 15 minutes before it is done. The pie's surface should have a flat finish, although the center will still be glossy.

5. Transfer the pie to a wire rack and let cool thoroughly. Cover with loosely tented aluminum foil and refrigerate for at least 2 hours before serving.

Recipe for Success

▶ You may be wondering why you need additional sugar to sweeten this pie when you're already using sweetened applesauce. The reason is that the amount of sugar used to make the sauce isn't likely to be enough to deliver a decidedly sweet flavor to the pie. That said, not all applesauces are sweetened equally. You may use less sugar than I've called for, then taste the filling and see if you want to add more. If so, just beat it right into the filling before it goes in the pie shell.

Aunt Marge's Apple Butter Pie

I have a soft spot for my wife Bev's aunt Marge. The first time I met her, she waited a respectable five minutes or so and then, in the direct manner I supposed was common to West Virginia women, said, "And just when are you going to make my niece an honest woman?" If I harbored any uncertainty up to that point, I quickly assured her it wouldn't be long. (And it wasn't.) Since I've known her, and well before that, Aunt Marge has been sending Bev large jars of homemade apple butter every fall, made by the ladies of her church, Fairview Methodist Church in Charleston, West Virginia. So large are the jars that I've always had enough extra to make a couple of these pies with each batch. The texture is something like a rich pumpkin pie, smooth and well spiced. Extra spice is seldom needed, because most apple butters have lots of it. Like pumpkin pie, this would be a great choice for Thanksgiving dinner. Serve it cold, with whipped cream.

MAKES 8 TO 10 SERVINGS

1 recipe Basic Flaky Pie Pastry, Single Crust (page 31), refrigerated

FILLING

3 large eggs, at room temperature

1/2 cup sugar

1 3/4 cups spiced apple butter (see Recipe for Success)

1/3 cup light cream or half-and-half

1/4 teaspoon salt

1 tablespoon fresh lemon juice

1 teaspoon grated lemon zest

1/2 teaspoon vanilla extract

1/4 cup (1/2 stick) unsalted butter, melted

GARNISH

Fresh Whipped Cream (page 605)

1. If you haven't already, prepare the pastry and refrigerate until firm enough to roll, about 1 hour.

2. On a sheet of lightly floured waxed paper, roll the pastry into a 12-inch circle with a floured rolling pin. Invert the pastry over a 9-inch standard pie pan, center, and peel off the paper. Tuck the pastry into the pan, without stretching it, and sculpt the edge so it is just slightly higher than the rim. Place in the freezer for 15 minutes, then partially prebake and let cool according to the instructions on page 16.

3. Combine the eggs and sugar in a large bowl. Using an electric mixer, beat on medium-high speed until thoroughly blended, about 30 seconds. Add the apple butter, cream, salt, lemon juice, and lemon zest. Beat again until smooth. Blend in the vanilla and butter. Carefully pour the filling into the cooled pie shell.

4. Place the pie on the center oven rack and bake for 15 minutes. Reduce the oven temperature to 350°F and continue to bake until the sides just start to puff and the filling is set, about 30 minutes. Rotate the pie 180 degrees, so that the part that faced the back of the oven now faces forward, about 15 minutes before it is done. The very center of the pie will probably look a little glossy compared to most of the perimeter.

5. Transfer the pie to a wire rack and let cool completely. Cover with loosely tented aluminum foil and refrigerate for at least 2 hours. Serve with a dollop of whipped cream.

Recipe for Success

▶ Since there are no uniform standards for making apple butter, taste the brand you choose to determine both how sweet it is and how well spiced. Then taste the filling, too, before it goes into the pan. You may decide that it needs more or less sugar than specified. As for the spices, if the apple butter doesn't have a distinctly spicy edge, you'll probably want to add a little ground cinnamon and cloves to the filling as well.

We Couldn't Agree More

"When you can make a good pie, you will have a special gift to give others that money can't buy."

—Marion Cunningham, *Cooking with Children* (Knopf, 1995)

Apple-Pear White Wine Pie

The soft, fruity flavor of a Chardonnay or Chenin Blanc is a wonderful enhancement for a pie made with apples and pears. I stir the sugar into the fruit, saturate the mixture with white wine, and let it sit for an hour to really juice well. Then I drain off the accumulated juice and boil it to concentrate the flavors of the fruit and wine. This is a classy fruit pie that's best served with—what else?—a glass of the same wine you used in the pie. (It's fun to see if anyone is able to taste the connection between the two.)

MAKES 8 TO 10 SERVINGS

1 recipe Basic Flaky Pie Pastry, Double Crust (page 31) or Tender Cream Cheese Pastry, Double Crust (page 46), refrigerated

FILLING

4 cups peeled, cored, and sliced apples (see pages 232–233 for recommendations)

3 cups peeled, cored, and sliced ripe fresh pears

1/3 cup plus 2 tablespoons sugar

1 cup Chardonnay, Chenin Blanc, or other fruity white wine

2 1/2 tablespoons cornstarch

1/2 teaspoon grated lemon zest

1/8 teaspoon vanilla extract

Big pinch of salt

2 tablespoons cold unsalted butter, cut into small pieces

1. If you haven't already, prepare the pastry and refrigerate until firm enough to roll, 1 to 1 1/2 hours.

2. On a sheet of lightly floured waxed paper, roll the larger portion of the pastry into a 12-inch circle with a floured rolling pin. Invert the pastry over a 9-inch standard pie pan, center, and peel off the paper. Gently tuck the pastry into the pan, without stretching it, and let the overhang drape over the edge. Place in the refrigerator for 15 minutes.

3. Combine the apples, pears, and 1/3 cup of the sugar in a large bowl. Mix well, add the wine, and mix again. Set aside for 1 hour, stirring occasionally.

4. Drain off all the juice and transfer it to a medium-size nonreactive saucepan. Bring to a boil, then continue to boil gently until reduced to 1/2 to 2/3 cup. Have a heatproof measuring cup nearby to check. Pour the reduced juice back over the fruit and mix well.

5. In a small bowl, combine the remaining 2 tablespoons sugar and the cornstarch, then stir the mixture into the fruit. Stir in the lemon zest, vanilla, and salt. Turn the filling into the chilled pie shell and dot the top with the butter.

6. Roll the other half of the pastry into a 10-inch circle on a sheet of lightly floured waxed paper. Moisten the outer edge of the pie shell with a pastry brush. Invert the top pastry over the filling, center, and peel off the paper. Press the top and bottom pastries together along the dampened edge. Using the back of a butter knife, trim the pastry flush with the edge of the pan. With the back of a fork, press the tines all along the edge to seal. Poke several steam vents in the top of the pie with the fork or a paring knife, including a couple along the edge so you can check the juices there later.

7. Place the pie on the center oven rack and bake for 30 minutes. Reduce the oven temperature to 375°F and rotate the pie 180 degrees, so that the side that faced the back of the oven now faces forward. Just in case, slip a large aluminum foil–lined baking sheet onto the rack below to catch any spills. Bake until the pie is golden brown, 25 to 30 minutes. When done, you may notice thick juices bubbling out of the steam vents along the edge.

8. Transfer the pie to a wire rack and let cool for at least 2 hours before serving.

Recipe for Success

▶ This is one pie where it pays to find a superior-tasting apple, best done in the fall and from a local grower. Some apples actually have a complex, winy flavor—not surprisingly, the Winesap variety stands out—that would be delicious in this pie. It's worth inquiring to see if someone in your area grows Winesap or other notable antique apples.

▶ I prefer not to serve this pie with whipped cream or ice cream. The richness can overwhelm the subtle flavors of the pie.

Sounds Like It's Worth the Detour

Every August, the little town of Braham, Minnesota, holds its annual pie festival. This isn't just any pie festival, but one befitting the "Homemade Pie Capital of Minnesota"—so declared by Governor Rudy Perpich back in 1990. The one-day affair draws more than 5,000 hungry visitors, to whom some 150 volunteers serve up more than 500 homemade baked fruit pies. If you can drag yourself away from the pie table long enough, you might be lucky enough to catch some tunes by the Apple Chords Barbershop Quartet or hear the Pie-Alluia Chorus performing at the south end of the town park.

Pie Birds

Pie birds—or pie funnels, as they're called in England—have been used by home cooks since Victorian times. Placed in the center of a pie, with the top pastry draped over the bird through a slit in the crust, this hollow ceramic figure helps support the crust and allow steam to escape through a vent in the bird's beak.

Not all pie birds are birds, incidentally. Some of them are chefs, bakers, pigs, elephants, frogs, golfers, witches, and Santas, to name just a few. Blackbirds, as you might imagine, are a perennial hot seller.

In recent years, pie birds have become highly collectible in the United States. A 97-cent "Benny the Baker" pie bird, produced in the 1950s by New Jersey's Cardinal China Company, is worth about $60 today. A 1950 "Black Chef" wearing a white chef's hat is worth about $150.

To use a pie bird, line your pie pan with pastry, place the bird in the center, and add the filling. Make a small slit in the center of the top pastry, then lower the pastry onto the pie, sliding the bird's head through the slit. With the head sticking through, pinch the pastry around the bird's shoulders. The vent will release steam as the pie bakes.

Nancy Byal's Cider-Infused Apple Pie

Smart pie bakers like Nancy Byal know that you can cram the most apples in your apple pie by partially precooking them first. Nancy, the former food editor of *Better Homes and Gardens* magazine, knows her way around her Iowa kitchen. And she knows apples, too. Her husband, Wayne, used to run an apple orchard that was started by his father and uncle in the 1930s. Back then, says Nancy, Iowa was a significant apple-producing state—something that changed virtually overnight in 1940 when the devastating Armistice Day blizzard killed many of the state's fruit trees. During that storm, the temperature dropped from 70°F to 0°F in a matter of hours.

As you might imagine, Nancy made many apple pies during her husband's tenure at the orchard. This was a family favorite—a thick apple pie made with cider-cooked apples, a little sugar and spice, and not much else. The cider is boiled down and added back to the pie, so it has a pure, clean apple flavor. Nancy likes to use Jonathan apples, a variety that she says is very traditional in Iowa.

MAKES 8 TO 10 SERVINGS

1 recipe Basic Flaky Pie Pastry, Double Crust (page 31), refrigerated

FILLING

12 cups peeled, cored, and sliced Jonathan, Golden Delicious, Rome, or other apples (see pages 232–233 for recommendations)

3/4 cup apple cider

3/4 cup sugar

1/3 cup all-purpose flour

1/2 teaspoon ground cinnamon

1/2 teaspoon ground nutmeg

Pinch of salt

1 tablespoon cold salted or unsalted butter, cut into small pieces

GLAZE

Milk or light cream

Sugar

1. If you haven't already, prepare the pastry and refrigerate until firm enough to roll, about 1 hour.

2. On a sheet of lightly floured waxed paper, roll the larger portion of the pastry into a 13-inch circle with a floured rolling pin. Invert the pastry over a 9½-inch deep-dish pie pan, center, and peel off the paper. Gently tuck the pastry into the pan, without stretching it, and let the overhang drape over the edge. Place in the refrigerator for 15 minutes.

3. Combine the apples and cider in a large nonreactive pot. Bring to a boil, cover, and cook over relatively high heat for 5 minutes, stirring once or twice. Drain the apples, reserving the juice. Transfer the juice to a small nonreactive saucepan and reduce over medium-high heat to ¼ cup. Combine with the apples in a large bowl and let cool.

4. Preheat the oven to 375°F. In a small bowl, combine the sugar, flour, cinnamon, nutmeg, and salt. Stir into the cooled apples and set aside.

5. On another sheet of lightly floured waxed paper, roll the other half of the pastry into an 11½-inch circle. Turn the filling into the chilled pie shell and smooth the top with your hands. Dot the filling with the butter. Lightly moisten the rim of the pie shell. Invert the top pastry over the filling, center it, and peel off the paper. Press the top and bottom pastries together along the dampened edge. Trim the pastry with scissors or a paring knife, leaving an even ½-inch overhang all around, then sculpt the overhang into an upstanding ridge. Poke several steam vents in the top of the pie with a fork or paring knife. Put a couple of the vents near the edge of the crust so you can check the juices there later. Using a pastry brush, brush the pie lightly with milk, then sprinkle with sugar.

6. Place the pie on the center oven rack and bake for 30 minutes, then rotate the pie 180 degrees, so that the part that faced the back of the oven now faces forward. Just in case, slide a large aluminum foil–lined baking sheet onto the rack below to catch any

drips. Continue to bake until the top of the pie is golden brown and any juices visible at the steam vents bubble thickly, 35 to 40 minutes. If the pie starts to get too dark, cover with loosely tented aluminum foil during the last 15 minutes.

7. Transfer the pie to a wire rack and let cool for at least 2 hours before serving.

Recipe for Success

▶ Nancy likes to use more than one type of apple in this pie, including those listed in the ingredients. Each, she says, has something to offer, and together they yield a pie with a well-rounded flavor and texture.

▶ Use more spices, if you like, but Nancy keeps it to a minimum so that the flavor of the apples shines through.

From My "Dubious Pie" File

This is a group of pie recipes I've seen or collected but somehow haven't gotten around to testing.

▶ PICKLE PIE: One Utah newspaper thought the recipe was good enough to print.

▶ SAUERKRAUT PIE: Vaguely intriguing, until I saw the crème de cacao, brandy, and Oreo crust.

▶ JICAMA PIE: So *that's* what you're supposed to do with the stuff!

▶ HORSERADISH APPLE PIE: Still under development, last I heard. I can hardly wait.

Love Apple Pie

Given the fact that I myself make a very delicious apple pie with fresh tomatoes, I should not have been surprised to learn of the existence of a pie made with ketchup. From what I can piece together of the story, sometime in the mid-1970s, the Heinz test kitchen developed a recipe for Love Apple Pie—love apples being another name for tomatoes. The idea seems not to have caught on, but Heinz gamely reintroduced the recipe in the late 1990s, hoping it would strike a chord among a new generation of American pie makers. Once I got over my misgivings, I made the pie and thought it was very good. It has the spicy sweetness of the ketchup, which doesn't seem at all out of place and is, in fact, virtually undetectable. The recipe here is a little different from the original. I sweetened it up a bit, using a little brown sugar in addition to the granulated sugar, and found it more to my taste.

MAKES 8 TO 10 SERVINGS

1 recipe Basic Shortening Pie Pastry, Single Crust (page 30) or Basic Flaky Pie Pastry, Single Crust (page 31), refrigerated

FILLING

1/3 cup Heinz ketchup

2 teaspoons fresh lemon juice

6 cups peeled, cored, and sliced tart apples

1/3 cup sugar

1 tablespoon firmly packed light brown sugar

CRUMB TOPPING

2/3 cup all-purpose flour

1/3 cup sugar

1 teaspoon ground cinnamon

1/3 cup unsalted butter or margarine, softened

1. If you haven't already, prepare the pastry and refrigerate until firm enough to roll, about 1 hour.

2. On a sheet of lightly floured waxed paper, roll the pastry into a 12-inch circle with a floured rolling pin. Invert the pastry over a 9-inch standard pie pan, center, and peel off the paper. Tuck the pastry into the pan, without stretching it, and sculpt the edge into an upstanding ridge. Place in the freezer for 15 minutes. Preheat the oven to 425°F.

3. Combine the ketchup and lemon juice in a large bowl. Add the apples and sugar and stir well. Scrape the filling into the chilled pie shell, smoothing the top with your hands.

4. To make the topping, combine the flour, sugar, and cinnamon in a large bowl, tossing it with your hands. Add the butter, rubbing it gently into the flour mixture until well mixed. Carefully dump the crumbs in the center of the pie, spreading them evenly over the surface with your hands. Tamp them down lightly.

5. Place the pie on the center oven rack and bake until the juices bubble thickly around the edge, 40 to 45 minutes. Rotate the pie 180 degrees halfway through the baking, so that the part that faced the back of the oven now faces forward. Slide a large aluminum foil–lined baking sheet onto the rack below to catch any drips. If the top of the pie starts to get a little too dark, cover loosely with aluminum foil during the final 10 minutes of baking.

6. Transfer the pie to a wire rack to cool. Serve barely warm or at room temperature.

Recipe for Success

▶ Good as this is, I wouldn't go announcing the secret ingredient until dessert is over. I think you run into less resistance that way.

Washington State Granny Smith Apple Pie

I called LaVerne Bergstrom of the Washington Apple Commission, whose job it is to promote Washington State apples, to ask if there's anything cooks in her state do to make a particularly delicious or notable pie with Granny Smith apples. As you might expect, she was quick to point out that many home bakers like Grannies for their tartness, juiciness, and complex flavor. That said, she told me that bakers in the know often use less than the usual amount of sugar to make a Granny Smith pie. The flavor of the apples is so good, she said, less sugar is required. She went on to describe a technique she likes for making a Granny Smith pie—one she once saw Martha Stewart demonstrate. You just layer Granny Smith apples in a pie shell and sprinkle a little sugar and thickener over them. I thought this sounded like an interesting approach, so I tried doing it myself, with excellent results. I added an easy crumb topping made with melted butter, but a top pastry crust would be an excellent choice, too.

MAKES 8 TO 10 SERVINGS

1 recipe Basic Flaky Pie Pastry, Single Crust (page 31), refrigerated

FILLING

1/3 cup sugar

1 1/2 tablespoons cornstarch

1/8 teaspoon salt

7 cups peeled, cored, and sliced Granny Smith apples (see Recipe for Success)

1 tablespoon fresh lemon juice

CRUMB TOPPING

6 tablespoons (3/4 stick) unsalted butter

1 1/4 cups all-purpose flour

1/2 cup sugar

1/4 teaspoon salt

1/2 teaspoon ground cinnamon

1. If you haven't already, prepare the pastry and refrigerate until firm enough to roll, about 1 hour.

2. On a sheet of lightly floured waxed paper, roll the pastry into a 13-inch circle with a floured rolling pin. Invert the pastry over a 9½-inch deep-dish pie pan, center, and peel off the paper. Tuck the pastry into the pan, without stretching it, and sculpt the edge into an upstanding ridge. Place in the freezer for 15 minutes. Preheat the oven to 400°F.

3. Mix the sugar, cornstarch, and salt together in a small bowl. Set aside. Combine the apples and lemon juice in a large bowl. Sprinkle about 1 tablespoon of the sugar mixture evenly over the chilled pie shell. Arrange a single, compact layer of apples, flat side down, in the shell. Sprinkle with 1 tablespoon of the sugar mixture. Arrange a second layer of apples over the first and sprinkle with another tablespoon of the sugar mixture. Continue until all the apples and sugar mixture have been used. Place the pie on the center oven rack and bake for 30 minutes.

4. Meanwhile, make the crumb topping. In a medium-size saucepan, melt the butter over very low heat. As it melts, combine the flour, sugar, salt, and cinnamon in a medium-size bowl. Pour the melted butter over the flour mixture and mix well with a fork. Using your fingertips, rub the mixture gently until it forms more or less even, damp crumbs. Set aside.

5. Remove the pie from the oven and reduce the temperature to 375°F. Carefully dump the crumb topping in the center of the pie and spread evenly over the surface with your hands. Tamp the crumbs down lightly. Return the pie to the oven, placing it so that the part that faced the back of the oven now faces forward. To catch any spills, slide a large aluminum foil–lined baking sheet onto the rack below. Bake until you see the juices bubbling thickly at the edge, about 35 minutes. If the top starts to get too brown, cover loosely with aluminum foil for the last 15 minutes.

6. Transfer the pie to a wire rack and let cool for at least 1 hour before serving.

Recipe for Success

▶ Not everyone likes Granny Smith apples for a pie, because they bake up soft. Although I've found that to be the case much of the time, I don't think soft apples are a bad thing. Indeed, I've spoken with many people over the years who much prefer a softer, saucy apple filling to a more textured one. You can always use a couple of Golden Delicious apples along with the Grannies to add a little texture to the pie.

Liz Reiter's All-Granny Slug-O-Bourbon Spiced Apple Pie

Liz Reiter is my pie-making editor pal from Kentucky and my expert on the pies in that neck of the woods. (Do read her fun sidebar on page 225.) Earlier in her career, Liz made pies for some restaurants in and around the Louisville area, including this apple pie, about which she has strong opinions (see Recipe for Success). Anyway, I know a thing or two about apple pie myself, and one thing I can tell you is that I was delighted to add this pie to my collection. It's spicy, bold, and has attitude; bourbon will do that. You'll want to give this one a try.

MAKES 8 TO 10 SERVINGS

1 recipe Basic Flaky Pie Pastry, Double Crust (page 31), refrigerated

FILLING

4 large or 3 extra-large Granny Smith apples, peeled, cored, and cut into chunks

3/4 cup sugar

2 tablespoons all-purpose flour

1/2 teaspoon ground cinnamon

1/4 teaspoon ground nutmeg

1/4 teaspoon ground cloves

Pinch of salt

Slug of bourbon (Liz calls it a "one-two count slug")

3 tablespoons cold unsalted butter, cut into small pieces

GARNISH

Sugar

1. If you haven't already, prepare the pastry and refrigerate until firm enough to roll, about 1 hour.

2. On a sheet of lightly floured waxed paper, roll the larger portion of the pastry into a 13-inch circle with a floured rolling pin. Invert the pastry over a 9½-inch deep-dish pie pan, center, and peel off the paper. Gently tuck the pastry into the pan, without stretching it, and let the overhang drape over the edge. Place in the refrigerator for 15 minutes.

3. In a large bowl, combine the apples, sugar, flour, spices, and salt. Mix well, then set aside for 15 minutes. Stir in the bourbon. Preheat the oven to 400°F.

4. Roll the other half of the pastry into an 11-inch circle on a sheet of lightly floured waxed paper. Turn the filling into the chilled pie shell, smoothing the fruit with your hands. Dot the filling with the butter. Lightly moisten the rim of the pie shell. Invert the top pastry over the filling, center, and peel off the paper. Press the top and bottom pastries together along the dampened edge. Using the back of a butter knife or pastry knife, trim the pastry flush with the edge of the pan and crimp the edge with a fork. Poke several steam vents in the top of the pie with a fork or paring knife. Put a couple of the vents near the edge of the crust so you can check the juices there later. To glaze the pie, sprinkle the top lightly with sugar.

5. Place the pie on the center oven rack and bake for 30 minutes. Reduce the oven temperature to 350°F and rotate the pie 180 degrees, so that the part that faced the back of the oven now faces forward. Just in case, slide a large aluminum foil–lined baking sheet onto the rack below to catch any spills. Continue to bake until the top is golden brown and any visible juices bubble thickly through the steam vents, about 30 minutes.

6. Transfer the pie to a wire rack and let cool for at least 2 hours before serving.

Recipe for Success

▶ Liz's pastry is a little different from my own, but similar enough that she said it would be fine to recommend the Basic Flaky Pie Pastry.

▶ Liz says, "I hate pastry blenders; they smoosh everything together." She prefers making her pastry with 2 knives or a food processor.

▶ And this: "I hate it when the apple slices are so thin that it makes applesauce. That's why I specify chunks."

A Slice of Kentucky (Pie) Culture

"In Kentucky, change comes slowly. Even young people may use the phrase 'a while back,' meaning not months or even years, but decades.

"At the *Courier-Journal*, people still call and ask for Cissy Gregg, a former food editor who retired in 1962. Told she's no longer there, they may laugh and say, 'Honey, it just doesn't seem like it's been that long.'

"And it really doesn't, once you're away from the highway, with chain restaurants clustered at every exit. In almost every small town, you can still walk into an unair-conditioned family restaurant with gray-haired wait staff and customers who seem like family.

"In this restaurant, there are usually some living room knickknacks or family pictures hanging on the walls to dress up the place. The aged floor will be freshly washed, and the air may smell faintly of bleach. And there's liable to be a counter lined with glass cake keepers.

"In at least one of these keepers, if you're lucky and the regular customers haven't already eaten it all, you'll see one of our real Kentucky pies.

"Maybe it's buttermilk, with soft filling oozing thickly. Maybe it's a so-sweet-only-a-southerner-could-stand-it coconut cream; a creamy, tart lemon meringue; or a gooey chocolate-nut. Whatever the case, it's sure to be as full of sugar as a Kentucky conversation.

"And after you've had a bit, you want more. You want to be able to make this anytime you please.

"'Our cook makes these every day,' the restaurant owner may say. 'She doesn't usually like to give people the recipes—they all came from her mama—but you can ask her.'

"You and the cook may drawl compliments at each other for a little while. Like any good southerner, she'll avoid a definite yes or no answer at first. But if you're lucky, and polite as can be, she'll take you into her confidence eventually.

"When you leave, the recipe scrawled onto a bit of notepaper or napkin, you'll never know if she shared everything. Maybe she kept just one ingredient secret.

"Even if you suspect such a sweet deception, however, you'll happily keep trying to re-create that glue-your-teeth-together sugary treat that is a real Kentucky pie."

—Liz Reiter, Assistant Food Editor, *Louisville Courier-Journal*

Cooked-Fruit Apple Pie

Frequently during my cooking classes and demonstrations, someone asks what they can do about eliminating the space that remains between the crust and the apples after they've baked an apple pie. Frankly, I say, there's not a whole lot you can do about it after the fact—although you might want to try the little trick I mention in the Recipe for Success on pages 146–147. But there is something you can do to eliminate that gap altogether: cook the apples ahead of time. Cooking the apples shrinks their mass by nearly one-half, so there is no gap when the pie is baked. The pastry just snuggles up to the apples and stays there. The key to preparing this pie is to cook the apples just enough but not too much. You want them to shrink but not lose their crunch and texture altogether. So pay careful attention to the precooking step here. I think you'll like this approach to apple pie. You may not care to do this all the time, but it's worth trying to see how the flavor and texture differ from the traditional approach.

MAKES 8 TO 10 SERVINGS

1 recipe Basic Flaky Pie Pastry, Double Crust (page 31), refrigerated

FILLING

2 tablespoons unsalted butter

8 cups peeled, cored, and thickly sliced (about 1/3 inch thick) Golden Delicious apples (see Recipe for Success)

1/2 cup sugar

1 tablespoon cornstarch

2 teaspoons fresh lemon juice

1/2 cup dark raisins

1/4 teaspoon ground cinnamon

1. If you haven't already, prepare the pastry and refrigerate until firm enough to roll, about 1 hour.

2. On a sheet of lightly floured waxed paper, roll the larger portion of the pastry into a 12-inch circle with a floured rolling pin. Invert the pastry over a 9-inch standard pie pan, center, and peel off the paper. Gently tuck the pastry into the pan, without stretching it, and let the overhang drape over the edge. Place in the refrigerator for 15 minutes.

3. Melt the butter in a very large skillet over medium-high heat. Add the apples and cook, stirring very often, for 3 to 4 minutes. Add most of the sugar, reserving a tablespoon or two, and continue to cook, still stirring often, for 2 to 3 minutes. As the apples cook, mix the remaining sugar with the cornstarch. Stir this mixture into the apples and cook for another minute. The apples should have shrunk by now, but they should still have some of their crunch. Transfer the apples to a large, shallow casserole. Stir in the lemon juice, raisins, and cinnamon. Spread the filling evenly in the casserole and let cool thoroughly. Preheat the oven to 400°F when it's almost there.

4. Turn the cooled filling into the chilled pie shell and smooth the top with your hands. Roll the other half of the pastry into a 10-inch circle on a sheet of lightly floured waxed paper. Moisten the outer edge of the pie shell with a pastry brush. Invert the top pastry over the filling, center, and peel off the paper. Press the top and bottom pastries together along the dampened edge. Using the back of a butter knife, trim the pastry flush with the edge of the pan. With the back of a fork, press the tines all along the edge to seal. Poke several steam vents in the top of the pie with the fork.

5. Place the pie on the center oven rack and bake until nicely browned, 40 to 45 minutes. Rotate the pie 180 degrees halfway through the baking, so that the part that faced the back of the oven now faces forward. You should not experience any trouble with the pie bubbling over, but just in case, slide a large aluminum foil–lined baking sheet onto the rack below.

6. Transfer the pie to a wire rack and let cool for at least 30 minutes before serving.

Recipe for Success

▶ Don't substitute another variety of apple unless you're certain it will hold up well in the cooking. Most apples will likely get too soft in the intense heat of the skillet. Northern Spy may work well, although I haven't actually tried it. Do spread the apples out, as directed. If you pile them up, they'll continue to cook from the surrounding heat, resulting in overly soft apples.

Sugar-Dusted Apple Strudel Pie

I've noticed that a number of apple pie recipes, including some previous winners from the American Pie Council's National Pie Championships (see page 387), call for the entire filling to be mixed ahead and then left in the fridge overnight. I wondered what this was all about—how leaving the filling to sit would affect the pie—so I tried it and liked the results. For one thing, the apples get very moist and soft, because they sit in their own juices for hours. They also settle, reducing in volume by as much as one-third. This makes for a compact, full-flavored pie that I quite like. The filling suggests a very light, flaky, and tender dough, so I use my favorite cream cheese pastry. Dusted with confectioners' sugar, this pie reminds me very much of a traditional apple strudel.

MAKES 8 TO 10 SERVINGS

FILLING

5 cups peeled, cored, and thinly sliced Granny Smith apples

1/4 cup granulated sugar

2 tablespoons all-purpose flour

1/4 teaspoon ground cinnamon

1 tablespoon fresh lemon juice

Pinch of salt

CRUST

1 recipe Tender Cream Cheese Pastry, Double Crust (page 46), divided as instructed in step 2 and refrigerated

GARNISH

Confectioners' sugar

1. Prepare the filling at least 4 hours or up to 12 hours before assembling the pie. Place the apples in a large bowl. In a small bowl, combine the granulated sugar, flour, and cinnamon, then stir the mixture into the apples. Stir in the lemon juice and salt and toss well. Cover the bowl with plastic wrap and refrigerate, stirring every hour or so, when you think of it. Remove the filling from the refrigerator about 1 hour before you plan to use it.

2. If you haven't already, prepare the pastry, dividing it into equal halves. Refrigerate for 1 to 1½ hours.

3. When you're ready to assemble and bake the pie, preheat the oven to 400°F. On a sheet of lightly floured waxed paper, roll half of the pastry into a 12-inch circle with a floured rolling pin. Invert the pastry over a 9-inch standard pie pan, center, and peel off the paper. Gently tuck the pastry down into the pan, without stretching it, and let the overhang drape over the edge. Place in the refrigerator for 15 minutes.

4. Roll the other half of the pastry into a 12-inch circle on a sheet of lightly floured waxed paper. Turn the filling into the chilled pie shell and smooth the top with your hands. Dampen the edge of the pie shell with a wet fingertip or pastry brush. Invert the top pastry over the filling, center, and peel off the paper. Press the top and bottom pastries together along the dampened edge. Trim the pastry, leaving an even ½-inch overhang all around, then sculpt the overhang into an upstanding ridge. Poke several steam vents in the top of

the pie with a fork or paring knife. Put a couple of the vents near the edge of the crust so you can check the juices there later.

5. Place the pie on the center oven rack and bake for 25 minutes. Reduce the oven temperature to 375°F and rotate the pie 180 degrees, so that the part that faced the back of the oven now faces forward. Continue to bake until the top of the pie is golden and the juices visible at the steam vents bubble thickly, 25 to 30 minutes. Since this pie is not prone to bubbling over, you probably won't need a baking sheet under it to catch drips.

6. Transfer the pie to a wire rack. While the pie is still hot, dust the top with confectioners' sugar. Let cool for at least 1 hour before serving.

Recipe for Success

▶ **Full-flavored Granny Smith apples are excellent here, but there are any number of other good choices. If apples are in season and the selection is wide, you might consider Northern Spy, Gravenstein, or Winesap, all of which have great flavor and a nice balance of tartness and sweetness.**

▶ **Dusting the pie with confectioners' sugar while it is still hot gives you 2 sugar layers.** The part closest to the pie more or less melts in place, while the sugar on top remains powdery. It's a nice touch that you'll miss if you wait until the pie is cool before dusting it.

Caramel Apple-Pecan Pie

A reporter from a large Illinois newspaper asked me if I thought the current caramel apple pie craze had anything to do with the resurgence of pie making in this country. I was clueless about the caramel apple pie craze, but I launched into a dazzling answer, as if I had been personally responsible for starting it. Then I hung up the phone and quickly started inventing my own recipe, basing it on one the reporter had recently tried and fallen in love with. So here is my version, which has a pecan crumb topping covered with a layer of caramel and pecans. It has great eye appeal—just like a caramel apple—and the pecan, apple, and caramel flavors couldn't be more delicious together. So have at it—and just remember, you read about it here first.

MAKES 8 TO 10 SERVINGS

1 recipe Basic Flaky Pie Pastry, Single Crust (page 31), modified as instructed in step 1 and refrigerated

10 caramels, each cut into 4 pieces

FILLING

7 cups peeled, cored, and sliced Golden Delicious apples (see Recipe for Success)

1/2 cup firmly packed light brown sugar

1 tablespoon fresh lemon juice

2 tablespoons granulated sugar

1 tablespoon cornstarch

1/2 teaspoon ground cinnamon

1 teaspoon vanilla extract

PECAN CRUMB TOPPING

3/4 cup all-purpose flour

3/4 cup pecan halves

1/2 cup granulated sugar

1/4 teaspoon salt

6 tablespoons (3/4 stick) cold unsalted butter, cut into 1/4-inch pieces

CARAMEL AND GARNISH

3 tablespoons unsalted butter, cut into pieces

1 tablespoon water

30 caramels

Large handful of pecan halves

1/2 cup chopped pecans

1. Prepare the pastry according to the recipe, using a total of 3 tablespoons sugar. Refrigerate until firm enough to roll, about 1 hour.

2. On a sheet of lightly floured waxed paper, roll the pastry into a 13-inch circle with a floured rolling pin. Invert the pastry over a 9½-inch deep-dish pie pan, center, and peel off the paper. Tuck the pastry into the pan, without stretching it, and sculpt the edge into an upstanding ridge. Scatter the caramel pieces in the pie shell and place in the freezer while you make the filling. Preheat the oven to 400°F.

3. Combine the apples, brown sugar, and lemon juice in a large bowl. Mix well, then set aside for 5 to 10 minutes to juice. Mix the granulated sugar and cornstarch together in a small bowl. Stir the mixture into the fruit along with the cinnamon and vanilla. Scrape the filling into the chilled pie shell, smoothing the fruit with your hands. Put the pie on the center oven rack and bake for 30 minutes.

4. Meanwhile, make the crumb topping. Combine the flour, pecan halves, granulated sugar, and salt in a food processor. Pulse several times, chopping the nuts coarsely. Scatter the butter over the dry mixture and pulse the machine again until the mixture resembles fine crumbs. Transfer the crumbs to a medium-size bowl and rub the mixture between your fingers to make damp, gravelly crumbs. Refrigerate until ready to use.

5. Remove the pie from the oven and reduce the temperature to 375°F. Carefully dump the crumbs in the center of the pie, spreading them evenly over the surface with your hands. Tamp them down lightly. Return the pie to the oven, placing it so that the part

that faced the back of the oven now faces forward. Just in case, slide a large aluminum foil–lined baking sheet onto the rack below to catch any drips. Bake until the juices bubble thickly around the edge, 30 to 40 minutes. If necessary, cover the pie with loosely tented aluminum foil for the last 15 minutes to keep the top from getting too dark.

6. Transfer the pie to a wire rack and let cool for about 1 hour.

7. While the pie is still warm—approaching the 1-hour mark—prepare the caramel. Combine the butter, water, and caramels in the top of a double boiler. Melt the caramels over, not in, barely simmering water. This may take 10 minutes or more. To facilitate the melting, press down on them as they start to soften and melt. When melted, whisk the mixture until it is smooth, then drizzle the caramel over the entire surface of the pie. Immediately press the pecan halves into the caramel in a random fashion, then sprinkle the chopped pecans over the top as well. Let cool for another hour before serving.

Recipe for Success

▶ Golden Delicious isn't the only variety of apple you can use here, but since it holds its shape well, I consider it a good candidate. Feel free to substitute 1 or 2 Granny Smith or other tart apples for contrast. See pages 232–233 for other recommendations.

▶ You can make this pie with walnuts, but I think the pecan halves give it a very attractive and classy look.

▶ Work quickly after you pour the caramel over the pie so that it doesn't firm up before you add the pecans.

Another One for the Record Books

In 1976, 16-year-old Kathy Wafler Madison of Wolcott, New York, pared her way into the history books by peeling the longest apple peel on record. According to the *Guinness Book of World Records*, the peel measured 2,068 inches, or roughly 172 feet, long—more than half the length of a football field. Using a special horticultural knife adapted by her father, Kathy spent 11 hours creating the record strand, which measured on average one-thirty-second inch wide. Asked if she had any advice for those who would care to break her record, she replied, "Get a big apple. And have a lot of patience."

Pie Apples at a Glance

I give quite a few apple pie–baking demonstrations each year, and many more interviews on the subject, and the question that always comes up is, Which kind of apples make the best pie? The fact is, most of them do—as long as they're fresh and juicy. A certain amount of tartness helps, too, as well as complexity of flavor. I delve into the subject of pie apples in detail in my book *Apple Pie Perfect* (Harvard Common Press, 2002), which includes a section on antique apples by my friend Mike Berst, one of the smartest apple experts in the country. It's worth consulting if, like me, you're an apple pie aficionado. Meanwhile, here are some observations to lead you in the right direction.

- **BALDWIN** An all-purpose red-skinned apple with a mild, sweet-tart flavor and crisp texture. Aromatic, it stores well and makes a commendable pie.

- **BRAEBURN** Varies in color from greenish gold to red with yellow markings. The flesh is smooth, juicy, and crisp, with a good flavor. Thumbs up.

- **CORTLAND** Common in the Northeast and one of Vermont's leading apples. For pies, the early ones are tarter and generally better than the later ones, which tend to be fairly sweet.

- **FUJI** One of the best-selling apples in Japan, it's a cross between a Red Delicious and a Ralls Janet. More prized as a dessert apple—one that's eaten out of hand—than a baking apple, it has a spicy flavor and juiciness that I quite like in pies.

- **GOLDEN DELICIOUS** A reliable, all-purpose apple with legions of both fans and detractors, the latter who don't care for the apple's sometimes bland flavor. The skin is soft enough to leave on, and the slices hold their shape well. When fresh and juicy, this is a fine pie apple.

- **GRAVENSTEIN** Thought to be one of the best early apples for pie makers, ripening in late August. It has a creamy, sweet-tart flesh and makes a delicious pie.

- **JONAGOLD** A cross between a Jonathan and a Golden Delicious, it doesn't store well but has a sweet, creamy, juicy flesh that tastes great in a pie.

- **JONATHAN** Some think it ranks as one of the best pie apples; others are less effusive. It has a soft, fine-textured flesh with a spicy flavor that I believe translates well into pies.

- **MACOUN** Developed in New York State, the Macoun is a cross between a McIntosh and a Jersey Black. Generally considered to be a dessert apple, some say it makes a much better pie apple than the McIntosh.

- **McINTOSH** Some love, others despise the McIntosh's fine-textured flesh, which tends to turn very soft when baked. I prefer the early Macs more than the later ones, as they're generally sweeter, firmer, and more distinctive.

- **NORTHERN SPY** Spies are for pies, the saying goes, and this is perhaps the quintessential pie apple—tart, tangy, juicy, and firm. Sometimes hard to find outside of farm stands, the Northern Spy is an excellent storage apple.

- **RED DELICIOUS** This is the one apple that, unequivocally, does *not* make a decent pie. Bred more for good looks than flavor or texture, it lacks the personality needed for a successful apple pie.

- **WINESAP** A superior, late-ripening apple with sweet-tart, winy, juicy flesh. The complex flavor has made it a favorite of cider makers for hundreds of years. Though hard to find, it's worth the look.

Mile-Deep Apple Ring Pie

You've heard of mile-high pies, of course, but here's a mile-deep one—a little stunt I accomplish by using a chicken fryer–like pan or deep cast-iron skillet to bake this top crust–only pie. The ideal pan should stand $3^1/4$ to $3^1/2$ inches tall, with a diameter of about 10 inches. Any deep-dish casserole or pan of those approximate dimensions will probably do nicely. One of the things I like best about this pie is its straightforward rusticity: it's just apple rings, sugar, thickener, and maple syrup. I top it with a butter pastry and bake. The pie slowly sinks as the apples cook down and settle. It reminds me of a simple country pie that a farm family might make in the fall, when fresh apples are plentiful. Kids like to help with this one because they get to core the whole apples to make the rings.

MAKES 8 TO 10 SERVINGS

1 recipe All-Butter Pie Pastry, Single Crust (page 28), refrigerated

FILLING

$1/3$ cup sugar

$1/4$ cup all-purpose flour

1 teaspoon ground cinnamon

7 or 8 good-size apples (see Recipe for Success; half of them should be Golden Delicious), peeled

$1/4$ cup pure maple syrup

2 tablespoons cold unsalted butter, cut into small pieces

GLAZE

Milk or light cream

Sugar

1. If you haven't already, prepare the pastry and refrigerate it until firm enough to roll, about 1 hour. Preheat the oven to 400°F. Get out your baking pan (see headnote) and butter it well.

2. Combine the sugar, flour, and cinnamon in a small bowl. Set aside.

3. Using an apple corer, core the apples, then slice them into rings about $1/4$ inch thick. Layer the apple rings in the pan, overlapping them slightly. Sprinkle each layer generously with the sugar mixture. Continue layering and sprinkling until you're within $1/2$ inch of the rim. Drizzle the maple syrup over the apples, then dot with the butter.

4. On a sheet of lightly floured waxed paper, roll the pastry into an 11- to 12-inch circle with a floured rolling pin; you want it slightly larger than the pan's diameter. Invert the pastry over the pan, center, and peel off the paper. Tuck the pastry down into the pan.

Using a fork or paring knife, make a few steam vents in the top. Brush the pastry with milk and sprinkle with sugar.

5. Place the pie on one of the lower oven racks and bake for 40 minutes. Reduce the oven temperature to 375°F and rotate the pie 180 degrees, so that the part that faced the back of the oven now faces forward. Continue to bake until the top is golden brown and the apples are tender, 30 to 40 minutes. Use a skewer or paring knife poked through the top crust to make sure the apples are done. Because of the depth of the pie, don't expect to see juices bubbling up along the edge.

6. Transfer the pie to a wire rack and let cool for at least 20 minutes before serving. Rather than cut this pie into slices, you may want to spoon it out, because it may be difficult to make neat cuts. That's part of the pie's rustic charm.

Recipe for Success

▶ **This is a good pie to use more than one type of apple—Golden Delicious for firmness, maybe a Granny Smith or two for tartness and juiciness. Don't be afraid to experiment. You'll likely end up with the best features of each apple in your pie.**

▶ **If you're not using a cast-iron pan, add 1 tablespoon fresh lemon juice to the apples. Don't use the lemon juice with cast iron because the juice may react with the iron and cause an off flavor.**

Calvados-Apple Custard Pie

The Normandy region of France is known for its fine dairy products, including smooth, rich cheese, butter, and crème fraîche. It's also a center of French apple production and thus cider, the basic ingredient in the twice-distilled apple brandy known as Calvados. This pie is a nod to Normandy, where Calvados-spiked apple tarts are common. In the French tradition, one would search high and low for the best fresh, crisp apples, whose complex flavor would dignify such a fine dessert. If you have access to antique apples, I suggest that you do the same. Otherwise, I recommend Northern Spy, Greening, or even Golden Delicious—the last not the equal of the others in terms of flavor, but it will hold up nicely in the pie. Serve this as the finale to a French-inspired menu—barely warm, if you prefer, or, the way I like it, chilled for several hours.

MAKES 8 TO 10 SERVINGS

1 recipe All-Butter Pie Pastry, Single Crust (page 28) or Basic Flaky Pie Pastry, Single Crust (page 31), refrigerated

FILLING

2 tablespoons unsalted butter

3 large apples (see headnote), peeled, cored, and thickly sliced (about 1/3 inch thick)

2 tablespoons plus 1/2 cup sugar

1/4 cup plus 2 tablespoons Calvados

11/4 cups heavy or whipping cream

3 large eggs

1/2 teaspoon vanilla extract

Big pinch of salt

1.   If you haven't already, prepare the pastry and refrigerate until firm enough to roll, about 1 hour.

2.   On a sheet of lightly floured waxed paper, roll the pastry into a 13-inch circle with a floured rolling pin. Invert the pastry over a 9½-inch deep-dish pie pan, center, and peel off the paper. Tuck the pastry into the pan, without stretching it, and sculpt the edge into an upstanding ridge. Place in the freezer for 15 minutes, then partially prebake and let cool according to the instructions on page 16. Reduce the oven temperature to 350°F.

3.   Melt the butter in a large, preferably nonstick nonreactive skillet. Stir in the apples and cook over medium-high heat, stirring often, for 2 minutes. Stir in 2 tablespoons of the sugar and cook for 1 minute. Add ¼ cup of the Calvados and continue to cook, stirring, until the liquid boils off, 1 to 2 minutes. Remove from the heat and scrape the apples onto a large plate to cool.

4.   Meanwhile, heat the heavy cream and remaining ½ cup sugar in a small saucepan over medium heat, stirring, until fairly warm, 2 to 3 minutes. Remove from the heat. Beat the eggs until frothy in a medium-size bowl, then stir in about ½ cup of the warm cream. Gradually stir in the rest of the cream along with the vanilla, salt, and remaining 2 tablespoons Calvados.

5.   Turn the cooled apples into the cooled pie shell, spreading them evenly. Ladle the custard over the apples. After the first couple of ladlefuls, move the apples around slightly to make sure the custard is flowing underneath them. Ladle on the rest of the custard, taking care that you don't overfill the pie shell.

6.   Place the pie on the center oven rack and bake for 25 minutes. Rotate the pie 180 degrees, so that the part that faced the back of the oven now faces forward. Continue to bake until the custard is set in the center, 20 to 25 minutes.

7. Transfer the pie to a wire rack and let cool. Serve barely warm or at room temperature, or cover loosely with aluminum foil, refrigerate, and serve cold.

Recipe for Success

▶ **When you're precooking the apples, make sure they don't get too soft. If that starts to happen, pick up the pace and get them off the heat and onto the plate as soon as possible.**

▶ **To check the pie for doneness, you may have to stick a paring knife down into the center of the custard. Simply find a gap between the apples and probe gently. It's fine if the custard looks barely set, but it should not be runny.**

Pennsylvania Dutch Sour Cream–Apple Pie

Custard pies such as this often show up in places like Wisconsin and Vermont, or just about anywhere apples and dairy farms coexist, sometimes side by side. The custard part of the equation is more typically made with heavy or light cream, but here we use sour cream, resulting in a tangy, more full-bodied custard. (You could, if you like, substitute a full-fat yogurt such as Stonyfield Farm.) It's all very rich and delicious, and even more so with the crunchy-sweet walnut topping.

MAKES 8 TO 10 SERVINGS

1 recipe Basic Flaky Pie Pastry, Single Crust (page 31) or All-Butter Pie Pastry, Single Crust (page 28), refrigerated

FILLING

1 1/4 cups full-fat sour cream

3/4 cup granulated sugar

1 large egg

1/4 cup all-purpose flour

1/4 teaspoon salt

2 teaspoons vanilla extract

7 to 8 cups peeled, cored, and thinly sliced Granny Smith, Northern Spy, or Golden Delicious apples

WALNUT STREUSEL TOPPING

1 cup all-purpose flour

1/2 cup granulated sugar

1/2 cup firmly packed light brown sugar

1 teaspoon ground cinnamon

Big pinch of salt

3/4 cup chopped walnuts

6 tablespoons (3/4 stick) unsalted butter, melted

1.   If you haven't already, prepare the pastry and refrigerate until firm enough to roll, about 1 hour.

2.   On a sheet of lightly floured waxed paper, roll the pastry into a 13-inch circle with a floured rolling pin. Invert the pastry over a 9½-inch deep-dish pie pan, center, and peel off the paper. Tuck the pastry into the pan, without stretching it, and sculpt the edge into an upstanding ridge. Place in the freezer for 15 minutes. Preheat the oven to 400°F.

3.   In a large bowl, whisk together the sour cream, granulated sugar, egg, flour, salt, and vanilla until evenly blended. Add the apples and mix well. Turn the filling into the chilled pie shell and smooth the top with your hands, laying the apple slices down flat.

4.   Place the pie on the center oven rack and bake for 15 minutes. Reduce the oven temperature to 350°F and bake for 30 minutes more.

5.   Meanwhile, make the topping. Combine the flour, sugars, cinnamon, salt, and walnuts in a large bowl. Add the butter and stir with a fork, then switch to your hands, rubbing the mixture gently between your fingers until it forms uniform crumbs. Refrigerate until ready to use.

6.   Remove the pie from the oven and carefully dump the streusel topping in the center, spreading it evenly over the surface with your hands. Tamp the topping down lightly. Return the pie to the oven, placing it so that the part that faced the back of the oven now faces forward. Just in case, slide a large aluminum foil–lined baking sheet onto the rack below to catch any spills. Continue to bake until the topping is golden brown, about 20 minutes.

7.   Transfer the pie to a wire rack and let cool for at least 2 hours before serving. I prefer to serve this pie chilled. If you do, too, when the pie is thoroughly cooled, cover with loosely tented aluminum foil and refrigerate for at least 2 hours.

Recipe for Success

▸   When an apple pie is cooked in a thick custard such as this, expect the apples to stay a little on the firm side. They never seem to get quite as soft as they do in an apple pie made without the custard.

▸   You'll notice that this streusel topping, made with melted butter, is crunchier than streusel made with solid butter. You can, if you like, substitute one of the many other crumb toppings in this collection.

The Mother of All Apple Pies

A couple of times each fall, I pull out my really big Emile Henry pie plate—I call it my Hummer of pie plates—and bake a mondo apple pie. I like doing it for the shock value, because pies this size seldom make public appearances. But I also do it out of need: I don't know what it's like around your house, but come autumn, we have apples multiplying like rabbits. The best way I know to use them is by making a pie. This pie will also answer a question I've heard frequently since writing my book *Apple Pie Perfect* (Harvard Common Press, 2002): can I mix different kinds of apples when I make an apple pie? My response is a resounding yes! Like kids who wind up with the best traits of both parents, a mixed-apple pie has the best qualities of all the apples used. I like a couple of Grannies for tartness, Golden Delicious for texture, Gala for flavor, and McIntosh for a bit of sauciness. But don't feel limited to those. By the way, the pan I use for this measures almost 12 inches across, is 2 inches deep, and holds a good 12 to 13 cups of sliced apples.

MAKE 12 TO 14 SERVINGS

1 recipe Basic Flaky Pie Pastry, Double Crust (page 31), modified as instructed in step 1 and refrigerated

FILLING

12 to 13 cups peeled, cored, and sliced apples (see headnote)

3/4 cup sugar

Juice of 2 lemons

1/3 cup all-purpose flour

1/2 teaspoon ground nutmeg

1/4 cup (1/2 stick) cold unsalted butter, cut into small pieces

PECAN CRUMB TOPPING

1 1/4 cups pecan halves

1 cup all-purpose flour

3/4 cup sugar

1/2 teaspoon salt

1 teaspoon ground cinnamon

1/2 cup (1 stick) cold unsalted butter, cut into 1/4-inch pieces

1. If you haven't already, prepare the pastry but don't divide it in half. Leave it whole and flatten the entire thing into a disk about 3/4 inch thick. Refrigerate until firm enough to roll, about 1 hour. Meanwhile, get out a pan like the one I describe in the headnote or a similar one. You may have a casserole dish that will work. Set aside.

2. Place two overlapping sheets of waxed paper on your counter to roll the pastry on. Dust with flour. Put the pastry on the seam and, using a floured rolling pin, roll it into a 17-inch circle (or thereabouts). Invert the pastry over the pan, center, and peel off the paper. Gently tuck the pastry into the pan, without stretching it, and sculpt the edge into an upstanding ridge. Place in the freezer or refrigerator while you make the filling. Preheat the oven to 400°F.

3.   In your largest bowl, combine the apples, sugar, and lemon juice. Set aside for 10 minutes. Stir in the flour and nutmeg. Turn the filling into the chilled pie shell, smoothing it with your hands so that the apple slices lie flat. Dot the top of the pie with the butter. Put the pie on the center oven rack and bake for 30 minutes.

4.   Meanwhile, make the crumb topping. Combine the pecans, flour, sugar, and salt in a food processor and pulse several times to chop the nuts coarsely. Scatter the butter over the dry mixture and pulse again until the mixture resembles fine crumbs. Transfer the topping to a large bowl and rub the mixture between your fingers to make damp, gravelly crumbs. Refrigerate until ready to use.

5.   Remove the pie from the oven and reduce the temperature to 375°F. Carefully dump the crumbs in the center of the pie, spreading them evenly over the surface with your hands. Tamp them down lightly. Return the pie to the oven, placing it so that the part that faced the back of the oven now faces forward. Just in case, slide a large aluminum foil–lined baking sheet onto the rack below to catch any spills. Bake until the juices bubble thickly around the edge, 35 to 45 minutes. If the top of the pie starts to get too brown, drape a piece of aluminum foil over it for the last 10 minutes of baking.

6.   Transfer the pie to a rack and cool. Serve barely warm or at room temperature.

Recipe for Success

▶ Don't be intimidated by the size of this pie or the outsize rolling job required for the pastry. It's no more difficult to roll a 17-inch circle than it is to roll a 12-inch one. Just take it nice and easy, and keep your pastry and pin floured.

▶ Especially when you bake a pie for an extended period, like this one, there's a chance the edge will get well browned. Either just forget about it—it affects very little of the pie crust—or make a customized aluminum foil shield to cover the edge of the crust.

We Think We'll Pass, Too, Thank You

"There's a truck stop along Interstate 80 in Western Pennsylvania that has a billboard claiming it serves the world's worst pie. I've been meaning to stop in for years, but . . . I haven't yet made it."

—Posting at www.roadfood.com

Rose Calello's Salem Cross Inn Apple Pie

For the past several years, the Salem Cross Inn in West Brookfield, Massachusetts, has sponsored the Best Apple Pie in New England Contest. All the contestants must bake their pies in the inn's old-fashioned wood-fired beehive oven, which presents challenges that few of us face with our modern ovens (see box, page 242). The following recipe is from Rose Calello, winner of the contest in 2000 and 2001.

MAKES 8 TO 10 SERVINGS

1 recipe Basic Shortening Pie Pastry, Double Crust (page 30), refrigerated (see Recipe for Success)

FILLING

8 cups peeled, cored, and thinly sliced Golden Delicious apples

1 tablespoon fresh lemon juice

2/3 cup sugar

2 1/2 tablespoons all-purpose flour

3/4 teaspoon ground cinnamon

1/4 teaspoon ground nutmeg

Pinch of salt

1 tablespoon cold unsalted butter, cut into small pieces

GLAZE

1 large egg white, lightly beaten

1. If you haven't already, prepare the pastry and refrigerate until firm enough to roll, about 1 hour.

2. On a sheet of lightly floured waxed paper, roll the larger portion of the pastry into a 12-inch circle with a floured rolling pin. Invert the pastry over a 9-inch standard pie pan, center, and peel off the paper. Gently tuck the pastry into the pan, without stretching it, and let the overhang drape over the edge. Place in the refrigerator for 15 minutes.

3. Combine the apples and lemon juice in a large bowl, tossing to blend. Stir in the sugar, flour, cinnamon, nutmeg, and salt. Set aside. Preheat the oven to 375°F.

4. On another sheet of lightly floured waxed paper, roll the other half of the pastry into an 11 1/2-inch circle. Turn the filling into the chilled pie shell; it will mound quite high in the shell. Smooth the filling with your hands, laying the apples slices down so they don't poke through the crust. Dot the top of the fruit with the butter. Lightly moisten the rim of the pie shell. Invert the top pastry over the filling, center, and peel off the paper. Press the top and bottom pastries together along the dampened edge. Trim the pastry with scissors or a paring knife, leaving an even 1/2-inch overhang all around, then sculpt the overhang

Salem Cross Inn Apple Pie Contest

The 300-year-old beehive brick oven used for the Salem Cross Inn's apple pie contest measures about 4 feet by 5 feet and consists of such a large thermal mass that it must be fired the day before the baking takes place. According to Martha Salem, the inn's owner, the oven is first loaded with pieces of hardwood, then the fire is set and left to burn for many hours. The remaining ash and coals are scraped into a built-in ash pit.

Martha and her brother, Robert, who presides over the oven, know that it is ready when a little flour tossed on the oven's floor turns just the right shade of toasted brown, and when an arm extended into the oven can be held there for precisely 8 seconds without singing a hair. This is admittedly a bit imprecise by modern standards, but the whole point of the contest, says Martha, is to celebrate the sort of intuitive baking our ancestors did so well on a regular basis.

The apple pies are hustled into the oven, then quickly removed and scrutinized by their creators, one from each New England state. Back into the oven they go—some for just a few minutes, others for much longer, according to individual design. Finally, the judges announce the winner, and everyone shares in the satisfaction of helping to re-create a slice of American culinary history.

(*Note:* Martha Salem has put the apple pie contest on hold for 2004 but plans to sponsor it again in the future. For the latest information, consult the inn's Web site, www.salemcrossinn.com.)

into an upstanding ridge. Poke several steam vents in the top of the pie with a fork or paring knife. Put a couple of the vents near the edge of the crust so you can check the juices there later. To glaze the pie, lightly brush the pastry with the beaten egg white.

5. Place the pie on the center oven rack and bake for 30 minutes, then rotate the pie 180 degrees, so that the part that faced the back of the oven now faces forward. Just in case, slide a large aluminum foil–lined baking sheet onto the rack below to catch any spills. Continue to bake until the juices bubble thickly through the side steam vents, another 30 to 35 minutes. If the top of the pie starts to get too dark, cover loosely with aluminum foil during the last 15 minutes.

6. Transfer the pie to a wire rack and let cool for at least 2 hours before serving.

Recipe for Success

▶ Rose uses part regular and part Butter Flavor Crisco to make the pastry for this pie. To make a pastry that's similar to Rose's, follow the directions for Basic Shortening Pie Pastry, but use ²/₃ cup Butter Flavor Crisco and ¹/₃ cup regular Crisco. In addition, substitute firmly packed light brown sugar for the granulated sugar.

Liz Smothers's Sugarless Apple-Berry Pie

Liz Smothers is the matriarch of the Julian Pie Company, with stores in Julian and Santa Ysabel, near San Diego, California. Liz, who inherited her mother's love for pie making, and her husband, Keith, opened their first small pie shop in Julian at the base of Volcan Mountain in 1986. Two years later, they bought an apple farm so they could grow the apples for their pies, and by 1992 they had opened a second, larger bakery to accommodate the great demand for their pies. You get the picture: Liz knows how to bake a fine pie. Those whose diets are sugar restricted will find this pie incredibly satisfying. Heck, I find it scrumptious, and, as you might have noticed, I'm not shy about using sugar. The apple juice concentrate Liz uses adds a certain sweetness to the pie, as do the fresh berries and apples. All told, this is a great recipe for just about any pie lover.

MAKES 8 TO 10 SERVINGS

1 recipe Basic Shortening Pie Pastry, Double Crust (page 30), modified as instructed in step 1 and refrigerated

FILLING

6 cups peeled, cored, and sliced Golden Delicious apples

1/3 cup frozen apple juice concentrate, thawed, or 3/4 cup apple juice

2 to 3 tablespoons all-purpose flour

1 teaspoon ground cinnamon

1 to 1 1/2 cups fresh blueberries (picked over for stems), raspberries, or hulled and sliced strawberries, to your taste

2 tablespoons cold unsalted butter, cut into small pieces

GLAZE

1 large egg white whisked with 1 tablespoon water

1. If you haven't already, prepare the pastry, omitting the sugar. Refrigerate until firm enough to roll, about 1 hour.

2. On a sheet of lightly floured waxed paper, roll the larger portion of the pastry into a 13-inch circle with a floured rolling pin. Invert the pastry over a 9 1/2-inch deep-dish pie pan, center, and peel off the paper. Tuck the pastry into the pan, without stretching it, and let the overhang drape over the edge. Place in the refrigerator for 15 minutes.

3. Combine the apples, apple juice concentrate, 2 tablespoons of the flour (3 tablespoons if using apple juice), and cinnamon in a large bowl. Set aside for 10 minutes. Preheat the oven to 350°F.

4. On another sheet of lightly floured waxed paper, roll the other half of the pastry into an 11-inch circle. Pour the berries into the chilled pie shell, making one thick layer.

Turn the apples into the shell and smooth the top with your hands. Dot the filling with the butter. Lightly moisten the rim of the pie shell. Invert the top pastry over the filling, center, and peel off the paper. Press the top and bottom pastries together along the dampened edge. Trim the pastry with scissors or a paring knife, leaving an even ½-inch overhang all around, then sculpt the overhang into an upstanding ridge. Poke several steam vents in the top of the pie with a fork or paring knife. Put a couple of the vents near the edge of the crust so you can check the juices there later. Brush the top of the pie with the egg white mixture.

5. Place the pie on the center oven rack and bake for 45 minutes, then rotate the pie 180 degrees, so that the part that faced the back of the oven now faces forward. Slide a large aluminum foil–lined baking sheet onto the rack below to catch any drips. Continue to bake until the top is golden brown, the apples are tender (check with a skewer), and the juices bubble through the vents at the edge, about 30 minutes.

6. Transfer the pie to a wire rack and let cool for at least 2 hours before serving.

Recipe for Success

▶ Liz is equally enthusiastic about all of the berries you might use for this pie. Your choice should depend on what's fresh, available, and tempting. A combination of berries would work well, too, if you have some of each on hand.

▶ Liz likes to bake her fruit pies longer and slower than I do. I generally start them at a higher temperature, then turn down the heat. Try both methods and see which you prefer.

Ozark Pie

This recipe and others like it are variously called Ozark Mountain pie, Ozark pie cake, and Ozark apple pie, but they're all very similar: an apple (and often nut) filling in a sweet batter that manages to form both a crusty top and a defined bottom crust. It's one of just a handful of pies I've included in this collection that make their own crusts. Notice the absence of butter. A few of the recipes I've seen do use butter, but that makes the pie more cake-like and less crusty, so I've left it out. If you have only one apple and a desire to make a simple pie, this one is for you.

MAKES 8 SERVINGS

1 large egg

1 large egg yolk

1/2 cup granulated sugar

1/4 cup firmly packed light brown sugar

1/2 teaspoon vanilla extract

1/2 cup plus 1 tablespoon all-purpose flour

1 1/2 tablespoons baking powder

1/2 teaspoon ground cinnamon

1/4 teaspoon ground nutmeg

1 large apple (any type), peeled, cored, and cut into chunks

1/2 cup chopped pecans or walnuts

GARNISH

Fresh Whipped Cream (page 605)

1. Butter a 9 1/2-inch deep-dish pie pan (see Recipe for Success). Set aside. Preheat the oven to 350°F.

2. Combine the egg, egg yolk, granulated sugar, and brown sugar in a large bowl. Using an electric mixer, beat until light and airy, about 2 minutes. Blend in the vanilla.

3. Sift the flour, baking powder, cinnamon, and nutmeg into a separate bowl. Stir into the batter along with the apple and nuts. Scrape the mixture into the prepared pan, smoothing the top with your hands.

4. Place the pie on the center oven rack and bake until the top is dark golden brown and crusted over, about 30 minutes. The apples will most likely be visible through the crust.

5. Transfer the pie to a wire rack and let cool. Serve barely warm or at room temperature, garnished with whipped cream.

Recipe for Success

▶ This is a fairly shallow pie, no more than about 1 inch tall. To make a higher pie, use a 9-inch standard pie pan and increase the baking time 5 to 8 minutes.

▶ Any apple will do here. Just use what you have on hand.

▶ This makes a very nice breakfast dish. To shorten the morning preparations, combine the dry ingredients the night before and also chop the apple. Toss the apple with a little lemon juice, cover, and refrigerate overnight.

The Original Ritz Mock Apple Pie

The original mock apple pie made with Ritz crackers is still, after all these years, the gold standard of the mock cracker pie genre and by far Nabisco's most requested recipe. Cool, I thought, but how does the pie taste? Like a throwback to another era? Or can it stand on its own merits? I started out with a serious skeptical streak—how could wet crackers double as apples?—but ended up a believer. Even my wife, Bev, guessed "apples" when I gave her a bite of this. It tastes most appley while it's still warm, so serve it thus, with a scoop of vanilla ice cream.

MAKES 8 TO 10 SERVINGS

1 recipe Basic Shortening Pie Pastry, Double Crust (page 30), refrigerated, or 2 store-bought refrigerated pie pastries

FILLING

36 Ritz crackers, coarsely broken (scant 2 cups)

1 3/4 cups water

2 cups sugar

2 teaspoons cream of tartar

2 tablespoons fresh lemon juice

Grated zest of 1 lemon

2 tablespoons cold unsalted butter or margarine, cut into small pieces

1/2 teaspoon ground cinnamon

GARNISH

Vanilla ice cream

1.   If you haven't already, prepare the pastry and refrigerate until firm enough to roll, about 1 hour.

2.   On a sheet of lightly floured waxed paper, roll the larger portion of the pastry into a 12-inch circle with a floured rolling pin. Invert the pastry over a 9-inch standard pie pan, center, and peel off the paper. Gently tuck the pastry into the pan, without stretching it, and let the overhang drape over the edge. If you're using a store-bought pastry, simply line the pie pan with it. Put the cracker crumbs in the prepared crust. Place in the refrigerator for 15 minutes.

3.   Bring the water, sugar, and cream of tartar to a boil in a medium-size saucepan over high heat. Reduce the heat to medium and simmer for 15 minutes. Remove from the heat and stir in the lemon juice and zest. Let cool to lukewarm.

4.   Slowly pour the cooled syrup over the cracker crumbs in the chilled pie shell. Dot the filling with the butter and sprinkle with the cinnamon. On a separate sheet of floured waxed paper, roll the other half of the pastry into a 10-inch circle. Lightly moisten the rim

of the pie shell. Invert the top pastry over the filling, center, and peel off the paper. Or drape the other store-bought pastry over the filling. Press the top and bottom pastries together along the dampened edge. Using the back of a butter knife or pastry knife, trim the pastry flush with the edge of the pan. Make several steam vents in the top of the pie with the tip of a paring knife.

5. Place the pie on the center oven rack and bake until the top crust is crisp and dark golden brown, 30 to 35 minutes.

6. Transfer the pie to a wire rack and let cool. Serve slightly warm with scoops of vanilla ice cream.

Recipe for Success

▶ I consider this a very casual pie and wouldn't hesitate to use store-bought pastry when preparing it.

▶ This is deviating from tradition, and I admit I haven't tried it, but if you substituted a little apple cider for the water, you'd probably have an even more authentic-tasting mock apple pie.

Iowa Pie Politics

Apparently, Congressman Dick Gephardt believes that presidential aspirations and a love for homemade pie go hand in hand. Gearing up for his 2004 presidential bid and the Iowa caucuses, the Missouri congressman launched the Great Gephardt Iowa Pie Challenge, calling on Iowans to help him find the "tastiest, flakiest, fruitiest, creamiest, most scrumptious slices of pie in Iowa." The candidate enjoyed "deep-dish" support from all Iowans, but especially those who made and loved Iowa pies. Voters were invited to visit his official Web site, where they could recommend a stop on his statewide pie tour and follow his progress on the site's "pie chart." Among the pies recommended were the mile-high pie at Stone's Restaurant in Marshalltown and the apple pies at Cronk's Café in Denison and the Chrome Diner in Algona.

Mrs. Smith's Pies

To the millions of Americans with neither the time nor the inclination to make their own pies, the name that means the next best thing to homemade is Mrs. Smith's. One of the nation's top bakeries, Mrs. Smith's enjoys an impressive 90 percent brand awareness in the United States. Indeed, we've all eaten a slice of Mrs. Smith's pie and, considering the millions the company turns out each year, you can't help but admire the way a mass-produced food product can maintain such a generous amount of homemade charm.

According to a company spokesperson, that's because the principles of quality that governed the real Mrs. Smith are still in practice today. In the early 1900s, a homemaker named Amanda Smith of Pottstown, Pennsylvania, started baking pies in her home kitchen. She enjoyed a reputation as a serious baker, with exacting standards, so the townsfolk would bring her their fruit. She, in turn, would bake it into pies, a service she provided in exchange for her customers' excess fruit. One day, on a whim, her son Robert thought he'd try selling some of her pies at the local YMCA. He quickly sold out, and before long he was delivering pies all over the area in his old Dodge coupe. A bakery icon had been born.

Today Mrs. Smith's pies are baked in facilities across the country and are available just about anywhere you look. If she were alive today, Amanda Smith would no doubt be tickled to learn that her fruit pies are still the company's biggest sellers, with good old apple accounting for 60 to 65 percent of the pies sold, followed by pumpkin, cherry, and berry. This all adds up to a great American success story and a delicious slice of our pie heritage.

To a lot of people, fall is more or less defined by two pies: apple and then, for

a day, pumpkin. Which is a fine start. But limiting your fall pie making to apple

and pumpkin is like narrowing your choices to vanilla and chocolate at the ice

cream parlor. There's a whole lot else going on here, and you neglect the pos-

sibilities at your pie-making peril. • Pears are near the top of my favorite fall

Cranberry, Pear, Pumpkin, and Other Classic Fall Pies

pie fruits, in some ways the equal of apples. Pears tend to be very juicy,

always an asset to fruit pies. Ripe pears have a soft, buttery flesh that makes

for a meltingly tender slice of pie. I find their aroma intoxicating, and they

match up well with other fruits, such as cranberries—one of fall's other pie

treasures. • An all-cranberry pie is a real treat, but more typically I like to use

cranberries as an accent, not the prevailing theme. Used judiciously, cran-

berries will not steal the show, but instead will highlight the flavors of other fruit. They add the tartness that's often lacking in store-bought fruit, and a splash of color that fits right in with both early fall and the holiday season.

Pumpkin and sweet potato pies are other fall standards I've included here. Perhaps more so than any other pies in this collection, these have had to pass the most rigid scrutiny: having tasted too many bland versions of both, I have pretty high standards in this category. You can rest assured that the pumpkin and sweet potato pies in the following pages are either rich, exotic, or otherwise jazzed up to capture my fancy—like Triple-Layer Pumpkin-Chocolate Pie on page 282.

So take a minute to thumb through this section and see what looks good. Once you've baked a few of these pies, I doubt that you'll ever again think of fall pie baking as just apple and pumpkin.

Tips for Baking Fabulous Fall Pies

- Choose pears that are weighty in proportion to their size, an indication of freshness and juiciness. Ripe pears will yield to moderate finger pressure. Pears often require further ripening at home, on the kitchen counter in a closed paper bag.

- If your pears seem unusually juicy, increase the amount of thickener slightly.

- Like apple pies and nearly all fruit pies, be sure not to underbake your pear pie, or the thickener won't have time to "set" the juices. Bake until any visible juices bubble thickly.

- Purchase cranberries that are bright red. Early in the season, you may notice berries that are half white and half red. They'll not have as much flavor as bright red ones.

- If you freeze your cranberries, bring them to room temperature before adding them to a pie filling. Frozen berries will make for sluggish baking and, likely, an overbaked crust.

- In most cases, pumpkin pies should be baked in a partially prebaked pie shell. If they are not, the bottom crust may not have a fully baked flavor.

- Don't freeze pumpkin pies. The filling and crust tend to separate when you do.

- Keep in mind that pumpkin is, more or less, a custard-type pie and therefore requires moderate heat. Never raise the temperature in an effort to accelerate the baking. One indication that you've overbaked a pumpkin pie is a watery filling when you cut into the pie.

All-Pear Pie with Maple and Candied Ginger

Pears have always been one of my favorite fruits. When I was a kid, my mom would often open up several cans of pears after dinner—dessert for me and my six siblings—and I'd quickly be in gourmet heaven. I still love pear desserts, especially this double-crust pie featuring maple syrup and candied ginger. As with the canned pears of my youth, I can't get enough of it. I like to make this in the fall, when pears are abundant and juicy, and I'll often bring it to a potluck or other special event. The all-pear filling never ceases to delight: it's just not a filling that many cooks consider. Note that I don't usually bother to peel pears, as the skins of most varieties are very soft and not chewy, unlike apple skins.

MAKES 8 TO 10 SERVINGS

1 recipe Basic Flaky Pie Pastry, Double Crust (page 31), refrigerated

FILLING

7 cups cored and sliced ripe pears, unpeeled

1/3 cup sugar

1/4 cup pure maple syrup (see Recipe for Success)

2 tablespoons quick-cooking tapioca

1/2 teaspoon vanilla extract

1 1/2 tablespoons fresh lemon juice

Grated zest of 1 lemon (optional)

1 tablespoon minced candied (crystallized) ginger or 1/2 teaspoon ground ginger

2 tablespoons cold unsalted butter, cut into small pieces

GLAZE

Milk or light cream

Sugar

1. If you haven't already, prepare the pastry and refrigerate until firm enough to roll, about 1 hour.

2. On a sheet of lightly floured waxed paper, roll the larger portion of the pastry into a 13-inch circle with a floured rolling pin. Invert the pastry over a 9 1/2-inch deep-dish pie pan, center, and peel off the paper. Gently tuck the pastry into the pan, without stretching it, and let the overhang drape over the edge. Place in the refrigerator for 15 minutes.

3. Combine the pears, sugar, maple syrup, tapioca, vanilla, lemon juice, lemon zest (if using), and ginger in a large bowl. Toss well and set aside. Preheat the oven to 400°F.

4. On another sheet of lightly floured waxed paper, roll the other half of the pastry into an 11 1/2-inch circle. Turn the filling into the chilled pie shell and smooth the fruit with your hands. Dot the top of the fruit with the butter. Lightly moisten the edge of the pie shell with a wet fingertip or pastry brush. Invert the top pastry over the filling, center, and peel off the paper. Press the top and bottom pastries together along the dampened edge. Trim the pastry with scissors or a paring knife, leaving an even 1/2-inch overhang all around, then sculpt the overhang into an upstanding ridge. Poke several steam vents in the top of the pie with a fork or paring knife. Put a couple of the vents near the edge of the crust so you can check the juices there later. Brush the top of the pie with a little milk and sprinkle with sugar.

5. Place the pie on the center oven rack and bake for 30 minutes. Reduce the oven temperature to 375°F and rotate the pie 180 degrees, so that the part that faced the back of the oven now faces forward. Just in case, slide a large aluminum foil–lined baking sheet onto the rack below to catch any spills. Continue to bake until the juices bubble thickly at the edge, 30 to 35 minutes.

6. Transfer the pie to a wire rack and let cool for at least 2 hours—preferably longer, since this is a juicy pie—before serving.

Recipe for Success

▶ This also makes a very good-looking lattice-top pie. (See page 71 for directions.)

▶ If you don't have any pure maple syrup on hand, substitute an equal amount of firmly packed light brown sugar.

Streusel-Topped Pear Pie with Walnut Crust

I'm a big fan of pear pies, as you might have guessed from the number of them scattered throughout this collection. Here's one that has a sturdy walnut pastry and is topped with what I call blond streusel—blond because it only has white or light ingredients, as opposed to the more typical cinnamon and brown sugar. Any good, juicy pear will do here. If you want to play up the pear flavor, add a tablespoon or two of pear brandy. Even better, keep the bottle out and serve some with the pie.

MAKES 8 TO 10 SERVINGS

1/2 recipe Nutty Pie Pastry (page 42) made with walnuts, refrigerated

FILLING

5 1/2 cups peeled, cored, and sliced ripe pears

1/2 cup sugar

2 tablespoons cornstarch

1 tablespoon fresh lemon juice

1 to 2 tablespoons pear brandy (optional), to your taste

1/4 teaspoon ground cinnamon

Pinch of ground nutmeg

Pinch of salt

BLOND STREUSEL TOPPING

1 cup all-purpose flour

2/3 cup sugar

1/4 teaspoon salt

6 tablespoons (3/4 stick) cold unsalted butter, cut into 1/4-inch pieces

1 tablespoon milk or light cream

1. If you haven't already, prepare the pastry and refrigerate until firm enough to roll, about 1 hour. It's best not to overchill nut pastries, or they can be difficult to handle.

2. On a sheet of lightly floured waxed paper, roll the pastry into a 13-inch circle with a floured rolling pin. Invert the pastry over a 9½-inch deep-dish pie pan, center, and peel off the paper. Gently tuck the pastry into the pan, without stretching it. Note that because of the walnuts, this pastry is a little more delicate than some and should be eased into the pan as carefully as possible. Sculpt the overhang into an upstanding ridge. Place in the freezer for 15 minutes. Preheat the oven to 400°F.

3. Place the pears in a large bowl. Mix the sugar and cornstarch together in a small bowl. Add the mixture to the fruit and stir well. Stir in the lemon juice, pear brandy (if using), cinnamon, nutmeg, and salt. Turn the filling into the chilled pie shell, smoothing the top with your hands. Place the pie on the center oven rack and bake for 35 minutes.

4. Meanwhile, make the streusel topping. Combine the flour, sugar, and salt in a food processor. Scatter the butter over the dry ingredients. Pulse until the mixture resembles fine crumbs. Add the milk and pulse again. Dump the mixture into a medium-size bowl and gently rub between your fingers to make large, buttery crumbs. Refrigerate until ready to use. (See Recipe for Success.)

5. Remove the pie from the oven and reduce the temperature to 375°F. Carefully dump the crumbs in the center of the pie, spreading them evenly over the surface with your hands. Press down gently to compact them. Return the pie to the oven, placing it so that the part that faced the back of the oven now faces forward. Just in case, slide a large aluminum foil–lined baking sheet onto the rack below to catch any spills. Continue to bake until the juices bubble thickly around the edge, 30 to 35 minutes. If necessary, cover the pie with loosely tented aluminum foil during the last 15 minutes, to prevent the streusel from getting too brown.

6. Transfer the pie to a wire rack and let cool for at least 1 hour before serving.

Recipe for Success

▶ Juicy pears can be very, well, juicy. That juice can sometimes present a problem when you're making a streusel-topped pie. The juice can saturate the topping, turning some of it to sludge. To prevent that from happening, about 5 minutes before I add the topping to the pie, I sprinkle a small handful of quick-cooking rolled oats over the juiciest parts. The oatmeal absorbs some of the excess juice and forms a sort of barrier between the filling and the topping. The result? Less streusel sludge and more streusel.

Pears for Your Pies

Provided they're fresh, juicy, and ripe, nearly all pears are excellent in pies. But their ripeness is sometimes difficult to judge, especially with the variety of skin colors available. Like peaches, pears are ripe when they yield to finger pressure, without feeling overly soft. Keep in mind that pears do not ripen well on trees. Pears are harvested mature but unripe—which is often how you'll find them in the market—and must be ripened after harvest. The easiest way to do this when you get them home is to place them in a paper bag and ripen them right on the counter. Check them daily to see how they're progressing. Store ripe pears in the fridge for two to three days.

Here are some pear varieties you'll want to try in your pies.

▶ BOSC Highly aromatic. Its dense flesh makes for great pies.

▶ COMICE Perhaps the sweetest, juiciest variety.

▶ RED BARTLETT Skin is bright red when fully ripe. Very sweet and juicy, excellent in pies.

▶ YELLOW BARTLETT Same flavor, texture, and qualities as Red Bartlett. Ripens to bright yellow.

Pear Pie with Almond Cake Topping

This is one of my favorite pies of all time—a medium-thick filling of soft pears topped with something like a delicate almond torte. (For a wonderful variation, you can replace the almonds with pecan halves.) It's no more difficult to make than a streusel-topped pie, since the almond cake topping is mixed right in the food processor. The topping makes this pie somewhat more refined, so consider serving it if you're entertaining. Top it with vanilla, butter pecan, or coffee ice cream.

MAKES 8 TO 10 SERVINGS

1 recipe All-Butter Pie Pastry, Single Crust (page 28) or Basic Flaky Pie Pastry, Single Crust (page 31), refrigerated

FILLING

5 1/2 cups peeled, cored, and thinly sliced ripe pears (see Recipe for Success)

1/3 cup plus 2 tablespoons sugar

1 tablespoon fresh lemon juice

1 teaspoon grated lemon zest

1 1/2 tablespoons cornstarch

Big pinch of ground nutmeg or cardamom

ALMOND CAKE TOPPING

1 cup whole almonds

1/3 cup sugar

3 tablespoons all-purpose flour

1/4 cup sweetened flaked coconut

1 teaspoon baking powder

1/4 teaspoon salt

1/4 cup (1/2 stick) unsalted butter, at room temperature but not soft, cut into 1/4-inch pieces

1 large egg

1/2 teaspoon vanilla extract

1/4 teaspoon almond extract (optional)

1.   If you haven't already, prepare the pastry and refrigerate until firm enough to roll, about 1 hour.

2.   On a sheet of lightly floured waxed paper, roll the pastry into a 13-inch circle with a floured rolling pin. Invert the pastry over a 9 1/2-inch deep-dish pie pan, center, and peel off the paper. Tuck the pastry into the pan, without stretching it, and sculpt the edge into an upstanding ridge. Place in the freezer for 15 minutes.

3.   Combine the pears, 1/3 cup of the sugar, the lemon juice, and lemon zest in a large bowl. Set aside for 10 minutes. Preheat the oven to 400°F.

4.   Combine the remaining 2 tablespoons sugar, the cornstarch, and nutmeg in a small bowl, then stir the mixture into the fruit. Scrape the filling into the chilled pie shell. Place the pie on the center oven rack and bake for 30 minutes, then reduce the oven temperature to 375°F and bake for 10 minutes more.

5.   Meanwhile, prepare the cake topping. Put the almonds, sugar, flour, coconut, baking powder, and salt in a food processor and pulse until the nuts are very finely chopped. Scatter the butter over the top and pulse until it is well incorporated and the mixture is crumbly. Whisk the egg, vanilla, and almond extract (if using) together in a small bowl. Add to the processor and pulse again, just until the mixture starts to gather around the blade. Scrape the cake batter into a bowl.

6.   Remove the pie from the oven. Using a soup spoon, dollop the cake batter more or less evenly over the fruit. Don't worry if it is lumpy or otherwise imperfect because it

will settle during baking. Return the pie to the oven, placing it so that the part that faced the back of the oven now faces forward. Continue to bake until the top is a rich golden brown and the batter is cooked through, 20 to 22 minutes. You most likely will not need to worry about the pie bubbling over, but if it starts to, slide a large aluminum foil–lined baking sheet onto the rack below.

7. Transfer the pie to a wire rack and let cool for at least 2 hours. This pie is best served barely warm or at room temperature

Recipe for Success

▶ You don't have to peel the pears, because their skins are so soft. I recommend it here, however, because this pie is a little more "formal" than some, and I prefer the refined look of no skins.

▶ If you plan to serve this pie for a party, make it the same day. This will help preserve the wonderful texture of the cake topping, because it won't have a chance to absorb any moisture from below. You want it to be a little on the dry side.

Pear and Jalapeño Jelly Pie

If you read a lot of recipes like I do, you've probably seen pears and black pepper teamed up on more than one occasion. I used to think this was a bit strange, but once I tried it—grinding black pepper onto sliced ripe pears and serving them with a bit of cheese—I realized just how good the combination is. My own forays into pear-pepper partnering led to this spicy pear pie, sweetened with jalapeño jelly and jazzed up with a little five-spice powder. The spices and jelly envelop the pears, leaving a warm and subtly exotic aftertaste. I think you'll be surprised at how good this is.

MAKES 8 TO 10 SERVINGS

1 recipe Basic Flaky Pie Pastry, Double Crust (page 31) or Basic Shortening Pie Pastry, Double Crust (page 30), refrigerated

FILLING

4¹/₂ to 5 cups peeled, cored, and sliced ripe pears

¹/₂ cup jalapeño jelly

2 tablespoons unsalted butter

¹/₄ cup sugar

2 tablespoons cornstarch

¹/₄ teaspoon Chinese five-spice powder

Big pinch of salt

GLAZE

Milk or light cream

Sugar

GARNISH

Vanilla or butter pecan ice cream

1. If you haven't already, prepare the pastry and refrigerate until firm enough to roll, about 1 hour.

2. On a sheet of lightly floured waxed paper, roll the larger portion of the pastry into a 12-inch circle with a floured rolling pin. Invert the pastry over a 9-inch standard pie pan, center, and peel off the paper. Gently tuck the pastry into the pan, without stretching it, and let the overhang drape over the edge. Place in the refrigerator for 15 minutes. Preheat the oven to 400°F.

3. Put the pears in a large bowl. Combine the jelly and butter in a small saucepan over medium heat. Heat until the butter melts, then whisk to smooth the mixture and pour it over the pears. Combine the sugar, cornstarch, five-spice powder, and salt in a small bowl. Stir the mixture into the fruit and set aside.

4. On another sheet of floured waxed paper, roll the other half of the pastry into a 10-inch circle. Turn the filling into the chilled pie shell, smoothing the top with your hands. Lightly moisten the rim of the shell. Invert the top pastry over the filling, center, and peel off the paper. Press the top and bottom pastries together along the dampened edge. Using the back of a paring knife, trim the pastry flush with the edge of the pan, then pinch the pastries together to seal. Poke several steam vents in the top of the pie with a fork or paring knife. Put a couple of the vents near the edge of the crust so you can check the juices there later. To glaze the pie, lightly brush the pastry with milk and sprinkle with sugar.

5. Place the pie on the center oven rack and bake for 30 minutes. Reduce the oven temperature to 375°F and rotate the pie 180 degrees, so that the part that faced the back of the oven now faces forward. Just in case, slide a large aluminum foil–lined baking sheet onto the rack below to catch any spills. Continue to bake until the top is golden brown and any visible juices bubble thickly through the side steam vents, 25 to 30 minutes.

6. Transfer the pie to a wire rack and let cool for at least 1 hour. Serve with scoops of ice cream.

Recipe for Success

▸ I imagine that there are any number of good jalapeño jellies on the market, but I use Knott's Berry Farm, available—I believe—at most supermarkets.

▸ If you like, you can substitute up to half sliced apples for an equal amount of sliced pears.

Five-Spice Pear-Apple Pie

In the winter, I love to make poached pears flavored with star anise, a flavor scheme I thought would adapt nicely to a pie. Anise is one of the more exotic spices in five-spice powder, and it really stands out in this mixed-fruit pie, lending a heady fragrance and warming flavor. I have made the same pie with a top and bottom crust, but I prefer the cornmeal streusel. It covers the pie with a light crunch and is the perfect complement to the spicy filling.

MAKES 8 TO 10 SERVINGS

1 recipe Whole Wheat Pie Pastry, Single Crust (page 33) or Basic Flaky Pie Pastry, Single Crust (page 31), refrigerated

FILLING

3 1/2 cups peeled, cored, and sliced Granny Smith, Cortland, Northern Spy, or other apples (see pages 232–233 for recommendations)

3 1/2 cups cored and sliced ripe pears, peeled or unpeeled

Grated zest of 1 lemon

1 tablespoon fresh lemon juice

2 tablespoons orange juice

3/4 cup granulated sugar

1 1/2 tablespoons cornstarch

2 teaspoons Chinese five-spice powder

CORNMEAL STREUSEL TOPPING

3/4 cup all-purpose flour

1/4 cup fine yellow cornmeal

2/3 cup firmly packed light brown sugar

1/4 teaspoon salt

1/2 cup (1 stick) cold unsalted butter, cut into 1/4-inch pieces

1. If you haven't already, prepare the pastry and refrigerate until firm enough to roll, about 1 hour.

2. On a sheet of lightly floured waxed paper, roll the pastry into a 13-inch circle with a floured rolling pin. Invert the pastry over a 9 1/2-inch deep-dish pie pan, center, and peel off the paper. Tuck the pastry into the pan, without stretching it, and sculpt the edge into an upstanding ridge. Place in the freezer for 15 minutes.

3. Combine the apples, pears, lemon zest, lemon juice, orange juice, and 1/2 cup of the granulated sugar in a large bowl. Set aside for 10 minutes. Preheat the oven to 400°F.

4. Mix together the remaining 1/4 cup sugar, the cornstarch, and five-spice powder in a small bowl. Stir the mixture into the fruit. Turn the filling into the chilled pie shell and smooth the filling with your hands to even it out. Place the pie on the center oven rack and bake for 30 minutes.

5. Meanwhile, make the topping. Put the flour, cornmeal, brown sugar, and salt in a

Keep Those Pie Spices Fresh

If you like to make pies, you probably spend a lot of money on spices. So you've probably noticed that they aren't as cheap as they used to be. Add up the cost of a few jars, and you might have been able to purchase a package tour to the exotic places they came from instead.

Under the circumstances, it pays to keep your spices in good shape after you get them home. Here are some guidelines for doing just that.

- Give your old spices the sniff test. If they don't tantalize your senses, throw them away and get fresh ones.

- Keep them away from the heat. The biggest mistake cooks make is keeping spices too near the stove. Heat destroys the volatile oils that give spices their distinctive flavor.

- Don't store them in the sunlight. Direct sunlight will also wreak havoc on their flavor. Find a dark, low-humidity cabinet to store them in.

- Rule of thumb: Don't buy any more of a given spice than you'll use in six to nine months.

- If you really want your pies to sparkle, get a spice grinder and use whole spices. Whole spices will last for years.

food processor and pulse several times to mix. Scatter the butter over the mixture and pulse until it resembles fine crumbs. Empty the crumbs into a medium-size bowl and rub them between your fingers to make large, buttery crumbs. Refrigerate until ready to use.

6. Remove the pie from the oven and reduce the oven temperature to 375°F. Carefully dump the crumbs in the center of the pie, spreading them evenly over the surface with your hands. Tamp them down lightly. Return the pie to the oven, placing it so that the part that faced the back of the oven now faces forward. Just in case, slide a large aluminum foil–lined baking sheet onto the rack below to catch any spills. Continue to bake until the juices bubble thickly around the edge, another 30 minutes.

7. Transfer the pie to a wire rack and let cool for at least 1 hour before serving.

Recipe for Success

- I recommend keeping a jar of five-spice powder on your spice shelf. In a pinch, if you'd like to approximate it with spices on hand, you can mix cinnamon, ground fennel seed, ground cloves, and ground white pepper—more of the first two, less of the cloves, and much less of the pepper. Use 1½ teaspoons of your homemade powder in this pie. Bury 2 whole star anise in the center of the pie (so that you can find and remove them when you cut the first slices).

Pear-Raspberry Lattice-Top Pie

My favorite pies for lattice tops are the ones with red fillings, like this one. Here we mix juicy sliced pears with fresh or frozen raspberries, which give the filling a deep, rosy blush. I've always loved the softness of pear fillings, and it's one of the things I like most about this pie. If you make this in early fall, you may be able to use all fresh fruit. When the local raspberries are no longer in season, use frozen.

MAKES 8 TO 10 SERVINGS

1 recipe Basic Flaky Pie Pastry, Double Crust (page 31), or All-Butter Pie Pastry, Double Crust (page 28), modified as instructed in step 1 and refrigerated

FILLING

5¹/₂ cups cored and sliced ripe pears, peeled or unpeeled

2 cups raspberries, fresh or individually frozen (not packed in syrup), partially thawed

³/₄ cup sugar

1 tablespoon fresh lemon juice

1 teaspoon grated lemon zest

¹/₄ teaspoon ground cardamom or ginger

2¹/₂ tablespoons cornstarch

2 tablespoons cold unsalted butter, cut into small pieces

GLAZE

Milk or light cream

Sugar

1.   Prepare the pastry as directed, shaping half of it into a disk and the other half into a square; both should be about ³/₄ inch thick. Wrap the pastry as usual and refrigerate until firm enough to roll, about 1 hour.

2.   On a sheet of lightly floured waxed paper, roll the disk of pastry into a 13-inch circle with a floured rolling pin. Invert the pastry over a 9¹/₂-inch deep-dish pie pan, center, and peel off the paper. Gently tuck the pastry into the pan, without stretching it, and sculpt the overhang into an upstanding ridge. Place in the refrigerator for 15 minutes.

3.   Combine the pears, raspberries, ¹/₂ cup of the sugar, the lemon juice, lemon zest, and cardamom in a large bowl. Mix well and set aside for 10 minutes. Mix the remaining ¹/₄ cup sugar and the cornstarch together in a small bowl, then stir the mixture into the fruit. Preheat the oven to 400°F.

4.   On another sheet of lightly floured waxed paper, roll the other piece of dough into a rectangle about 12 inches long and 10 inches wide. Using a pastry wheel or pizza cutter, cut the pastry into 8 lengthwise strips, each about 1¹/₄ inches wide and 12 inches long. Set aside.

5. Turn the filling into the chilled pie shell, taking care to smooth the top so that no pear slices jut up, which could tear the lattice. Dot the top of the pie with the butter. Lay 5 pastry strips vertically across the pie, evenly spaced, as shown in figure 1. Fold back strips 2 and 4, then lay another strip directly across the center of the pie, as shown in figure 2. Unfold the folded dough strips, then fold back strips 1, 3, and 5. Lay another perpendicular strip across the pie as shown in figure 3. Unfold the folded strips, then fold up strips 1, 3, and 5 on the other side of the pie. Place another perpendicular strip across the pie, as shown in figure 4, then unfold strips 1, 3, and 5. Trim the strips, then pinch the ends into the edge of the pastry. Lightly brush the pastry strips with milk and sprinkle the pie with sugar.

6. Place the pie on the center oven rack and bake for 25 minutes, then reduce the oven temperature to 375°F and rotate the pie 180 degrees, so that the part that faced the back of the oven now faces forward. Just in case, place a large aluminum foil–lined baking sheet on the rack below to catch any spills. Continue to bake until the top of the pie is golden brown and any visible juices bubble thickly, 35 to 40 minutes.

7. Transfer the pie to a wire rack and let cool for at least 2 hours before serving.

Recipe for Success

▶ **Read about lattice-top pies (see page 72) before making this.**

▶ **If you're unfamiliar with cardamom, pick up a jar at the market. It tastes particularly good with pear baked goods. Don't overdo it, though; a little goes a long way.**

▶ **Blackberries are excellent in place of the raspberries in this pie.**

Figure 1

Figure 2

Figure 3

Figure 4

National Pie Day

You knew there had to be one, right? So mark your calendars accordingly: January 23. Created by the American Pie Council, National Pie Day is dedicated to the celebration of pie, plain and simple. The council says it's the perfect opportunity to pass on the love and enjoyment of pie eating and making to future generations. How best to do this? Here are a few of the council's suggestions.

> Make pie. Bake your favorite, and share it with a friend.

> Teach pie making. Go to a local school, senior center, or civic club and show the people there how it's done.

> Hold a pie night. Invite a number of your friends to bring their favorite pies for an irresistible pie buffet.

> Throw a pie-making contest. Invite everyone in your community to participate. Ask local chefs and cooking teachers to be judges and award fanciful prizes.

> Hold a pie auction. Donate the proceeds to a worthy cause.

And in general, do as much fun pie stuff as possible on this special day.

Pear and Fig Pie with a Pine Nut Crust

Anytime I see a recipe with pears and figs—a combination I just adore—I pay attention. So when I came across Mary Ann Esposito's recipe for a dried fig, pear, and pine nut pie in her book *Celebrations Italian Style* (William Morrow, 1995), I had to make it. That delicious pie turned out to be the inspiration for this one. The filling is what might loosely be called a Mediterranean mincemeat, with a little tangerine zest and juice added to brighten the dried and fresh fruits. Pine nuts are used twice, in the filling and embedded in the crust. It's a handsome touch for a tasty pie.

MAKES 8 TO 10 SERVINGS

1 recipe Basic Flaky Pie Pastry, Double Crust (page 31), refrigerated

FILLING

3 large ripe pears, peeled, cored, and sliced crosswise

1 cup stemmed and diced dried figs

1/4 cup sugar

1/2 cup fresh tangerine or orange juice (see Recipe for Success)

1 teaspoon grated tangerine or orange zest

2 tablespoons honey

1 tablespoon fresh lemon juice

3/4 cup pine nuts

GLAZE

Milk or light cream

Sugar

1. If you haven't already, prepare the pastry and refrigerate until firm enough to roll, about 1 hour.

2. On a sheet of lightly floured waxed paper, roll the larger portion of the pastry into a 13-inch circle with a floured rolling pin. Invert the pastry over a 9½-inch deep-dish pie pan, center, and peel off the paper. Gently tuck the pastry into the pan, without stretching it, and let the overhang drape over the edge. Place in the refrigerator for 15 minutes.

3. Combine one-third of the pears, the figs, sugar, tangerine juice, and tangerine zest in a medium-size nonreactive saucepan. Bring to a boil over medium heat, then reduce the heat slightly, cover, and simmer for about 10 minutes, until the fruit has absorbed most of the liquid. Remove from the heat and stir in the remaining pears, the honey, lemon juice, and ½ cup of the pine nuts. Set aside. Preheat the oven to 400°F.

4. On a fresh sheet of lightly floured waxed paper, roll the other half of the pastry into an 11-inch circle. Strew the remaining ¼ cup pine nuts over the pastry. Using your rolling pin, gently roll the nuts into the pastry, embedding them deeply.

5. Turn the filling into the chilled pie shell, moistening the edge of the shell with a pastry brush or finger. Invert the top pastry onto your outstretched hand or another sheet of waxed paper, then invert it over the filling, nut side up. Press the top and bottom pastries together along the edge to seal. Trim the pastry with scissors or a paring knife, leaving an even ½-inch overhang all around, and sculpt it into an upstanding ridge. Poke several steam vents in the top of the pie with a fork or paring knife. Put a couple of the vents near the edge of the crust so you can check the juices there later. To glaze the pie, brush lightly with milk and sprinkle with sugar.

6. Place the pie on the center oven rack and bake for 20 minutes. Reduce the oven temperature to 375°F and rotate the pie 180 degrees, so that the part that faced the back

A Slice of Sara Lee

Sara Lee is one of the nation's top producers of quality baked goods. Many of us grew up eating Sara Lee cheesecake or pound cake for dessert and hearing the company's catchy jingle—"Nobody doesn't like Sara Lee!"—on TV. And did you know that the company's founder, Charles Lubin, named his bakery business after his daughter? How sweet!

Pies are no small part of Sara Lee's business. During the holiday season, Sara Lee bakes more than 20 million pumpkin pies to keep up with the demand. In late 2002, Sara Lee's Traverse City, Michigan, bakery produced its 3 billionth pie. Here are some other interesting tidbits:

▶ Sara Lee's facility in Traverse City bakes more than 420,000 pies each day. If you placed one year's worth of Sara Lee pies side by side, the line would stretch nearly around the world.

▶ Sara Lee's pie shopping list for a year includes 60 million apples; more than 20 million pounds of cherries, blueberries, strawberries, peaches, pumpkins, and rhubarb; more than 40 million pounds of flour; and 75 million eggs.

To learn more about Sara Lee and find some pie preparation tips, go to www.saralee.com.

---

of the oven now faces forward. Just in case, slide a large aluminum foil–lined baking sheet onto the rack below to catch any drips. Continue to bake until the juices bubble thickly at the steam vents and the top is golden brown, 35 to 45 minutes. If the top starts to get too dark, cover it with loosely tented aluminum foil during the last 10 to 15 minutes.

7. Transfer the pie to a wire rack and let cool for at least 2 hours before serving.

Recipe for Success

▶ Dried figs can vary greatly in their degree of dryness. If yours seem quite dry—maybe after sitting for months in your cupboard—increase the tangerine or orange juice to ³/₄ cup.

Pear and Fig Pie with Hazelnut Crumb Topping

As much as any pie in this book, this one has several distinctive elements—figs, pears, and hazelnuts—that add up to more than the sum of its parts. It's classy, too. I often serve it if I'm looking for a pie that's a little more sophisticated and refined than most. Since good fresh figs can be difficult to procure, I always use dried and poach them to add flavor, tenderness, and juiciness. The poaching liquid—pear juice, which you may have to buy at a health food store— is then reduced and used to sweeten and flavor the pie. The figs are mixed with ripe pear slices and baked with a toasted hazelnut topping. It's all so delicious together, I think you'll agree that these flavors were made for one another.

MAKES 8 TO 10 SERVINGS

1 recipe Basic Flaky Pie Pastry, Single Crust (page 31), refrigerated

FILLING

2 cups dried Black Mission figs, stemmed

About 2 cups pear juice

4 large ripe pears, peeled, cored, and sliced

1/3 cup plus 3 tablespoons sugar

2 1/2 tablespoons cornstarch

1 tablespoon fresh lemon juice

Grated zest of 1 orange

HAZELNUT CRUMB TOPPING

1 cup hazelnuts, toasted (see page 163)

2/3 cup sugar

3/4 cup all-purpose flour

1/4 teaspoon ground cinnamon

1/4 teaspoon salt

1/2 cup (1 stick) cold unsalted butter, cut into 1/4-inch pieces

1.   If you haven't already, prepare the pastry and refrigerate until firm enough to roll, about 1 hour.

2.   On a sheet of lightly floured waxed paper, roll the pastry into a 13-inch circle with a floured rolling pin. Invert the pastry over a 9½-inch deep-dish pie pan, center, and peel off the paper. Gently tuck the pastry down into the pan, without stretching it, and sculpt the edge into an upstanding ridge. Place in the freezer for 15 minutes.

3.   Halve the figs or cut them into quarters if they're very large. Place them in a medium-size nonreactive saucepan and add enough pear juice to cover by about ½ inch.

Bring to a boil, reduce the heat to low, cover, and gently simmer for 30 minutes. Preheat the oven to 400°F.

4. Using a slotted spoon, transfer the figs to a large bowl. Increase the heat and boil any remaining liquid until it becomes syrupy and just covers the bottom of the pan. You should have ¼ to ⅓ cup. Pour this over the figs and mix. Add the pears and ⅓ cup of the sugar and toss well. In a small bowl, mix the remaining 3 tablespoons sugar with the cornstarch. Add the mixture to the fruit and mix again. Stir in the lemon juice and orange zest. Turn the filling into the chilled pie shell and smooth the top with your hands to even it out. Place the pie on the center oven rack and bake for 35 minutes.

5. Meanwhile, make the hazelnut crumb topping. Place the toasted hazelnuts and sugar in a food processor and pulse until the nuts are well chopped but not overly so. Add the flour, cinnamon, and salt and pulse again to mix. Scatter the butter over the dry ingredients and pulse until the mixture resembles medium-fine crumbs. Empty the crumbs into a medium-size bowl and rub between your fingers to make large, buttery crumbs. Refrigerate until ready to use.

6. Remove the pie from the oven and reduce the temperature to 375°F. Carefully dump the crumbs in the center of the pie, spreading them evenly over the surface with your hands. There will be a lot of crumbs, but use them all. Tamp them down lightly. Return the pie to the oven, placing it so that the part that faced the back of the oven now faces forward. Just in case, place a large aluminum foil–lined baking sheet on the rack below to catch any spills. Continue to bake until the juices bubble thickly around the edge, 35 to 40 minutes. If necessary, cover the pie loosely with aluminum foil during the last 10 to 15 minutes of baking to keep the top from browning too much.

7. Transfer the pie to a wire rack and let cool for at least 1 hour before serving.

Recipe for Success

▶ Often when I'm baking a pie such as this that involves an extra step or two—in this case, poaching the figs—I'll try to get those steps done the day before. Here the figs can be poached up to 2 days ahead and kept in the refrigerator. Don't be concerned if they soak up much of the liquid as they sit; that won't affect the outcome of the pie. If you think of it, bring the figs to room temperature before you proceed with making the filling. Don't forget, too, that the pastry can always be made—or made, rolled, and put in the pie pan—the day before as well.

Very Cranberry-Pear Pie

I think cranberries are one of the most underused pie fruits, perhaps because of their reputation as being quite tart. In fact, that tartness is easily balanced with the correct amount of sugar and contributes to the delicious, full flavor of this brightly colored pie. Finely chopping the cranberries, as I do here, makes for a compact pie. And letting them sit in the sugar for a while allows them to start juicing and accelerates the cooking process. A top crust could be used, but I prefer a thick nut crumb topping; either walnuts or pecans work beautifully. This is an excellent pie for the holidays.

MAKES 8 TO 10 SERVINGS

1 recipe Basic Flaky Pie Pastry, Single Crust (page 31), refrigerated

FILLING

3 cups fresh cranberries, picked over for stems

1/2 cup plus 1 tablespoon granulated sugar

2 large ripe pears, unpeeled, cored, and coarsely chopped

1 tablespoon fresh lemon juice

Finely grated zest of 1 orange

1 1/2 tablespoons cornstarch

1/4 teaspoon ground cinnamon

1/4 teaspoon ground cardamom

NUT CRUMB TOPPING

1 cup walnut or pecan halves

1/3 cup granulated sugar

1/3 cup firmly packed light brown sugar

3/4 cup all-purpose flour

1/4 teaspoon salt

1/2 cup (1 stick) cold unsalted butter, cut into 1/4-inch pieces

1.   If you haven't already, prepare the pastry and refrigerate until firm enough to roll, about 1 hour.

2.   On a sheet of lightly floured waxed paper, roll the pastry into a 13-inch circle with a floured rolling pin. Invert the pastry over a 9 1/2-inch deep-dish pie pan, center, and peel off the paper. Gently tuck the pastry into the pan, without stretching it, and sculpt the edge into a short upstanding ridge. Place in the freezer for 15 minutes.

3.   Combine the cranberries and 1/2 cup of the sugar in a food processor and pulse 5 or 6 times, until the cranberries are well chopped. Transfer to a large bowl and mix in the pears, lemon juice, and orange zest. Mix well and set aside for 20 minutes to juice. Preheat the oven to 400°F.

4.   In a small bowl, mix the remaining 1 tablespoon sugar with the cornstarch, cin-

Just Put It There in the Corner, Next to the Flour

Is the thought of all that rolling, mixing, and crimping just too much to handle sometimes? Maybe you ought to consider buying a Colborne Straight Line Pie System, like the big boys use.

Colborne is the largest manufacturer of commercial pie-making equipment in the country. The company's first pie machines were invented by founder Oliver Colborne in the early 1900s. Even he would be impressed by the 9D Colborne sells today. Basically an all-in-one pie maker, the fully automated unit does everything a human pie maker does—shape the dough, roll it, and get it into the pan. It also deposits the filling, crimps the edges, puts on a lattice top (that and the streusel depositor will cost you extra), and delivers the pie to the oven. This to the tune of some 120 to 200 pies *per minute*. All you need is about 50 feet of floor space in your kitchen and about $1.6 million to pay for the machine. Save your pennies, because you also need a 100-foot-long tunnel oven to handle the output.

namon, and cardamom. Add to the fruit and mix well. Turn the filling into the chilled pie shell. Smooth the top with your hands to even it out. Place the pie on the center oven rack and bake for 35 minutes.

5. Meanwhile, make the crumb topping. Put the nuts, sugars, flour, and salt in a food processor and pulse several times to mix. Scatter the butter over the top and pulse until the mixture resembles medium-fine crumbs. Transfer to a large bowl, then rub the crumbs between your fingers to make large, buttery crumbs. Refrigerate until ready to use.

6. Remove the pie from the oven and reduce the temperature to 375°F. Carefully dump the topping in the center of the pie, spreading the crumbs evenly over the surface with your hands. Tamp them down lightly. Return the pie to the oven, placing it so that the part that faced the back of the oven now faces front. Just in case, slide a large aluminum foil–lined baking sheet onto the rack below to catch any spills. Continue to bake until the juices bubble thickly around the edge, 30 to 35 minutes. If necessary, cover with loosely tented aluminum foil during the last 10 to 15 minutes to keep the crumbs from browning too much.

7. Transfer the pie to a wire rack and let cool for at least 1 hour before serving.

Recipe for Success

▶ **If you like cranberry pie, do what I do and buy a case of cranberries in the fall, when they're on sale, and freeze them. That way, you can make this and other cranberry pies throughout the year.**

Cranberry-Cherry Peekaboo Pie

Here's a fun way to make a see-through pie—by cutting a number of holes in the top crust. If you don't have one, you'll need to pick up a small round cutter between 1 and 1½ inches in diameter. If you're using the larger size, it looks better if you cut in some sort of a regular pattern—perhaps eight holes around the edge, to fall in the center of each slice, with another grouping in the middle. With the smaller cutter, the holes can be more random. In any case, the holes make great little windows to view the deep red filling and give the pie a special folk art feel. Did I mention that this cranberry-cherry filling tastes great? If holes aren't your thing, just use the top crust without the holes.

MAKES 8 TO 10 SERVINGS

1 recipe Basic Flaky Pie Pastry, Double Crust (page 31), Tender Cream Cheese Pastry, Double Crust (page 46), or All-Butter Pie Pastry, Double Crust (page 28), refrigerated

FILLING

3 cups fresh cranberries, picked over for stems

3 cups pitted fresh sweet cherries, fresh or individually frozen (not packed in syrup), partially thawed

1 cup sugar

1 tablespoon fresh lemon or orange juice

Grated zest of 1 orange

2½ tablespoons cornstarch

GLAZE

Milk or light cream

Sugar

1. If you haven't already, prepare the pastry and refrigerate until firm enough to roll, about 1 hour.

2. On a sheet of lightly floured waxed paper, roll the larger portion of the pastry into a 13-inch circle with a floured rolling pin. Invert the pastry over a 9½-inch deep-dish pie pan, center, and peel off the paper. Gently tuck the pastry into the pan, without stretching it, and let the overhang drape over the edge. Place in the refrigerator for 15 minutes.

3. On a separate sheet of floured waxed paper, roll the other half of the pastry into an 11-inch circle. Lift the paper and slide the paper and pastry onto a small baking sheet. Place in the freezer for 15 minutes.

4. In a large bowl, combine the cranberries, cherries, ¾ cup of the sugar, the lemon juice, and orange zest. Mix well and set aside for 15 minutes. Mix the cornstarch and remaining ¹/₄ cup sugar together in a small bowl, then stir the mixture into the fruit. Preheat the oven to 400°F.

5. Remove the top pastry from the freezer. Using a round 1- to 1¹/₂-inch cutter, cut a number of holes in the pastry (see headnote), none of them within 1 inch of the edge. Remove the holes (see Recipe for Success), keeping the pastry nearby. Scrape the filling into the chilled pie shell and smooth the top with your hands to even it out. Using a pastry brush, lightly moisten the edge of the pie shell. Invert the top pastry over the filling, center, and slowly and carefully peel off the paper. Press the top and bottom pastries together along the dampened edge. Trim the pastry with scissors or a paring knife, leaving an even ¹/₂-inch overhang all around, then sculpt the overhang into an upstanding ridge. Brush the top with a little milk and sprinkle lightly with sugar. Take care not to drag your brush over the exposed fruit, or you'll streak the top pastry.

6. Place the pie on the center oven rack and bake for 30 minutes. Reduce the oven temperature to 375°F and rotate the pie 180 degrees, so that the part that faced the back of the oven now faces forward. To catch any spills, slide a large aluminum foil–lined baking sheet onto the rack below. Continue to bake until the top crust is dark golden brown and the juices bubble thickly, 30 to 35 minutes.

7. Transfer the pie to a wire rack and let cool for at least 2 hours before serving.

Recipe for Success

▶ There are several things you can do with the circles you cut out of the top pastry. You can pack them together, refrigerate, and save for making a small pie (a good option if you have kids who like to bake). Or you can offset them over the holes, so that the holes are partially covered. Put them in place after you've brushed the pastry with milk but before you sprinkle it with sugar. Or you can cut them in half and decorate the edge of the pie with them. If you do this, press the edges of the top and bottom pastries together to seal, then trim flush to the edge without making an upstanding ridge. Crimp the pastries together with a fork, then arrange the half circles, evenly spaced or in any pattern that pleases you, around the edge.

The Simplest Cranberry-Apple Crumb Pie

One of the magazines I write for frequently is *FamilyFun*, for which I am a contributing editor. (If you have youngsters in the 8- to 12-year-old range, it's a must read.) A while back, one of the editors there asked me to come up with the easiest cranberry-apple pie I could, one that used a store-bought pastry, for the sake of convenience. And it had to have one of those crumb toppings, because, as she put it, "those are so yummy." This is the pie. She loved it, and I hope you will, too.

MAKES 8 TO 10 SERVINGS

1 store-bought refrigerated pie pastry

FILLING

2 cups fresh cranberries, fresh (picked over for stems) or frozen (partially thawed)

2 large apples (any type), peeled, quartered, cored, and thinly sliced crosswise

²/3 cup sugar

1 tablespoon fresh lemon juice

1¹/2 cups all-purpose flour

CRUMB TOPPING

¹/2 cup all-purpose flour

¹/2 cup sugar

¹/4 teaspoon ground cinnamon

¹/4 cup (¹/2 stick) cold unsalted butter, cut into ¹/4-inch pieces

1. Line a 9-inch standard pie pan with the pastry, turning the top edge back and sculpting it into an upstanding ridge. Place in the freezer for 15 minutes. Preheat the oven to 400°F.

2. Put the cranberries in a large bowl and add the apples, stirring to combine. Stir in the sugar, lemon juice, and flour. Set aside for 10 minutes.

3. Scrape the filling into the chilled pie shell and smooth the top with your hands. Bake on the center oven rack for 30 minutes.

4. Meanwhile, make the topping. Combine the flour, sugar, and cinnamon in a medium-size bowl. Add the butter and rub it into the dry ingredients until the mixture resembles coarse crumbs. Refrigerate until ready to use.

5. Remove the pie from the oven and reduce the temperature to 375°F. Sprinkle the topping over the filling and press gently to compact. Return the pie to the oven, placing it so that the part that faced the back of the oven now faces forward. Just in case, slide a large aluminum foil–lined baking sheet onto the rack below to catch any spills. Continue

to bake until the topping is golden brown and the juices bubble thickly around the edge, 25 to 30 minutes.

6. Transfer the pie to a wire rack and let cool for at least 1 hour before serving.

Recipe for Success

▶ **For a refresher on pie apples, see pages 232–233.**

▶ **To make this even simpler, use a store-bought frozen pie shell, but keep in mind that it won't hold as much filling. Reduce each filling ingredient by roughly one-quarter.**

Cranberry-Apple-Orange Freeform Pie

Sometimes I get the urge to make a simple pie like this one—no top crust or crumb topping, just a large bottom crust that gets folded up to partially enclose the filling. You can apply this technique to just about any fruit pie with great results. Here's one fall version I'm particularly fond of.

MAKES 8 TO 10 SERVINGS

1 recipe Basic Flaky Pie Pastry, Single Crust (page 31), refrigerated

FILLING

2 cups fresh cranberries, picked over for stems

2/3 cup sugar

3 large Golden Delicious, Northern Spy, Granny Smith, or other firm apples (see pages 232–233 for recommendations), peeled, quartered, cored, and sliced crosswise

1/3 cup orange juice

Grated zest of 1 orange

1/2 teaspoon vanilla extract

3 tablespoons all-purpose flour

1/4 teaspoon ground cinnamon

1. If you haven't already, prepare the pastry and refrigerate until firm enough to roll, about 1 hour.

2. Combine the cranberries and sugar in a food processor and pulse until the cranberries are coarsely chopped. Transfer to a large bowl and add all the remaining filling ingredients, tossing well to combine. Set the mixture aside for 30 minutes. Preheat the oven to 400°F a few minutes before you start to assemble the pie.

3. On a sheet of lightly floured waxed paper, roll the pastry into a 14-inch circle with a floured rolling pin. The pastry will extend about 1 inch beyond the edge of the paper. Invert the pastry over a 9½-inch deep-dish pie pan, center, and peel off the paper. Gently ease the pastry into the pan, simultaneously lifting up on the edge of the pastry as you tuck it into the pan. Let the pastry drape over the edge. Turn the filling into the pie shell and smooth the top. Fold the overhanging dough up over the filling. The dough will self-pleat as you do this, and you'll have a 3- or 4-inch "window" of exposed filling in the center.

4. Place the pie on the center oven rack and bake for 30 minutes. Reduce the oven temperature to 375°F and rotate the pie 180 degrees, so that the part that was facing the back of the oven now faces forward. Continue to bake until the juices bubble thickly up through the center of the pie, 30 to 35 minutes.

5. Transfer the pie to a wire rack and let cool for at least 1 hour before serving.

Recipe for Success

▶ You can do a couple of fun things with the gap in the center of the pie, where the pastry doesn't cover the filling. The simplest is a mini mountain of Fresh Whipped Cream (page 605), spooned right into the hole. The other is a serious pool of Crème Anglaise (page 606) poured into the hole; this will ooze over the fruit and seep throughout the pie. In either case, let the pie cool considerably, until barely warm, before adding the garnish, so that the heat doesn't destabilize it.

Jellied Cranberry-Pecan Pie

Fresh cranberries go into a lot of my fall and winter pies. I buy bags of them on sale and store them in the freezer. Dried cranberries are wonderful in pies, too. But did you know that you can also use canned cranberry sauce in pies? It makes a delicious alternative. I call this a jellied pie because the filling—flavored with lemon zest, vanilla, and a splash of maple syrup—has a jelly-like consistency and color, contributed to in part by the cranberry sauce. The pecans give it an additional autumn emphasis and a bit of crunch to boot. Consider this one for your Thanksgiving holiday lineup.

MAKES 8 TO 10 SERVINGS

1 recipe Whole Wheat Pie Pastry, Single Crust (page 33), Lard Pie Pastry, Single Crust (page 36), or Basic Flaky Pie Pastry, Single Crust (page 31), refrigerated

FILLING

1/2 cup firmly packed light brown sugar

3 tablespoons all-purpose flour

1/8 teaspoon ground cinnamon

1/8 teaspoon salt

3 large eggs

1/4 cup (1/2 stick) unsalted butter, melted

1/2 cup light corn syrup

2 tablespoons pure maple syrup or honey

1/2 teaspoon vanilla extract

1 teaspoon grated lemon zest

1 cup chopped pecans

1 cup whole-berry cranberry sauce (see Recipe for Success)

1. If you haven't already, prepare the pastry and refrigerate until firm enough to roll, about 1 hour.

2. On a sheet of lightly floured waxed paper, roll the pastry into a 12-inch circle with a floured rolling pin. Invert the pastry over a 9-inch standard pie pan, center, and peel off the paper. Tuck the pastry into the pan, without stretching it, and sculpt the edge so it is just slightly higher than the rim of the pan. Place in the freezer for 15 minutes, then partially prebake and let cool according to the instructions on page 16. Reduce the oven temperature to 350°F.

3. In a large bowl, combine the brown sugar, flour, cinnamon, and salt. Rub them together well, breaking up any clumps of sugar. Whisk in the eggs, followed by the butter, corn syrup, maple syrup, vanilla, and lemon zest. Stir in the pecans and cranberry sauce. Carefully pour the filling into the cooled pie shell.

4. Place the pie on the center oven rack and bake until the filling is set, 40 to 45 minutes, rotating the pie 180 degrees halfway through the baking, so that the part that faced the back of the oven now faces forward. When done, the filling should not be soupy in the center. Give the pie a little nudge to check.

5. Transfer the pie to a wire rack and let cool to room temperature. Serve immediately, or cover with loosely tented aluminum foil and refrigerate for several hours before serving.

Recipe for Success

▶ Don't measure the cranberry sauce directly from the can because the jellied part tends to settle to the bottom. Empty the entire can into a small bowl, stir well, and then measure it.

Libby's Famous Pumpkin Pie

When I write cookbooks, I don't normally lift recipes right off the box top or can. But when the recipe is as reliable and famous as this one—by rights, the most frequently made pie in America—it's worth adding to a collection as inclusive as this. There are no real tricks or secrets here, just a straightforward approach to making a very pumpkiny pumpkin pie, with a familiar taste and creamy texture. The liquid is evaporated milk, which—because it contains less water than fresh milk—contributes to the smooth texture. It's just a fine recipe all around, and it's reprinted here with the permission of Nestle. Don't use a store-bought frozen pie shell; it's not large enough to hold all of the filling. However, you can use a 9-inch standard pie pan lined with store-bought refrigerated pastry.

MAKES 8 SERVINGS

1 recipe Basic Flaky Pie Pastry, Single Crust (page 31), refrigerated

FILLING

$3/4$ cup sugar

$1/2$ teaspoon salt

1 teaspoon ground cinnamon

$1/2$ teaspoon ground ginger

$1/4$ teaspoon ground cloves

2 large eggs

One 15-ounce can Libby's 100% Pure Pumpkin

One 12-ounce can Nestlé Carnation evaporated milk

GARNISH

Fresh Whipped Cream (page 605; optional)

1. If you haven't already, prepare the pastry and refrigerate until firm enough to roll, about 1 hour.

2. On a sheet of lightly floured waxed paper, roll the pastry into a 12-inch circle with a floured rolling pin. Invert the pastry over a 9-inch standard pie pan, center, and peel off the paper. Tuck the pastry into the pan, without stretching it, and sculpt the edge into an upstanding ridge. Place in the freezer for 15 minutes. Preheat the oven to 425°F.

3. Combine the sugar, salt, and spices in a small bowl. Beat the eggs in a large bowl. Stir in the pumpkin and sugar-spice mixture. Gradually stir in the evaporated milk. Pour into the chilled pie shell.

4. Place the pie on the center oven rack and bake for 15 minutes. Reduce the oven temperature to 350°F and rotate the pie 180 degrees, so that the part that was facing the back of the oven now faces forward. Continue to bake until a knife inserted near the center comes out clean, 40 to 50 minutes.

Cranking Out Those Holiday Pies

If you're like me, what comes to the table *after* the Thanksgiving meal is as important as what comes to the table *during* the meal. What comes after, of course, is pie, and no doubt you've experienced times when the demand has put a strain on both your and your kitchen's ability to keep up with the meal and juggle the pies. Here are some suggestions to keep those pies coming.

- Remember that nearly all pie pastries freeze well and can be made at least a month ahead of when you'll need them. Take them out of the freezer the day before and thaw in the refrigerator.

- Decide on your pie menu a week ahead and check your supply of staples. Buy plenty, knowing that you'll need extra flour, sugar, vanilla, butter, and the like in the weeks to come. Overlooked ingredients will try your patience and tax your time with extra trips to the grocery store.

- To save time, compartmentalize your movements. Don't make one pastry, then the filling, then the pastry for the next pie. Make all the pastry you need, plus an extra portion for good measure.

- To avoid oven congestion on Thanksgiving Day, bake your pies the day before. Unless your oven is very large, avoid baking them more than one at a time, if possible, so that they bake as evenly as possible. Fruit and pumpkin pies—the ones you'll most likely be making—will hold up fine for 24 hours. Pumpkin pies should be refrigerated overnight, but fruit pies will be fine if you simply keep them cool. Protect them well and store them in the cellar, mudroom, or pantry.

- Cool or cold fruit pies can be warmed in a low oven for about 20 minutes before serving. This will loosen the juices and take off the cold edge.

5. Transfer the pie to a wire rack and let cool for 2 hours. Serve immediately, or cover with loosely tented aluminum foil and refrigerate before serving. Garnish with whipped cream, if desired.

Recipe for Success

- I mentioned above that there is too much filling here for a store-bought frozen pie shell. However, as it mentions on the Libby's label, you can bake 2 shallow pies by dividing the filling between 2 such shells. Bake at 425°F for 15 minutes, then reduce the oven temperature to 350°F and bake for 20 to 30 minutes.

- Also from the Libby's can: (1) Do not freeze the pie, as this will cause the crust to separate from the filling. (2) You can substitute 1³/₄ teaspoons pumpkin pie spice for the other spices, but the taste will be a little different.

Maple Pumpkin Pie

I've always had to work at loving pumpkin pie. I mean, I like it, but to really love it, I've had to make some special provisions over the years—such as sweetening them with maple syrup, as I do here. The two flavors—pumpkin and maple—seem to have a certain affinity for each other. When I lived in New England, I often made a side dish of mashed pumpkin with a touch of maple syrup for sweetener. It's delicious alongside baked ham and roast chicken. I recommend dark, cooking-grade maple syrup here, because the deep, caramel flavor comes through and flatters the pumpkin. I also use dark brown sugar, as a frugal cook such as myself has a hard time adding a full cup of expensive maple syrup to anything.

MAKES 8 TO 10 SERVINGS

1 recipe Basic Flaky Pie Pastry, Single Crust (page 31), refrigerated

FILLING

3 large eggs

1 cup light cream or half-and-half

1/2 cup pure maple syrup, preferably dark

1 teaspoon vanilla extract

1/2 cup firmly packed dark brown sugar

1 1/2 tablespoons all-purpose flour

1 teaspoon ground ginger

1/2 teaspoon ground cinnamon

1/4 teaspoon ground cloves

1/4 teaspoon ground nutmeg

3/4 teaspoon salt

One 15-ounce can or 1 3/4 cups fresh (see page 286) pumpkin puree

GARNISH

Fresh Whipped Cream (page 605)

1. If you haven't already, prepare the pastry and refrigerate until firm enough to roll, about 1 hour.

2. On a sheet of lightly floured waxed paper, roll the pastry into a 13-inch circle with a floured rolling pin. Invert the pastry over a 9 1/2-inch deep-dish pie pan, center, and peel off the paper. Tuck the pastry into the pan, without stretching it, and sculpt the edge until it is even with the rim. Place in the freezer for 15 minutes, then partially prebake and let cool according to the instructions on page 16. Reduce the oven temperature to 350°F.

3. Beat the eggs lightly in a medium-size bowl. Whisk in the cream, maple syrup, and vanilla. Combine the brown sugar, flour, spices, and salt in a small bowl. Add the mixture to the wet ingredients and stir well to combine. Add the pumpkin and blend well with a whisk. Carefully pour the filling into the cooled pie shell.

4. Place the pie on the center oven rack and bake for 25 minutes, then rotate the pie 180 degrees, so that the part that was facing the back of the oven now faces forward. Continue to bake until the filling is set, about 25 minutes. When the pie is done, the center will not be soupy. The outer area will have puffed a little, and the edges of the pie will have a slight sheen, although the center portion may not.

5. Transfer the pie to a wire rack and let cool. Serve warm or at room temperature. Or cover with loosely tented aluminum foil and refrigerate until well chilled. Serve garnished with whipped cream.

Recipe for Success

▶ Do look for the subtle sheen differences on the surface of the pie, as described in step 4. If you can get the pie out of the oven while the center still has a shiny surface, it should be perfectly baked.

Spiced Pumpkin Indian Pudding Pie

A cross between Indian pudding and pumpkin pie, this has a cornmeal-thickened base that's cooked on the stovetop before being blended with eggs, sugar, pumpkin, and spices. Served warm, it has a pudding-soft consistency. Served cold, it's more like pumpkin pie, with a firmer, custard-like filling. This makes a large pie that will be greeted warmly at any Thanksgiving or holiday dinner.

MAKES 8 TO 10 SERVINGS

1 recipe Basic Flaky Pie Pastry, Single Crust (page 31), refrigerated

FILLING

2 cups whole or reduced-fat (2%) milk

1/3 cup fine yellow cornmeal (see Recipe for Success)

1/4 teaspoon salt

2 tablespoons unsalted butter, cut into 1/2-inch pieces

1/2 cup granulated sugar

1/2 cup firmly packed light brown sugar

1 cup pumpkin puree, canned or fresh (see page 286)

1 teaspoon vanilla extract

1/2 teaspoon ground cinnamon

1/2 teaspoon ground ginger

1/2 teaspoon ground nutmeg

1/4 teaspoon ground cloves

3 large eggs, lightly beaten

GARNISH

Fresh Whipped Cream (page 605) or vanilla ice cream

1. If you haven't already, prepare the pastry and refrigerate until firm enough to roll, about 1 hour.

2. On a sheet of lightly floured waxed paper, roll the pastry into a 13-inch circle with a floured rolling pin. Invert the pastry over a 9½-inch deep-dish pie pan, center, and peel off the paper. Tuck the pastry into the pan, without stretching it, and sculpt the edge so it is just slightly higher than the rim. Place in the freezer for 15 minutes, then partially pre-bake and let cool according to the instructions on page 16. Increase the oven temperature to 400°F.

3. Combine the milk and cornmeal in a medium-size saucepan and bring to a simmer over medium heat, whisking frequently. Don't let the liquid reach a rapid boil. As the mixture starts to thicken, continue to whisk virtually nonstop until it reaches the consistency of thin hot cereal, 1 to 2 minutes. Transfer to a medium-size bowl and whisk in the salt, butter, and sugars. Let cool for 10 minutes, then whisk in the pumpkin, vanilla, and spices. Add the eggs, whisking to blend. Slowly pour the filling into the cooled pie shell.

4. Place the pie on the center oven rack and bake for 15 minutes, then reduce the oven temperature to 350°F and rotate the pie 180 degrees, so that the part that faced the back of the oven now faces forward. Continue to bake until the filling is set in the center, about 30 minutes. To check the pie, give it a quick little nudge. It should wobble but not seem soupy in the center.

5. Transfer the pie to a wire rack and let cool. Serve barely warm, or let cool to room temperature, cover with loosely tented aluminum foil, and refrigerate before serving. Garnish with a dollop of whipped cream or a scoop of ice cream.

Recipe for Success

▶ Be sure to use fine cornmeal here. Coarse-ground cornmeal will not give the pie the same sort of smooth, uniform texture.

▶ If you substitute ¼ cup each unsulfured molasses and pure maple syrup for the brown sugar, this will taste even more like Indian pudding.

Ben's Pumpkin Cheesecake Pie

The sort of pumpkin pie I like best tastes more like cheesecake than traditional pumpkin pie. Years ago, finding the texture of pumpkin pie a little too dry for my taste, I started adding cream cheese to my recipes and found the result much to my liking. You can bake this in any pastry, but I like the earthiness of the cornmeal crust here; it's a good match for the pumpkin. If you're pressed for time, you don't have to prebake the pastry, but you'll get a better result if you do, possibly avoiding that slightly underbaked taste. The recipe is named for my oldest son, Ben, whose taste in pumpkin pie runs close to my own.

MAKES 8 TO 10 SERVINGS

1 recipe Cornmeal Pie Pastry, Single Crust (page 40), refrigerated

FILLING

One 8-ounce package full-fat cream cheese, softened

1/2 cup granulated sugar

1/2 cup firmly packed light brown sugar

2 large eggs, at room temperature

1 large egg yolk, at room temperature

1/2 teaspoon vanilla extract

Finely grated zest of 1 lemon

1/2 teaspoon ground cinnamon

1/2 teaspoon ground nutmeg

1/4 teaspoon ground ginger

1/4 teaspoon salt

1 cup pumpkin puree, canned or fresh (see page 286)

2/3 cup light cream or half-and-half

1. If you haven't already, prepare the pastry and refrigerate until firm enough to roll, about 1 hour.

2. On a sheet of lightly floured waxed paper, roll the pastry into a 13-inch circle with a floured rolling pin. Invert the pastry over a 9½-inch deep-dish pie pan, center, and peel off the paper. Tuck the pastry into the pan, without stretching it, and sculpt the edge so it is slightly higher than the rim. Place in the freezer for 15 minutes, then partially prebake and let cool according to the instructions on page 16. Reduce the oven temperature to 350°F.

3. Using an electric mixer, cream the cream cheese, gradually beating in the sugars. Blend in the eggs and egg yolk, one at a time, on medium speed. Blend in the vanilla, lemon zest, spices, and salt. Add the pumpkin and cream and blend until smooth and evenly mixed. Pour the filling into the cooled pie shell and smooth the top.

4. Place the pie on the center oven rack and bake for 20 minutes. Rotate the pie 180 degrees, so that the part that faced the back of the oven now faces forward. Bake for about 20 minutes more, until the top has puffed slightly and perhaps cracked around the perimeter. The center may seem a little wobbly, but it should not be soupy.

5. Transfer the pie to a wire rack and let cool to room temperature. Cover with loosely tented aluminum foil and refrigerate for at least 4 hours or overnight before serving.

Recipe for Success

▶ Occasionally, I add a thick chocolate glaze to the top of this pie. It's a delicious touch. Prepare a batch of Warm Mocha Sauce (page 607), then let it cool until thick but still pourable. It will still be slightly warm. Pour most or all of the sauce over the pie, tilting it to spread the sauce evenly. Refrigerate for at least 30 minutes before serving.

Triple-Layer Pumpkin-Chocolate Pie

Now here's a pumpkin pie that will get you rave reviews, at least in part because the slices have such a handsome profile. We begin with a cheesecake-like pumpkin filling, half of which is blended with a good amount of semisweet chocolate. The chocolate portion goes into the shell first, then is briefly baked to stabilize it. The "plain" pumpkin filling goes on top, and the pie is baked some more. The topping is a thin layer of sweetened sour cream. Once cooled, the pie has three colorfully distinct layers and tastes delicious, much to the surprise of those—and there have been a few—whom I've had to assure that chocolate and pumpkin are perfect partners on the dessert plate. Try this; I think you'll like it.

MAKES 10 TO 12 SERVINGS

1 recipe Basic Flaky Pie Pastry, Single Crust (page 31), refrigerated, or Graham Cracker Crumb Crust (page 51), or 1 large store-bought graham cracker crust

FILLING

2 tablespoons unsalted butter

4 ounces semisweet chocolate, coarsely chopped

Four 3-ounce packages full-fat cream cheese, softened

1 1/2 cups sugar

2 large eggs, at room temperature

1 cup pumpkin puree, canned or fresh (see page 286)

1/2 teaspoon vanilla extract

1/4 teaspoon ground cinnamon

1/4 teaspoon ground nutmeg

1/4 teaspoon ground cloves

1/4 teaspoon salt

1 cup full-fat sour cream

1. If you are using the pastry and haven't already prepared it, prepare it now and refrigerate until firm enough to roll, about 1 hour. If you are using the graham cracker crust, prepare the crust and press it into the bottom and up the side of a 9 1/2-inch deep-dish pie pan. Refrigerate, prebake, and let cool as directed. Or simply prebake a store-bought crust as directed on the package and let cool.

2. On a sheet of lightly floured waxed paper, roll the pastry, if using, into a 13-inch circle with a floured rolling pin. Invert the pastry over a 9 1/2-inch deep-dish pie pan, center, and peel off the paper. Tuck the pastry into the pan, without stretching it, and sculpt the edge into an upstanding ridge. Place in the freezer for 15 minutes, then partially prebake and let cool according to the instructions on page 16.

3. Reduce the oven temperature to 350°F. Place the butter in the top of a double boiler set over, not in, barely simmering water. When the butter is partially melted, add the chocolate. Heat for 5 to 7 minutes, until melted, then whisk until smooth. Remove the top of the double boiler and set it aside to partially cool the chocolate.

4. Using an electric mixer, cream the cream cheese on medium speed in a large bowl, gradually adding 1 1/4 cups of the sugar. Beat in the eggs, one at a time, then blend in the pumpkin, vanilla, spices, and salt until evenly combined. Pour slightly less than half of the filling into a separate bowl and stir in the melted chocolate until evenly blended. Pour the chocolate filling into the cooled pie shell and gently shake the pan to settle the filling.

5. Place the pie on the center oven rack and bake for 20 minutes. Transfer to a wire rack and let cool for 15 minutes.

6. Carefully ladle the remaining plain pumpkin filling over the cooled chocolate layer. Shake the pan gently to settle the filling. Return to the oven, placing the pie so that the part that faced the back of the oven now faces forward. Bake until the pumpkin layer is set, 35 to 40 minutes. When done, the perimeter of the filling will have puffed somewhat but not so much that it develops large cracks.

7. Transfer the pie to a wire rack and let cool until the filling settles down and flattens out, 30 to 45 minutes.

8. Combine the sour cream and remaining ¼ cup sugar in a small saucepan over very low heat and warm, stirring often, for 2 to 4 minutes. When the sour cream is fairly thin—and slightly warmer than body temperature, carefully pour it over the top of the pie. Immediately shake and tilt the pie to cover it with the topping. Return the pie to the rack and let cool thoroughly, then cover with loosely tented aluminum foil and refrigerate for at least 3 hours before serving.

Recipe for Success

▶ The chocolate layer is partially prebaked to maintain its integrity when the plain pumpkin layer is added. The prebaking firms up the chocolate, and the short cooldown allows a slight skin to form, which helps keep the pumpkin layer from sinking into the chocolate. Keep all of this in mind as you're handling the pie. To emphasize the break between layers, you also might sprinkle a fairly dense layer of chopped walnuts or pecans over the chocolate as soon as the pie comes out of the oven, pressing them ever so gently to embed them in the chocolate.

Diane's Pumpkin-Praline Pie

There are pumpkin pies for purists, bereft of fanfare and flourishes. And then there are over-the-top pumpkin pies, for when you want to wow the crowd. This falls into the second category. Indeed, I would say it crowns the category. When I asked Diane Rossen Worthington, a celebrated California cook and cookbook author, if she'd be kind enough to let me include her "most requested" holiday pie in this collection, she quickly gave me the go-ahead. The thick, creamy pumpkin layer would make a great pie on its own, but Diane goes one better—first cooling the pie, then topping it with a brown sugar–pecan praline mixture, which she caramelizes under the broiler. The pie is gorgeous to slice—first carving into the crunchy praline, then the soft pumpkin. Once you've tried it, plain pumpkin pie won't taste the same. Please note that I've made one small change to Diane's spices: I use a little cinnamon and cloves in place of the allspice she prefers.

MAKES 8 TO 10 SERVINGS

1 recipe Basic Flaky Pie Pastry, Single Crust (page 31), refrigerated

FILLING

3 large eggs, at room temperature

2/3 cup sugar

One 15-ounce can or 1 3/4 cups fresh (see page 286) pumpkin puree

1/4 cup light cream or half-and-half

1/2 teaspoon salt

1/2 teaspoon ground ginger

1/2 teaspoon ground nutmeg

1/4 teaspoon ground cinnamon

1/4 teaspoon ground cloves

3 tablespoons bourbon or 1 teaspoon vanilla extract

PRALINE TOPPING

1 1/4 cups chopped pecans

3/4 cup firmly packed light brown sugar

1/4 cup (1/2 stick) unsalted butter, melted

2 tablespoons heavy or whipping cream

1/4 teaspoon ground cinnamon

GARNISH

Fresh Whipped Cream (page 605)

1. If you haven't already, prepare the pastry and refrigerate until firm enough to roll, about 1 hour.

2. On a sheet of lightly floured waxed paper, roll the pastry into a 13-inch circle with a floured rolling pin. Invert the pastry over a 9½-inch deep-dish pie pan, center, and peel off the paper. Tuck the pastry into the pan, without stretching it, and sculpt the edge into an upstanding ridge. Place in the freezer for 15 minutes, then partially prebake and let cool according to the instructions on page 16. Reduce the oven temperature to 350°F.

3. Combine the eggs and sugar in a large bowl. Using an electric mixer, beat on high speed until light and lemon-colored, about 3 minutes. Add the pumpkin, light cream, salt, spices, and bourbon and blend on low speed until evenly mixed. Pour the filling into the cooled pie shell.

4. Place the pie on the center oven rack and bake for 20 minutes, then rotate the pie 180 degrees, so that the part that faced the back of the oven now faces forward. Continue to bake until the filling is set, 40 to 45 minutes. When done, the perimeter of the pie will have puffed very slightly. Also, the very center will look a little glossy compared to the perimeter, which will have a flatter finish.

Homemade Pumpkin Puree

Most of the time, I reach for canned pumpkin when I want to make a pumpkin pie. Canned gets high grades for both flavor and convenience; it would take one sophisticated palate to tell the difference between canned and fresh pumpkin puree.

Come October, however, many of us get the urge to bake a real pumpkin and make a genuine pumpkin pie from scratch. Here's a simple way to do just that.

Select a small pumpkin of the sort generally referred to as a sugar pie pumpkin. These are smaller than carving pumpkins and have a denser, sweeter flesh. Preheat the oven to 375°F. Wash off the pumpkin, then cut it in half crosswise and scoop out the seeds. (The seeds can be roasted separately, by the way. They make a great snack.) Put about 1/2 cup water in a large roasting pan, then add the pumpkin cut side up or down—it doesn't much matter. Bake until the flesh is very tender when pierced with a paring knife, 45 to 60 minutes. Let the pumpkin cool, then scoop out the flesh and discard the skin. Puree the flesh in a food processor before adding it to your recipe. That's all there is to it.

5. Transfer the pie to a wire rack and let cool completely. The praline can be added once the pie has cooled, or the pie can be covered and refrigerated until you're ready to add the praline. The praline will need to stabilize for at least 10 minutes before serving.

6. When you're ready to add the praline, preheat the broiler. Adjust one of the oven racks so that it is 6 to 8 inches away from the broiler. Combine all the topping ingredients in a medium-size bowl and stir well. Scrape the praline evenly over the pie and smooth with a spoon. Place the pie on a baking sheet and set it under the broiler (see Recipe for Success) until the topping is melted and bubbly. As it bubbles, move the baking sheet a couple of times, changing the position of the pie slightly so that it browns evenly. This entire process may take less than 1 minute—do not walk away from the oven!

7. Transfer to a wire rack and let cool at least 10 minutes. Or let cool thoroughly, cover with loosely tented aluminum foil, and refrigerate. Serve with whipped cream.

Recipe for Success

▶ Diane says to watch the pie like a hawk when you put it under the broiler, because it can bubble and brown very quickly and take you by surprise. Don't leave the stove area, and do consider leaving the oven door open so that you can both hear what is going on and moderate the intense broiler heat just a little.

▶ Diane likes to press some additional pecan halves right into the warm praline as soon as the pie comes out of the oven for a pretty garnish.

Muirhead Pumpkin Butter and Pecan Pie

I seldom write a recipe around a product that isn't widely available in most supermarkets, but I'm going to make an exception for something called Pecan Pumpkin Butter made by a New Jersey company named Muirhead. (You can find Muirhead online at www.muirheadfoods.com.) Muirhead's pumpkin butter is pureed pumpkin cooked to a thick, delicious paste, then combined with finely chopped pecans, sugar, lemon juice, and spices. It's mainly a spread for biscuits, toast, and English muffins, but after one taste, you'll know why I love it as the base for this creamy, perfectly spiced pie. This is one of my favorite fall desserts.

MAKES 8 TO 10 SERVINGS

1 recipe Basic Flaky Pie Pastry, Single Crust (page 31), refrigerated

FILLING

3 large eggs, at room temperature

One 13.5-ounce jar (about 1 1/3 cups) Muirhead Pecan Pumpkin Butter

1/2 cup heavy or whipping cream

1/4 cup light cream or half-and-half

3 tablespoons sugar

1/4 teaspoon salt

1 1/2 cups coarsely chopped pecans

1. If you haven't already, prepare the pastry and refrigerate until firm enough to roll, about 1 hour.

2. On a sheet of lightly floured waxed paper, roll the pastry into a 12-inch circle with a floured rolling pin. Invert the pastry over a 9-inch standard pie pan, center, and peel off the paper. Tuck the pastry into the pan, without stretching it, and sculpt the edge into an upstanding ridge. Place in the freezer for 15 minutes, then partially prebake and let cool according to the instructions on page 16. Reduce the oven temperature to 350°F.

3. Whisk the eggs in a large bowl just until frothy. Add the pumpkin butter, heavy cream, light cream, sugar, and salt and whisk well to combine. Stir in the pecans, then turn the filling into the cooled pie shell. Using a fork, gently rake through the filling to distribute the nuts evenly.

4. Place the pie on the center oven rack and bake for 25 minutes, then rotate the pie 180 degrees, so that the part that faced the back of the oven now faces forward. Continue to bake until the filling is barely set in the center, 15 to 20 minutes. When done, the edge of the pie may have puffed slightly.

5. Transfer the pie to a wire rack and let cool. The pie can be served slightly warm or at room temperature. Or it can be thoroughly cooled, covered with loosely tented aluminum foil, and refrigerated before serving.

Recipe for Success

▶ For an even nuttier flavor, toast the pecans in a preheated 350°F oven until fragrant, 7 to 8 minutes, before adding them to the pie.

▶ Do not substitute canned pumpkin puree for the pumpkin butter—it will not work.

Honey Pumpkin-Date Pie with Golden Marshmallow Topping

Here's an over-the-top pumpkin pie that's as fetching as it is delicious. The creamy filling is sweetened with honey and speckled with soft dates. The real treat, though, is the golden marshmallow topping. Just before serving, spread mini marshmallows over the pie, then quickly brown them under the broiler. This is best served chilled, with the warm marshmallows on top, so plan on making the pie the day before you plan to serve it, or very early the same day, then finish it right before serving.

MAKES 10 TO 12 SERVINGS

1 recipe Graham Cracker Crumb Crust (page 51)

FILLING

1 1/4 cups pumpkin puree, canned or fresh (see page 286)

3 large eggs, at room temperature

3/4 cup heavy or whipping cream

1/2 cup full-fat sour cream

1/2 cup honey

2 tablespoons unsulfured molasses

1 teaspoon ground ginger

1 teaspoon ground cinnamon

1/2 teaspoon ground cloves

1/2 teaspoon ground nutmeg

1 cup soft dates, pitted and cut into bite-size pieces

GOLDEN MARSHMALLOW TOPPING

2 to 2 1/2 cups mini marshmallows

1. Prepare the crust and press it into the bottom and up the side of a 9 1/2-inch deep-dish pie pan. Refrigerate, prebake, and let cool as directed. Increase the oven temperature to 400°F.

Those First Pumpkin Pies

From a multitude of sources, we know that the earliest settlers learned to make pumpkin "pie" from the Native Americans. It wasn't pumpkin pie as we know it today. The filling would have likely been a primitive medley of bread pieces, nuts, honey, and, in time, milk and spices, tucked in a hollowed-out pumpkin and baked over ashes. If all this sounds austere, it must have tasted heavenly to families struggling for survival.

According to Waverly Root and Richard de Rochemont in their book *Eating in America* (William Morrow, 1976), the first American cookbook to contain a recipe for "pompkin" pie was Amelia Simmons's *American Cookery*, published in 1796. Credited as being the first true American cookbook, it became something of a bestseller in its day, gaining wide popularity through a number of editions.

2. In a large bowl, combine the pumpkin, eggs, heavy cream, sour cream, honey, and molasses. Using an electric mixer, blend briefly on medium-low speed until evenly mixed. Blend in the spices, then stir in the dates. Slowly pour the filling into the cooled pie shell, raking the dates with a fork to distribute them evenly.

3. Place the pie on the center oven rack and bake for 20 minutes. Reduce the oven temperature to 325°F and rotate the pie 180 degrees, so that the part that faced the back of the oven now faces forward. Continue to bake until the filling is set but still somewhat jiggly in the center, 25 to 30 minutes.

4. Transfer the pie to a wire rack and let cool thoroughly, then cover with loosely tented aluminum foil and refrigerate for at least 3 hours or overnight.

5. When you're ready to serve the pie, preheat the broiler. Spread the marshmallows evenly over the top of the pie in a single, tightly packed layer. Slide the pie onto a rack under the broiler and lightly brown the marshmallows. Keep a close eye on the pie; the marshmallows will brown quickly (see Recipe for Success). Slice and serve right away.

Recipe for Success

▶ Given the richness of this pie, the dramatic topping, and the near imperative that it be eaten right out of the oven, think of it as one you'd prepare for a crowd. Obviously, Thanksgiving is a good occasion. This does, incidentally, reheat nicely. Just put the pie in a hot oven for 3 to 4 minutes, and the marshmallows will be crisp on the outside and soft on the inside.

▶ The marshmallows will go from golden to gone in seconds. Don't even close the oven door when you're browning them, and position the oven rack at a comfortable distance from the broiler.

Five-Spice Winter Squash Pie

For the most part, winter squash and pumpkin can be used interchangeably in pies. That said, there are a few differences. I find most cooked winter squash to be a little drier than pumpkin. The color is a paler orange, and the flavor is milder, too. One advantage of squash over pumpkin is that a squash is a little smaller and easier to cut and handle, and therefore easier to bake. Of course, none of this makes much difference if you're using canned squash. But given the quality and availability of winter squash in the fall, it's fun—once in a while—to bake your own and turn it into a pie. My favorite version of squash pie contains a good amount of Chinese five-spice powder, which is a little like pumpkin pie spice with ground star anise added. It lends the pie a warming and festive flavor and makes this a good candidate for a Thanksgiving dessert.

MAKES 8 TO 10 SERVINGS

1 recipe Basic Flaky Pie Pastry, Single Crust (page 31) or Whole Wheat Pie Pastry, Single Crust (page 33), refrigerated

FILLING

1 large butternut squash, 2 large delicata squash, or one 15-ounce can squash puree

1 cup firmly packed light brown sugar

3 large eggs, at room temperature

3/4 cup light cream or half-and-half, at room temperature

2 teaspoons Chinese five-spice powder

1/4 teaspoon salt

1 tablespoon all-purpose flour

1 teaspoon vanilla extract

GARNISH

Fresh Whipped Cream (page 605)

1.   Before you prepare the pastry, if you're using fresh squash, preheat the oven to 400°F. Cut off a little of the stem end of the squash and halve it lengthwise. Scoop the seeds out of the cavity. Place the squash flat side down in a large, shallow oiled casserole and add just enough water to cover the bottom. Cover loosely with aluminum foil and bake for about 50 minutes. Remove the foil and continue to bake until the squash is very tender (test it with a paring knife), about 10 minutes. Transfer the squash to a plate and let cool.

2.   If you haven't already, prepare the pastry and refrigerate until firm enough to roll, about 1 hour.

3.   On a sheet of lightly floured waxed paper, roll the pastry into a 13-inch circle with a floured rolling pin. Invert the pastry over a 9½-inch deep-dish pie pan, center, and peel

off the paper. Gently tuck the pastry into the pan, without stretching it, and sculpt the edge so it is just slightly higher than the rim. Place in the freezer for 15 minutes, then partially prebake and let cool according to the instructions on page 16. Reduce the oven temperature to 350°F.

4.   When the squash is cool enough to handle, spoon 1³/₄ cups firmly packed flesh out of the skin and put it (or the canned puree) in a food processor with the brown sugar. Process briefly, until smooth. Add the eggs, light cream, five-spice powder, salt, flour, and vanilla and process briefly. Slowly pour the filling into the cooled pie shell.

5.   Place the pie on the center oven rack and bake for about 50 minutes, rotating the pie 180 degrees halfway through the baking, so that the part that faced the back of the oven now faces forward. When done, the perimeter of the pie will be somewhat risen and puffy, though not so much that it develops large cracks. The filling will be set and generally have a flat finish, although the center may be shiny.

6.   Transfer the pie to a wire rack and let cool. Serve slightly warm or at room temperature. Or cover with loosely tented aluminum foil, refrigerate, and serve cold. Garnish with a dollop of whipped cream.

Recipe for Success

▸   You'll end up with a creamier pie if you don't bake the squash in too much water. That's why I recommend using just a little water in the pan, then removing the foil when the squash is almost done, so that any excess water evaporates. If you use more water, the squash will soak it up, and your pie will be watery and not as creamy.

Traditional Sweet Potato Pie

Sweet potato pie may not be the national icon that pumpkin pie is, but it has much to recommend it. Like pumpkins, the meaty texture of sweet potatoes makes for a wonderfully dense filling with a creamy consistency. The flavor is unique and sweet, and the color is similarly lovely. To help keep this recipe distinct from those for pumpkin pie, I don't repeat all the traditional pumpkin pie spices, but rather limit the spices here to cinnamon and nutmeg.

MAKES 8 TO 10 SERVINGS

1 recipe Basic Flaky Pie Pastry, Single Crust
(page 31), refrigerated

FILLING

2 large sweet potatoes

1/3 cup granulated sugar

1/3 cup firmly packed light brown sugar

2 large eggs

1 large egg yolk

1 cup light cream or half-and-half

1 teaspoon vanilla extract

1 teaspoon fresh lemon juice

1/2 teaspoon ground cinnamon

1/2 teaspoon ground nutmeg

Scant 1/2 teaspoon salt

1. If you haven't already, prepare the pastry and refrigerate until firm enough to roll, about 1 hour.

2. Meanwhile, bake the sweet potatoes. Preheat the oven to 400°F. Put the sweet potatoes on a large baking sheet. Pierce them deeply with a paring knife several times. Bake until tender throughout (check with a paring knife), about 1 hour. Set aside to cool. When cool enough to handle, scoop the flesh into a food processor and process until smooth. Dump the puree into a medium-size bowl. Return 1 1/2 cups of the puree to the food processor. Don't worry if you come up a little short. If you have extra, save it for another use.

3. On a sheet of lightly floured waxed paper, roll the pastry into a 12-inch circle with a floured rolling pin. Invert the pastry over a 9-inch standard pie pan, center, and peel off the paper. Tuck the pastry into the pan, without stretching it, and sculpt the edge into an upstanding ridge. Place in the freezer for 15 minutes, then partially prebake and let cool according to the directions on page 16. Reduce the oven temperature to 350°F.

4. Add the sugars, eggs, and egg yolk to the food processor and process with the sweet potato puree until smooth. Add the cream, vanilla, lemon juice, cinnamon, nutmeg, and salt and process again until smooth. Carefully pour the filling into the cooled pie shell.

5. Place the pie on the center oven rack and bake for 30 minutes, then rotate the pie 180 degrees, so that the part that faced the back of the oven now faces forward. Continue to bake until the center is set and the edge has risen slightly, 15 to 20 minutes.

6. Transfer the pie to a wire rack and let cool. Serve barely warm or at room temperature. Or cover with loosely tented aluminum foil, refrigerate, and serve cold.

Recipe for Success

▶ Since you're baking sweet potatoes anyway, why not bake a couple of extras and use them to thicken soups or stews or for making muffins or quick breads. Or simply serve them mashed, as a side dish. Consult a general cookbook such as *Joy of Cooking* for recipes and serving ideas.

▶ To keep the color of the pie as bright as possible, use $^2/_3$ cup granulated sugar and leave out the brown sugar.

▶ Remember that this is essentially a custard pie, and, like other custard pies, it will turn watery if overbaked. Keep a close eye on it during the last 15 minutes of baking and remove it from the oven as soon as it is done.

Pass a Slice of That Sweet Potato Pie, Lover Boy

"In the case of the sweet potato, it is probable that its honeyed taste helped it to achieve quick popularity in Europe and America. When it first reached Europe, imported at the beginning of the sixteenth century by the Spaniards, who named it *batata*, it was endowed, quite gratuitously, with the reputation of being an aphrodisiac. For this or other reasons, it appealed to Henry VIII, who imported sweet potatoes from Spain and ate them in the form of pies, very sweet and heavily spiced; by the end of the sixteenth century many of his subjects were following suit."

—Waverly Root and Richard de Rochemont, *Eating in America* (William Morrow, 1976)

Fancy Sweet Potato Pie

Sweet potato pie, a southern specialty, has been an American tradition for more than 100 years. Like pumpkin pie, sweet potato pie tends to have a meaty, firm-bodied texture, although the flavor is somewhat more delicate and elusive than pumpkin, and it has a lighter orange hue. Pie makers reach into their pumpkin pie bag of tricks to nudge a sweet potato pie toward greatness. The same pumpkin pie spices make the rounds in sweet potato pies, as well as eggs, milk or cream, and a good measure of sweetener in the form of molasses, brown sugar, or even maple syrup. Our fancy version is a little light on the spices, but we include orange zest—a festive touch—and an optional splash of hazelnut or almond liqueur, to give this earthy pie an appropriately nutty flavor. I think it's best served cold, but it's also very good warm.

MAKES 8 TO 10 SERVINGS

1 recipe Basic Flaky Pie Pastry, Single Crust (page 31), refrigerated

FILLING

2 medium-large sweet potatoes

1/2 cup granulated sugar

1/2 cup firmly packed light brown sugar

3 tablespoons unsalted butter, melted

1/4 teaspoon ground nutmeg

1/4 teaspoon ground cloves

1/4 teaspoon ground cinnamon

Scant 1/2 teaspoon salt

2 large eggs

1 large egg yolk

Grated zest of 1 orange

2 tablespoons hazelnut or almond liqueur (optional)

1 cup light cream or half-and-half

GARNISH

Fresh Whipped Cream (page 605)

1.   If you haven't already, prepare the pastry and refrigerate until firm enough to roll, about 1 hour.

2.   On a sheet of lightly floured waxed paper, roll the pastry into a 13-inch circle with a floured rolling pin. Invert the pastry over a 9½-inch deep-dish pie pan, center, and peel off the paper. Tuck the pastry into the pan, without stretching it, and let the overhang drape over the edge. Trim the pastry flush with the outside edge of the pan, then crimp the edge with the tines of a fork. Place in the freezer for 15 minutes, then partially pre-bake and let cool according to the instructions on page 16. Leave the oven on.

3. Put the sweet potatoes on a large baking sheet. Pierce them deeply with a paring knife several times. Bake until tender to the center (check with a paring knife), about 1 hour. Set aside for 10 to 15 minutes to cool. Reduce the oven temperature to 350°F.

4. Spoon the sweet potato flesh into a liquid measuring cup, measuring out $2\frac{1}{2}$ cups. (Don't worry if you're a little over or under.) Place in a food processor, add the sugars and butter, and process until smooth. Add the spices, salt, eggs, egg yolk, and orange zest. Process until combined. Add the liqueur, if using, and light cream. Process until smooth. Pour the filling into the cooled pie shell and smooth the top with a spoon.

5. Place the pie on the center oven rack and bake for 45 to 50 minutes, rotating the pie 180 degrees halfway through the baking, so that the part that faced the back of the oven now faces forward. When done, the filling should have puffed and cracked slightly around the perimeter. The center may wobble slightly, but it should still seem set. The center may look shiny, but the edge will have a flat finish.

6. Transfer the pie to a wire rack and let cool. Serve barely warm or at room temperature. Or cover with loosely tented aluminum foil, refrigerate, and serve cold. Garnish with whipped cream.

Recipe for Success

▶ In my sweet potato pie trials, I both boiled and baked the potatoes and found that I prefer the results when baked. Baking takes longer, but it seems to concentrate the flavor without adding excess moisture to the pie. You get a creamier, fuller-bodied pie when the moisture comes from the cream and eggs. If you like, you can accelerate the pie-making process by baking the sweet potatoes the day before—perhaps when you have something else in the oven. Refrigerate them after they have cooled.

Carrot Custard Pie

If you think carrot pie sounds like a gimmick, not so fast: sweet carrots are every bit as delicious as pumpkin in a pie. I take the light approach here, using enough carrots to give the pie an unmistakable flavor, but not so many that it tastes like a contest to include as much of the vegetable as possible. This lighter hand, I find, makes this much more inviting as a dessert pie. Serve this delicious, creamy pie for Thanksgiving or anytime you can get your hands on good fresh carrots.

MAKES 8 TO 10 SERVINGS

1 recipe Basic Flaky Pie Pastry, Single Crust (page 31), refrigerated

FILLING

1 1/2 cups peeled and thinly sliced carrots

1/2 cup granulated sugar

1/2 cup firmly packed light brown sugar

2 large eggs

1 large egg yolk

3/4 cup light cream or half-and-half

1/2 cup heavy or whipping cream

1/2 teaspoon vanilla extract

1/2 teaspoon ground ginger

1/8 teaspoon ground nutmeg

1/8 teaspoon salt

1.   If you haven't already, prepare the pastry and refrigerate until firm enough to roll, about 1 hour.

2.   On a sheet of lightly floured waxed paper, roll the pastry into a 12-inch circle with a floured rolling pin. Invert the pastry over a 9-inch standard pie pan, center, and peel off the paper. Tuck the pastry into the pan, without stretching it, and sculpt the edge so it is just slightly higher than the rim. Place in the freezer for 15 minutes, then partially prebake and let cool according to the instructions on page 16. Reduce the oven temperature to 350°F.

3.   Put the carrots in a saucepan with enough lightly salted water to cover generously. Bring to a boil, then continue to boil until the carrots are very soft, 10 to 15 minutes. Drain and then let cool for 10 minutes.

4.   Combine the carrots and sugars in a food processor and process until smooth. Add the eggs and egg yolk and process again until smooth. Scrape the mixture into a large bowl and whisk in the light cream, heavy cream, vanilla, ginger, nutmeg, and salt. Carefully pour the filling into the cooled pie shell.

5. Place the pie on the center oven rack and bake for 30 minutes, then rotate the pie 180 degrees, so that the part that faced the back of the oven now faces forward. Continue to bake until the filling is set and the edge has risen slightly, 20 to 25 minutes. When done, the center of the pie should not be soupy; a little wobbly is fine. Give the pie a little nudge to check. The filling should shake, not move in waves.

6. Transfer the pie to a wire rack and let cool to room temperature. Cover with loosely tented aluminum foil and refrigerate for several hours before serving.

Recipe for Success

▶ Buy the sweetest, freshest carrots you can get. Late-summer, freshly dug carrots are the best and will make the sweetest, most flavorful pie.

▶ This pie tastes very nice with a honey or maple syrup accent. Substitute either for the brown sugar in equal measure.

▶ As with any custard pie, take special care not to overbake the pie or the filling will become watery. At the very first indication that the center is set, remove the pie from the oven.

Spiced Parsnip Pie

This will not be everyone's idea of a dream pie, but some people—including gardeners and hearty country folk—may find it very appealing. To give the idea a context, think of pumpkin pie, but replace the pumpkin flavor with the sweetness of parsnips. To be sure, parsnips have a very dense, meaty texture, so it takes a bit of finesse to elevate them to sweet pie status. In plain English, that means plenty of sugar, spices, and light cream. These are blended with the pureed parsnips and a dash of vanilla, then poured into a large pie shell and baked to a turn. Think of this pie around the holidays, but don't rule it out in the spring either. Gardeners know that spring-dug parsnips are always the sweetest and best-tasting.

MAKES 10 TO 12 SERVINGS

1 recipe Extra-Flaky Pie Pastry, Single Crust (page 34) or Basic Shortening Pie Pastry, Single Crust (page 30), refrigerated

FILLING

4 cups trimmed, peeled, and coarsely chopped parsnips (about 1 3/4 pounds)

1 1/4 cups light cream or half-and-half

3 large eggs

1 cup firmly packed light brown sugar

1/3 cup granulated sugar

1/4 cup (1/2 stick) unsalted butter, melted

1 tablespoon fresh lemon juice

2 teaspoons grated lemon zest

1 teaspoon ground cinnamon

1/2 teaspoon ground cloves

1/2 teaspoon ground nutmeg

1/2 teaspoon ground ginger

3/4 teaspoon salt

1 teaspoon vanilla extract

GARNISH

Fresh Whipped Cream (page 605)

1.   If you haven't already, prepare the pastry and refrigerate until firm enough to roll, about 1 hour.

2.   On a sheet of lightly floured waxed paper, roll the pastry into a 13-inch circle with a floured rolling pin. Invert the pastry over a 9 1/2-inch deep-dish pie pan, center, and peel off the paper. Gently tuck the pastry into the pan, without stretching it, and sculpt the overhang into an upstanding ridge. Place in the freezer for 15 minutes, then partially pre-bake and let cool according to the directions on page 16.

3.   Put the parsnips in a large saucepan with just enough lightly salted water to cover. Bring to a boil, then continue to boil gently until tender, 12 to 18 minutes. Test a large chunk with a paring knife to be sure they are done. Drain in a colander and let cool for 10 minutes.

4.   Combine the parsnips and light cream in a food processor and process until smooth. Add the eggs, sugars, butter, lemon juice, and lemon zest and process until smooth. Add the spices, salt, and vanilla and process again until smooth. Set aside, leaving the filling in the processor bowl. Preheat the oven to 375°F.

5.   Process the filling for several seconds to mix, then pour into the cooled pie shell, smoothing the top with a spoon. Place on the center oven rack and bake for 30 minutes. Reduce the oven temperature to 350°F and rotate the pie 180 degrees, so that the part that faced the back of the oven now faces forward. Continue to bake until the edges have puffed and started to crack, 20 to 25 minutes. When done, the center of the pie will be firmly set.

Hold a Pie Auction

In these days of downsizing and slashed budgets, you have to be creative to fund a new school library, much-needed fire truck, or other worthy cause. In towns from Maine to California, citizens are turning to old-fashioned pie auctions as a source of income. Lest you think we're talking chump change here, think again: a pie auction can raise hundreds or even thousands of dollars for your pet project.

The idea is pretty simple. Participating bakers are asked to donate one or more of their best home-made pies. There's usually an entry fee, and often the pies are judged for appearance by a special panel and prizes are awarded. That same day, the pies are auctioned off at a special event. Looks are important: the best-looking pies often garner the biggest bucks. Pies baked by local celebrities, such as the mayor, usually do well, too.

Those in the know have some advice for would-be pie auctioneers. First, find a good auctioneer—a fast talker who has a sense of humor and can cajole the crowd into parting with their hard-earned dollars.

Second, encourage contestants to think beyond apple. A variety of attractive pies yields the best results.

And third, get the word out. Send out press releases and pie recipes, put up posters—anything to ensure a successful event.

6. Transfer the pie to a wire rack and let cool. Serve slightly warm, at room temperature, or—my favorite way—slightly chilled. Garnish with whipped cream.

Recipe for Success

▸ Judith and Evan Jones, in their informative *The L.L. Bean Book of New New England Cooking* (Random House, 1987), have a wonderful recipe for a parsnip pie sweetened with maple syrup, which would work well in this version. If you'd like to try it, substitute up to $1/2$ cup pure maple syrup for an equal amount of the brown sugar.

▸ This may look done—and appear set in the center—after just 30 minutes. Nonetheless, continue to bake the pie as directed for an additional 20 to 25 minutes.

Green Tomato–Mincemeat Pie

As a former New Englander, I know that green tomatoes aren't only a bittersweet harbinger of fall; they're also prime pie pickings. Indeed, no New Englander, or frugal home gardener anywhere, for that matter, would let a handful of not-gonna-ripen green tomatoes rot on the vine—not when there are delicious pies like this to be made. If you have doubts about cooking with green tomatoes, one bite of this pie will banish them forever. This is sweet-tart and spicy and tastes nothing like raw green tomatoes. In fact, about the only thing I can compare it to is mincemeat—thus the pie's name. It's perfect for all your fall get-togethers, including tailgate parties, and goes great with hot or cold apple cider.

MAKES 8 TO 10 SERVINGS

1 recipe Cornmeal Pie Pastry, Double Crust (page 40) or other double-crust pie pastry, refrigerated

FILLING

4 cups quartered, cored, seeded, and very thinly sliced green tomatoes

1/2 cup dark raisins

1/2 cup chopped walnuts or pecans

1/2 cup chopped pitted dates

1/3 cup granulated sugar

1/3 cup firmly packed light brown sugar

1/4 cup cider vinegar

3 tablespoons all-purpose flour

1/2 teaspoon ground cinnamon

1/2 teaspoon ground ginger

1/2 teaspoon ground cloves

Scant 1/2 teaspoon salt

1 teaspoon grated lemon zest

2 tablespoons cold unsalted butter, cut into small pieces

GLAZE

Milk or light cream

Sugar

1. If you haven't already, prepare the pastry and refrigerate until firm enough to roll, about 1 hour.

2. On a sheet of lightly floured waxed paper, roll the larger half of the pastry into a 13-inch circle with a floured rolling pin. Invert over a 9½-inch deep-dish pie pan, center, and peel off the paper. Tuck the pastry into the pan, without stretching it, and let the overhang drape over the edge. Place in the refrigerator for 15 minutes.

3. In a large bowl, combine the tomatoes, raisins, nuts, dates, and sugars and mix well. Add the vinegar, flour, spices, salt, and lemon zest and mix again. Set aside for 10 minutes. Preheat the oven to 400°F.

4. Roll the other half of the pastry into an 11-inch circle on a sheet of lightly floured waxed paper. Turn the filling into the chilled pie shell, smoothing the top with your hands or a spoon. Dot the filling with the butter. Lightly moisten the rim of the shell. Invert the top pastry over the filling, center, and peel off the paper. Press the top and bottom pastries together along the dampened edge. Using the back of a paring knife, trim the pastry flush with the edge of the pan and crimp the edge with a fork. (Or don't trim the pastry and sculpt the edge into an upstanding ridge.) Poke several steam vents in the top of the pie with a fork or paring knife. Put a couple of the vents near the edge of the crust so you can check the juices there later. To glaze the pie, lightly brush the pastry with milk and sprinkle with sugar.

5. Place the pie on the center oven rack and bake for 30 minutes. Reduce the oven temperature to 375°F and rotate the pie 180 degrees, so that the part that faced the back of the oven now faces forward. Just in case, slide a large aluminum foil–lined baking sheet onto the rack below to catch any spills. Continue to bake until the top is golden brown and any visible juices bubble thickly through the steam vents, no more than 25 to 30 minutes.

6. Transfer the pie to a wire rack and let cool for at least 1 hour. Serve warm or at room temperature.

Recipe for Success

▶ Green tomatoes can seem so rock hard that you may wonder if they'll ever soften as they bake. They will. Just slice them as thinly as possible, and they'll be fine.

▶ Some green tomatoes will have a few red spots on them, indicating the first signs of ripening. That's fine.

▶ Another test worth mentioning is to insert a sharp paring knife through the top crust in several places and down into the tomatoes to check for tenderness. When the pie is done, the tomatoes will offer little or no resistance.

Green Tomato–Cranberry Pie with Cornmeal Crumb Topping

Given the prevalence of green tomatoes and maple syrup in New England, pies like this aren't really all that unusual in the region, although this one, with its cornmeal crumb topping, is perhaps more unusual than most. The dried cranberries are a pleasant surprise, as is the Chinese five-spice powder.

MAKES 8 TO 10 SERVINGS

1 recipe Basic Shortening Pie Pastry, Single Crust (page 30) or Basic Flaky Pie Pastry, Single Crust (page 31), refrigerated

FILLING

4¹/2 cups quartered, cored, seeded, and very thinly sliced green tomatoes

¹/2 cup sweetened dried cranberries (sold as Craisins)

¹/3 cup firmly packed light brown sugar

¹/3 cup pure maple syrup

2 tablespoons fresh lemon juice

1 tablespoon cider vinegar

1 teaspoon Chinese five-spice powder

Scant ¹/2 teaspoon salt

3 tablespoons all-purpose flour

CORNMEAL CRUMB TOPPING

¹/3 cup all-purpose flour

¹/4 cup fine yellow cornmeal

¹/2 cup sugar

¹/4 teaspoon ground cinnamon

¹/4 teaspoon salt

¹/4 cup (¹/2 stick) cold unsalted butter, cut into ¹/4-inch pieces

1.   If you haven't already, prepare the pastry and refrigerate until firm enough to roll, about 1 hour.

2.   On a sheet of lightly floured waxed paper, roll the pastry into a 12-inch circle with a floured rolling pin. Invert over a 9-inch standard pie pan, center, and peel off the paper. Gently tuck the pastry into the pan, without stretching it, and sculpt the overhang into an upstanding ridge. Place in the freezer for 15 minutes. Preheat the oven to 400°F

3.   In a large bowl, combine the green tomatoes, cranberries, brown sugar, maple syrup, lemon juice, and vinegar and mix well. Stir in the five-spice powder, salt, and flour. Turn the filling into the chilled pie shell, smoothing the top with your hands. Bake on the center oven rack for 30 minutes.

4.   Meanwhile, make the topping. In a food processor, combine the flour, cornmeal, sugar, cinnamon, and salt and pulse several times to mix. Scatter the butter over the top and

pulse until the mixture resembles fine crumbs. Empty the crumbs into a large bowl and rub them between your fingers to make large, buttery crumbs. Refrigerate until ready to use.

5. Reduce the oven temperature to 375°F, loosely drape a piece of aluminum foil over the pie, and bake for 10 minutes.

6. Remove the pie from the oven and spread the crumb topping over the pie. Tamp down lightly to compact the crumbs. Return the pie to the oven, placing it so that the part that faced the back of the oven now faces forward. Just in case, slide a large aluminum foil–lined baking sheet onto the rack below to catch any spills. Continue to bake until the topping is golden brown and the juices bubble thickly around the edge, 23 to 25 minutes.

7. Transfer the pie to a wire rack and let cool. Serve just slightly warm or at room temperature.

Recipe for Success

▶   **For a filling with a more mincemeat-like texture, you can chop the tomatoes coarsely after you slice them.**

▶   **If you don't have any Chinese five-spice powder but you'd like to make the pie with ingredients on hand, substitute the spices used in Green Tomato–Mincemeat Pie (page 300).**

▶   **Another way you can do this is to use Cornmeal Pie Pastry (page 40) and make a double-crust pie.**

Crock-Pot Fall Fruit Pie

Like a lot of cooks I know, I like my slow cooker. I may not use it as often as some, but once or twice a month, I unload all the odd utensils I store in it and make a mean stew or brisket. A while ago, I ran across an unlikely recipe for a Crock-Pot apple pie. I was, of course, a little incredulous: how could you make a pie, which requires dry heat, in a slow cooker, which is essentially a steamer? Turns out the result is pretty darn good—not really a pie in the traditional sense, with a crisp-dry crust and separate filling, but more of an apple pudding, with a moist top and bottom "crust." Indeed, it was good enough, and certainly interesting enough, to adapt and turn into a fall fruit pie, made with apples, pears, and cranberries. I think you'll like it very much. You have two options: prepare it late the night before for breakfast or make it in the morning for dinner.

MAKES 8 TO 10 SERVINGS

4 cups peeled, cored, and sliced Golden Delicious, Granny Smith, Northern Spy, Jonagold, or Gravenstein apples

3 cups peeled, cored, and sliced ripe pears

1 cup fresh cranberries, picked over for stems

1 teaspoon ground cinnamon

1/4 teaspoon ground cardamom

1/4 teaspoon ground nutmeg

1/8 teaspoon salt

1 1/2 cups baking mix (such as Bisquick)

3/4 cup whole or reduced-fat (2%) milk

3/4 cup granulated sugar

2 large eggs

3 tablespoons unsalted butter, softened

1/2 teaspoon vanilla extract

1/3 cup firmly packed light brown sugar

3 tablespoons cold unsalted butter, cut into 1/4-inch pieces

GARNISH

Fresh Whipped Cream (page 605) or cold light cream or half-and-half (optional)

1. Lightly butter or grease a 5- to 6-quart slow cooker. Add the apples, pears, and cranberries. Sprinkle the spices and salt over the fruit. Toss well to combine.

2. In a large bowl, combine 1/2 cup of the baking mix, the milk, granulated sugar, eggs, softened butter, and vanilla. Mix well, then pour over the apples.

3. In another bowl, combine the remaining 1 cup baking mix and the brown sugar. Add the cold butter and rub the mixture between your fingers until crumbly. Sprinkle evenly over the fruit.

4. Cover and cook on the low setting for 7 hours. When done, the fruit will be quite soft.

5. Unplug the pot and let cool for about 30 minutes. If you can't wait that long, cool briefly in individual bowls. Serve with whipped cream or light cream, if desired.

Recipe for Success

▸ A few options to consider: (1) Use equal amounts of apples and pears and leave out the cranberries. (2) Add a handful of raisins, chopped dried figs, apricots, or other dried fruit. (3) Use sweetened dried cranberries (sold as Craisins) instead of fresh.

▸ With such prolonged cooking, don't expect the apples and pears to hold their shape all that well, no matter what kind you use. They'll likely be quite soft, maybe even mushy, when the pie is finished cooking.

Splenda Fall Fruit and Cherry Pie

Quite often when I'm giving a pie-baking demonstration, someone will ask me about sugar-free pies and pies that diabetics can eat. Diabetic cooking isn't, frankly, something I'm well versed in, but I've learned—usually from diabetics in the crowd—what sweetener they like. Splenda comes up frequently. It tastes like sugar, because it's made from sugar, but it is then converted into a sweet, granular, sugar-like product that's fine to use in a diabetic diet. In pie fillings and other baking, you can substitute Splenda measure for measure for sugar, and the results are impressive. I've made a number of pies with it, and all have been delicious. Here's one I particularly like. Use fresh pears and apples but frozen cherries.

MAKES 8 TO 10 SERVINGS

1 recipe Basic Flaky Pie Pastry, Double Crust (page 31), modified as instructed in step 1 and refrigerated

FILLING

4 cups peeled, cored, and sliced Granny Smith, Northern Spy, or other tart apples

3 cups peeled, cored, and sliced ripe fresh pears

1 cup individually frozen pitted sweet cherries (not packed in syrup), partially thawed

1/2 cup Splenda sugar substitute

1 tablespoon fresh lemon juice

1 1/2 tablespoons cornstarch

1/4 teaspoon ground cinnamon

1/4 teaspoon ground nutmeg

1. If you haven't already, prepare the pastry, omitting the sugar. Refrigerate until firm enough to roll, about 1 hour.

2. On a sheet of lightly floured waxed paper, roll the larger portion of the pastry into a 13-inch circle with a floured rolling pin. Invert over a 9 1/2-inch deep-dish pie pan, center, and peel off the paper. Gently tuck the pastry into the pan, without stretching it, and let the overhang drape over the edge. Place in the refrigerator for 15 minutes.

3. Combine the fruit, Splenda, and lemon juice in a large bowl and toss well to combine. Set aside for 10 minutes to juice. Stir in the cornstarch, cinnamon, and nutmeg (see Recipe for Success). Preheat the oven to 400°F.

4. On another sheet of lightly floured waxed paper, roll the other half of the pastry into an 11-inch circle. Turn the filling into the chilled pie shell and smooth the fruit with a spoon. Lightly moisten the rim of the shell. Invert the top pastry over the filling, center, and peel off the paper. Press the top and bottom pastries together along the dampened edge. Trim the pastry with scissors or a paring knife, leaving an even ½-inch overhang all around, then sculpt the overhang into an upstanding ridge. Poke several steam vents in the top of the pie with a fork or paring knife. Put a couple of the vents near the edge of the crust so you can check the juices there later.

5.   Place the pie on the center oven rack and bake for 30 minutes. Reduce the oven temperature to 375°F and rotate the pie 180 degrees, so that the part that faced the back of the oven now faces forward. Just in case, slide a large aluminum foil–lined baking sheet onto the rack below to catch any drips. Bake until the juices bubble thickly at the steam vents and the top is golden brown, 35 to 45 minutes. If the top starts to get too dark, cover it with loosely tented aluminum foil during the last 10 to 15 minutes.

6.   Transfer the pie to a wire rack and let cool for at least 2 hours before serving.

Recipe for Success

▶   You've probably noticed that I typically mix the sugar and cornstarch together before adding it to fruit fillings, to get any lumps out of the cornstarch. Here the cornstarch is added separately, so make sure you mix the filling well to eliminate any lumps.

▶   In large measure, the quality of the fruit you use will determine the flavor score for this pie. If you make it with the best fall apples and pears, it will be as good as any fruit pie you could possibly bake—sugar or not.